The Blackwell Guide

Metaphysics

—— Blackwell Philosophy Guides ——

Series Editor: Steven M. Cahn, City University of New York Graduate School

Written by an international assembly of distinguished philosophers, the *Blackwell Philosophy Guides* create a groundbreaking student resource – a complete critical survey of the central themes and issues of philosophy today. Focusing and advancing key arguments throughout, each essay incorporates essential background material serving to clarify the history and logic of the relevant topic. Accordingly, these volumes will be a valuable resource for a broad range of students and readers, including professional philosophers.

1 The Blackwell Guide to Epistemology
Edited by John Greco and Ernest Sosa

2 The Blackwell Guide to Ethical Theory
Edited by Hugh LaFollette

3 The Blackwell Guide to the Modern Philosophers
Edited by Steven M. Emmanuel

4 The Blackwell Guide to Philosophical Logic
Edited by Lou Goble

5 The Blackwell Guide to Social and Political Philosophy
Edited by Robert L. Simon

6 The Blackwell Guide to Business Ethics
Edited by Norman E. Bowie

7 The Blackwell Guide to the Philosophy of Science
Edited by Peter Machamer and Michael Silberstein

8 The Blackwell Guide to Metaphysics
Edited by Richard M. Gale

9 The Blackwell Guide to the Philosophy of Education
Edited by Nigel Blake, Paul Smeyers, Richard Smith, and Paul Standish

The Blackwell Guide to
Metaphysics

Edited by

Richard M. Gale

Blackwell Publishers

© 2002 by Blackwell Publishers Ltd
a Blackwell Publishing company

Editorial Offices:
108 Cowley Road, Oxford OX4 1JF, UK
Tel: +44 (0)1865 791100
350 Main Street, Malden, MA 02148-5018, USA
Tel: +1 781 388 8250

First published 2002 by Blackwell Publishers Ltd

Library of Congress Cataloging-in-Publication Data has been applied for.

ISBN 0-631-22120-4 (hardback); ISBN 0-631-22121-2 (paperback)

A catalogue record for this title is available from the British Library.

Set in 10 on 13 pt Galliard
by SNP Best-set Typesetter Ltd., Hong Kong
Printed and bound in Great Britain
by T.J. International, Padstow, Cornwall

For further information on
Blackwell Publishers, visit our website:
www.blackwellpublishers.co.uk

Contents

List of Contributors   vii

Preface   viii

1 Physics, Metaphysics, and Method in Newton's Dynamics   1
   Lawrence Sklar

2 Causation   19
   Wesley C. Salmon

3 What Events Are   43
   Jonathan Bennett

4 Time, Temporality, and Paradox   66
   Richard M. Gale

5 A Thomist Metaphysics   87
   John J. Haldane

6 The Concept of Ontological Category: A New Approach   110
   Lorenz B. Puntel

7 Universals and Predication   131
   Bruce Aune

8 Composition as a Fiction   151
   Gideon Rosen and Cian Dorr

9 What Do We Refer to When We Say "I"?   175
   Peter van Inwagen

10 Personal Identity: The Non-Branching Form of "What Matters"   190
   Jennifer E. Whiting

11 Idealism   219
    T. L. S. Sprigge

12 An Idealistic Realism: Presuppositional Realism and Justificatory
    Idealism   242
    Nicholas Rescher

13 Overcoming a Dualism of Concepts and Causes: The Basic
    Argument of "Empiricism and the Philosophy of Mind"   263
    Robert Brandom

14 Metaphysical Realism and Logical Nonrealism   282
    Panayot Butchvarov

15 The Metaphysics of Possibilia   303
    William G. Lycan

16 The Actual and the Possible   317
    Alexander R. Pruss

Index   334

Contributors

Bruce Aune, Professor, University of Massachusetts.

Jonathan Bennett, Professor Emeritus, Syracuse University.

Robert Brandom, Distinguished Service Professor, University of Pittsburgh.

Panayot Butchvarov, Professor, University of Iowa.

Cian Dorr, Graduate Student, Princeton University.

Richard M. Gale, Professor, University of Pittsburgh.

John J. Haldane, Professor, University of Saint Andrews.

William G. Lycan, Professor, University of North Carolina.

Alexander R. Pruss, Assistant Professor, Georgetown University.

Lorenz B. Puntel, Professor, University of Munich.

Nicholas Rescher, University Professor, University of Pittsburgh.

Gideon Rosen, Associate Professor, Princeton University.

Wesley C. Salmon, University Professor Emeritus, University of Pittsburgh.

Lawrence Sklar, Professor, University of Michigan.

T. L. S. Sprigge, Professor, University of Edinburgh.

Peter van Inwagen, Professor, University of Notre Dame.

Jennifer E. Whiting, Associate Professor, Cornell University.

Preface

Just as the best way to learn how to hit tennis strokes is to watch good players in action, the best way, in fact the only way, to learn how to do metaphysics is to be exposed to paradigm cases of metaphysics in action and then try to answer in kind. The purpose of this volume is to supply students of philosophy with just such paradigm displays so that they can begin doing metaphysics on their own. It is not an accident that none of the included essays attempts to say what metaphysics is, to describe the methods for doing it and the rules or criteria for assessing the success of a metaphysical theory. For all such metaphilosophical attempts have failed miserably. But the history of metaphysics, as well as the essays in this volume, shows that one can successfully engage in the metaphysical language-game even though one cannot articulate the rules of the game in virtue of which we can keep score and thus determine who wins and who loses.

Not all philosophers accept this favorable evaluation of the history of metaphysics. Whereas I view it as one of the glories of our species, one of our greatest cultural achievements, there are deconstructionists of traditional metaphysics who see it as a shocking scandal because it is a history of perennial and intractable disagreements. The disputants cannot even agree upon a decision procedure for resolving their disagreements. This demand for a cognitive discipline to have a decision procedure for determining who is right smacks of scientism in which the methods employed by the sciences, as well as the way in which they use concepts, are taken to be legislative for all contexts and disciplines, a discipline's failure to measure up to these scientific standards showing that it is bogus. The only effective response to the deconstructionist's scientistically-based indictment of metaphysics as meaningless is to do more metaphysics. I hold that the essays in this volume constitute just such a response. In spite of the hype job of various intellectual historians that we are in a post-this or post-that era, it is still business as usual within philosophy. Metaphysics is alive and kicking.

Chapter 1

Physics, Metaphysics, and Method in Newton's Dynamics

Lawrence Sklar

Newton's masterful scientific achievement was constructed under the influence of much previous philosophical discussion and controversy that went beyond the limits of scientific debate narrowly construed. Much that Newton says in the *Principia* also ranges beyond the confines of experimental or even theoretical science and into the realm of what we usually think of as philosophy. And Newton's work gave rise, possibly more than any other work of science before or since (excepting just possibly the work of Darwin and Einstein) to vigorous philosophical as well as scientific discussion. Let us look at some of the philosophical issues behind, within, and ensuing from Newton's work.

It is convenient to group the discussions into three broad categories. First, there is the "metaphysical" debate over the nature of space, time, and motion. Next there is the debate over what can be properly construed as a scientific explanation of some phenomenon. Lastly, there is the controversy over what the appropriate rules are by which scientific hypotheses are to be credited with having reasonable warrant for our belief. We will discuss these three broad topics in turn.

The Metaphysics of Space, Time, and Motion

There are passages in Aristotle that some read as an anticipation of the doctrine about space and time called "relationism," as when he speaks of the place of an object in terms of the matter surrounding it or talks of time as the "measure of motion." But the full-fledged doctrine of relationism is a product of the scientific revolution. The doctrine is first explicitly stated by Descartes in his later work, is accepted by Huyghens, and is worked out in great detail by Leibniz. In one of the most curious episodes in the history of scientific and philosophical thought, Newton, who all along was philosophically predisposed against relationism, changes the whole character of the metaphysical debate about the nature of space

and time by offering a scientific, almost an "experimental," refutation of the relationist's claims.

In the ancient tradition there is a sense in which there is no real debate going
on about the absolute or relational notion of motion. Motion is taken to be a
property of an object that is not a merely relative property. An object is either at
rest or in motion, and one need not supplement assertions about the state of the
object by noting that the rest or motion is being posited with respect to some reference object that one has in mind. On the other hand, given the belief that the
earth is at rest in the center of the universe, the earth itself, with its cosmic position, provides the standard of rest relative to which objects are adjudged to be at
rest or in motion.

The strong impetus toward relationism arose out of the desire, beginning with
Copernicus himself, to make the earth's rotational motion creditable. In defend-
ing his views against his critics, Copernicus speaks of earthly things as sharing in
the earth's natural motion. In trying to back up Copernicanism Galileo points out
how physical experiments fail to distinguish smooth motions in a straight line on
the earth's surface. After all, a ball dropped from the mast of a ship, although in
motion with respect to the pier, is at rest with respect to the ship itself. No wonder,
then, that it drops to the foot of the mast.

Descartes generalized this to the claim that it was nonsensical to speak of an
object being at rest or being in motion *simpliciter*. An object could be at rest or
in motion only with respect to some other object taken as the reference relative
to which rest or motion, and kind of motion, was to be specified. Descartes used
the doctrine of the relativity of motion, combined with the suggestion that we
usually speak of things as moving when they are in motion with respect to the
things continuous with them, to claim that his theory of the earth driven in a
vortex of the plenum about the sun could be properly said to be at rest. Descartes'
relationism is plainly also motivated by the new anti-Aristotelian view of the space
of the cosmos. Instead of a finite realm marked out by an earth at the center and
the starry sphere at the boundary, the cosmos is, for Descartes, as for Giordano
Bruno, an infinite Euclidean three-dimensional space. In such a space, alike at
every point and in every direction, nothing in the nature of "space itself" provides
a reference frame for position or for motion.

Leibniz gives a worked out account of a metaphysics of space and time that is
relationist through and through. A nice presentation of his views can be found in
a series of letters he exchanged with Samuel Clarke, a disciple of Newton and
defender of Newton's absolutism. Leibniz's views of space and time are actually a
portion of a deeper metaphysics on his part about which we can only make the
briefest remarks. Partly as a response to the difficulty of imagining a causal relationship between mind and matter, and partly motivated by thoughts about perception and its relation to the world that drove later philosophers to varieties of
idealism and phenomenalism, Leibniz posits a world composed solely of spiritual
beings and their properties, the monads. These basic constituents have no causal
relations to one another. But they experience coherent lives due to a "pre-

established harmony" instilled in them by God at their creation, which leads each of them to a programmed existence corresponding to the evolution of each other monad.

But we can understand much of Leibniz's space–time relationism by working in a scheme in which material events occur and material things exist. Events bear temporal relations to one another, they occur before or after one another, and different amounts of time separate their occurrences. Objects existing together at one time bear spatial relations to one another. They are above or below one another, one object can be between two others, they have certain specifiable distances between them. There are, then, two "families" of relations, the temporal relations among events and the spatial relations among things.

But what there is not, according to Leibniz, is "time itself" or "space itself." To imagine such "entities" is as foolish as to imagine that in a family of people who bear familial relations to one another, there is something that exists as an entity in its own right above and beyond the existing people. No, only the people exist, although they do bear many familial relations to one another. Similarly, events occur, and they bear temporal relations to one another. Material objects exist (in the misleading version of Leibniz we are dealing with) and they bear spatial relations to one another. But there is no time itself and no space itself that would exist even if no material events occurred and no material objects existed.

Leibniz offers a series of arguments designed to show that the opposite view, say that space exists as a substance in its own right, is manifestly absurd. All of the arguments rest upon the idea that if time and space existed in their own right, then to ask when things happened in time and where things happened in space would be meaningful. But, Leibniz argues, such questions are absurd.

Suppose substantival space exists. Then God could have created the entire material world somewhere other in space than where he put it. But in doing so he would have had to act without a "sufficient reason" for putting the material world in one place rather than another. But, according to a fundamental metaphysical principle of Leibniz, nothing happens without sufficient reason. So substantival space cannot exist.

Suppose substantival space exists. Now imagine two possible worlds, alike save that the entire material world occupies different places in space itself in the two worlds. These worlds would be, according to the substantivalist, distinct possible worlds. But they would be alike in every qualitative respect. Here Leibniz is operating under the assumption, of course, that every point in space itself is like every other, and every direction in space itself is like every other, that is that space is homogeneous and isotropic. But another Leibnizian fundamental principle is that if A and B have all qualitative properties alike, then A is the same thing as B (the Identity of Indiscernibles). So the two worlds must be, contrary to substantivalism about space, the same possible world. So substantivalism is wrong.

Finally, were the material world somewhere else in substantival space, this would make no difference whatever in any of our possible empirical experiences of things. But it is nonsense to speak of differences in the world that are totally immune from any observational consequences whatever. So substantival space doesn't exist.

What is time? Time is an order of occurrences, that is a set of relations among material happenings. What is space? Space is an order of relations holding among material things considered as existing at the same time. Actually it isn't quite that simple, for time and space are orders of *possibilities*. Let us just deal with space. There is empty space in the world (if, that is, you don't agree with Descartes that all space is filled with matter). But how can we speak of empty space, say between here and the sun, if there is no such thing as space? Well although nothing material is between the sun and the earth (let us suppose), something *could* be there. To speak of the empty space of the world, even of its geometric properties, is to speak of what the family of spatial relations would be like were there material objects occupying the places of space that are in fact empty. It is these "relations in possibility" that constitute what we are talking about when we talk of empty space, and not some mysterious space substance waiting to have material stuff coincide in position with it.

But not everyone before Newton or contemporaneous with him is a relationist. Indeed, two clear influences on Newton's thought were Henry More and Isaac Barrow. Both taught at Cambridge and it was Barrow, Newton's direct teacher, who ceded his professorial chair to his more brilliant student.

More, called the "Cambridge Platonist," was an ardent exponent of the doctrine that space existed in its own right. "It is infinite, incorporeal and endowed only with extension." Space, according to More, is "one, simple, immobile, eternal, perfect, independent, existing by itself, incorruptible, necessary, immense, uncircumscribed, incomprehensible, omnipresent, incorporeal, permeating and embracing all things, essential being, actual being, pure actuality." Indeed, God is always and everywhere present in space itself. Space is a substance in that it exists in its own right. Even if there were no matter in it, space would still have its same being. And this being is an actuality, not a mere mode of possible relations among material things. The echo of More can be clearly heard again and again in Newton's own philosophical remarks about the nature of space.

There are interesting purely philosophical arguments that can be adduced to support such a substantivalist position against Cartesian–Leibnizian relationism. For example, if there were no such thing as space itself with its own existing actual structure, what would provide the ground for the law-like behavior of the possible spatial relations among things, made so much of by Leibniz? If there were no actual space obeying the laws of geometry, why would it be the case that whatever material things existed, with whatever spatial relations they had to one another, those relations would have to conform with the laws of geometry? Arguments in this style are the stock in trade of the substantivalist objections to relationism. We shall not pursue them, focusing instead on Newton's novel "scientific" refutation of relationism.

Barrow also believes in an infinite, eternal space that exists before the material world and beyond it. And, he insists, "so before the world and together with the world (perhaps beyond the world) time was and is . . ." Sometimes his language takes on a "modal" cast not unlike that of Leibniz, as when he says that time "does not denote an actual existence, but simply a capacity or possibility of permanent existence; just as space indicates the possibility of an intervening magnitude . . ." But, he is insistent, time is not a mere abstraction from motion or change. There is a "flow" of time which is uniform and unchanging. Even if all motion and change in the universe ceased, time would continue to elapse at its steady rate. We can measure the lapse of time with clocks that are more or less adequate, but no material clock is a perfect measurer of the lapse of time. He is a little vague on how we know the real rate at which time elapses, but suggests that it is through a kind of "congruence" among our various measures that we infer the real rate at which time is elapsing. Barrow's very words are often discernible in Newton's remarks.

Newton had many things to say about the metaphysics of space and time. In the unpublished work "*De Gravitatione*" he speaks of absolute place and motion in terms familiar from More. He often has theological things to say about space and time as well, taking the Deity to be eternal and ubiquitous, existing at all time in all places. In one notorious passage he speculates about space being the "sensorium" of the Deity, God's visual field, as it were. In other places he puzzles over the metaphysical nature of space, sometimes saying it is like a substance, sometimes thinking of it as an attribute (of the Deity), and in other places saying that it has a nature of its own unlike ordinary substance or accident. But it is not in espousing any such "absolutist" doctrines about space and time, nor for rehearsing the usual philosophical arguments for them, that Newton draws our attention. For Newton provides a wholly novel argument in favor of the existence of space as an independent entity over and above material things, and for an absolute measure of the "rate of flow" of time. His argument rests upon bringing to the surface a blatant contradiction latent in Descartes.

Descartes' one fully correct contribution to dynamics was in his version of what became Newton's First Law of Motion. Objects not acted upon by external forces persist in uniform motions in a straight line. But the truth of that law, indeed, the very comprehensibility of what the assertion of the law means, requires that we be able to say what it is to move with constant speed and what it is to move in a straight line. But if we can choose measures of the lapse of time as we wish, any motion can be regarded as at constant speed or at variable speed as we wish. Constant speed means the same distance covered in the same time, and that implies, if constant speed is not to be arbitrarily asserted or denied of an object, that our measure of the sameness of time intervals be absolute, or at least invariant up to a linear transformation (that is, a choice of zero point and choice of scale for time intervals). And to say that something moves in a straight line also implies some standard of reference relative to which motion is genuinely straight. Be allowed to choose any reference frame that is fixed in a material object that moves however you like, and any motion can be construed, relative to some selected frame, as straight-line or not straight-line as one chooses. To make the first law of motion meaningful requires an absolute standard of lapse of time and an absolute reference frame relative to which uniform straight-line motion is to be counted as genuine uniform straight-line motion.

As Newton argues in the "Scholium to the Definitions" of the *Principia*, we can easily detect deviation from inertial motion experimentally. He chooses his examples from rotation (the non-flatness of the surface of the spinning water in the bucket, the tension on the rope holding together the spheres in rotation about the center of the rope), but examples from linear acceleration would suffice as well. Deviations from uniform, straight-line motion show up by the presence of inertial forces. Therefore uniform straight-line motion is not arbitrarily chosen but fixed by nature and empirically discernible. It is that motion which continues unabated when no forces act on the moving object and it is that motion which generates no inertial forces.

One could put an object into relative acceleration by leaving it alone and applying forces to the reference object relative to which the motion of the test object is to be judged. But such relative acceleration is not absolute acceleration. For an object to be truly accelerated, absolutely accelerated, forces must be applied to the object itself. But if acceleration is absolute, there must be, Newton believes, absolute place and absolute change of place. For only then could absolute acceleration even be defined.

Finally, absolute motion as revealed by its dynamical effects must be attributed to the earth along with all the other planets. Only by considering the earth in truly accelerated motion in its elliptical orbit about the sun can we understand the need for the mutual attractive force sun and earth exert on each other, which serves as the "tether" keeping the earth from following its otherwise natural, inertial, straight-line motion. So much the worse for Descartes' attempt at keeping on good terms with the Inquisition by using relationism to defend a claim of the earth being at rest.

Newton's "experimental proof" of the existence of substantival space becomes the subject of several centuries of ongoing controversy. It is the core critical element a relationist such as Ernst Mach must deal with in the nineteenth century, and it is central to twentieth-century attempts at characterizing an appropriate metaphysics for space–time. Suffice it to say here, though, that Newton is certainly right that any espousal of a dynamical theory that places inertial motion at the very center of its theoretical apparatus cannot be compatible with the kind of spatial and temporal relationism espoused by Descartes and Leibniz. Flat-out relationism as they intended it is not easily reconcilable with the existence of special states of motion that reveal themselves as dynamically distinguished in nature.

Leibniz tried to respond to the Newtonian argument, as it was presented to him by Clarke in their correspondence, but his final response to the Newtonian arguments is quite weak. Leibniz says, "I grant there is a difference between an absolute true motion of a body, and a mere relative change in its situation with respect to another body. For when the immediate cause of change is in the body, that body is truly in motion; and then the situation of other bodies, with respect to it, will be changed consequently, though the cause of that change not be in them." But consider a wheel spinning for all eternity in an otherwise empty universe. There is no relative motion of the wheel with respect to other bodies at all. And there is a sense in which there is no "cause" that sets the wheel in motion. Yet, if Newton's science is right (and Leibniz is not disagreeing with it), the wheel's rotation will show up in its internal stresses. To be sure, each point of the wheel suffers internal forces from the other points of the wheel. These are the forces that simultaneously deviate each point from its inertial motion and hold the wheel together. But Newton will insist that the need for such forces to keep the points of the wheel on their circular orbits must be accounted for in terms of something special about the motion of those points, something kinematically and not dynamically characterized. Otherwise the need for the forces could only receive a circular explanation: "The forces are needed because the points of the wheel are in the kind of motion for which forces are needed." And to characterize what is special about the motion of the points in terms that do not themselves invoke the needed forces can only be to assert that the motion of the points requires those forces because the points of the wheel are deviating from uniform motion in a straight line. And that deviation implies the existence of space as the reference frame relative to which such deviation is real, true, absolute deviation.

It is fascinating to see how Huyghens responds to the Newtonian arguments. Huyghens once said that straight-line motions were all merely relative, but that circular motions had a criterion that identified them – the tension in the rope needed to keep the object in its circular orbit, for example. He later tries to give a relationist account of circular motion in terms of points on a wheel on opposite sides of the axle moving in opposite directions relative to one another. But this won't do, for in a reference frame fixed in the wheel, all the points on the wheel are simply at rest. Huyghens is just assuming the description of the system from the point of view of an inertial reference frame. Furthermore, linear accelerations show up dynamically as well. When the emergency brake is pulled and the train screeches to a halt at a station, it is the coffee in the cups held by the passengers on the train that sloshes out of the cups, not the coffee in the cups held by people on the station platform. Yet relationistically speaking, the platform is just as much accelerated relative to the train as the train is to the station.

There are, of course, deeply problematic aspects to Newton's account. Although absolute acceleration reveals itself dynamically, absolute place and absolute uniform motion do not. If we accept Leibniz's claim, anticipating later positivism, that it is nonsensical to speak of features of the universe that have no observational consequences whatsoever, how can we tolerate a theory that posits the existence of both absolute place and absolute uniform motion, but which, on its own terms, declares them as having no empirical import whatever? Newton was clearly aware of the problem of the empirical irrelevance of states of absolute uniform motion. He himself points the important facts out in Corollary V to the Laws of Motion in the *Principia*. The best he can do to repair this gap in his theory is to propose the peculiar Hypothesis I of Part III of the *Principia*, which rests on what "all agree to," that the center of the solar universe is at rest, and to use that hypothesis to then fix the center of mass of the solar system as being at rest. Corollary VI to the Laws shows that there is an even deeper problem in the Newtonian system, in that even some accelerated motions may have no dynamical effects. Both corollaries rest upon implicit assumptions that go beyond Newton's Laws of Motions, the assumptions to the effect that the motions will not change the interactive forces among the particles of the moving systems. Both results will play deep roles in later dynamics. The equivalence of all inertial frames will later be fundamental in special relativity and in the reconstruction of Newtonian theory from a space–time point of view (Galilean or neo-Newtonian space–time), and the empirical irrelevance of uniform universal acceleration will play its role in the foundations of general relativity and in the space–time reconstruction of the Newtonian theory of gravity.

Issues Concerning Explanation

Philosophers try to characterize the general notion of the nature of a scientific explanation. Usually it is assumed that we can say what it is for something to count as having the right character to be a scientific explanation without paying much attention to what the actual contents of some particular science are in which the explanations are being offered. That is, it is often assumed that we can make sense of unpacking the *form* of what an explanation must be like in indifference to the particular *contents* of particular explanations offered in particular scientific theories.

But is that really so? Or is it the case, rather, that our very idea of what sorts of things are to count as explanatory is conditioned by the particular contents of what we take to be our best available explanatory theories? This issue can be nicely illustrated by looking at some of the debates about the nature of scientific explanation that arose out of the Newtonian synthesis in dynamics. But to understand these we must first look at the account of explanation most popular among knowledgeable scientists immediately prior to Newton's great work.

The ideals of scientific explanation arising out of Newton's work are best understood in contrast to the explanation ideals promulgated by Descartes and his followers, where the model of scientific explanation offered was proposed as an alternative to what were taken to be, rightly or wrongly, the ideals of explanation of Descartes' predecessors. The Cartesians are constantly contrasting their "modern" notion of scientific explanation with the outworn and foolish ideas, they think, of their Aristotelian or "Peripatetic" opponents.

The Aristotelians believed in species of natural motions as well as forced motions. Natural motions consisted in the attempt of objects to return to their natural places in the universe, such as the motion of falling earthly things, and the perfect, eternal circular motions of the heavenly bodies. All other motions are forced. For Cartesians natural motions are motions at constant speed in a straight line – inertial motions. All other motions are forced.

For Aristotelians, the world is a place of substance and properties. There are many kinds of properties of things, and properties can inhere in things both in actuality and in mere potentiality. For Cartesians there are only two substances, mind and matter. And only two kinds of general properties, thought and extension. For Aristotelians there are many kinds of changes, comings into being and passings out of being, as properties come and go in actuality. Motion, properly so-called, is only one kind of change. These changes are to be accounted for in terms of the four causes: the formal, material, efficient and final causes of the change. For Cartesians there is only one kind of change in the realm of matter, that is change describable in terms of the basic notions of time and space alone. For the Cartesians, that is, all material change is motion in the narrower sense of change of spatial place in time.

For Aristotelians, at least in the version of them favored by their Cartesian critics, explanation is often in terms of properties of things that are hidden from our direct observational awareness. Peripatetic physics, the Cartesians say, is incessantly resorting to the attribution of "occult," hidden, qualities to things to explain their behavior. But Cartesian physics denies the reality of such hidden causes, or even the meaningfulness of attributing them to objects. For Cartesians all explanatory features must be "manifest," directly open to our observational awareness.

For the Cartesians all explanation of all change, that is of all motion, must take one of two forms. The motion may be natural motion, that is inertial motion, in which case no further explanation of it is needed. If the motion is not inertial, it must deviate from uniform motion in a straight line only because some other motion has directly impinged upon the moved object. A ball is accelerated when another moving ball collides with it. A planet moves in an orbit only because it is dragged along by the vortex of the medium in which it resides. Non-inertial motion is always the result of other, contiguous motion. And the fundamental rule governing this causation of one motion by another is that motion is conserved. The accelerated ball has its motion changed only to the degree that its gain or loss of motion is compensated by the gain or loss of motion of the ball impacting it.

Any explanatory account of the world that deviates from the Cartesian pattern must not only fail to be scientifically correct, it must fail to meet the conditions necessary for something to be a genuine scientific explanation at all. The account Newton gives of the motion of the planets fails in many ways to meet the proper standards for explanation as the Cartesians see it. Their response is twofold, even though, curiously, their two objections are often quite at odds with one another. On the one hand, Newton is often accused by the Cartesians of a kind of reactionary resort to justly condemned, outmoded forms of explanation. He invokes, say the Cartesians, the infamous occult properties of the Aristotelians. Worse yet, he allows explanations of motion that do not themselves invoke previous motion as the explanatory element, and he tolerates mysterious influences of objects on one another even when the objects are not contiguous to one another. On the other hand, Newton is often accused by the Cartesians of merely describing the motions of things, and not offering an explanation of their motions at all!

Consider some contrasts between the Newtonian and the Cartesian explanatory schemes. The one element they clearly have in common is the postulation of uniform speed in a straight line as the natural state of motion of things, although as we have seen, Newton takes the posit of such natural motions to be blatantly inconsistent with Descartes' relationist theory of space and time.

Newton invokes both quantity of matter, mass, and force as fundamental concepts in his descriptive scheme. In fact he believes in other primitive qualities of matter as well, such as hardness and impenetrability. There is no obvious way that Newtonian physics can be characterized solely in terms of the kinematic notions of place, time and motion, to which the Cartesian is conceptually restricted. Whether these apparent primitive concepts are really needed in the Newtonian theory is something much debated in Machian and later reconstructions of Newtonian theory. Neither mass nor force are obviously "manifest" properties, as Cartesians take relative place and motion to be. Furthermore, Newton invokes the notions of absolute place and absolute time interval. Here the basic concepts are purely kinematic in nature, but they are, once again, not manifest as relative place and clock-measured time would be.

For Newton the fundamental explanation of change of motion is force, the force an object exerts upon another, be it a force of contact impulse or the action, at a distance, of gravitational attraction. Motion need not be accounted for in terms of antecedent motion. Indeed, Newton expresses grave reservations about the correctness of any comprehensive posit of the conservation of all motion, remarking how motion can be generated where none was before and how, by means of friction and like effects, it can disappear from the world. This is so even though Newton was quite aware of how the conservation of linear momentum for point particles acting on each other by forces followed from his Third Law; and even though, as we shall discuss later, other "conservation of motion" results either follow from Newton's original theory or become deeply integrated into its later formalisms.

This invocation of the notion of force in the Newtonian sense traces back to Galileo. It was in his work that the notion of force invoked in statics, primarily in the form of weight that impinged on some static framework, was invoked as the originator or generator of motion in dynamics.

And of course, motion need not require, at least in the first instance, an explanatory account in which all causes are taken as acting contiguously in space. We will note below, Newton's own preference for explanatory accounts that eschew any genuine action at a distance, but at least on the surface the actions of the heavenly bodies on each other, of gravitational attraction – the actions that govern the whole motion of the cosmos – seem plainly to violate Cartesian precepts that all causes are immediately next to their effects.

Newton is very sensitive to the charges laid against him by the Cartesians. On the one hand he is adamant that his account of motion does not resort to "occult qualities." He sometimes argues that when he speaks of the gravitational attraction one object exerts upon another, he is not positing some hypothetical cause of the motions or changes of motions of objects. He is, rather, merely noting the observable deviations from inertial motions that are induced when objects are in one another's proximity. That deviation is, for both objects, proportional to the product of their inertial masses and inversely proportional to the square of the distance between them. And it is directed along the line connecting the objects. From that, the law of gravitational "force" follows, and that is all the law is committed to. If anyone is dealing in the "hidden," Newton says, it is those who propose particular "mechanisms" to account for this mutual gravitational influence bodies have on one another (such as the not-directly observable vortices in the plenum that account for the cosmic motions, in Descartes' theory).

There is no simple way to characterize Newton's methodology. On the one hand his restriction, within the main body of the work, to the mathematical description of the motions of things summarized in general laws, with its eschewal of the search for hidden mechanisms, makes Newton seem quite the positivist. On the other hand nothing more infuriates the positivistically minded philosophers of his day, or of later eras, than his postulation of absolute space and absolute time.

Anxious to avoid what he takes to be the pointless and endless controversies that rage between scientists and philosophers, Newton, famously, asserts in the *Principia* that he does not "frame hypotheses" about the nature of the mechanism of gravitational attraction. As we shall see, he claims that all of the assertions he has made in the Laws of Motion and the Law of Universal Gravitation rest on far firmer grounds than any mere "hypothesis."

Nonetheless, Newton does frame hypotheses – about gravity and about many other things as well. In the "General Scholium" that forms the last section of the *Principia*, in the "Queries" section to his famous work *Opticks*, and elsewhere, Newton makes many proposals about the possible mechanisms that might result in gravitational attraction, that might account for light showing the properties that it displays (many experimentally determined for the first time by Newton himself), and that might explain the various structural and behavioral features of matter of various kinds. His hypotheses about gravity, for example, often have a very Cartesian flavor to them, as they postulate "ethers" that fill the universe with various fluid properties of pressure and resistance, and whose relation to matter (perhaps of lower pressure where matter is present, resulting in a "push" that moves matter toward matter) might, possibly, explain the law-like behavior of gravitational attraction. Such "mechanisms" might also remove from gravity the taint of action at a distance. It is worth noting here that the elements that later function to suggest the replacement of "action at a distance" theories by theories that propose an ontology of "fields" intermediate between the interacting objects, that is to say the time lapse in inter-particle actions and the violation in conservation of energy that results if one is not very careful in framing an "action at a distance" theory, play no role in the controversies embroiling Cartesians and Newtonians in Newton's time.

Some of Newton's hypotheses remain only curiosities in the history of science. Others, such as his particle theory of light, remain, if not really correct, important contributions to the development of later science. Still others, such as his hypothesis expressed in the "Queries" to the *Opticks* that there might be other forces along with that of gravity by which matter influences matter, and that these other forces might account for such things as the structure and behavior of materials, are prophetic insights into what became large components of the future growth of scientific understanding.

In any case, though, Newton is always careful to distinguish what he is guessing at or speculating at, that is, what he is "hypothesizing," from that which he thinks he has established by experiment, observation, and the kind of legitimate inferences from these upon which he thinks the core law-like assertions of the *Principia* are based.

Philosophically the most important thing to notice about this whole debate is the way in which scientists and philosophers become committed to a doctrine about the very nature of what a scientific explanation is, depending on which particular theories about that nature they hold at the time. For Cartesians, what they called "mechanical" explanations were constitutive of what any scientific explanation had to be. Any "explanation" that violated their precepts of being framed solely in manifest kinematic terms, of relying on motion only to generate motion, and of demanding contiguity of cause and effect, was not explanatory at all. It was either "mere description" without explanatory force, or it was pseudo-explanation resorting to rejected Peripatetic mumbo-jumbo. As we have seen in the case of Newton's account of motion under the influence of gravity, both accusations were made simultaneously.

With the triumph of the Newtonian dynamical scheme, however, came a wholly new idea of what any putative explanation must be like in order that it be a genuine scientific explanation. If an account of a phenomenon did not resort to natural motions being changed by interactive mutual forces among particles, it could not be a genuinely scientific, or sometimes, "causal," or sometimes, "mechanical" explanation of what was going on.

Just as Newton's science, in not fitting the Cartesian pattern of appropriate explanation by triumphing scientifically, cast grave doubt upon the very Cartesian demands for the structure of explanation in general, later science, in not easily fitting into a Newtonian pattern, led methodologists to become skeptical of what had become the Newtonian standard of the necessary conditions to be met by any scientific explanation. This becomes crucial in the critiques of generalized Newtonianism in science, put forward by Mach and others in the nineteenth century, and in later positivism.

It is worthwhile noting here that the Cartesian criteria of legitimacy in explanation suffered an additional blow from ongoing developments in dynamics that was not the result of the Newtonian synthesis. Along with occult qualities, Cartesians demanded the total rejection of the notion of "final cause" applied to the physical world. For Aristotelians each event was explicable both in terms of its immediate, driving predecessors – its efficient causes – and in terms of the obtainment of some goal or end, a final cause; for Cartesians, in the physical realm at least, only efficient causes were to be tolerable as legitimate explainers.

But the reintroduction into optics of a least time principle by Fermat seemed to provide a place for final causes in that branch of physics. Such principles, originally explored by Hero of Alexandria in the case of reflection and invoked by Fermat to account for the Descartes–Snell law of refraction, seemed to the Cartesians to smack badly of the forbidden Aristotelian idea of nature acting for an end or purpose. When Maupertuis discovered that a principle of least action could serve as a general foundational principle for dynamics, and when that principle was given decisive rigorous form by Euler, the reappearance of final causes threatened to be one more "reactionary" blow delivered to the failing body of Cartesian "progressive" dogma about the restrictions to be applied to the domain of legitimate explanatory methods in physics.

Newton's "Rules of Reasoning in Philosophy"

Newton had framed dynamics in terms of his three fundamental laws of motion and had applied dynamics to a theory of the heavenly motions by supplementing the dynamical laws with a law of universal gravitation. But why should we believe in the truth of the Newtonian account?

Newton himself was highly sensitive to criticism and deeply concerned to anticipate what he expected to be angry and vituperative attacks on his masterwork, the *Principia*. First there were the perpetual battles over precedence in discovery endemic to the science of Newton's day and of our own as well. Newton is careful to give generous credit where he thinks it is due, to Galileo on inertia, on the fact that constant force generates equal changes of motion in equal times, and on the fact that the acceleration due to gravity is independent of the size and constitution of the falling object; to Huyghens, Wallis and Wren on the conservation of momentum in collisions; to Huyghens on the magnitude of centrifugal force; and to Bouilleau, Wren and others on the inverse square diminution of the force holding planets to the sun. Sometimes, though, he is less than generous, failing to note Descartes' first fully correct statement of the inertia law and Descartes' first statement of a principle of the conservation of motion (even if Descartes got the principle wrong); and also failing to give Hooke enough credit for being, perhaps, the first person to state correctly that the motion of the heavenly bodies required only inertia and centripetal force alone. Since much of the *Principia* can be considered a sound refutation of everything Descartes said about the structure of the universe the less than generous stance toward Descartes can, perhaps, be understood. Since Hooke falsely claimed credit not only for getting elliptical orbits out of an inverse-square law, but for anticipating Newton's invention of the reflecting telescope as well, Newton's stinginess in granting him credit can also be understood. Hooke's nasty controversy with Newton over the nature of light also played a role, as we shall see, in Newton's framing of his methodological remarks in Book III of the *Principia*.

But it is not quarrels over precedence that most concern Newton. In 1671 Newton presented to the Royal Society the results of his wonderful experiments on the refraction and dispersion of light. These were published along with some of Newton's speculations about the corpuscular composition of light. Hooke responded immediately with a critical attack, offering his own "hypotheses" about the nature of light to contend with those of Newton. The resulting quarrelsomeness so upset Newton that he withdrew from publishing virtually any of his work until finally persuaded to come out with the *Principia* by Halley. Newton was well aware that his views in the *Principia* were likely to start another round of even greater controversy, especially at the hands of defenders of the Cartesian scheme of explanation.

As we have seen, Newton did not cease "hypothesizing," even within the *Principia* itself, where, in the "General Scholium" speculative thoughts about the mechanism of gravity receive their due. But he is careful throughout the work to isolate such "hypotheses" from the far more important work of developing his mathematically formulated laws of dynamics and of gravity, and using them to ground the laws governing the motions of the heavenly bodies. He also takes pains in several places to let the reader know that his grounds for believing in the truth of his laws are not the guesswork of hypothesis, but something that he thinks provides a far more secure basis for scientific belief. If the reader accepts these claims, then the core developments of the work will remain immunized from squabbles of the sort that arise when one bit of speculative scientific guesswork is confronted by other "hypotheses" of the same nature.

One thing Newton does not try to do is to show that his laws can be established by some kind of purely rational thought, that is by *a priori* reasoning or by Descartes' "clear and distinct ideas." He affirms the role of pure mathematics in his work and the soundness of his reasoning that follows from its use. But he is well aware of the fact that the soundness of the system as a whole is only as sure as the soundness of its "first principles." These, he insists, are derived not by any mode of pure thought, but by inference from the facts nature presents to our observation and experiment.

In the "Scholium to the Laws," Newton says, "Hitherto I have laid down such principles as have been received by mathematicians, and are confirmed by abundance of experiments." Galileo had, Newton suggests, discovered the Law of Inertia and the Second Law in his experiments on gravity and motion and had derived from them the famous results on the paths of projectiles. Wren, Wallis and Huyghens, Newton goes on, had discovered the truth of the Third Law in their work on collisions. Here Newton realizes that his generalization of that principle beyond collisions and into the realm of attractions is on more dubious experimental ground, and so he offers both deductive reasons why the law must extend to such phenomena and a confirming experimental test using floating magnets.

The laws, then, are supposed by Newton to be established by observation and experiment, which is then generalized from particular experiences to all phenomena by what is commonly called inductive reasoning. To be sure, the philosopher, especially one coming after David Hume and Nelson Goodman, will realize how many pitfalls stand in the way of someone who wants to underpin their beliefs on the grounds of the sole combination of observation and induction. But Newton is surely right in contrasting the support his laws of dynamics receive from quite direct experience projected by universalization, with the more tenuous kind of support an hypothesis that involves the widespread positing of "hidden" entities, properties and mechanisms would receive from its indirect confirmation only by its ability to predict confirming results at the observational level. Whatever the problems with induction may be, there is a sense in which inductive reasoning can be distinguished from more general "hypothetico-deductive" reasoning, and there is good reason to agree with Newton that his laws of motion receive their support from the narrower, and hence allegedly more secure, kind of inference.

Newton's most self-conscious reflection on methodology, in particular on the grounds for belief in a fundamental physical proposition, comes in an initial prefatory section to Book III of the *Principia* that gives its title to this section. The material is plainly intended to provide the basis for the reasoning that will support the inference to the universal law of gravitation. It is the grounds for that law that provides the content of the first part of Book III, and the application of that law in conjunction with the dynamical laws in order to account for the laws describing the heavenly motions that is the bulk of the remaining content of that Book.

There are four famous "Rules of Reasoning":

Rule I: We are to admit no more causes of natural things than such as are both true and sufficient to explain their appearance.

Rule II: Therefore, to the same natural effects we must, as far as possible, assign the same causes.

Rule III: The qualities of bodies which admit neither intensification nor remission of degrees, and which are found to belong to all bodies within the reach of our experiments, are to be esteemed the universal qualities of all bodies whatsoever.

Rule IV: In experimental philosophy we are to look upon propositions inferred by general induction from phenomena as accurately or very nearly true, notwithstanding any contrary hypotheses that may be imagined, till such time as other phenomena occur, by which they may be made more accurate, or liable to exceptions.

It would be a mistake to think of Newton as here proposing some general grand epistemology in the manner, say, of Descartes. He is, rather, adducing just those rules he thinks will appeal to all rational readers as unquestionably sound, and which will be sufficient to allow him to justify his claims to the effect that it is universal gravitation that is sufficient to provide the needed dynamical basis for all the heavenly motions, and to defend those claims from possible "alternative hypotheses" likely to be flung at him by Cartesian opponents of his work.

Rules I and II are invoked in Proposition IV, the proposition that first associates earthly gravity with a cosmic dynamical force. We can infer from the work of Book I that the cosmic forces are centripetal, for they obey the "equal area" law of Kepler. We can infer that this cosmic force diminishes with distance as the inverse square, for the orbits of the heavenly bodies are ellipses with the attracting center as a focus (and by other subtler facts in the case of the moon). But measurement of the acceleration of gravity at the surface of the earth shows that such gravity at the distance of the moon, having fallen off by the inverse square of distance, will be just the amount of cosmic, centripetal force needed to hold the moon in its orbit. So the force holding the moon in its orbit must be just that gravity: "And therefore (by Rules I and II) the force by which the moon is retained in its orbit is the very same force which we commonly call gravity; for, were gravity another force different from that, then bodies descending to the earth with the joint impulse of both forces would fall with a double velocity . . . altogether against experience." We need only the amount of the one accelerative force to get the correct acceleration of rock on earth and of the moon in the heavens, and since the effect is "the same" in both cases (appropriately modified in magnitude by the inverse square law) the cause of the acceleration must be the same.

In Proposition V it is argued that the similarity in effect of the moons of Jupiter, the moons of Saturn, and the planets in their relation to Jupiter, Saturn and the sun respectively, to that of the moon in its relation to the earth tells us, by Rule II, that it is "no other than a gravitating force" that retains all these other satellites in their orbits as well. This is defended in a "Scholium" to the proposition by reference to Rules I and II, and to Rule IV as well. Presumably the reference to the last rule is to deny the opponent the right to suggest that some other hypothesis could also do justice to the behavior of the satellites other than the earth's moon. For in their cases we don't have the argument that backed up gravity as the force used in Proposition IV. But here Rule IV tells us that we need not hesitate in our induction just because of the mere presence of other hypotheses as possible explanations of the phenomena.

Rule III is especially interesting. Its purpose is expressed in an exegesis immediately following the presentation of the rule itself. First it is argued, presumably against Cartesian rationalism and its skepticism of the reliability of the senses, that "all qualities of bodies are known to us by experiments." According to the Rule then, "we are to hold for universal all such as universally agree with experiments." Here quantity of matter (*vis insita*, inertial mass) is likened to such other properties as spatial extension, hardness and impenetrability, and mobility. That all bodies have such features, Newton claims, "we gather not from reason, but from sensation."

"Lastly, if it universally appears, by experiments and astronomical observations, that all bodies about the earth gravitate toward the earth, and that in proportion to the quantity of matter which they severally contain; that the moon likewise, according to the quantity of its matter, gravitates toward the earth; that, on the other hand, our sea gravitates toward the moon; and all the planets toward one another; and the comets in like manner toward the sun; we must, in consequence of this rule [Rule III], universally allow that all bodies whatsoever are endowed with a principle of mutual gravitation. For the argument from the appearances concludes with more force for universal gravitation than for their impenetrability; of which, among those in the celestial regions, we have no experiments, nor any manner of observation."

From observation we learn of the irreducible primary properties of matter available to hand for experimentation. By observation we can extend some of our attributions even to the heavens. Then, by the universalizing permitted by Rule III, we can finally arrive at the full attribution of the relevant properties to all matter in general. Thus we are able to project our earthly experience into a general description of the heavens as well.

What about the curious "which admit neither intensification nor remission of degrees" qualification in the statement of Rule III? It isn't completely clear what Newton is concerned about here, but perhaps the last sentence of the discussion following the statement of the rule gives us a clue: "Not that I affirm gravity [that is, weight] to be essential to bodies: by their *vis insita* I mean nothing but their inertia. That is immutable. Their gravity is diminished as they recede from the earth."

Newton is aware of just how subtle the connection is of mass to weight. In the "Definitions" of Book I he told us that we could measure the quantity of matter in a thing by its weight. And in his discussion of gravity he is brilliantly clear on the fact that both the passive and active gravitational charges of an object must also equal its inertial mass. But the mass is not the weight. The weight is a matter of a *relation* between the object, and the earth that is gravitationally attracting the object. Change the spatial relation of object to earth and you change the object's weight. But the object's mass (and its intrinsic gravitational charges for that matter) do not change. Our "universalizing" of the properties of what is in hand to properties of things everywhere and anywhere must confine itself to those properties intrinsic to the object, and not be applied to those which hold of the object only because of its special relations to objects external to it and which may "intensify or diminish" as those relations change.

Of course Newton has not provided any infallible recipe to tell us which of the properties we experience as universal of things in our experience really are "intrinsic," and which might very well turn out to be, in the end, merely relational. It was, after all, a great discovery of Newton and his contemporaries that weight was in fact not intrinsic but relational. But, as has been said, it would be misleading to think of Newton's rules as proposals for the foundations of epistemology. They are safeguards against polemic and misguided skepticism toward the results of his mathematical physics, especially toward his revelation of the universal law of gravitational attraction and its role in accounting for the heavenly motions.

18 *Lawrence Sklar*

Suggested Reading

For an introduction to Aristotle on motion see J. Barbour, *Absolute or Relative Motion?*, Cambridge: Cambridge University Press, 1989, ch. 2, "Aristotle: the First Airing of the Absolute/Relative Problem." On Descartes' relationism see D. Garber, *Descartes' Metaphysical Physics*, Chicago: University of Chicago Press, 1992, ch. 6, "Motion," and Barbour, ch. 8, "Descartes and the New World." For Leibnizian relationism see H. G. Alexander, *The Leibniz–Clarke Correspondence*, Manchester: Manchester University Press, 1956, especially the editor's introduction and Leibniz's 3rd. paper. For Cambridge Platonism and its influence on Newton see A. Koyré, *From the Closed World to the Infinite Universe*, Baltimore: Johns Hopkins University Press, 1957. For an outline of the development of Newton's metaphysics of space and time see Barbour, ch. 11, "Newton II: Absolute or Relative Motion?" Newton's reflections on space and time in his mature work can be found in I. Newton, *Newton's Principia*, translated and edited by F. Cajori, Berkeley: University of California, 1947, Book I, "Definitions," and, especially, "Scholium to the Definitions." See again Barbour, ch. 11, "Newton II: Absolute or Relative Motion?" For some contemporary philosophical commentary on the Newton–Leibniz controversy over the nature of space and time see L. Sklar, *Space, Time and Spacetime*, Berkeley: University of California, 1974, ch. III, "Absolute Motion and Substantival Spacetime," and J. Earman, *World-Enough and Space–Time*, Cambridge, MA: MIT, 1989, ch. 6, "Substantivalism: Newton versus Leibniz." For Huyghens difficulties with the issues of relationism see Barbour, ch. 9, "Huyghens: Relativity and Centrifugal Force." Newton's thoughts on method in science can be found in Newton, *Principia*, Book I, "Scholium to the Laws," and Book III, "Rules of Reasoning in Philosophy." To see how Newton applies his rules to justify his theory of universal gravitation see *Principia*, Book III, "Phenomena," and, especially, "Propositions (I through VII)." Newton's "hypothesis" about the nature of matter and forces in general can be found in I. Newton, *Opticks*, New York: Dover, 1952, "Query 31." For a condensed history of the "least action" principle and the difficulties it raised for the Cartesians, see R. Dugas, *A History of Mechanics*, New York: Dover, 1988, Part III, ch. 5, "The Principle of Least Action."

—————— Chapter 2 ——————

Causation

Wesley C. Salmon

You awaken to the sound of your alarm clock; you get out of bed to turn it off. Causal relations enter your life at the beginning of your day, even before you are fully conscious. The noise of the clock caused you to wake up and get out of bed; turning it off caused the sound to stop. The same sort of thing is repeated innumerable times throughout the day. Under normal conditions – you hope today is normal! – turning the key in the ignition causes your car to start. After you get going, pressure of your foot on the brake pedal causes the car to slow down. Causation is involved in virtually everything anyone does, day in and day out, year in and year out.

Down the street, a carpenter hits a nail with a hammer, causing it to penetrate some wood. An electrician flips a switch, causing a bunch of lights to go on. At the city morgue, a forensic pathologist tries to figure out what caused a particular person to die. Millions of years ago, the last of the dinosaurs died; scientists have long wondered why. In recent years, they have theorized that the collision of a massive body with our planet caused conditions in which they could not survive. In this case, no humans were involved. Astronomers make extremely precise measurements of the movements of a star; they conclude that its behavior is caused by a planet in orbit around it. Perhaps conditions conducive to the emergence of intelligent life exist out there beyond the confines of our solar system.

So what's the big problem? We all understand causation, don't we? Why should philosophers write long articles on the subject? For an answer, we have to go back to the eighteenth century, and consider what David Hume had to say about it. Whether he was right or wrong, his writings on this subject are the most important.[1]

Hume's Problem

Hume discussed many examples, but his favorite is the behavior of billiard balls. Suppose that we have one ball lying at rest on the table, and another moving rapidly toward it. They collide. It's logical, isn't it, for the one at rest to start moving as a result of the collision? Well, no, he says, it's easy to imagine that the one at rest remains in that state, while the other ball returns in the direction from which it came. But what does Hume's imagination have to do with it? If it were a matter of pure logic, from the description of the cause we should be able to deduce the nature of the effect.[2] Hume shows that this entailment doesn't hold; alternative outcomes are conceivable without any contradiction. Suppose, for ex-ample that the ball at rest is securely bolted to the tabletop. In this case, if the first ball hits the second precisely head on, we surely expect it to come back to where it started. If there's any question, we can set up these conditions and perform the experiment.

Wait, you say. Hume's example didn't include anything about the ball being bolted to the table. True. But the only way we changed Hume's example was by adding some further conditions. Having done this, we see that the new descrip-tion is logically consistent, because that's what would actually happen. Surely, what's actual is possible, that is, logically consistent. Now, if we have a logically consistent group of statements, and then remove one of them, the result *cannot* be self-contradictory. The *only* way to make a consistent set of statements self-contradictory is to *add* a statement that conflicts with something already contained in that set. Having added a statement to Hume's description of the situation, *without assuming it was consistent*, we can now take it away again. The result is a demonstration that what Hume imagined as logically possible is logically possible.[3]

The point of this example can be generalized. From a description of a cause, it is impossible to deduce what its effect will be. Hume gives many other examples to support this point. In addition, he makes the same point in reverse; from a description of an effect, it is impossible to deduce what its cause was. Place a large diamond (if you happen to have one handy) in the freezing compartment of your refrigerator. After it has been brought down to 32°F, take it out and put it beside an ice cube. How, Hume asks, could anyone who has not had prior experience with such objects deduce that one of them is produced – caused – by extremely high temperature and high pressure, whereas the other would be completely destroyed by such conditions? He concludes that distinct events, including causes and effects, are logically independent of one another. No valid deductive infer-ences can be made from the existence or nature of one object from nothing more than a list of the properties of the other.[4] Consider an example in which an entail-ment relation does obtain. Someone might say, "High unemployment is caused by a lot of people being out of work." The word "cause" is certainly out of place; what we have is a definition of "high unemployment," not a cause–effect relation. Definitions govern the use of terms; they do not describe physical relations among events.

Having established his point that causal relations are not logical relations, Hume asks whether we can find any physical relation, such as the power of one event to produce another, or a necessary connection of a nonlogical sort between causes and effects. Let's return to the billiard ball example and examine it carefully. Now we are not looking for a logical relation between cause and effect; we are trying to observe a factual relation between cause and effect. We observe three aspects. First, we notice that the cause comes before the effect; the collision with the moving billiard ball comes before the motion of the ball that was at rest. Second, there is contiguity; the collision and the initiation of motion are close together in space and time. Third, we notice that the same sequence of events will occur every time we set up the same conditions. "Beyond these three circumstances of contiguity, priority, and constant conjunction I can discover nothing in this cause" (1955 [1739–40], p. 187).

What Hume failed to discover is far more important than what he found. A pair of events can satisfy the conditions of temporal priority and spatiotemporal contiguity by sheer coincidence. For instance, a loud thunderclap might have sounded immediately before your alarm went off. The pair of sounds exhibits priority and contiguity, but they bear no causal relations to one another. So we have to appeal to constant conjunction to determine whether these events are causally connected. Repeated experience reveals that thunderclaps are heard when no alarm rings immediately thereafter, and alarms ring when there is no immediately preceding thunderclap. Now, Hume argues, if we observe just one collision of two billiard balls, there is no feature of the situation that reveals the power of the collision to produce the subsequent motion. Moreover, if we have just one case of the thunderclap immediately preceding the ringing of the clock, there is no observable factor whose absence allows us to perceive the lack of causal connection.[5] It is only repetition that enables us to tell the difference. There is no objectively observable aspect of the events that discriminates between causes and coincidences. If we observe additional identical collisions of billiard balls, we will not notice some new characteristic that reveals the causal relation between the events.

After careful extended argumentation, which we have barely sketched, Hume concludes that the constant conjunction, which reveals nothing about the causal relations in the physical situation, has an influence on our minds. If we observe the same pattern of billiard-ball collisions several times, we come to expect the pattern to be repeated. When we see the collision, "habit" – Hume's term – leads us to expect motion to occur in the ball initially at rest. Notice, however, that this conclusion puts the connection between cause and effect in the human mind, not in the physical world. Our idea of causal efficacy is what we now call a conditioned response. It is exemplified by a famous experiment, performed in 1905, by Ivan Petrovich Pavlov. In this experiment, Pavlov rang a bell just as he was feeding his dogs. After this process was repeated a number of times, Pavlov rang the bell without providing any food. The dogs salivated when the bell rang, showing clearly that they expected food. This, according to Hume, is exactly what causation amounts to.

This conclusion is shocking. If causal connections exist only in our minds, then there were no causal connections before humans or other forms of intelligent life (remember Pavlov's dogs) existed, or in places that are not available for observation by such beings. I happen to believe that the Grand Canyon in northern Arizona is an effect of erosion by the Colorado River hundreds of millions of years ago. Not even dinosaurs were present at the time. So, according to Hume, there was no causal relation between the flowing water and the erosion of the earth at that place and time. You can see this more clearly if you imagine that an event – like the one that destroyed the dinosaurs 65 million years ago – had occurred much earlier, permanently eliminating all higher forms of life on earth. In that case, no organisms capable of forming habits would have been around to impute a *causal relation* between the motion of water over stone and the erosion of the stone.

If you're not uncomfortable at this point, you should be. There just has to be some way to escape this paradoxical view of causation. One idea, proposed by John Locke before Hume's time, is that we can directly perceive causal power in certain circumstances. Hume's prime example involves two material objects existing outside of our minds. We should, however, consider cases where conscious intentions are involved. In your philosophy class, you decided to raise your hand to ask a question. Your hand went up. Didn't you feel the power of your will to cause your hand to move? No, said Hume, in answer to Locke. Lots of things had to happen between your wish to raise your hand and the motion of your hand. Somehow brain processes had to send a signal through appropriate nerves to the arm muscles that must contract in order for your hand to move. You were not consciously aware of these intermediate processes, so you couldn't have directly perceived the power to move your hand. In order to learn what's involved in this example, you'd have to study neurophysiology, a highly technical field of contemporary science. However, even learning about all of these physiological details wouldn't really help. Even if you learn that a certain chemical process stimulates an electrical impulse to travel in a nerve, Hume's question comes back at you. What have you found in this situation other than a constant conjunction between a chemical reaction and an electrical response? It's hard to see how you could have perceived a power of the kind that Hume and Locke were talking about.

Classic Responses to Hume

According to Hume's successor, Immanuel Kant, these challenging notions sent him a real wake-up call.[6] By intricate and difficult reasoning, Kant concluded that our sense experience is necessarily organized in certain ways by our minds. His prime example is geometry; we must spatially arrange our perceptions in ways that conform to Euclidean geometry. He classified geometric knowledge as *synthetic a priori*. It is a priori because it can be established by pure reason alone, without the aid of sense experience. Euclid's axioms seemed self-evidently true, and the other propositions follow from the axioms with logical necessity.[7] Therefore, geometry is a priori. But geometry is synthetic because it contains useful information about the physical world; even the ancient Egyptians used it for such practical ends as architecture and surveying. Thereupon, Kant extended his idea of synthetic a priori principles to include causality as well as geometry: "Everything that happens (begins to be) presupposes something from which it follows according to some rule."[8] Even if we were to accept this principle – which is extremely dubious in the light of modern science – it would not be very helpful. Suppose that lightning strikes a tree and we seek its cause. According to Kant it follows from *something*, but there's no clue about what that thing is or where to look for it. Moreover this unknown something is connected to the lightning strike by *some* rule, but again there's no hint as to what kind of rule it is. It's as if someone tells us that there is oil below the seas, without telling us how to find it or how to extract it.

In the middle of the nineteenth century, John Stuart Mill gave us five rather useful rules for discovering or proving cause–effect relations; in fact, they are still in use. First, the *method of agreement* applies to situations in which an effect occurs in many different circumstances, which have only one feature in common. For example, if all of the students in a particular dormitory, who have eaten the same dorm dinner, suffer severe gastrointestinal distress on the same night – and that is the only food that all of them consumed that day – there's a good chance that contaminated food in the dinner caused their digestive systems to behave so disagreeably.

Second, the *method of difference* is used in situations where all antecedent factors except one are the same – that is, some factor is present in some of these cases but absent in others. Moreover, an effect follows in cases in which the factor in question is present but fails to occur when it is absent. In these circumstances, there's a good chance that the factor that differs among the antecedent conditions is the cause of the one that differs among the subsequent circumstances. In one of my first forays into a shop to buy some music on CDs, for example, I made my selections and then headed for the men's room prior to checking out. *Stupid!* As I entered a short hallway, a loud alarm sounded; it nearly scared me out of my wits. A rapid analysis of the situation enabled me to conclude that taking CDs into rest rooms is not allowed and that I had set off the alarm. A quick survey of the situation showed that my crossing the boundary with the CDs was the only difference relevant to the sounding of the alarm. I'm happy to say that the staff readily concluded that it was only my ignorance that led me to carry them in; it was not a case of attempted shoplifting.

Third, the *joint method of agreement and difference* – as the name indicates – is a combination of the foregoing two, and it is more powerful than either by itself. To begin, you get many different cases where the result is present, and many others in which the result is absent. We can see how this works by an actual example similar to the dorm illness case. On an overseas airline flight on a jumbo-jet, two different dinners were offered – one was meat, the other seafood. Everyone who chose the seafood dinner became sick; no one who chose the meat was adversely affected. There can hardly be any doubt that some ingredient in the seafood dinner was tainted.

Fourth, the *method of concomitant variation* applies to situations in which the factors involved are neither completely absent nor completely present to a fixed degree. Instead, some causal factor varies in degree along with a variation in some effect. For example, you might find that the amount of natural gas you use in your household each month varies with the average daily temperature. Clearly there is a cause–effect relation between the outdoor temperature and the amount of gas you use.[9]

Although Mill didn't mention it, perhaps the most important kind of concomitant variation is a variation in frequencies of certain types of occurrences. Tests have shown, for example, that a smaller percentage of men who take an aspirin tablet every day suffer heart attacks than of those who don't. Taking aspirin reduces the risk of a heart attack. It isn't a case of all or nothing. Men who take aspirin do get heart attacks; men who don't take aspirin escape such attacks. It's a matter of percentages. Testing causal hypotheses through the use of such controlled experiments is a powerful tool of modern science that is widely used today.

Fifth is the *method of residues*. If we have a list of possible causes of some phenomenon, and if we have in some fashion ruled out all but one, then the remaining possible cause is likely to be the genuine cause. For example, the planets in the solar system travel around the sun in nearly elliptical paths, but they deviate somewhat from perfect ellipses because of gravitational attraction of other planets. In the nineteenth century, it was noticed that the orbit of Uranus differed from the path calculated by taking account of the influence of other planets, especially Jupiter and Saturn. Since the other known planets could not account for all of the deviations, a previously unknown planet, Neptune, was postulated as the cause; it was observed telescopically not long thereafter.

There is no question that, even though Mill's methods have their limitations, they are useful for distinguishing genuine causal relations from relations that only appear to be causal. Hume didn't help us much with this aspect of causation, but he was interested in a different kind of problem. Hume was asking what causality is. What precisely is the power of a cause to bring about an effect? What kind of relation binds effects to their causes? These are profound questions, and philosophers are still trying to find answers to them. Mill's methods are not particularly helpful in answering the kinds of questions Hume raised. They don't go much beyond the notion that causation amounts to constant conjunction, as Hume had said, but they are useful tools for determining which conjunctions are constant and which are not.

Mill's great work, *A System of Logic*, is *the* classic nineteenth-century work on causation. The twentieth-century classic is J. L. Mackie's *The Cement of the Universe*. Its title is a phrase used by Hume; it poses the question of what holds the universe together. It attempts to show the nature of this cosmic glue that we call "causation." Mackie offers penetrating analyses of the works of Hume, Kant, and

Mill, as well as many others. To understand his work, we must introduce some standard terminology.

Sentences having the form, "If *A* then *B*," are called *conditional statements.* They say that if the condition *A* is present, then the consequence *B* will also hold. In this case, *A* is called a *sufficient condition* of *B*. For example, in the title of an old song – "If you've got the money, honey, I've got the time" – your possession of money is *sufficient* for the availability of my time. Another kind of conditional statement has the form, "If not-*A* then not-*B*." In this case, it says that if the condition *A* is *not* present, *B* will *not* hold. In this case, *A* is a *necessary condition* of *B* – *B* will not occur unless *A* does. The concluding line of the aforementioned song is, "If you run out of money, honey, I'll run out of time." This says that your possession of money is *necessary* for the availability of my time. If both of these statements are true, we say that *A* is a *necessary and sufficient condition* of *B*. According to the song, then, your possession of money is *necessary and sufficient* for the availability of my time.

Conditional statements of the foregoing sorts are often construed as generalizations, i.e., the symbols "*A*" and "*B*" are taken to refer to classes or types of events. Given this interpretation, to say that *A* is a sufficient condition of *B* means that in every case in which an event of *type A* occurs an event of *type B* will also occur. Similarly, to say that *A* is a necessary condition of *B* means that whenever an event of *type A* fails to occur, no event of *type B* will occur. For example, having one's head cut off is a sufficient condition of dying; it is not a necessary condition because there are many other causes of death besides decapitation. Having oxygen to breath is a necessary condition for staying alive. In the absence of oxygen, a person dies. But having oxygen to breathe is not a sufficient condition of life; without food and water as well a person cannot continue to live.

A philosophical account of causation according to which causal relations can be analyzed entirely in terms of sufficient conditions, necessary conditions, or any combination of such conditions is a *regularity theory*. Those who hold regularity theories understand such conditions as generalizations, and they usually require that if an instance of *A* is a cause of an instance of *B*, it precedes that instance of *B*. Hume's theory, as explained above, makes his view a regularity theory. In addition to temporal priority and constant conjunction, he also requires spatiotemporal contiguity. However, it isn't clear from his various statements whether he regards causal regularities as sufficient conditions, necessary conditions, or both. That's not especially important because any simple regularity theory faces serious difficulties.[10] Many regularities that fit the description cannot be considered *causal* regularities; for example, day regularly precedes night, but day doesn't cause night. The regular succession of day and night is caused by the rotation of Earth.

Although Mackie does not, himself, advocate a regularity theory, a major part of this theory would qualify as an extremely sophisticated regularity account.[11] It can best be explained by a concrete example. Suppose that a barn burns down. Speaking loosely, we would say that there are many possible causes, e.g., a lighted cigarette dropped by a careless smoker, a stroke of lightning, deliberate arson, a spark from a workman's torch, and many others. Since there are many possible causes, none of the foregoing can qualify as a necessary condition. Suppose, for the moment, that the careless disposal of a cigarette is (a part of) the actual cause. It cannot, by itself, be a sufficient condition, because other factors must be present. It must land on some inflammable material, such as dry straw, rather than on a clean concrete floor. This straw must be located near other inflammable material, such as wood, in order for the fire to spread. No one who would have put out the fire before it spread could have been present. And so on. A fairly complex *set of conditions* must be fulfilled in order to make up a genuine sufficient condition. At the same time, the dropping of the cigarette is an indispensable part of this set of conditions.

Mackie (1974, p. 62) adopts the acronym INUS – standing for an Insufficient but Nonredundant part of a condition that is Unnecessary but Sufficient – to designate such causal factors as the careless tossing of the cigarette. The complex of conditions containing the improper disposal of a burning cigarette is a sufficient, but not necessary, condition of the burning of the barn; the dropping of the lighted cigarette does not, by itself, constitute a sufficient condition for the burning of the barn, but it is a necessary part of that complex of conditions.

A natural question arises at this point. Why do we pick out the dropping of the cigarette as the cause, rather than another indispensable part of the entire sufficient condition – e.g., the presence of dry straw? According to Mackie, this decision often depends on what is considered usual or unusual in the circumstances. In our particular case, it may be that dry straw is usually present; what is unusual is its contact with a burning cigarette. In some barns, however, the presence of dry straw might be an unusual circumstance (depending on what the barn is normally used for). If the barn had been of the latter kind, the presence of dry straw might be cited as the cause. It, too, is an INUS condition. As Mackie clearly notes, the selection of one INUS condition rather than another as *the cause* depends strongly on the context. Human interests, purposes, and knowledge play a large part in the selection of the cause.

As we saw, Hume's analysis locates causation "in the mind (imagination)." Mackie's aim is to find causation "in the objects" – i.e., in the external world as it exists independently of the human mind. Contexts are determined by the human point of view; conceptions of causation that depend on context don't succeed in finding causation "in the objects." Realizing this point, as Mill had done before, Mackie tries to analyze "the *full* cause" in terms of the set of all of the possible sufficient causes, each of which is spelled out in detail as a conjunction of factors that have to be present in order to insure the sufficiency of each term. In our discussion of the burning of the barn, we obviously left out many possible causes, e.g., spontaneous combustion in hay stored in the barn, burning debris from a nearby forest fire falling on the roof, being struck by a meteor, etc. Mackie (1974, p. 76) realizes that we don't usually know all of the possible causes, so the *full cause* will be represented by an "*elliptical* or *gappy* universal" statement. However, this doesn't solve the problem. Such universals aren't really statements at all; they are *forms of statements* containing blanks that have to be filled in. The blanks reflect our ignorance of the exhaustive list of sufficient conditions – the list that represents the full cause.

Regularity theories in general face a further problem, namely, *causal preemption*. It can be illustrated by the barn example. Suppose that our careless smoker tosses his lighted cigarette toward the dry straw (and that all the other attendant conditions are fulfilled). Suppose, however, that lightning strikes the barn, which is unprotected by a lightning rod, just before the cigarette reaches the straw. The tossing of the cigarette is still an INUS condition by Mackie's formal definition, but the lightning is the cause of the fire. The literature on causation is full of examples of causal preemption; I don't think any version of the regularity theory has a satisfactory resolution of this difficulty.

One of Hume's definitions of causation suggests a different analysis, namely, one in terms of *counterfactual conditionals*. A counterfactual conditional statement is an "if . . . then . . ." statement whose antecedent clause is false. An old nursery rhyme (which I'm extending a bit) contains a sequence of counterfactual conditionals: "For want of a nail, the shoe was lost; for want of a shoe, the horse was lost; for want of a horse, the rider was lost; for want of a rider, the message was lost; for want of the message, the battle was lost; for want of the battle, the war was lost; for want of a victory, a kingdom was lost. All for want of a nail." If the nail had not been missing, the horseshoe would not have been lost – the missing nail *caused* the horseshoe to be lost. If the horseshoe had not been lost, the horse would not have been lost – the missing horseshoe *caused* the unavailability of the horse. And so on.[12]

The problem with counterfactual conditionals is that they are highly context-dependent. In the preceding case, the series of counterfactuals conjures up an overall picture of a military situation with many implicit assumptions about the surrounding conditions. It assumes that there was no means of communication except by the delivery of a message by a rider; it could not have been carried by a runner or sent by a carrier-pigeon. It assumes that no other horse and rider were available to carry the message. It vaguely assumes conditions of battle in which the receipt of a message means the difference between victory and defeat. Because of the dependence on contextual factors, it is extremely difficult to specify objective conditions that determine the truth or falsity of counterfactuals. Therefore, any attempt to analyze causality in terms of counterfactual statements will fall short of locating causality "in the objects." If there is any question about this, consider the difficulty of specifying precisely the situation in which the lack of a horseshoe nail could *actually cause* the loss of a kingdom. Philosophers have made many attempts to solve the problems raised by counterfactuals, but none has been clearly successful.

The approaches to causation that we have considered so far all share a fundamental feature, namely, they analyze the relation between causes and effects in terms of *sentential connectives* – that is, terms like "if . . . then . . ." or "unless" whose function is to join complete sentences together to form more complicated sentences. Regularity views, such as those advocated by Hume, Mill, and Mackie,[13] rely on statements of the form, "If anything is an *A*, then it is a *B*." Counterfactual theories require statements of the form, "If *X* had not occurred, then *Y* would not have occurred," or, equivalently, "*Y* would not have occurred unless *X* had occurred." Sentential connectives are *logical* terms. Perhaps we should be looking for a different kind of relation.[14] Hume had looked, without success, for "necessary connections" and "secret powers." We should look again. As we shall see, the connections need not be necessary and the powers need not be secret. I believe they can be discovered in the physical world and that *they can be objectively characterized entirely in terms of noncausal concepts.* This is the task to which I now turn. Mackie – in his effort to find causation "in the objects" – tried without success to accomplish this goal. He did not succeed. Your philosophy instructor probably believes that it can't be done.

Causation in the Objects – Causal Processes

You see a friend across the street, but she is looking in a different direction, so she doesn't see you. You shout "Hi, Mary!" The sound waves you created travel toward her; she turns and waves to you. Light reflected from her hand reaches your eyes. You know that she has heard your greeting and has recognized you. Stripping this encounter down to its bare essentials, we have three events, namely, your shout, Mary's turning and waving, and your seeing her wave. They are connected by two processes, namely, the sound waves that travel from your mouth to her ears and the light rays that travel from her hand to your eyes. The three events are *causally connected* by these processes. In the end, I shall claim that processes of various types are precisely the causal connections that Hume sought and failed to find, but several key concepts need to be clarified in order to explain this idea.

To begin, we must understand, at least in a fairly rough way, what is meant by the term "process." According to the dictionary, the core meaning of this term designates something that goes on continuously over a span of time. Frequently, it transpires over a spatial distance as well. Some examples will help. As we have already noted, sound waves and light rays are processes. Material objects, such as Hume's famous billiard balls, are processes. An airplane flying through the air is a process, and so is the shadow it casts on the ground on a sunny day. A paperweight that is motionless on your desk is a process because it endures through a span of time – well, it's motionless with respect to your room, but it moves with the Earth as the Earth rotates on its own axis and in its orbit around the Sun. A football being passed by one player to another is a process; so is the motion of the image of the same football if you are watching a movie of the game.

As this term is commonly used, a process is something that is related to some particular goal, whether or not it is designed for this purpose. For example, the process of annealing is designed by humans to make steel softer and less brittle by heating and cooling it. The process of sedimentation produces fertile plains by a river's depositing of silt in a valley. This process was not designed by humans. While we recognize that many processes are picked out because of notable or desired results, we shall not limit our concept to them.[15]

Our notion of a process is similar to Bertrand Russell's concept of a *causal line*. "A causal line may always be regarded as the persistence of something – a person, a table, a photon, or what not. Throughout a given causal line, there may be constancy of quality, constancy of structure or gradual change in either, but not sudden change of any considerable magnitude" (1948, p. 459; pt. VI, ch. 5 is entitled "Causal Lines"). Our concept of process will become much clearer as we proceed. For now, we need to distinguish two kinds of processes, namely, *causal processes* and *pseudo-processes*. Unfortunately, Russell did not make this distinction. We will aim to show how causal processes transmit *causal influence*, whereas pseudo-processes do no such thing. Suppose that you are driving along a road on a sunny day. Both your car and its shadow are processes, but the car is a causal process and the shadow is a pseudo-process. One way to make the distinction is by noting what happens to these two processes if they encounter obstacles. If the shadow meets a stone pillar standing at the roadside, it is temporarily distorted, but as it passes beyond the pillar it resumes its former shape as if nothing had happened. If, however, your car collides with a stone pillar, it will bear the marks of the encounter long after it has moved past the pillar (assuming that it is capable of going on). This means that the causal process (the car) can transmit the marks of the collision beyond the place where it occurred, whereas the pseudo-process cannot transmit any such mark.

Because the distinction between causal processes and pseudo-processes is so fundamental to this approach to causation, let's look at another example. In my office hangs a picture of the famous lighthouse that stands at the port of Genoa, Italy. Like the many other lighthouses all over the world, it is lit at night and its beacon rotates, sending beams of white light in all directions. As I stood at the window of my hotel room one evening during a visit to Genoa, I watched as it sent a beam periodically in my direction. As the light turned, it cast a moving spot of light across the wall of my hotel. As it pointed in other directions the spot of light moved across clouds in the distance. The light sent out in any given direction by the beacon was a causal process; if a piece of red glass had been placed in the beam anywhere between the lighthouse and my hotel window, I would have seen a flash of red light. The color of the white beam would have been changed in its encounter with the red filter, and that change (a mark) would have been transmitted by the pulse of light traveling from the beacon to my window. In contrast, if I had covered my window with transparent red plastic, I would have marked the spot of light traversing my window, but the mark would not have persisted as the spot of light moved on. The mark could have been imposed at one place, but it would not have been transmitted by the moving spot. The moving spot was a pseudo-process; it could not transmit that mark or any other mark.

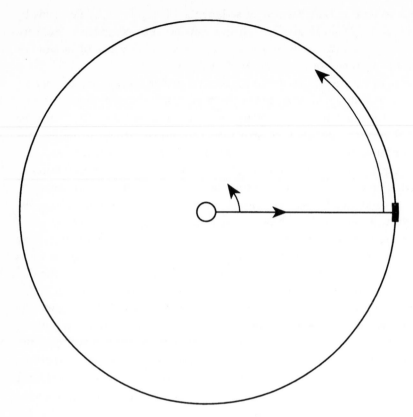

Figure 2.1   Rotating beacon

Causal vs. pseudo-processes

The processes we observe on a movie screen or a TV tube are pseudo-processes. If a passionate (quite possibly drunk) fan of one particular football team – desperately hoping to prevent completion of a pass – were to draw a pistol and fire it into the image of the football on the cinema screen, a hole would be made in the ball at one particular point, but the hole *in the ball* would not persist as the image moved across the screen. Again, the mark could be made, but it could not be transmitted. Shooting the image of the football on the screen would have no effect whatever as far as the completion of the pass was concerned. A similar shot at the image of the football on a TV screen would simply terminate that pseudo-process and all of the others that would have constituted the rest of the TV game as well.

In Hume's lifetime, no fundamental reason existed for the distinction between causal processes and pseudo-processes. The situation changed radically early in the twentieth century – 1905 to be precise – when Albert Einstein formulated his special theory of relativity. People often say that, according to that theory, nothing can travel faster than light.[16] This is simply wrong, unless the term "thing" is construed very carefully. The correct statement is that no causal process can transpire faster than light. Pseudo-processes can go at arbitrarily high velocities. Recall the

Genoa lighthouse. Imagine that it is surrounded by a circular wall around which the spot of light moves. The spot must traverse the entire circle each time the beacon makes a single complete rotation. The larger the circle, the faster the spot must travel to complete its course in the required time. Here is a much more dramatic example. In the Crab nebula, 6,500 light years from Earth, a neutron star (a pulsar) rotates thirty times per second. It sends out a beam of light just as the lighthouse does. The "spot" of light that zips past us traverses the "circle" whose radius equals our distance from the pulsar in one-thirtieth of a *second*; the time it takes for *light* to cross the diameter of this circle is 13,000 *years*. As the spot passes us, it is traveling at approximately $4 \times 10^{13} \times c$ (the speed of light).

Causal processes – in contrast to pseudo-processes – are the means by which causal influence is transmitted from one place and time to another. If a process can transmit a mark, it can transmit information, just as a radio signal can transmit messages, orders, and music. Causal processes – again, in contrast to pseudo-processes – can also transmit energy, momentum, electric charge, and various other physical quantities. A causal process is a process that persists on its own, without contributions from any outside source. Once a pulse of light is emitted from the neutron star, for example, it travels vast distances without any *external* influence. It is, so to speak, self-propelled. Pseudo-processes, in contrast, depend for their continuing existence upon something supplied from an external source. The spot of light created by the rotating beacon of the lighthouse will vanish almost immediately if the light is turned off.[17]

Causation in the Objects – Causal Interactions

When two processes intersect, there are two possibilities. On the one hand, both processes might be altered in ways that pass beyond the locus of the intersection. If, as in the example of the auto and the stone pillar, your car collides with the pillar, the car will carry scrapes and dents until you get it to the body shop to have it repaired. The pillar might be marked by some paint scraped off your car, or some of the stone might be chipped. This is a classic case of a causal interaction. On the other hand, if you avoid hitting the pillar with the car and only the shadow touches it, the shadow will be distorted (marked) at the place in which the intersection occurs, but this change will not persist beyond that location. This is an example of an intersection that does not qualify as a causal interaction.

As a second example, consider two airplanes that are flying on intersecting courses at different altitudes on a sunny day. Their shadows will intersect on the ground below, but no alteration of the shape will persist beyond the intersection. The shadows are pseudo-processes; they cannot interact with one another. A genuine causal interaction requires causal processes.[18] If the airplanes were traveling at the same altitude, the result would be a mid-air collision, and both planes would be altered – perhaps disastrously – in lasting ways.

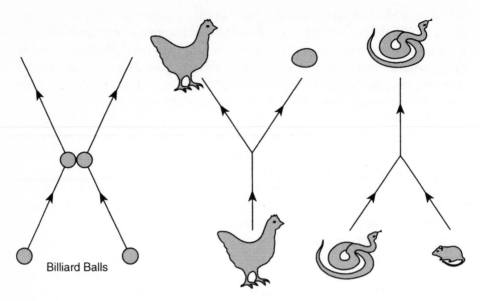

Figure 2.2   Types of causal interaction

The intersections mentioned so far have been cases in which two processes enter and two processes exit. Let's refer to them as *X-type intersections*. Two other basic configurations should be considered. Sometimes a single process splits into two parts. This sort of thing happens when a single-celled organism (e.g., an amoeba) splits into two by fission. We can call this a *Y-type intersection*. A hen laying an egg is another case. At first, we have a single organism, the hen, and later we have two entities, the hen and the separate egg. To be sure, the egg develops inside of the hen, but at some stage two processes exist. For simplicity, I've taken the moment of separation between the hen and the egg as the locus of the intersection.

A mirror image sort of intersection occurs when two processes come together and merge into one. This happens, for example, when a snake ingests a mouse. Following the strategy of the hen–egg example, we can say that the two processes have become one when the mouse is completely inside of the snake. The lower-case Greek letter lambda – which is somewhat similar to an inverted Y – serves as a handy schema. We can call this a *λ-type intersection*.

The criterion of mark transmission that we applied to the X-type intersection doesn't work very well for either the Y-type or the λ-type, so we need a different criterion for distinguishing mere spatial intersections from genuine causal inter-actions. At this point we have to introduce a tiny bit of basic physics. Don't panic – it's really simple. We've already mentioned energy, momentum, and electric charge; these are familiar examples of *conserved quantities* in physics. Take linear momentum, which is defined as the velocity of a body times its mass. The law of conservation of momentum states that momentum is neither created nor destroyed; for example, when Hume's billiard balls collide, the total momentum of the two balls before the collision is equal to their total momentum after the collision. What does happen in the collision is that momentum is *exchanged*. Prior to the collision, the momentum of the ball initially at rest is zero; in the collision some of the momentum of the moving ball is transferred to the one at rest. After the collision, the two balls retain their new quantities of momentum until some new interaction produces further change.

The point of this example can be generalized: *whenever processes exchange a conserved quantity in an intersection, that intersection qualifies as a causal interaction.* This criterion applies equally to the X, Y, and λ types of intersection. If, in any intersection of processes, the outgoing values of a conserved quantity in these processes differ from the incoming values, then, and only then, does the intersection of processes constitute a *causal interaction*. For example, when a hen lays an egg, the incoming process (the hen) has a different mass from either the hen or the egg after the two have been separated.[19] Likewise, the mouse and the snake each have a different mass from the mass of the snake that has swallowed the mouse.[20]

Note carefully an important philosophical point. In the preceding paragraph, the concept of *causal interaction* is explained entirely in terms of *noncausal* concepts. The key notions are *process* and *intersection*. The distinction between causal processes and pseudo-processes is *not* used. Intersection is essentially a geometrical notion (in four-dimensional space–time). On this approach, *causal interaction* is the most fundamental causal concept. *Very roughly speaking*, if processes intersect, and changes that persist beyond the locus of intersection arise, we have the most fundamental causal phenomenon – a causal interaction. Causal interactions *produce* changes; such changes are *propagated* by causal processes. The remaining question is what constitutes causal propagation.

Causation in the Objects – Causal Transmission

About 2,500 years ago, the Greek philosopher Zeno of Elea asked a simple question that turned out to be exceedingly difficult to answer. In fact, this was one of many paradoxes he posed. How can an arrow travel from the bow of the archer to its target? If it could actually move, then, at any place in its (supposed) path, it would be exactly where it is. It would be occupying a space equal to itself, so there would be no extra space in which to move. Moreover, at any moment or point of time, it is where it is. The moment is indivisible, so the arrow couldn't be at one place in one part of the moment and at another place at another part of the moment. It simply would have no space or time in which to move. At every point in its trajectory it would be at rest; therefore, it can't possibly move. Motion, Zeno concluded, is an illusion.

If you've studied even a little bit of differential calculus, you're likely to realize that, in calculus, it's easy to make a distinction between being in motion at a point

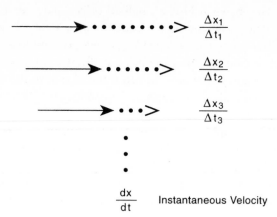

$$\frac{\Delta x_1}{\Delta t_1}$$

$$\frac{\Delta x_2}{\Delta t_2}$$

$$\frac{\Delta x_3}{\Delta t_3}$$

$$\frac{dx}{dt} \quad \text{Instantaneous Velocity}$$

Figure 2.3   Zeno's Arrow

and being at rest at a point. (If you haven't studied calculus, don't worry; the point will become clear very soon.) Pick one point in the arrow, say its center of mass. Then, the motion of the arrow is defined by the position of that point at each moment of time. The calculus defines instantaneous velocity as the derivative of space with respect to time, i.e., dx/dt. The value of the derivative at time t is the instantaneous velocity at that time. If $dx/dt = 0$, the arrow is not moving at t.

Early in the twentieth century, Bertrand Russell showed that, because of the definition of the derivative, this answer to Zeno begs the question. To define the derivative at time t_0 we consider the distance the object travels in a *finite time span* Δt, which includes t_0. The ratio $\Delta x/\Delta t$ is its *average speed* in the *time span* Δt. The operation is repeated for smaller and smaller values of Δt. The derivative at the moment t_0 is the limit of the ratio $\Delta x/\Delta t$ as Δt goes to zero. Thus, the definition of the derivative requires consideration of motions over finite stretches of space and time, precisely the kind of motion Zeno claimed to be impossible. To define the derivative, we have to assume that the conclusion of Zeno's argument is false. This would only evade the problem, not answer it.

Russell then offered an alternative solution. As we have already noted, the motion of the arrow can be represented by noting the position of its center of mass at each moment in the duration of its flight. Russell proposed an "at–at" theory of motion. To say that the arrow moves from A to B *means* that it *occupies* each point in its trajectory at each corresponding moment of time. He doesn't say that it zips rapidly through these points. If you consider the arrow's state of motion at just one moment, without taking into account its position at any other time, the instantaneous velocity has no meaning.[21] If you ask how the arrow gets from the beginning of the path A to the midpoint C, he answers that it is by occupying each point between these two points at the appropriate time. If you ask how the arrow gets from one point to the next, he reminds us that there is no *next* point – between any two points in its continuous path there are infinitely many others.

I find Russell's solution to the arrow paradox completely satisfactory. In addition, it suggests an analogous approach to the concept of causal transmission. Instead of an arrow, think of a bullet shot from a gun. As readers of mystery stories know, when the bullet leaves the gun, marks are made upon it that enable experts to identify the gun from which the bullet was shot. The moving bullet is a causal process; the marks are transmitted. Once the marks have been imposed by the interaction of the bullet with the gun, they remain on the bullet as it travels. To say that the mark is transmitted *means* that it is *at* the appropriate place in the process *at* the appropriate time. Also, the bullet transmits mass, a conserved quantity in this nonrelativistic context. It possesses a certain mass when it exits from the gun, and it continues to possess that same mass without any further interactions to replenish mass. The mass in question is *at* the appropriate place *at* the appropriate stage in the evolution of this process. Thus, we can adapt Russell's "at–at" theory of motion to an "at–at" theory of causal transmission. Note that the bullet transmits information – the marks identifying the gun from which it was shot. It also transmits causal influence. If the bullet strikes a person, it will produce a wound – possibly a fatal wound.

As an additional example of causal transmission, consider a pulse of white light sent out by a beacon. We noted earlier that, if a red filter is placed in the path of this white pulse, the light becomes red and remains red from that point on without any further interactions. The color red is *at* the appropriate place in this process *at* the appropriate stage of its travel.

Complete Causal Structures

Now that we have the three fundamental concepts – causal interaction, causal transmission, and causal process – at our disposal, we can answer the question about causation "in the objects." If we want to give an objective causal account of any spatiotemporal region of the universe, we must take account of all of the causal processes in that region and all of the interactions among them. This includes, of course, all of the causal processes entering and leaving this region. Recall the speeding bullet. As it travels from the gun to the target it collides with a huge number of molecules in the air. Light waves also strike it. This is an extremely complex set of processes and interactions. For most practical purposes much of this can be ignored, but if we want the full causal story, none can be left out. This is a pretty simple case. If we enlarge the sphere of discussion to include the operation of the gun and the effects on the target, the story becomes much more complex.

The complexity is even more evident in an example given earlier, namely, the starting of your car. Light rays impinging on your eyes let you see the ignition switch. A complicated set of nerve stimuli and muscular motions enables you to insert the key and turn it. An electrical contact is made that allows electricity to flow to the starter and to the spark plugs that ignite the fuel in the cylinders. The fuel injector must be activated, so that fuel enters the cylinders in the proper order; the timing mechanism has to coordinate the injection of fuel with the spark. This simple everyday situation is exceedingly complex when we consider the complete causal structure. Fortunately, seldom, if ever, do we need to appeal to all of the complexities of the complete causal structure. One manifestation of the possibility of omitting details of the complete causal structure is the fact that for some purposes a given process may be taken as simple, while for other purposes it is a complicated structure involving many processes and interactions. For a traffic engineer, the motion of a car along a street might be taken as a simple process. In contrast, as we have just seen, for an automotive engineer, the car is an exceedingly complicated set of processes and interactions.

To be quite clear on the status of the complete causal structure, let us recapitulate its construction. Philosophically speaking, the first step is the definition of *causal interaction*. As already mentioned, this concept was introduced without the aid of any other causal concept. We used the notion of a process, without making a distinction between causal processes and pseudo-processes. We used the entirely geometrical concept of an intersection, without distinguishing causal interactions from mere noncausal intersections. We referred to changes in properties, without presupposing that such changes are causal. We then defined causal interactions as intersections of processes in which changes occur that persist beyond the locus of intersection. When we think in terms of marks, we can say that interacting processes produce marks in one another that persist beyond the marking location. When we think in terms of conserved quantities – which, following Dowe, I consider preferable to marks – we say that causal interactions are intersections in which conserved quantities are exchanged.

The next causal concept is *transmission*; *causal interaction* is the only causal concept we use to introduce it. We say that a mark is transmitted by a process if it is present in the process beyond the point of introduction by an interaction *without any additional interactions*. We say that a conserved quantity is transmitted by a process over a finite interval if that process possesses a certain amount of that quantity over that span *in the absence of any additional interactions within that interval*.

Our third basic causal concept is *causal process*; the only causal concept required is *causal transmission*. A process is causal if it is capable of transmitting a mark, or if it actually transmits a conserved quantity. Since you might think that *capability* is a further causal concept, I much prefer the conserved quantity alternative.

Using these three causal concepts, introduced in the manner just described, we have everything necessary to define a *complete causal structure*. The result, in my view, is a genuine characterization of causation *in the objects*.

Causes and Effects

You may have noticed that, in sections 3–6, the terms "cause" and "effect" were hardly used at all. Instead, we referred to processes, interactions, and transmission. The complete causal structure is characterized entirely in terms of these latter concepts. However, the "cause–effect" terminology occurs frequently in everyday life and in science. It is used mainly to select those parts and aspects of the complete causal structure that are relevant to a given situation. This means that cause–effect relations are context dependent, and for that reason, they are not independent of human knowledge, interests, and desires. Thus, while processes, interactions, and transmission are "in the objects," cause–effect relations are not entirely so because of their context-dependence.

Two sorts of configurations are commonly regarded as cause–effect relations. The first involves simply the interaction between two (or more) causal processes. Hume's example of the colliding billiard balls is a good illustration – in Hume's words, "As perfect an instance of the relation of cause and effect as any which we know either by sensation or reflection" ([1748] 1955, p. 186). Each ball is a causal process; the collision is a causal interaction. The motion of each ball is changed in the intersection, and these motions persist after the collision. Notice how much is left out of Hume's description. The interactions between the air molecules and the balls are ignored. The friction of the balls moving on the billiard table is also ignored. Even the spin on the moving ball prior to the collision is left out. Hume tells us that the second ball is initially at rest, but afterward is moving, but he tells us nothing about the motion of the first ball after the collision. That depends sensitively on its spin before the collision. Hume has told us all we need to know to understand his example and the point he is trying to make.[22]

The second common configuration involves two events connected by a causal process. Suppose that some children are playing baseball in a vacant lot. The child at bat hits a ball that crashes through a window of a neighboring house. One event is the collision of the bat with the ball. The ball, traveling from the bat to the window, is a causal process. The second event is the ball striking and breaking the window. We can invoke Hume's remark again. "This is as perfect an instance of the [second type] of the relation of cause and effect as any which we know. . . ." Note again how much is left out. The collisions with air molecules are omitted; so are the positions of the glass shards on the floor of the house.[23] Suppose the batter, observing the direction of the ball, shouts "Oh, no!" (or words to that effect). The sound waves might reach the window at the same time as the ball; however, they would not be considered relevant.

As Mackie pointed out in connection with his INUS conditions, we often make causal judgments in terms of what is usual or unusual in a given case. If dropping cigarettes on the floor were customary in some particular barn and dry straw on the floor very unusual, we might say that the presence of the straw was the cause of the fire. Mackie strongly emphasizes the context dependence of such causal judgments.

Having discussed the context dependence of cause–effect language, I must now emphasize the fact that, *given a particular context*, cause–effect relations may be entirely objective. If water comes through a hole in your roof and damages some of your books, the roofer needs to find the hole and fix it. You need to find out how much it will cost to replace the damaged books. Given the context, each of these questions has an objective answer.

I have no intention of suggesting even for one moment that cause–effect terminology is defective or should be banished; quite the contrary. My principal aim has been to establish the objective nature of causation, and to investigate the ways in which our causal claims can legitimately be applied in the contexts in which they are important. Obviously, we want objective answers to questions about causes of airplane crashes and the onset of diseases, as well as a plethora of other phenomena. Causal explanation sheds light on questions of this sort.

Causal Explanation

It is pretty obvious that causal knowledge is sought both for intellectual under-standing and for practical control. As already mentioned, most scientists investigating the extinction of dinosaurs now believe that the collision of a massive body – a comet or an asteroid – with the Earth produced atmospheric conditions under which the dinosaurs and many other species could not survive. This is a causal explanation of the extinction, and one I find extremely interesting, but I don't see any practical application of this piece of causal knowledge. Nevertheless, it is satisfying to understand the history of our planet and the forms of life that have inhabited it.

In a more practical vein, airplanes crash, leading to death and destruction. We want to discover the causes of such accidents in order to prevent them in the future. If a crash is a result of pilot error, we seek to understand the error in order to show other pilots how to avoid it. If a crash is caused by wind sheers, we seek better ways of detecting them, and we issue orders that places where they are occurring should be avoided. There is nothing we can do about the wind sheer; that is beyond our control, but measures can be taken to lessen their danger to life and property. If the cause is a mechanical failure, we try to ascertain its precise nature in order to make modifications that will prevent such failures in the future.

Where diseases are concerned, causal understanding may enable us to prevent or cure them. Smallpox has been eliminated from the human population by means of an effective vaccine. Antibiotics can cure many kinds of infections. The knowledge that diseases are caused by germs, not mysterious vapors, has been enormously beneficial to humans and other animals.

Causal information plays a crucial role in assigning legal or moral responsibility. If, for example, someone is injured as a result of falling down a flight of stairs, it's essential to find out whether the victim was pushed by an enemy or tripped on a piece of loose carpet. In the former case, the other person is responsible; in the latter case, the landlord would be at fault. Often, of course, many causes combine to bring about an event. If two cars collide at an intersection, both drivers may be equally responsible because of failure to pay attention to other traffic.

Causal knowledge is useful, not only for preventing undesirable states of affairs, but also for producing desired results. During World War I, it was found that soldiers whose wounds were infested with maggots had a survival rate greater than those whose similar wounds were free of maggots. Disgusting? Perhaps, but that's not so important where life and death are at issue.[24]

Further Topics

In this article, we have looked at causation at a fundamental metaphysical level. Almost all of the examples have been taken from physical science. Two questions remain open. First, we have omitted consideration of social causation. Is there such a thing as causation where social institutions are involved, and does it differ from the physical causation we have discussed? One point is surely true. There could be no social causation without physical means of communication. This is an important area for application of transmission via causal processes. However, I am not drawing reductive conclusions. I am *not* saying that all social causation can be reduced to physical causation of the sort I've discussed. Since I know of no satisfactory answer to the mind–body problem,[25] I must, in honesty, remain agnostic on this issue. It is a question for philosophers of psychology and the social sciences to confront. Second, in the social and biological sciences, functional explanations play important roles – e.g., elephants have huge ears because they fulfill the function of controlling body temperature. Can such explanations be analyzed in terms of physical causation?[26]

During the closing decades of the twentieth century, philosophers became increasingly aware of the need to analyze *probabilistic* or *indeterministic* forms of causation. This might initially seem like an incoherent or self-contradictory concept, but it is commonly used in science and everyday life. In discussing Mill's method of concomitant variation, for example, I mentioned the taking of aspirin as a preventative measure against heart disease. I pointed out that it does not prevent heart disease in every case, but it lowers the chances of contracting that malady. Similarly, we have known for many years that heavy cigarette smoking causes lung cancer, but not every heavy smoker is a victim. In fact, in the daily papers and TV news, we frequently find reports of some new medication designed to prevent or cure some disease, where it is obvious that, at best, it will be effective for some percentage of people who try it.[27] We have not been able to pursue this topic; there is an extensive and relatively technical body of literature on this subject.[28]

Twentieth-century physics has established beyond reasonable doubt that causation, at least as we naturally think of it, does not hold in the realm of quantum mechanics. My personal opinion is that there are noncausal mechanisms, which we don't really understand, that operate in the quantum domain.[29] Consequently, our analysis of causation does not apply even to all domains of our world, let alone in all possible worlds.

Our aim has been to learn what causality *is* in this world, to whatever extent it operates. Ours has been an exercise in empirical metaphysics, not an analysis of the uses of linguistic expressions. Naturally, we need some understanding of the meanings of the words "cause," "effect," and their cognates as they are actually used in English in order to be confident that we are dealing with the right concept. It must not turn out, for example, that lung cancer causes heavy smoking or that behavior of the barometer causes storms. Given this sort of initial semantic information, we have tried to find out precisely what our causal terms designate. We have sought to understand basic facts about how the world works, not semantic truths about the language used to describe it. I hope that we have discovered answers to the profound questions Hume raised.

Notes

1 Hume's *Enquiry Concerning Human Understanding* is an excellent classic text for beginning students of philosophy. Sec. IV, Pt. 1 and Sec. VII, Pts. 1–2 contain his central thoughts on causation.

2 Logical purists who object to the notion of entailments between descriptions may substitute phrases such as "a statement that an event of a certain description occurs" or "a statement that an object satisfying a certain description exists" wherever it is required in this essay.

3 Descartes, who is usually considered the first modern philosopher, used a priori causal principles in his proof of the existence of God. This comes at an absolutely fundamental point in his philosophy. He maintains that, by "the natural light of reason," we know that a cause must have at least as much reality as its effect. His book *Meditations*, in which that argument is offered, is another excellent classic text for beginning students of philosophy.

4 Of course, relational properties, such as *being the cause of* or *being the effect of* something else are not allowed as part of the description; to put the matter more generally, the properties in the description are confined to those that are observable by the time the event in question occurs.

5 My dissertation advisor, Hans Reichenbach, reported an incident from his own experience. He was sitting in a theater in Los Angeles watching a film. Just as a major explosion occurred in the film, the theater began to shake. Instinctively, he said, he felt that the explosion depicted on the screen caused the theater to tremble. What happened in fact was that a minor earthquake occurred by chance just when the explosion occurred on the screen.

6 Kant said that Hume had "awakened him from his dogmatic slumbers."

7 In saying that these propositions are self-evident or necessary, Kant did not mean to say that no other logically consistent type of geometry could exist. If he had said that Euclidean geometry is the only consistent geometry, he would have to have concluded

that the statements of Euclidean geometry are *analytic*, not synthetic. He was saying, instead, that Euclidean geometry provides the only framework in which we can visualize spatial relations among the objects in our world. Shortly after Kant's death, non-Euclidean geometries were discovered and shown to be consistent (if Euclidean geometry is consistent), but this did not refute Kant's thesis. However, the use of non-Euclidean geometry in Einstein's general theory of relativity to describe the physical space of our universe shows that spatial relations can have a non-Euclidean structure.

8   Smith (1933), p. 218.

9   If you have gas appliances in addition to a gas furnace, your gas consumption will not go to zero even in the warmest months.

10   Mill made this point in the nineteenth century.

11   Mackie requires an analysis of *causal* priority that is independent of *temporal* priority. This additional requirement does not affect our discussion of the "regularity part" of his theory.

12   David Lewis (1973) is the most famous advocate of the counterfactual account.

13   I am referring, of course, to the "regularity part" of Mackie's analysis.

14   Donald Davidson (1967) argued this thesis convincingly, in my opinion.

15   We will use the word "process" as a noun; however, it also occurs in everyday usage as a verb or an adjective. For instance, a processor in a computer *processes* information in some useful way; I'm writing this article using a word-processor. Process cheese is the result of mixing different kinds of cheese together. I've used *Webster's Ninth New Collegiate Dictionary* (1989) as the basis of these remarks about usage, but I've consulted other dictionaries as well.

16   Light travels at different speeds in different media; the maximum speed is the speed of light in a vacuum.

17   I say "almost" because the last bit of light from the beacon takes some time to travel from the source to the wall. As a pretty good approximation, we can say that light travels at one foot per nanosecond. In the case of the pulsar, "almost immediately" would be a gross error because it takes light 6,500 *years* to get to us.

18   However, causal processes can intersect without interacting. If two light rays intersect, they *interfere* in the locus of the intersection, but they continue beyond as if nothing had happened.

19   In this nonrelativistic situation, mass can safely be taken as a conserved quantity. This supposition is retained throughout the remainder of this essay.

20   The conserved-quantity approach to physical causation was introduced by Phil Dowe. His *Physical Causation* (2000) presents his most recent and most fully developed account.

21   Russell claims that these considerations actually vindicate Zeno. However, Russell points out, even if the arrow is at rest at each point of its trajectory, it doesn't follow that it is always in the same place. To say that what applies to each member of a class holds of the class itself is an example of the elementary fallacy of composition.

22   To a serious player of billiards, the behavior of the first ball after the collision is crucial.

23   If we were concerned with the curve ball thrown by the pitcher, the interactions with the air molecules would be highly relevant.

24   The practical applications of causal knowledge are so prominent that some philosophers have attempted to analyze causality in terms of manipulability; Gasking (1955) is the classic source.

25   This problem is eloquently stated by Descartes in his *Meditations*.
26   Wright (1976) defends the affirmative answer.
27   Some TV ads state explicitly, "Individual results may vary."
28   Patrick Suppes (1970) is the classic starting point for current discussions. Salmon
      (1980) contains a critical survey of various approaches.
29   See d'Espagnat (1979) for a clear and elementary discussion of the quantum
      situation. Mermin (1981, and more colorfully in 1985) offers another clear exposition.

Bibliography

Davidson, Donald (1967). "Causal Relations," *Journal of Philosophy*, 64, pp. 691–703.
Descartes, *Meditations*.
d'Espagnat, Bernard (1979). "The Quantum Theory and Reality," *Scientific American*,
      241, No. 5 (November), pp. 158–81.
Dowe, Phil (2000). *Physical Causation*. Cambridge: Cambridge University Press.
Fair, David (1979). "Causation and the Flow of Energy," *Erkenntnis*, 14, pp. 219–50.
Fales, Evan (1990). *Causation and Universals*. New York: Routledge.
French, Peter A., et al., eds. (1984). *Midwest Studies in Philosophy*, 9. Minneapolis:
      University of Minnesota Press.
Gasking, Douglas (1955). "Causation and Recipes," *Mind*, 64.
Hume, David [1739–40] (1888). *A Treatise of Human Nature*. Ed., L. A. Selby-Bigge.
      Oxford: Clarendon Press.
——. An Abstract of *A Treatise of Human Nature*, in Hume [1748] (1955), pp. 183–98.
——[1748] (1955). *An Enquiry Concerning Human Understanding*. Indianapolis:
      Bobbs-Merrill.
Lewis, David (1973). "Causation," *Journal of Philosophy*, 70, pp. 556–67.
Mackie, John L. (1974). *The Cement of the Universe*. Oxford: Clarendon Press.
Mermin, N. David (1981). "Quantum Mysteries for Anyone," *Journal of Philosophy*, 78,
      pp. 397–408.
——(1985). "Is the Moon Really There When Nobody Looks? Reality and the Quantum
      Theory," *Physics Today*, 38 (April), pp. 38–47.
Mill, John Stuart (1843). *A System of Logic*. London: John W. Parker.
Russell, Bertrand (1943). *The Principles of Mathematics*, 2nd ed. New York: W. W. Norton.
——(1948). *Human Knowledge: Its Scope and Limits*. New York: Simon and Schuster.
Salmon, Wesley C., ed. (1970). *Zeno's Paradoxes*. Indianapolis: Bobbs-Merrill.
——(1980). "Probabilistic Causality," *Pacific Philosophical Quarterly*, 61, pp. 50–74.
——(1998). *Causality and Explanation*. New York: Oxford University Press.
Smith, Norman Kemp (1933). *Immanuel Kant's Critique of Pure Reason*. London:
      Macmillan.
Sosa, Ernest, and Michael Tooley, eds. (1993). *Causation*. Oxford: Oxford University Press.
Suppes, Patrick (1970). *A Probabilistic Theory of Causality*. Amsterdam: North-Holland.
Wright, Larry (1976). *Teleological Explanations*. Berkeley: University of California Press.

Chapter 3

What Events Are

Jonathan Bennett

1 Introduction

The furniture of the world includes planets and pebbles, hopes and fears, fields and waves, theories and problems, births and deaths. As metaphysicians, we want to understand the basic nature of these and other kinds of item; and my topic is the basic nature of births and deaths – more generally, of *events*. If events are things that happen, what differentiates them from sticks and stones, which are things that exist but do not happen? Do events constitute a fundamental onto-logical category, or is our event concept just a way of organizing material that could be handled without its aid?

With questions like those in the background, I ask: what sort of things are events? Locke and Leibniz knew the answer to this; then Kim rediscovered it; but his rediscovery did less good than it might have because it was ambushed by an error. I shall explain.

A sparrow falls. That fall of that sparrow is a particular, located in space and time. It occurs where the sparrow is when it falls, and it occurs just then. It is, then, closely linked to the sparrow, and even more closely to the fact that the sparrow falls there and then. Witness the opening of this paragraph, where I said that a sparrow falls, and went straight on to speak of "that fall." That the fall exists (= occurs) is a logical upshot of the fact that the sparrow falls. Every event results logically from some such underlying fact: there was a fight because some animals fought, there was a storm because wind and water moved thus and so. In section 12, I shall discuss the rival view that some animals fought because there was a fight.

What metaphysical categories have a role in the fact that a certain sparrow fell? Can any of them be identified with *the sparrow's fall*? I shall consider five candi-dates: a fact, a thing, a temporal part of a thing, a property, and a property-instance.

(a) **The fact that the sparrow falls.** One simple reason why an event cannot be a fact is that events have positions in space–time, whereas facts do not. There is also another reason. Suppose that the sparrow, blown about by blustery winds, falls irregularly. Then its fall is irregular: one fall occurs, irregularity being one of its features. Another feature is that the fall goes right to the ground (unlike another sparrow that fell but then recovered in mid-air and flew up again). In contrast with this, the fact that the sparrow falls differs from the fact that it falls irregularly, and each differs from the fact that it moves right down to the ground. With the "that P" method for naming facts, what you see is what you get: if you vary such a fact-name so as to alter its logical force, no matter how slightly, you name a different fact. That is because facts correspond to true propositions, one for one; indeed, some hold that facts are true propositions. Either way, propositional difference carries fact difference with it. Here are some clear symptoms of this: She was surprised that the sparrow fell irregularly, but not that it fell; he hoped that the sparrow would move to the ground, but not that it would fall to the ground; the shadows on the wall are explained by the fact that the sparrow moved irregularly, but not by the fact that it fell. Whenever a statement applies an operator to a fact or proposition, its truth value can be affected by tiny changes in the propositional component; this shows that the change leads to the naming of a different proposition or fact. To suppose that all these differences created differences of events leads to implausible consequences: the sparrow suffered many falls at that time; some but not all were irregular, some but not all went right to the ground, and so on. Now, one good philosopher (Jaegwon Kim) has maintained precisely this, and in section 3 I shall explain why. I now merely point out how implausible it is.

(b) **The sparrow.** We cannot identify this with the fall, if only because the sparrow lasts for months while the fall takes only a few seconds. Well, then:

(c) **The sparrow-stage** – by this I mean the temporal part of the sparrow that stretches from the beginning to the end of the fall. Many philosophers hold that whereas falls and performances and earthquakes have temporal parts, sparrows and sopranos and mountains do not. Even if there are object-stages, however, it seems wrong to identify an event with the corresponding stage of the thing that is its subject.[1] Consider a cannon-ball which arcs its way over the wall of a city while rotating on an axis; it is plausible to suppose that the ball's *journey* is one event and its *rotation* another; but the present proposal identifies each event with the very same ball-stage, which makes them not two events but one. This is hard to swallow. Perhaps there is a richer event made up of the journey and the rotation; indeed, I think there is, though I have no ready name for it. But we want elbow-room in which to distinguish the journey from the rotation, which we cannot do if each is a ball-stage. I shall return to this matter in section 9.

(d) **Falling.** I mean this as a property, a universal, something that can be predicated of anything that falls. This cannot be what the fall of the sparrow is, because when another sparrow falls – or when this sparrow falls again – another fall occurs, another event; but it is the very same property of falling. Properties are universals; events are particulars. Well, then, finally:

2   Events are Property-Instances

(e) **The instance of falling.** I shall introduce this concept of "instance" through a different example. According to many philosophers down the ages, the fact that this pebble is round has involved not only *the pebble* (a concrete particular) and *roundness* (an abstract universal) but also *the roundness of this pebble*, which is an abstract particular. The roundness of this pebble, unlike the property *roundness*, is particular, pertaining only to this pebble; and unlike the pebble it is abstract, involving no property except roundness. (I use "abstract" in the good, Lockean sense of something not saturated with detail; not in any of the *mélange* of contemporary senses – existing necessarily, being out of space–time, lacking causal power, and so on.) Here are four uses that philosophers have made of property-instances.

(i)   Some late medieval philosophers thought that in sense perception a property-instance – sometimes called a "sensible species" – gets from the object to the percipient, which explains how roundness comes to be represented in my mind when I see something round. This entails that a property-instance can exist without anything's having it, as Berkeley implied when he said that a mind is not extended although extension exists in it, because it is "in the mind . . . not by way of mode or attribute but only by way of idea."

(ii)   Some philosophers have thought that causation involves the transfer of a property-instance from one thing to another. This lies behind Locke's remark that even in the familiar impact of body on body something "inconceivable" occurs, namely one thing's giving motion to another. It does not imply that a property-instance can exist when nothing possesses it, but it does imply that a single property-instance can be owned by first one thing and then another.

(iii)   Many philosophers right through to today have worried about the concept of *thing*; we can enumerate all the properties of a thing, they have thought, but how should we understand the thing that has the properties? One popular answer to this says that no separate thing has the properties, because things are bundles of properties, nothing more. In one version of this theory, a thing is a bundle of universals; in a different version – less fraught with difficulties – it is a bundle of property-instances. This view can, but does not have to, be advanced as part of the stronger thesis that basically there are only property-instances, a thing being one kind of aggregate of them and a universal property being another.

(iv)   Events are property-instances. That seems to have been Locke's view of them. Although he sometimes takes "modes" to be universal properties, he often thinks of them rather as instances, and then he tends to identify them with events or with one species of events, namely actions: "The greatest part of mixed modes, being actions which perish in their birth, are not capable of a lasting duration, as [are] substances, which are the actors" (1690, p. 465; see also pp. 289–90, 390, 429). Leibniz understood him in that way, and agreed:

> Locke's spokesman: Of all our various ideas, only the ideas of substances have proper, i.e., individual, names. For it seldom happens that men need to make frequent references to any individual quality or to some other accidental individual. Furthermore, individual actions perish straight away, [unlike] substances.

> Leibniz's spokesman: In certain cases, though, there has been a need to remember an individual accident, and it has been given a name. So your rule usually holds good but admits of exceptions. Religion provides us with some: for instance, the birth of Jesus Christ, the memory of which we celebrate every year; the Greeks called this event "Theogony", and gave the name "Epiphany" to the event of the adoration of the Magi. (1705, p. 328)

The phrases "individual quality" and "accidental individual" come from the mouth of Locke's spokesman, but Leibniz put them there. He evidently had no doubt that Locke meant to be deploying the concept of a property-instance, and does not hesitate to identify such instances with events.

Of the above four theories the first is clearly false; I am sceptical about the second and agnostic about the third. The fourth, however, seems to be exactly right. If the sparrow's fall is a particular instance of the property *falling*, that explains all the facts about why, when, and where it occurs. It explains why the sparrow's fall is so intimately linked with

- a fact (its existence is implied by the fact that the sparrow falls),
- a thing (it is possessed by the sparrow for a while),
- a thing-stage (it is possessed by the relevant sparrow-stage throughout its existence), and
- a property (it is an instance of the property *falling*),

without being identical with any of them. It also explains how there can be a rich event made up of two more abstract ones each occupying exactly the same spatio-temporal zone, e.g., the event composed of the cannon-ball's journey and its rotation. Just as a property can be composed of two more abstract properties, so a property-instance can be composed of instances of two more abstract properties.

3   Kim's Metaphysics and Semantics of Events

The theorist of events who has given most play to this view of events is Jaegwon Kim, who calls events "property exemplifications" (Kim, 1966, 1969, 1973,

1980). By this he seems to mean that they are property-instances. I have publicly interpreted him in that way, and have criticized an inference he makes from his account of what events are; Kim in reply has defended his inference, without suggesting that I had its premise wrong (Bennett, 1988: chapter 5; Kim, 1991).

Before proceeding, let us amend our language: in place of Kim's "property-exemplification" and my "property-instance" I now adopt the term "trope," which D. C. Williams (1953) invented to replace "property-instance."

Kim's insight that events are tropes did not do as much good as it should have, because of the wrong inference from it which I mentioned. As applied to the sparrow example, the inference goes like this:

> Falling is a different property from falling irregularly; so an instance of falling differs from an instance of falling irregularly; so when the sparrow falls, at least two falls occur, one an instance of falling and the other of falling irregularly.

These answers are not based on mere intuitions about what sounds right. Knowing that the answers are correct is part of elementary competence in the use of this part of our language. If a theory says that any of the answers is not strictly true, that is a defect in it. If on the other hand all three answers are true, then the kick he gave her was the assault he made on her; so Kim's conclusion is false.

His premise, however, is true: events are indeed tropes. So there must be something wrong with Kim's inference, and I now explain what it is. Although each event is a trope, I contend, an event name ("the sparrow's fall," "his assault on her") need not wear on its face every detail of the trope that it names. In this respect, names of events resemble names of physical objects: "the book on the table over there" says nothing about many features of the book to which it refers; to know the rest of the facts about it, you must turn from the name to the book. Exactly analogously, "his assault on her" says nothing about many features of the assault to which it refers; you cannot learn whether it was a kick (for instance) just by thinking about the name you have used for it; to know whether it was a kick or a punch you must investigate it out there in the world. In conclusion: events are tropes, and standard event names – I mean ones like "the kick that he gave her" and "the tornado that swept through this county last month" – tell you *something but not everything* about what trope the event is. They tell you one of the properties of which it is an instance, but not all of them. Someone who agrees with Kim about that might explain away its counterintuitive nature as follows: "One fall includes the other; indeed, one maximal fall includes all the others that occur at that time and place. When we count 'falls' in informal contexts we are really counting maximal falls. That is why Kim's conclusion strikes us as false when really it is true." In plenty of cases, though, our intuitions cannot be explained in that way. For example, he assaulted her by kicking her: with him as subject and her as object, there was a kick and an assault. Kim's inference makes these out to be different acts (and thus different events) because they are instances of different properties; and neither includes the other, so that the concept of maximalness gets no grip, and cannot be used to explain why we think it right to identify the kick with the assault.

I have mentioned our intuitive reactions to some things that Kim says; but my claim that the kick is the assault has a solider basis than that. Appeals to shallow and unexamined linguistic intuitions run all through the literature on events, and I want no part of them. Suppose that these are the facts:

> He assaulted her once, which he did by kicking her, and at no other time did he either assault her or kick her.

That, I contend, makes the following answers to these questions inevitable:

> How many kicks did he give her? One.
> How many assaults did he make on her? One.
> Was that kick that he launched at her a feint? No, it was an assault.

What else should we expect, given that events are contingently existing particulars? Why on earth would such things be referred to by expressions that tell the whole truth about them?

4   Kim's Inescapable Truism

Kim (1991) has resisted this critique of his inference. By accepting his premise and rejecting his conclusion, he has argued, I have come into conflict with an "uninformative but inescapable truism," namely:

> "The exemplification of property P by substance S at time T" (if it names anything) names the exemplification of P by S at T.

I would rather not deny this! But I do not accord it the power that Kim thinks it has, and I now explain why.

The phrase "the exemplification of P" can be taken in either of two ways. (1) Understood as a partial describer, an item can truthfully be called "the exemplification of P by S at T" even if it is also – still in the partial describer sense – the exemplification by S at T of some other property Q. We would be using the phrase in this partial-describer sense if we characterized the divorce of Elizabeth and John at T as "the exemplification by Elizabeth and John at T of *executes a legal procedure*"; we would not be meaning to rule out its also being an exemplification by them at that time of other properties, such as *ends a marriage*. (2) Alternatively, we could understand "the exemplification of P by S at T" as a complete describer, meaning that the item referred to cannot also be an exemplification of some other property Q. On this complete-describer reading of it, the phrase in question refers to some item the whole truth about which is that it is an exemplification of P by

S at T. In ordinary English we would never use "exemplification of . . ." etc. in this complete-describer fashion; that is why I cannot make it sound natural or find idiomatic examples of it. Still, the concept is clear enough.

To get a sense of how it works, consider a complete-describer terminology that we *do* actually have, namely the "that P" way of referring to facts. The fact that

he ran for about three minutes at about six miles per hour

is not the fact that

he ran for two minutes and fifty-nine seconds at about six miles per hour

or the fact that

he ran for about three minutes at exactly six miles per hour;

nor is it to be identified with any fact that we name by slightly altering the logical content of that first fact-naming sentence – increasing or decreasing precision, adding or subtracting descriptive color, whatever. Any change in content yields a different fact; the initial fact-name presents the entire intrinsic truth about the fact which it names. Well, that is how it would have to be with "exemplification of . . ." names of events if they were understood as complete describers. In each terminology, what you see is what you get.

The basic issue between Kim and myself is that when we both say that the sparrow's fall is a trope, he wants to call it "the exemplification of *falling* by that sparrow at T" with this meant as a complete describer; whereas I hold that that phrase fits the fall only when taken as a partial describer.

Now, I accept Kim's truism in each of its two clean readings. I accept the following:

When "the exemplification of P by S at T" is used as a partial describer, if it names anything it names the exemplification of P by S at T,

when its final phrase is also used as a partial describer. I also accept this:

When "the exemplification of P by S at T" is used as a complete describer, if it names anything it names the exemplification of P by S at T,

when its final phrase is also used as a complete describer. Each of those is indeed a truism. Kim must mean the final phrase to work as a complete describer: only thus can he distinguish the exemplification of *kicking* from the exemplification of *assaulting*, and so on. Very well, then: I accept Kim's inescapable truism on its complete-describer reading. Does this push me towards his semantics?

It does not. I say that the kick he gave her was the assault he made on her; I also say that the kick is a trope or property exemplification and (of course) so is the assault. When I call the kick "an instance of *kicking*," I mean this as a partial describer; I do not offer that phrase as telling the whole truth about the kick. To come to terms with Kim's argument, however, I must use the language of instances or exemplifications in the complete-describer manner. I can do that, but I must be careful. Suppose that I want to use a complete describer to refer to the kick that he gave her: I mean the real kick out there in the world, the one that was also an assault, a mistake, a betrayal, and so on. I characterize it not as "an exemplification of *kicking*" but rather as "an exemplification of . . ." some much richer property of which *kicking* is one component. To discover its other components, I must investigate what happened between him and her at that time. The result may be something that starts like this:

> The kick that he gave her was an exemplification of: *kicking hard with the right foot as an assault* . . . etc.

Similarly, the assault that he made on her was an exemplification not of *assaulting* but of a richer property with that as a component. After due inquiry it may turn out that

> The assault that he made on her was an exemplification of *assaulting by kicking hard with the right foot* . . . etc.

When fully spelled out, the two will be equivalent; they will refer to the very same property; so the kick that he gave her was the assault that he made on her, and this can be said and established purely in terms of the complete-describer use of "exemplification of . . .". So I stand by the thesis that events are tropes or property exemplifications, yet am not drawn into Kim's semantics of event names.

In showing how to tell the truth about events using complete-describer language, I do not endorse the latter. It is in fact a bad way of referring to any contingently existing particular. Imagine confining ourselves to complete describers in referring to people or islands or shoes!

5   How to Distinguish Events From Facts

As well as maintaining that his metaphysic of events entails his semantics for their names, Kim has defended the semantics on independent grounds. I shall explain how. When she asked him "Do you want to get out of this relationship?" he shouted "*Yes!*" He produced an answer, and also a shout; most of us would say that the shout was the answer, i.e., that only one event occurred, he performed only one act. Kim thinks differently, but he does not say so in quite these terms. Rather, he says things like "His shouting at her is not the same as his answering her." Now, that is persuasive: it seems clearly right to distinguish his shouting at her from his answering her. Then does Kim have a point after all?

No. We can (i) distinguish his shouting at her from his answering her without (ii) distinguishing his shout from his answer; for (ii) concerns events while (i) has nothing to do them. The phrases "his shouting at her" and "his answering her" refer not to events but to facts. Consider these two statements:

(a)   The fact that he answers her is not the same as the fact that he shouts at her.
(b)   His answering her is not the same as his shouting at her.

Nobody would dispute (a), which is obviously true. Most people find (b) plausible too, which explains why Kim uses it in argument; but not everyone has seen that it is plausible because it is strictly equivalent to (a). I now proceed to defend this, arguing that "his answering her" refers to the fact that he answers her.

With minor grammatical adjustments, "his answering her" and "that he answers [answered, will answer] her" can be interchanged in all *factual* contexts (I shall explain that at the end of this section), as can "his shouting at her" and "that he shouts at her":

It surprised me that he shouted at her, but not that he answered her;

His shouting at her surprised me, but not his answering her.

That he shouted at her constituted harassment, but not (the fact) that he answered her;

His shouting at her was harassment, but not his answering her.

That he shouted at her is one fact about his behavior, that he answered her is another;

His shouting at her is one thing, his answering her is another.

I knew that he shouted at her, but not that he answered her.

His shouting at her was known to me, but not his answering her.

I was aware that he shouted at her, but not that he answered her.

I was aware of his shouting at her, but not of his answering her.

On and on it goes. "His answering her" is a so-called *imperfect nominal*. It is a nominal, a noun phrase, which can serve as the subject of a sentence, as it does in the above examples. It is imperfect because in it the gerund "answering" retains many features of the verb from which it comes. Compare:

direct object: he answers her – his answering her
adverb: he loudly answers her – his loudly answering her
tense: he has answered her – his having answered her
modals: he has to answer her – his having to answer her.

In all these ways the gerund "answering" ("having answered," "having to answer" etc.) behaves like a verb; it has, as Zeno Vendler neatly puts it, a verb alive and kicking inside it. There is nothing surprising about the grammatical similarities between "his answering her" and "he answers her," given that they both name a single item.

None of this holds for *his answer* (meaning his action, not his words or their meaning). The noun "answer" takes adjectives not adverbs; it cannot be modified by tenses or modalities; it cannot have an indirect object – we cannot say "his answer her" but only "his answer to her." It is perfectly a noun, with no grammatical traces of its parent verb; and, consistently with that, we use it to refer not to his answering her but to the answer that he made, not to a fact but to an event. So his answer can be a shout: it is just false to say that his answer was one event and his shout another; nobody would entertain such a thought for a moment if some philosophers had not conflated his answer with his answering her, confusing an event with a fact.

Sometimes things get even worse, and philosophers use pathological phrases such as "the event of his answering her," as though you could turn a fact name into an event name by putting "the event of" in front of it. If the phrase had been "the event, his answering her" this would be bad enough: it would be like writing "the physical object seven" or "the comedy *Hamlet*" – false labeling. The phrase "the event *of* his answering her" is even worse: it is not English but philosophers' pidgin.

I said that an imperfect nominal and the corresponding that-P clause are routinely interchangeable "in all *factual* contexts." The sentences I gave as examples – including

It surprised me that he shouted at her,
That he shouted at her constituted harassment,
I knew that he shouted at her

– are all factual, in the sense that they all imply that he shouted at her. That is not implied by the likes of

They believe that he shouted at her, and
I hope that he shouted at her,

which therefore count as non-factual uses of the that-P form.[2] Significantly, they cannot be expressed with imperfect nominals.

6 Perfect and Imperfect Gerundial Nominals

Another source of error is more widespread in the literature; though more excusable than the "event of [imperfect nominal]" nonsense, it is equally harmful to talking sense about events. As well as imperfect gerundial nominals, which stand for facts, there are also perfect gerundial nominals, which stand for events. The difference between the two kinds of nominal has been noted by many grammarians and linguists; it was Zeno Vendler who discovered its alignment with the fact/event difference, and I am relying on his work here (Vendler, 1967; also Zucchi, 1993).

I shall start up a new example to illustrate how the two sorts of nominal differ. Datum: he pushed the rock, thereby dislodging it from the hole in which it lay half-buried. The fact that he pushed the rock is entirely distinct from the fact that he dislodged it: neither entails the other; and their relations to surprise, belief, expectation, gladness, regret and so on can be quite different, as can their roles in explanations. We can also say this using imperfect nominals: his pushing the rock is one fact, his dislodging it is another; his pushing it was legal, his dislodging it criminal; and so on.

Now consider the phrase "his pushing of the rock." This is a perfect nominal, in which the gerund bears no grammatical marks of its origin in a verb. The word "of" indicates this: the object is now genitive, not direct. Whereas "his pushing the rock" is a natural partner of "He pushes the rock," "his pushing of the rock" is grammatically like "the surface of the rock." Can the insertion of a mere "of" make much difference? It certainly can! If he pushed the rock strenuously, that can be reported by putting an adjective into the perfect nominal: "his strenuous pushing of the rock." We cannot use the adverb "strenuously" here. Tenses and modals have no place with the perfect nominal, either, as you can easily verify for yourself. On the other hand, perfect nominals do have plural forms and (connected with that) they can take definite and indefinite articles: "pushings of the rock," "a pushing of the rock," "the pushing of the rock." Try those with the imperfect "pushing the rock" and you will find that it cannot be done.

I chose to start with the genitive-object feature of perfect nominals, but it has no privilege. Take instead the phrase "the pushing": the definite article enforces its perfect-nominal status, keeping out adverbs, tenses, direct objects, and so on. Or start with "strenuous pushing": the mere fact of the adjective lets in articles and plurals, keeps out direct objects, and so on. The members of this tight cluster of grammatical features stand or fall together.

In all of these respects, the perfect gerundial "pushing of the rock" behaves exactly like the noun "push" as in "push that he gave the rock." It also turns out that "his pushing of the rock" and "the push that he gave the rock" can be interchanged in all contexts. The case for regarding perfect nominals as names of events is strong.

With that in mind, consider this interchange between Kim and Donald Davidson. Kim first:

> It is not at all absurd to say that Brutus's killing Caesar is *not the same as* Brutus's stabbing Caesar. Further, to explain Brutus's killing Caesar (why Brutus killed Caesar) is not the same as to explain Brutus's stabbing Caesar (why Brutus stabbed Caesar). (1966, p. 232n)

Davidson responded thus:

> I turn . . . to Kim's remark that it is not absurd to say that Brutus's killing Caesar is
> not the same as Brutus's stabbing Caesar. The plausibility of this is due, I think, to
> the undisputed fact that not all stabbings are killings . . . But [this does not show]
> that this particular stabbing was not a killing. Brutus's stabbing of Caesar did result
> in Caesar's death; so it was in fact, though not of course necessarily, identical with
> Brutus's killing of Caesar. (1969, p. 272)

Kim reported this later by saying: "Davidson and I disagree about . . . whether
Brutus's stabbing Caesar is the same as Brutus's killing Caesar (1980, p. 125).
Notice the switch from Kim's imperfect nominals to Davidson's perfect ones, followed by Kim's switch back again. That change of terminology enables Kim to
say true things about facts and Davidson to respond by saying true things about
events. The audible *click!* as the change occurs evidently passed unheard by both
writers.

Summing up: We have four kinds of expression to consider: (1) Ones containing complete sentences – "(The fact that) she kissed him tenderly." (2) Imperfect
nominals: "her kissing him tenderly." (3) Perfect nominals: "her tender kissing of
him." (4) So-called derived nominals, as in "the tender kiss that she gave him."
Everyone agrees that category 1 name facts while 4 name events. I have argued,
following Vendler, that 2 goes with 1, and 3 with 4. Though superficially similar,
2 and 3 are unlike in their syntactical properties; and grasping that frees one to
admit the plain evidence that they are also semantically unalike: 2 name facts,
3 name events. Many philosophers still have trouble with the difference
between 2 and 3, naively offering expressions like (2) "my daughter's eating all
the brownies" as names of events. If you want to write about events and to protect
yourself from clumsy misunderstandings, I suggest that you avoid (3) perfect
gerundial nominals altogether, and stay with (4) such event sortals as "accident,"
"answer," "birth," "blow," "circumcision," "coronation," "death," "eclipse,"
"explosion."

Having cited an example about stabbing and killing, I should report a debate
about that. Some writers who do not side with Kim across the board, and who
think that an answer can be a shout, nevertheless distinguish Brutus's stabbing
of Caesar from his killing of him on the grounds that the stabbing is complete
before the killing is (Cleland, 1991, pp. 392–4). That assumes that the time
of the killing runs on until the victim dies, which means that it could run on
until after the killer has died! A better solution is this: a killing is an action which
has a certain relational (causal) property; it occurs at the time and place where the
person makes the relevant movements; but it may acquire that relational property
after it is all over, i.e., after the event in question has ceased to exist. There is no
philosophical difficulty about this: it is logically on a par with someone's posthu-
mously becoming a great-great-grandfather. (For a full discussion, see Bennett,
1973.)

7 Tropes That Are Not Events

It has been maintained that all events must be changes (Lombard, 1986, ch. 6). That entails that each event must involve the instantiation of one property and then later of a different one, which means that each event must stretch through time. That debars starts and finishes – construed as instantaneous – from counting as events. It also implies that, although when a monument decays over centuries there occurs a protracted event which we might call *its decay*, no corresponding event occurs when a monument remains unchanged for centuries. You may find one or both of these plausible; I have no strong views about either, and do not want any. Each case involves a trope; and questions about whether this or that trope counts as an event are of no metaphysical interest.

Contrast this with the metaphysical theory that a physical object is an aggregate of spatiotemporal zones. Someone who finds that plausible, as Newton and Spinoza did and as I do (Newton, 1664; Bennett, 2001, sections 53–5), will not say that every aggregate of zones is a physical object; he will want to understand what it takes for an aggregate to satisfy the rather stern constraints that our concept of a physical object lays down. Our evidence about these comes not from shapeless intuitions of verbal propriety but from plain hard structural facts about what inferences are valid, what statements are self-contradictory, and so on. There are such facts because the physical object concept does a great deal of central, disciplined work for us. Not so our event concept. We use it to give small, vague gobbets of information about what goes on – the storm lasted for three days, the battle raged fiercely, he has been through two divorces – but when we want precision and detail we pay off the event concept and employ other parts of our conceptual repertoire instead. That is why the issue about which tropes are events is so thin.

Similarly, it has been maintained that relational tropes are not events: there was no such event as Xantippe's entry into widowhood, because if there were it would be an instance of the relational property: being married to a man who dies (Lombard, 1986, 123f). This implies that such phrases as "Foreman's loss of his title" are not strictly proper, for that claims to name an event, which would have to be a relational trope. We might live with this if it were implied by our best theory to cover the central facts about how our event concept behaves, but no-one has demonstrated any such backing for it.

Again, some have thought that a single event must be a trope possessed by a single object. This implies that there is no such event as a conversation, because two or more people don't constitute an object (Lombard, 1986, p. 239). That is also fiercely counterintuitive, and the supposed theoretical basis for it is weak. Granted that an event is a trope, and even granted that a trope can exist only at a zone where *something* has the property, it does not follow that what has the property must be *some one object* rather than a scattered aggregate of objects, for example, or a spatiotemporal zone. As before, these considerations should give way in face of solid theoretical advantages for the thesis that a single event must be tied to a single object; but nobody has shown, or even tried to show, that there are any such.

8 Zonal Fusion of Events

The cannon-ball's journey and its rotation occupy exactly the same spatiotemporal zone: the ball journeys when and where it rotates, and only then and there. If there is a single qualitatively richer event E that consists of these two, we call E the *non-zonal fusion* of the two. It is non-zonal because E results not from combining items from different zones, but from putting together qualitatively different items from one zone. If two events do not occupy the same zone, then an event which consists of those two must be spatially and/or temporally larger than either of them; such an event is called the *zonal fusion* of the two smaller events. From now on I shall use the unadorned "fusion" as short for "zonal fusion."

It is clearly all right to allow some fusions: a speech is the fusion of many briefer episodes, a riot is the fusion of many spatially smaller episodes (unless there is no such event as a riot because it does not have a single "object" as its subject). Some theorists of events – notably Judith Jarvis Thomson – hold that for any set of events there is a unique event that is the fusion of all of them (Thomson, 1977, pp. 78–9). This implies the existence of some pretty exotic events, such as the fusion of all the impolite utterances ever made by people with an "h" in their names.

Thomson remarks: "I have no argument for the Principle of Event Fusion. But it seems to me that there is no argument against it either" (1977, p. 82). Actually, her book on events is a kind of argument for it: the book presents an elaborate metaphysical theory of events, the building-blocks of which are the concepts of *event*, *cause*, and *part*; and it relies on the assumption that there are almost no restrictions on the fusion of events. This theory, however, has not won much acceptance; so the door is open to some rival metaphysic that does justice to our actual handlings of our event concept, is cleaner and more economical than any of its unrefuted rivals, and owes some of its success to restrictions that it places on fusion. That would be evidence that not all fusions of events are events.

So far nothing has come through that door. All we have been offered are "intuitions" – that is, quick appeals to episodes of naive astonishment – sometimes expressed with the all-purpose word "surely."[3] In this area of philosophy, as in every other, intuitions are of value only if they point the way to results that are theoretically solid. *Mere* intuitions are worthless.

One might argue for some more restricted principle of fusion, something saying that if $R(e_1, e_2)$ then there is an event that is the fusion of e_1 and e_2 – for some suitable R. Here are some plausible candidates: – (1) e_1 spatially or temporally overlaps e_2. If that sufficed for there to be an event fusing the two, events would be on a par with continuous, or unbroken, portions of matter. (2) e_1 is an immediate, or direct, cause of e_2. That would yield fewer events, but it would imply that every unbroken causal chain is an event (unless there is action at a spatial or temporal distance). (3) Given certain standing conditions, the occurrence of e_1 logically necessitates the occurrence of e_2. For example, given that Socrates was married to Xantippe, has dying absolutely necessitated her becoming a widow; and so the occurrence of his death necessitated the occurrence of her entry into widowhood. If relational tropes can be events, then clearly we have two events here – two tropes with different subjects in different places. On the present proposal we shall allow that there is also a single event that fuses those two.

I am sympathetic to all three of those proposals, but I know of no thick reasons – as distinct from paper-thin intuitions – for preferring any one of them, or indeed for rejecting Thomson's virtually unconstrained approach to zonal fusion.

9   Event-Identity: Non-Duplication Principles

The term "identity" is imposing and sounds deep and central, but when philosophers have discussed "identity conditions for events" they have generated more heat than light. This is partly because some of them have not been clear about what the problem is, wandering so far astray as to ask (absurdly) what the conditions are under which "two events are the same," or to ask (trivially) which events are identical with which.

However, we can do better. One objective is to discover sufficient conditions for event-identity, that is, values of R for which it is true and not trivial that

For any event x and for any y: if R(x,y) then x is y.

The problem here is to discover values of R that make this true but not trivial. Any success in this search must involve *a relation which no event can have to anything else*. Some proposals about this have involved relations of likeness: no event can be similar in such-and-such a way to anything but itself. Davidson, for example, has suggested that no two events can be related by R_{ce} = having the very same causes and effects, which means that if x is an event and $R_{ce}(x,y)$ then x is y. Such theses are non-duplication principles; they say that an event cannot be duplicated in a certain manner by another event.

It has often been remarked that Davidson's thesis could not help anyone who was trying to get a first hand-hold on event-identity, because a grasp of that is needed in establishing what the causes and effects of a given event are. Anyway, nobody has done anything interesting with this thesis, apart from some significant attempts to refute it (Brand, 1977, p. 366; Thomson, 1977, p. 70). Nor have discussions of it ever hooked into any metaphysical issues about what events are.

The same does not hold for the only other non-duplication principle that has been proposed, namely Quine's thesis that no two events be related by R_{st} = having the very same position in space–time. This says that if x is an event and $R_{st}(x,y)$

then x is y. It does have a metaphysical thrust; for it amounts to identifying events with stages of their subjects, and thus denying that the cannon-ball's rotation can be one event and its arcing across the sky another. I reject that. Each of the two salient facts about the cannon-ball attributes to it a property (one relational, one monadic), so to each there corresponds a trope; so there is every reason to say that there are two events here. That is not to deny that the (non-zonal) fusion of those two events is also an event, a trope consisting of an instance of the property *arcs across the sky while rotating*.

Non-duplication principles all concern sufficient conditions for event-identity: sameness of causes and effects (Davidson) or of spatiotemporal location (Quine) is said to *suffice* for identity. What about necessary conditions for identity? Do they present us with interesting theses that are mirror-images or logical duals of non-duplication principles? They do not. If it is interesting to be told that if x is like y in such-and-such respects then x is y, the interest lies in what the relevant respects are. But if x is y then x is like y in *every* respect; there is no space here to do philosophy in.

10   Event-Identity: Parts and Wholes

Of the remaining questions about "event-identity" that rattle around in the literature, most are about parts and wholes. A months-long battle around and (eventually) in Stalingrad had temporal parts, of which one occurred in September 1942 and another in February 1943. We can refer to the big long battle through descriptions pointing to either of these parts, and that enables us to come up with an identity-statement: "The battle being fought around Stalingrad in September 1942 was the battle being fought there in February 1943." This is logically like the statement: "The ocean that washes the beaches of California is the one that pounds against the east coast of New Zealand."

Similarly with spatial parts of events: the storm that is wrecking Galveston is the one that is making life miserable in Houston.

Although these are identity-statements, it is not helpful to think of them primarily in terms of "conditions for the identity of events." What makes any of them true is a pair of considerations. (1) The principles governing the (zonal) fusion of events under sortals – e.g., governing when two battles are parts of a larger battle, two fires parts of a larger fire, and so on. (2) The principles governing when one can refer to an event through a description that fixes on some part of it. Once those are grasped, and the relevant contingent facts are established, the statements about event-identity roll out automatically. There is nothing here about "event-identity" understood as something that we have to get straight about if we are to understand what an event is.

There is nothing deep in (1) the principles governing fusion under sortals. Wanting to know when

two episodes of combat count as parts of a single battle,
two conflagrations count as parts of a single fire, or
two festive episodes count as parts of a single picnic,

we have to consult the ordinary meanings of "battle," "fire," and "picnic." The
answers to our questions owe everything to semantics and nothing to metaphysics.
Was there a single fire that burned down your house on Monday and mine on
Tuesday (or yours and at the same time mine on the next street)? We do not
answer Yes unless some continuous spatiotemporal zone linking the two inciner-
ations is fiery throughout. But we handle "same battle" differently: we allow that
armies can sleep and then resume their battle; so a single battle can stretch across
two days even if the two episodes are not linked by a spatiotemporal zone that is
actively combative throughout. This difference between fires and battles is conventional; we can imagine handling "same battle" differently. Nothing of philosophical interest is going on here.

As for (2) the question of when it is all right to refer to a large event through
a reference to one of its parts: I suspect that it is always all right to do this, but I
have nothing useful to say on the topic.

Parts and wholes come into a different range of identity-statments about events,
such as these: "When he answered at the top of his voice, his shout was his answer";
"When he dislodged the rock by pushing it, the push that he gave it was his dislodgment of it." These involve *non*-zonal parts of events. A certain qualitatively
thick event, which is a push and a dislodgment, occupies a spatiotemporal zone
which is also occupied by a thinner event which is just a push, and another thinner
event which is just a dislodgment. These are qualitative or non-zonal parts of the
thicker event, just as the property of *pushing* is part of the richer property *dislodging by pushing*.

Here again we can ask (1) when two zonally coincident events count as parts
of a single qualitatively "larger" event, and (2) when it is all right to refer to an
event through a description that fixes on some qualitative (non-zonal) part of it.
I imagine that everyone would answer question (1) by saying that any such pair
of events are qualitative parts of a single qualitatively thicker event. Whatever
tropes occur at a given zone, there is always *the totality of what goes on at that
zone*, and there is no conceivable reason for denying that that is an event. There
is, however, controversy about how to answer question (2). Kim holds that it is
never correct to refer to an event through a description that picks out some qualitative part of it, so that we cannot use "The push he gave the rock" and "His
dislodgment of the rock" each to refer to a single thick event which was both a
push and a dislodgment. I have explained in section 3 why I disagree with this. It
is not, however, in any significant sense an issue about event-identity, but only one
about what can be meant by certain phrases. Kim's metaphysic of events is just
fine; only his semantics of event names is wrong.

Once we stop confounding events with facts, that frees us to hold that it is
sometimes all right to refer to an event through a phrase which gives only some

of the truth about it, that is, immediately refers to some non-zonal part of it; and when we have two such references to a single event we can formulate such identity-truths as that the shout was the answer, the kiss was the greeting, the picnic was the celebration, and so on.

We might hope to establish some general principles governing event-identities of this kind, but there is no prospect of that. Given that two things go on at a zone, the question of whether an expression naming one of them can also be used to name the fusion of them is a *purely* semantic one, and there seem to be no strong general principles governing the answer to it.

11   Events and the "by"-locution

One class of identity-statements about events needs separate mention. It concerns one species of events, namely acts. G. E. M. Anscombe once suggested, and Davidson later asserted, that if someone φs by ψing then the act which makes it the case that he φs is the act which makes it the case that he ψs (Anscombe, 1957, pp. 37–47; Davidson, 1971). If she signaled by lifting her arm, then the signal was the gesture; if he saved the village by diverting the river, then his rescue of the village was his diversion of the river; and so on. There has been much discussion of the "Anscombe thesis," as it has been called – I am guilty of adding to it myself. In fact, the thesis should have been strangled at birth, because the "by"-locution has nothing to do with acts or, therefore, with events. (For more details than I can give here, see Bennett, 1994.)

(1) One reason for that concerns scope. In many instances of the "by"-locution, the second half – the part that follows "by" – does not involve any act that the person performed. "He fulfilled her fears by never once thinking of her during the whole voyage." "He did his duty by continually remaining sensitive to any slights to her good name." In these perfectly normal "by"-statements, the phrases "[his] never once thinking of her during the whole voyage" and "[his] continually remaining sensitive to any slights to her good name" do not report on acts. Countless further examples could be given. (Those sentences report facts about the person's conduct – possible subjects of deliberation beforehand and recrimination or congratulation afterwards – so they pertain to the province of *action* (mass term). But they do not report *actions* (count term) or acts.)

(2) The other reason for being skeptical about the Anscombe thesis concerns logical form. "She signaled by raising her hand" passes the scope test: it does entail that she performed two acts, a signal and a gesture. But it contains no trace of the act concept; to bring the latter into the story we must reel it in on a line of logic. The sentence has the surface form of all "by"-statements:

(i)   a fully sentential clause ("She signaled . . .")
(ii)   the word "by," and
(iii) a subjectless gerundial nominal (". . . raising her hand").

Such triples give us "He broke the record by pushing a railroad car at 10 m.p.h. on level ground," "He let the apples spoil by leaving them in the barrel," and "She signaled by raising her hand." The first item, obviously, states a whole proposition about how the person behaved. That proposition might involve the act concept – "She gave him a kick" – but usually it does not.

What about the third item, the noun phrase containing a gerund? In "She signaled by raising her hand" the gerundial phrase is short for "*her* raising her hand," with "her" being deleted because it co-refers with the subject of the whole sentence. (To stop the co-reference, put the first clause into the passive – "A signal was given . . ." – and then we have to put "her" back in: "A signal was given by her raising her hand." Analogously, we delete "himself" from "He wants himself to go to the concert" but we do not delete "her" from "He wants her to go to the concert.") So we should see "She signaled by raising her hand" as ending with the complete gerundial nominal "her raising her hand" – an imperfect nominal which refers to the fact that she raised her hand.

The "by"-locution as such, we now see, does not involve the act concept anywhere. It has the form: *a proposition about behavior – "by" – a proposition about behavior.*

I now offer an analysis of the locution which dances to the tune of its logical form. The first clause always means something of the form: "Some fact about x's behavior had RP," where RP is a relational property. The remainder of the "by"-statement produces an instance, a value of the "Some fact . . ." which makes the initial clause true. Thus, "he broke a promise . . ." means that *some* fact about his behavior conflicted with a promise he had made, and ". . . by coming home late" says what it was. Thus,

He broke a promise – – – by – – – coming home late

analyzes into

Some fact about his behavior conflicted with a promise he had made – – – namely the fact that – – – he came home late.

Similarly, "He overcooked the stew . . ." says that some fact about his behavior causally led (in a certain way) to the stew's being overcooked, and ". . . by leaving it on the fire for too long" says what.

This "namely" story is the only analysis, so far, which covers all the territory. An ingenious account by Judith Jarvis Thomson applies only to cases where RP involves causation; as does a more recent one by Francken and Lombard.[4] Neither of those analyses applies to the likes of "He divorced her by signing a document" or "He tried to escape by disguising himself" or "He fished by throwing hand grenades into the water." The signing does not cause the divorcing, nor does his disguising himself cause his trying to escape, or his throwing of grenades cause his fishing.

The "namely" analysis lay hidden for so long because we did not think to dig into the initial clause of the "by"-locution so as to uncover the existential quantifier; until that comes into the open, "namely" has nothing to grab onto. The idea of digging came easily, once I had realized that "by"-statements do not interrelate human *acts* but rather *facts* about how people behave.

The vigor of the Anscombe thesis in the literature probably comes from its being true of a certain subset of cases. When someone ϕs by ψing, and

(1) his ϕing implies that he performed a K_1 action, and
(2) his ψing implies that he performed a K_2 action, and
(3) what makes it the case that he performed a K_2 action is that his ϕing had a certain causal consequence,

then his K_1 action is his K_2 action. I briefly defended this at the end of section 6, in connection with stabbing and killing. This is not to endorse the Anscombe thesis, but only a limited corner of it. It is not really about the "by"-locution, but rather about the relational properties of events.

12   Events and Adverbs

Anything useful we can say with the event concept we can say without it; it is everywhere dispensable. Truths about events supervene logically, and in a simple way, on truths about things and their properties: there was a quarrel because some people quarreled; there was a shower because rain fell; and so on.

Or so I maintain, but Davidson has argued on the contrary that "Adam and Eve quarreled" unpacks into "There was a quarrel, and Adam and Eve took part in it," not vice versa; that "Rain fell" derives from "There was a shower" rather than conversely, and so on (Davidson, 1967).

He has an ingenious reason for this. That they quarreled furiously entails that they quarreled, and Davidson has wanted to represent obvious entailments as holding in first-order quantificational logic. That logic cannot handle adverbs. It cannot do better than to represent "Adam quarreled with Eve" in the form $F(a,e)$, and "Adam quarreled furiously with Eve" as $G(a,e)$; and those, with their formally unrelated dyadic predicates, do not exhibit the entailment between the two propositions. Davidson proposes to remedy this by understanding "Adam quarreled furiously with Eve" as having the form

For some x: Quarrel(x) & Antagonists(x,a,e) & Furious(x).

Informally: there was a quarrel in which Adam and Eve were the antagonists, and it was furious. We get from this to "Adam quarreled with Eve" by representing the latter as

For some x: Quarrel(x) & Antagonists(x,a,e).

Informally: there was a quarrel in which Adam and Eve were the antagonists. First-order predicate logic captures the inference to this from the other, for it involves simply dropping a conjunctive clause in an existential statement.

Davidson offers this not as a mere technical device – a way of regimenting adverb-dropping inferences – but as a contribution to psychology. He claims to be laying bare the logical principles that guide us in our handling of adverbs. Someone tells me "... Danton gestured derisively to Robespierre ...," and on the strength of that I tell someone else "... Danton gestured to Robespierre." Davidson holds that I have inferred that Danton gestured from the premise that he gestured derisively by understanding the premise to mean "There was a gesture and it was derisive ..." and the conclusion to mean "There was a gesture ...". It would be absurd to maintain this only when there is an adverb in the vicinity; the claim has to be that *whenever* we say "He gestured ..." we mean "There was a gesture ...". That is hard to believe. It implies that if someone were brought up in ignorance of the fraction of English that involves the event concept – having no acquaintance with count nouns such as "fall," "kiss," "fight," "gesture," and their kin – he would have an impaired command of statements such as "That sparrow just fell" and "She kissed him" and "They fought with one another." I do not believe it.

Anyway, the theory is not strongly enough motivated, because a rival way of handling adverb-dropping inferences does better (Parsons, 1980; Bennett, 1988, pp. 168–78). The rival has to go outside the bounds of first-order logic, which may be a disadvantage; but as well as being believable considered as psychology, it has the further merit that it handles many adverbs which Davidson's theory does not touch.

Acknowledgments

This essay is based on one with the same title in Casati and Varzi (1996, pp. 137–51). I am grateful to the Dartmouth Press for permission to reuse that material, which here appears in an improved and enlarged form. Most of the improvements flow from comments by Richard Gale.

Notes

1 The identification of events with object-stages can be found in Quine (1960: 171). It is discussed at length in Bennett (1988, ch. 7).

2 Richard Gale helped me to an awareness that I need to bring in the factual/non-factual difference here. For a profound exploration of it, especially as concerns knowing and believing, see Vendler (1972, pp. 89–119).

3 "Events sometimes sum to yield a further and distinct one; yet intuition balks at the notion that such summing is universally permissible (there is surely no one event comprising both Lennon's death and Charles's wedding)." Taylor (1985, p. 25).
4 Thomson (1977, p. 204, formula T-S$_7$, and p. 218, formula T-S$_{12}$); Francken and Lombard (1992, p. 39). For other attempts, see Austin (1962, Lecture 10); Goldman (1970, ch. 2); Ginet (1990, pp. 16–17).

Bibliography

Anscombe, G. E. M. (1957). *Intention*. Oxford: Blackwell.

Austin, J. L. (1962). *How to Do Things with Words*. Cambridge, MA: Harvard University Press.

Bennett, Jonathan (1973). "Shooting, killing, and dying," reprinted in Casati and Varzi 1996: 319–27.

——(1988). *Events and their Names*. Oxford: Oxford University Press.

——(1994). "The 'Namely' analysis of the 'by'-locution." *Linguistics and Philosophy*, 17: 29–51.

——(2001). *Learning from Six Philosophers*. Oxford: Oxford University Press.

Brand, Myles (1977). "Identity conditions for events," reprinted in Casati and Varzi 1996: 363–71.

Casati, Roberto and Achille C. Varzi (eds.) (1996). *Events*. Aldershot: Dartmouth.

Cleland, Carol (1991). "On the individuation of events," reprinted in Casati and Varzi 1996: 373–98.

Davidson, Donald (1967). "The logical form of action sentences," reprinted in Casati and Varzi 1996: 3–17.

——(1969). "The Individuation of events," reprinted in ibid.: 265–83.

——(1971). "Agency," reprinted in his *Essays on Actions and Events*. Oxford: Oxford University Press, 1980: 43–61.

Francken, Patrick and Lawrence Brian Lombard (1992). "How not to flip the switch with the floodlight," *Pacific Philosophical Quarterly*, 73: 31–43.

Ginet, Carl (1990). *On Action*. Cambridge: Cambridge University Press.

Goldman, Alvin A. (1970). *A Theory of Human Action*. Princeton, NJ: Princeton University Press.

Kim, Jaegwon (1966). "On the psycho-physical identity theory." *American Philosophical Quarterly*, 3: 227–35.

——(1969). "Events and their descriptions: some considerations," in N. Rescher et al. (ed.), *Essays in honor of Carl G. Hempel*. Dordrecht: Reidel: 198–215.

——(1973). "Causation, nomic subsumption, and the concept of an event." *Journal of Philosophy*, 70: 217–36.

——(1980). "Events as property exemplifications," reprinted in Casati and Varzi 1996: 117–35.

——(1991). "Events: their metaphysics and semantics." *Philosophy and Phenomenological Research*, 51: 641–6.

Leibniz, G. W. (1705). *New Essays on Human Understanding*, ed. P. Remnant and J. Bennett. Cambridge: Cambridge University Press, 1996.

Locke, John (1690). *An Essay concerning human understanding*, ed. P. H. Nidditch. Oxford: Oxford University Press, 1975.

Lombard, Lawrence Brian (1986). *Events: a Metaphysical Study*. London: Routledge & Kegan Paul.

Newton, Isaac (1664). *De Gravitatione et aequipondio fluidorum*, in A. R. and M. B. Hall (eds.), *Unpublished Scientific Papers of Isaac Newton*. Cambridge: Cambridge University Press, 1962: 89–156.

Parsons, Terence (1980). "Modifiers and quantifiers in natural language." *Canadian Journal of Philosophy*, suppl. vol. 6: 29–60.

Quine, W. V. (1960). *Word and Object*. New York: MIT Press.

Taylor, Barry (1985). *Modes of Occurrence*. Oxford: Blackwell.

Thomson, Judith Jarvis (1977). *Acts and Other Events*. Ithaca, NY: Cornell University Press.

Vendler, Zeno (1967). "Facts and events," in his *Linguistics in Philosophy*. Ithaca, NY: Cornell University Press: 122–46.

——(1972). *Res cogitans: an Essay in Rational Psychology*. Ithaca, NY: Cornell University Press.

Williams, Donald C. (1953). "The Elements of being," reprinted in his *Principles of Empirical Realism*. Springfield, IL.: Thomas: 109–74.

Zucchi, Alessandro (1993). *The Language of Propositions and Events*. Dordrecht: Kluwer.

Chapter 4

Time, Temporality, and Paradox

Richard M. Gale

There are two kinds of perennial philosophies – those of temporality and those of timelessness. Whereas the former take reality to be temporal, the latter either deny the reality of time altogether, as have mystics throughout the ages, or locate true being in something that is timeless, such as Plato's forms, Aristotelian essences, God, or the Absolute of the idealists. Time sometimes is ontologically downgraded to Plato's moving image of eternity, an endless repetition of some timeless pattern or divine archetypes, which is a sophistication of the cyclical views of time and history that were prevalent in all archaic civilizations, or time might be nothing but the unfolding of some Absolute system of categories. Sometimes time is relegated to the junk heap of a mind-dependent appearance, thus having a second-class type of existence. Another form that the ontological downgrading of time takes is to make it nothing but a temporal series of events, completely analogous to a one-dimensional spatial ordering of events, devoid of any dynamic or transitory aspect.

The temporalists have a hard row to hoe, since time has been an endless source of perplexity. Part of this perplexity is due to the elusive nature of time. It is too fundamental to admit of verbal definition in terms of anything more basic. Definitions of it, such as "the measure of motion" (Aristotle) or "the advance of the soul" (Plotinus), invariably use temporal notions, thus rendering them viciously circular. Ostensive definitions also do not work, since there is nothing that we can point to or grab hold of. Yet we think there should be, since our language of time is rife with spatial and process metaphors, such as "the river of time" and "time flies." But more serious than its elusiveness is the paradoxes and puzzlements that break out when an attempt is made to analyze it. This has played into the hands of mystically inclined metaphysicians' intent on proving its unreality. In fact, the history of the philosophy of time can be written in terms of these paradoxes and the different responses to them.

Temporal Paradoxes

Intellectual mysticism is an attempt to give rational arguments, based on the paradoxical nature of time, for what mystics accept on unargued experiential grounds – that time is unreal. This tradition begins with Parmenides who argued that reality must be changeless and therefore timeless as well, given that time requires at least the possibility of change. Change is absurd, since it requires us to think about or refer to that which is not. This is because any change must involve a transition from a state of nonbeing to being, for example the poker's not being hot and then its being hot. But nonbeing, supposedly, cannot be named or referred to. Another argument against change is that it involves some event coming out of nothing, but something cannot come out of nothing. Our senses systematically deceive us into believing that change is real; but, for Parmenides, rather than seeing being believing, we must learn to turn our back on our senses and trust our reason.

Parmenides' henchman, Zeno of Elea, advanced arguments to show that reality must be changeless. Whether time is dense (between any two moments there is another moment) or discrete (every moment has an immediate successor and predecessor), change is impossible. In a dense time an object can traverse a unit distance only if it first traverses half of that distance, but before it can do so it must traverse half of that distance, and so on *ad infinitum*, thus making it impossible for it to get started (or to finish, if the regress is taken as coming at the end rather than the beginning). This argument can be deployed directly against the possibility of time itself lapsing; for before any temporal interval lapses, half of it must lapse, and so on *ad infinitum*. On the other hand, if time is discrete, the movement of an object through some unit distance consists of a finite number of moments at each of which it is immobile and therefore at rest. But since the object is always at rest, it does not move.

There have been four prominent answers to the argument against a dense time. Aristotelians argue for a mere *potential infinity* of finite spatial and temporal intervals within any given spatial extension or temporal duration, thereby excusing the object that traverses a spatial interval from having to go through each and every one of an infinite number of nonoverlapping spatial intervals. Another prominent response is based on a droplet theory of temporal passage, according to which what comes to pass is a temporally finite event, containing within itself a dense ordering. There is, as Whitehead said, "a becoming of continuity but not a continuity of becoming." A third answer is based on the mathematical theory of limits, the assumption being that what makes mathematical sense can be true of reality as well. Finally, there is the mystically-based response of Bergson and James that denies any sort of ordering between events, be it dense or discrete, and holds that instead there is a mushing together of successive events, so that they do not have separate identities. So-called "process philosophy" is advertised by its proponents as the only way to escape Zeno's paradoxes. A standard rebuttal of the paradox based on a discrete ordering is that an object cannot be said to be at rest at a single moment of time, and, even if it could be, it would be a commission of the fallacy of division to say that a change must be composed of changes.

Even those who did not set out to prove time unreal have unwittingly presented arguments against its reality. Saint Augustine puzzled over how time could be measured. For we can measure only what is present, but the present must have a zero duration (for if it were to have a finite duration it would have successive phases, but because these phases are copresent, they would not be successive!). He attempted to escape from this paradox by reducing time – the past, present, and future – to conscious acts of representation that take place in the present, those being memory, perception and anticipation, respectively. What he did not realize is that his problem about measuring time could be generalized to all events, resulting in the disappearance of all events and therefore of time itself. Events occur only when they are present. But they take a finite time in which to occur, unless they be terminal events that mark the beginning or end of some process or state that itself is noninstanteous. And, given that the present is of zero duration, it follows that no events occur. This applies even to his mental acts of representing the past, present and future, since they also require a finite time in which to occur. Another paradox that results from imputing a zero duration to the present is that there cannot be a finite duration, since it is made up of present moments, each of zero duration. Supposedly, this paradox has been resolved by the discovery (invention?) of the mathematical continuum.

The troubling concepts of the past, present and future underlie J. M. E. Mc-Taggart's argument, in 1908, for the unreality of time, which argument set off a rash of critical responses that are still going on today. His argument begins by distinguishing between two different ways in which events can be temporally located. They can be located either in the "*B*-series," the generating relation of which is *later than*, or in the "*A*-series," which is determined by the tensed distinctions of past, present, and future. The *B*-series is permanent, because events can never change in their temporal relations of precedence and subsequence to each other; but the *A*-series is dynamic, because events continually change with respect to their being past, present or future due to the fact that the present shifts to ever later events in the *B*-series. Such change is called "temporal becoming or passage." Time cannot consist in only the *B*-series, since events can stand in temporal relations to each other only if they are themselves past, present or future, just as there cannot be a harmonic relation between notes unless each note possess an absolute pitch. That event e_2 is later than event e_1 entails the following disjunction of tensed propositions: *either* e_1 is past and e_2 present *or* e_1 is past and e_2 future *or* e_1 is present and e_2 future *or* e_1 is more past than e_2 *or* e_1 is less future than e_2.

The *A*-series turns out to be unreal because it harbors a contradiction, since every event in it is past, present and future, assuming that there is no end or beginning of time. And when an attempt is made to escape this apparent contradiction by holding that no event has two or more of these tensed determinations at one and the same time, but rather has them successively at different moments of time, the apparent contradiction is transferred to these moments, which themselves must form an *A*-series, thus occasioning the same apparent contradiction that we began with. This is the first step in an infinite regress that is vicious because the very same apparent contradiction that infected the initial step in the regress breaks out anew at every one of the infinitely many successive steps.

Two different theories of time have emerged from the attempts to rebut McTaggart's argument. The "*B*-theorists" hold that time is nothing but the *B*-series, change being nothing but an object's having a property at one time that it lacks at another. Since the A-series is not necessary for the reality of time, they need not worry about whether it harbors a contradiction. "A-theorists" agree with McTaggart's positive claim that the A-series is necessary but attempt to divest it of contradiction or absurdity. They would deny that there is any apparent contradiction that needs to be explained away; for it is not true of any event that it is past, present, and future. Rather it is the case, for example, that an event is now present, was future, and will be past.

McTaggart could respond that the A-theorist's way out presupposes the reality of time through the use of these tensed distinctions, which begs the question against his argument, since it amounts to denying the very conclusion of his argument – that time is unreal. Time is the way of avoiding contradictions when an entity changes in its properties. Recall that Aristotle's formulation of the law of noncontradiction recognized this when he said that a given property couldn't both adhere and not inhere in one and the same substance *at the same time* and in the same respect. While it is not question-begging to escape from the apparent contradiction of a table being red and not red by pointing out that it is red at one time and not red another, thereby escaping from an argument to show that it is impossible for a substance to have incompatible properties, it is question-begging to escape from an argument for the unreality of time by invoking different times. This is because the former argument, unlike the latter, is not directed at establishing the very unreality of time. The A-theorists, in turn, could charge McTaggart with begging the question against them by not allowing them to invoke different times. Thus, McTaggart wins not a victory but a stalemate, which is a victory of sorts, given how hopeless his doctrine of the unreality of time initially appeared.

Many *B*-theorists go on to charge the concept of temporal becoming with being incoherent or contradictory, thereby agreeing with McTaggart that the A-series is unreal. If the present shifts to ever later times in the B-series, it must do so at a certain rate. But since it shifts along the time axis, the rate involves a change of time over time! To respond that it shifts at the rate of one second per second is to abuse the concept of a rate of change. Furthermore, the entity that does the shifting is an I-do-not-know-what sort of transcendental entity in relation to which events in the B-series change with regard to their being past, present or future. Yet another absurdity is that temporal becoming denies the necessity of identity; for if the present – this very moment of time – were to shift to later times, it would cease to be identical with itself. To respond, as have many A-theorists, that temporal becoming is *sui generis* and must be understood phenomenologically, is unsatisfying, since it does nothing to neutralize these apparent contradictions and absurdities.

The B-theorist, after having thoroughly trashed the concept of temporal becoming, concludes that space and time are completely analogous, there no more being an advancing *here* along a row of coexistent objects than there is an advancing *now* along a series of successive events. This conclusion is buttressed by the claim that the temporal indexical expression "now" ("this time", "the present") is analogous to the spatial indexical expression "here." It will be argued that *now* and *here* are modally disanalogous in ways that capture what is intended by the metaphor of temporal becoming. A modal disanalogy requires that the spatial or temporal analogue to a given sentence or proposition has a different modal status, in which a spatial or temporal analogue to a given sentence is formed by substituting for every temporal term in it a corresponding spatial one and vice versa. In forming analogues the temporal indexical term "now" and "this time" are to be replaced respectively by "here" and "this place" and a date expression by a proper name of a place. For the time being we will agree to substitute "in front of" for "later than." It will be seen that it does not matter if "to the rear (right, left) of" is substituted instead.[1]

I will follow a three-stage format in my pursuit of these disanalogies. I begin with our untutored common-sense beliefs, often expressed in metaphorical and pictorial terms, as to how time and space differ. Next, I refine these beliefs by translating them into more precise literal statements, being careful to make explicit all of their temporal and spatial commitments. Finally, I attempt to explain and justify these beliefs by unearthing the underlying modal disanalogies that serve as their cash backing. Sometimes these disanalogies will be formulated in the formal mode in which explicit mention is made of words and their rules of use. I will attempt to unearth them within our concepts of *agency* and *objectivity*.

Agency-Based Disanalogies

Whether an agent fills space and time in modally disanalogous ways, will depend crucially on how we define an "agent." I will be making a somewhat technical or jargonistic use of "agent," the justification for which will come at the end of this section when I discuss the connection of my use of "agent" with certain forensic uses of "person." According to my use, it is required that an agent, in addition to being rational and self-conscious, has as its overriding goal to achieve self-realization. An agent will rationally deliberate about the best way to achieve this goal and will then intentionally carry out her decisions in a free, morally responsible manner. Since an agent's *summum bonum* is to be an active and free cause of her own self-realization, an agent accepts a causal theory of value in which the goodness of an outcome, result, upshot, denouement, or culmination depends in part upon its being brought about in the right way, the right way involving the agent as an active and free cause. Means and ends interpenetrate, each deriving its meaning and value from its functional relation to the other. As is the case with other causal theories, such as those for perception, memory, and reference, we are able to recognize in many cases when a given sequence is or is not of the right sort, but notoriously are not able to specify in general what is the right sort of causal sequence.

To summarize, an agent is a rational self-conscious being who deliberates about the best way to achieve self-realization and then intentionally carries out her decisions in a free, morally responsible manner. For the time being we will accept this as a merely stipulative definition for the sake of the ensuing discussion. It now is to be shown that this concept of agency entails striking modal disanalogies between the manner in which an agent exists in space and time consisting in there necessarily being a direction to time but not space, regardless of its dimensionality.

Some important and startling modal disanalogies concerning an agent's axiological commitments follow logically from my concept of an agent when it is conjoined with the following modal disanalogies concerning causation and the dependent notions of deliberation and choice:

T1.   An action performed now can bring about something later but not earlier than now.[2]
S1.   An action performed here can bring about something in front of but not to the rear of here.

in which the "can" is the weakest one of mere logical or conceptual possibility. No difference is made if "to the rear (right, left) of here" is substituted for "in front of here" in S1," as will be the case with all of the modal disanalogies to follow.

The T1–S1 modal disanalogy entails this modal disanalogy:

T2.   An agent can now deliberate about and make choices and have intentions in respect to her conduct later but not earlier than now.
S2.   An agent can here deliberate about and make choices and have intentions in respect to her conduct in front of but not to the rear of here.

There might be circumstances in which I have the capacity and opportunity to bring about things only to the front but not to the rear of here – I would literally have my back to the wall – but it is still *logically* possible that I bring about something to the rear of here and thus *logically* possible that I deliberate about doing so. And thus T2 and S2 differ modally, T2 alone being necessarily true. Similar considerations hold for T1 and S1, provided their use of "can" is interpreted as expressing logical possibility.

Given that an agent's *summum bonum* or primary project is to be the right sort of cause of her own self-realization and that causation cannot go temporally backwards though it logically can go in any spatial direction, it follows that an agent, in virtue of being rational, will have axiological commitments that are modally disanalogous between space and time. These disanalogies hold only for my "agents," not for human beings in general; for it is well known that human beings in different cultures and socio-economic groups value the past, present, and future differently, some being more future oriented, while others give greater importance to the past or present. For this reason, the following would not express a modal disanalogy:

T3.   *Human beings* care more about what befalls them later rather than earlier than now.

S3.   *Human beings* care more about what befalls them in front of rather than to the rear of here.

1.   Let us begin with the old saws, "All's well that ends well" and "Consider no man fortunate until after he is dead." That it sounds funny to say that all's well that spatially terminates well in front of here or that you should count no man fortunate except from a place in front of where he dies is some indication that we have modal disanalogies in these cases, but it is not easy to give an explicit formulation of them.

Plainly, the following pair of analogues will not do, since they both seem to be *contingent* generalizations and false ones to boot:

T4.   A temporal succession of events is good if it temporally terminates later than now in a good state of affairs.

S4.   A spatial order of events is good if it spatially terminates in front of here in a good state of affairs.

Lynne McFall has presented me with numerous counter-examples to T4, consisting in cases in which a death-bed conversion or final moment of beatific bliss does not render good or valuable a life that prior to that was one of long and unremitting immorality or suffering. The moral of these examples is that the length and intensity of evil that leads up to the favorable upshot or culmination must be taken into account.

The McFall-type counter-examples might be met by requiring that the earlier succession of events is both the right sort of an agent-cause of the terminating state and is morally outweighed by it, resulting in:

T5.   A temporal succession of events is good if it temporally terminates later than now in a state of affairs that morally outweighs it and for which it is the right sort of agent-cause.

S5.   A spatial order of events is good if it spatially terminates in front of here in a state of affairs that morally outweighs it and for which it is the right sort of agent-cause.[3]

Whereas T5 seems a plausible candidate for being a necessary truth, S5 does not, since an agent does not necessarily give greater axiological value to any one particular spatial direction over the others.

There are other ways of reformulating T6 that might work as well as or even better than the T5 way, as for example:

> T6.   An agent holds that if it is better to be in state Y than state X, then it is better to be in state X now and state Y later rather than earlier than now, provided that she brings Y about out of X in the right sort of agency manner.
>
> S6.   An agent holds that if it is better to be in state Y than state X, then it is better to be in state X here and state Y in front of rather than to the rear of here, provided that she brings Y about out of X in the right sort of agency manner.

T6, for example, requires that an agent who believes that it is better to be a philosophy professor than a pickpocket believe that it is better to be a pickpocket now and a philosophy professor later than now rather than vice versa, provided that she agency-causes the professorial state to evolve from the pickpocket one in the right way, as, for example, by using her ill-gotten gains to pay her way through graduate school. But without any additional information, our agent will be indifferent between being a pickpocket here and a philosophy professor in front of here rather than vice versa. Given additional information, the agent might prefer the former, since here could be New York City, a good place for a pickpocket, and Pittsburgh could be in front of here, a good place for a philosophy professor but a bad place for a pickpocket due to its being economically depressed. But this hardly shows that S6 is a *necessary* truth, for this preference is based on extra non-spatial information of a contingent sort, whereas the preference in T6 is not based on any extra non-temporal information of a contingent sort, thereby showing that T6, unlike S6, is logically necessary.

It is interesting to note that the T6–S6 modal disanalogy underlies the prevalent soul-building theodicy, which holds that God is justified in permitting past evils if they serve as a necessary condition for an agent to grow freely in morally desirable ways. In determining the goodness of a world we do not just mechanically add up the goods and evils in it, but also consider the temporal plot into which they enter. Their spatial plot or concatenation is irrelevant. The greater value that T8 accords to the future does not mean that progress is inevitable or that future persons are to be given a privileged status when formulating social policies, a point that was forcefully made in discussion by George Kline.

Phil Quinn has presented me with a counter-example to T6's necessity that indicates the need to further qualify it. He imagines an agent of 60 who has been in poor health all his life reasoning as follows.

> It is better for me to be rich then to be poor, for wealth is bound to be helpful in the project of self-realization if wisely used. But clearly it is not better for me to

be poor now and rich later, provided I earn my wealth, than for me to be poor
now and rich earlier. Even if I can still earn a fortune at my age, by the time I
have done so I will be too old and feeble to make much use of it in advancing
my project of self-realization. But if I had a fortune when I was a mere youth, I
would have spent it all on my project of self-realization and would have made a lot
more progress in this project than I actually did, which in turn would have given me
internal resources I do not now have to enable me to make the best of my present
poverty.

One way to meet this ingenious counter-example is to require that we consider
only the intrinsic value of the successive states X and Y in T6, thereby precluding
consideration of their instrumental value in promoting other goods, such as that
of self-realization, which is what Quinn's 60-year-old man does. A technical device
for assuring that only the intrinsic values of X and Y be considered is to require
that they be described in "temporally pure" ways. A descriptive predicate "F" is
temporally pure just in case the proposition expressed by "A is F at time t_7," in
which "A" is a non-descriptive denotator of an individual, is such that it (i) does
not entail that there are any times other than t_7 and (ii) is compatible with there
being any number of instances of F at times other than t_7. Condition (i) rules out
"drinking the fatal glass of beer" since it entails that the drinker dies at some future
date as a result of the drinking and (ii) does so for "drinking the first (last) glass
of beer" since this entails that the drinker does not drink a glass of beer at any
earlier (later) time.

 2.   Another agency-based axiological asymmetry between past and future that
has no modally equivalent spatial analogue concerns this differences between an
agent's attitudes toward her past and future finitude:

 T7.   An agent regrets that her existence does not extend beyond some time
 later than now but does not regret in the same way that her existence does not
 extend beyond some time earlier than now.
 S7.   An agent regrets that her existence does not extend beyond some place
 in front of here but does not regret in the same way that her existence does
 not extend beyond some place to the rear of here.

The reason for the "in the same way" qualification will emerge from the ensuing
discussion. S7 is not a necessary truth; for, an agent's regret that she does not
exist at some place in front of here is based on contingent considerations that are
not necessary for her being an agent; e.g., Las Vegas could be in front of here and
she loves to gamble in different casinos and thus would regret her never existing
in Vegas. But is T9 necessary?

 To establish the necessity of T7 it must be shown to be a logical consequence
of my definition of an *agent*. Since an agent has as its *summum bonum* her own
self-realization and there is no upper limit on the possibility for the development
of one's character, knowledge, ability, and talents, etc., an agent ought to regret

its future demise.[4] To be sure, it might take only a finite future time for an agent to realize all of her present first-order intentions, but because there is no upper bound to an agent's potential for self-realization it is of the very essence of an agent always to be on the make, always to be incomplete. Thus, at every time, an agent has a second-order intention always to have a new intention, always to have its projected horizon recede as it succeeds in satisfying former intentions; and, thus, death always represents a cutting off of its possibility for a fuller self-realization of its inherent potentialities.

Annette Baier has pointed out that there could be extra-temporal contingent considerations that could lead an agent not to regret her death, such as her now suffering from an incurable illness that prevents her from progressing now or in the future in her self-realization project. This problem could be met by stipulating that her agency is not impaired later than now.

T8.   An agent regrets that her existence does not extend beyond some time later than now but does not regret in the same way that her existence does not extend beyond some time earlier than now, *provided nothing prevents her from functioning as an agent later than now.*

But, in contradistinction from T8, a necessary truth does not emerge when the analogous restriction is made in S7:

S8.   An agent regrets that her existence does not extend beyond some place in front of here but does not regret in the same way that her existence does not extend beyond some place to the rear of here, *provided nothing prevents her from functioning as an agent in front of here.*

An agent might grow weary of being an agent for non-medical reasons and thus no longer want an unlimited future. This, however, is just a case of an agent no longer being an agent, and thus not a counter-example to T8.

An agent might regret that her past existence is finite – she is an historian of ancient Greece and thus regrets having been born too late to have been an eye-witness to the goings-on in that era. But while her past finitude limits her knowledge, it does not limit in any way her opportunity to realize herself and, in particular, as an historian, her excellence as an historian is not being diminished by her not having certain data that it is not possible for her to obtain. Since the agent's regret at having a finite future is not topic-specific, unlike the historian who regrets that her past is finite, T8's temporal asymmetry between past and future is unscathed by this example. This is the reason for the *does not regret in the same way* qualification in T8.

T8 ceases to be a necessary truth when applied to human beings in general. Mystical individuals seem to have no asymmetry in their attitudes to birth and death, since they take time to be unreal. Derek Parfit has argued that we would be happier if we lacked the T8-type of temporal bias. He imagines a passive, contemplative sort of chap, named "Timeless" who is not concerned with being an agent but only with finding a psychologically satisfying way of viewing the world around him. Timeless is someone

> who takes life's pleasures as they come. And, to the extent that we are like this . . . we would be happier if we lacked the bias towards the future. We would be much less depressed by aging and the approach of death. If we were like Timeless, being at the end of our lives would be more like being at the beginning. At any point within our lives we could enjoy looking either backward or forward to our whole lives. . . . I have claimed that, if we lacked the bias towards the future, this would be better for us. . . . On any plausible moral view, it would be better if we were all happier.[5]

Timeless poses no threat to T8's necessity, since he is not an agent. Whether it is better to be an agent, and thereby have a T8-type bias, is an entirely different matter. No doubt Timeless has more peace of mind, is in a more mellow mood, than an agent. He is happier in the feeling-happy sense. But whether it is better to have the sort of psychological happiness of a Timeless than be in the mentally perturbed state of a striving, incomplete agent is irrelevant to the truth of T8. I happen not to share Parfit's "ethical" intuitions. I believe that those who have a capacity to become agents have an obligation to do so, even at the expense of their *ataraxia*.

3. It is an empirical fact that most human beings prefer that their painful experiences be in the past and their pleasurable ones in the future but do not have the analogous spatial preference, it mattering not at all whether their pains and pleasures occur in any particular direction from here. It does not seem to be necessary that *human beings* have these preferences, but is it necessary that *agents* do? Is the following a modal disanalogy?

> T9. An agent prefers that her painful experiences occur earlier than now and her pleasurable experiences later than now.
> S9. An agent prefers that her painful experiences occur to the rear of here and her pleasurable experiences in front of here.

While it is obvious that S9 is not necessary, that T9 is must be argued.

Before attempting this, the descriptions of the painful and pleasurable experiences in T9 must be restricted to temporally pure ones, so that no demands are made on what obtains or fails to obtain at times earlier or later than that at which the pleasure or pain occurs. Without such a restriction the following sort of counter-example can be produced. It is reasonable for an agent to prefer that a painful amputation of her leg occur in the future instead of the past, since this gives her more time in which she has use of the leg and thereby a leg up on her self-realization project. But the description of a pain as "the pain of having one's leg amputated" is temporally impure because it entails that one has this leg before the painful experience and lacks it afterwards.

It is very difficult to show why T9 is necessary, assuming that it is. Plainly, we can't do so by saying that a past pain, since it already has become present, is of no moment whereas a future one, since it has yet to do so, is. For this is just to say that the past pain has already happened while the future one has not yet happened, leaving unexplained why this difference should be significant. And, for reasons already given, we cannot explain why T9 is necessary by invoking the notion of temporal becoming that involves a shift of the present moment to ever later times.

Given that it is better to be in a pleasurable than a painful state, it could be claimed that T9 is a special instance of

T6.   An agent holds that if it is better to be in state Y than state X, then it is better to be in state X now and state Y later rather than earlier than now, provided that she brings Y about out of X in the right sort of agency manner.

The problem with this derivation is that an agent's T9 preference does not seem to require that she be a causal agent in respect to the painful and pleasurable experiences in question. Thus, there is a possible range of cases to which T9 applies but T6 does not, and therefore the necessity of T9 is yet to be explained.

Another possible way of grounding T9 in the concept of an agent is supplied by the following phenomenological insight of William James:

the fact is that our consciousness at a given moment is never free from the ingredient of expectancy. Every one knows how when a painful thing has to be undergone in the near future, the vague feeling that it is impending penetrates all our thought with uneasiness and subtly vitiates our mood even when it does not control our attention; it keeps us from being at rest in the given present.[6]

It could be objected that James's phenomenological generalization is at best a contingent truth about human beings, and thus cannot establish the necessity of T9. But agents, unlike human beings, are not as a contingent matter of fact expectors and anticipators but are essentially so. And anticipation of an impending harm is not only upsetting but, more important, distracting, thereby undermining their efficiency as agents. Furthermore, a future pain is harmful to their self-realization in a way in which a past pain is not. Thus, it is fitting and proper for an agent to have T9-type preferences. This defense requires that T9 be restricted to anticipated and remembered pleasures and pains.

It is not hard to tell a story in which a future pain is not deleterious to an agent's self-realization but even necessary for it. In such a case an agent does not prefer that the pain is in the past. Therefore, it seems necessary to add yet another restriction to T9, requiring that the pleasures and pains are respectively beneficial and deleterious for self-realization.[7] My defense of T9's necessity is starting to take on too many epicycles to be very convincing, but, unfortunately, it is the best that I am able to do right now.

In concluding this section, I will consider Richard Bernstein's very trenchant objection to my general procedure for deriving agency-based modal disanalogies: My stipulatively defining "agent" in such a way that it entails the desired axiological modal disanalogies is nothing but a trivial exercise in gerrymandering. The plums that I gleefully pull out of my pie have been put there by me. My response is in two stages. Even if I am gerrymandering, my task hardly is trivial, since, as the preceding discussion attests, it is no easy matter to show that my concept of an agent entails these disanalogies. One of the major tasks for philosophy, going back to Plato's science of "dialectics," is to articulate the logical interconnections between different concepts. Furthermore, my concept of an agent isn't all that gerrymandered. It is similar to a prevalent definition of what a person is in the normative or forensic sense, the sense which qualifies a person to be a bearer of rights, such as to be treated always as an end and never as a mere means. Thus, my concept is not made up out of the blue solely for the purpose of establishing modal disanalogies but is modeled on an important tradition for understanding the normative concept of personhood. That my agency-based analysis of personhood is controversial is readily granted but that is not grounds for the charge of gerrymandering.

Objectivity-Based Disanalogies

The doctrine of temporal becoming as involving a shifting now was supposed to offer a theoretical explanation for our gut feeling that our past–present–future perspective is objective in a way in which our here–there one is not. Because this doctrine is contradictory and thus explains nothing, it does not follow that we must give up our gut beliefs that there is a sense in which we are prisoners of time but not space, are spatially but not temporally free and rangy, and the like, which is what the metaphor of temporal becoming was trying to get at, its cash value. You can choose to leave Pittsburgh for a wild weekend in Ambridge or McKeesport but can't choose to leave the twentieth century for a high old time in the seventeenth century. It is just such beliefs in the coercive power of time that caused some of our forefathers to prostrate themselves before a god of time but not one of space. Our fear of heights, or in the case of the comedian Steven Wright, widths, is an entirely different matter. I will now attempt to legitimize these beliefs by unearthing the objectivity-based modal disanalogies that underlie them.

Our concept of objectivity comprises two components: being non-selective or imposed independently of our will; and being common to or shared by different observers. It will be shown that for each component there are modal disanalogies between space and time.

Non-selectivity disanalogies

There are three different sorts of non-selectivity disanalogies: (i) perceptual; (ii) referential; and (iii) locomotive.

(i) For the sake of simplicity the discussion will be confined to visual perception, but it admits of generalization to the other senses. Space is an order of co-existent objects and time an order of successive events. Visual experience presents us with coexistent objects but not successive events.[8] At any given time we can see only those events and objects that happen or exist at that time. This gives rise to the following modal disanalogy:

> T10.   I can now see only what is happening now.
> S10.   I can here see only what is happening here.

in which "can" again is that of mere logical possibility, thus rendering it irrelevant whether I have a stiff neck that prevents me from turning my head.

While it is clear that S10 is not necessary, there is cause to doubt that T10 is necessary, due to the fact that light signals have a finite velocity, resulting in what is seen being earlier than the seeing of it. One way to meet this difficulty is to revise T10–S10 as:

> T11.   I can now see only what happens now or earlier than now.
> S11.   I can here see only what happens here or to the rear of here.

Because perception is a causal process, this modal disanalogy rests on the T1–S1 one concerning the impossibility of backward causation.

Another way to circumvent the problem is to adopt the convention that "now" in T10 refers to the class of events that are directly perceivable by me, the observer, i.e., all those events that are causally connectible with my here–now by a recti-linear light ray. This convention for saving the necessity of T10 squares with the Special Theory of Relativity and is less cumbersome, and therefore will be adopted in what follows. Thus a tokening of "now" or "this time" refers to the simul-taneity class of events that stand in this light-ray relation to the time and place of the tokening.

The T10–S10 modal disanalogy, in turn, gives rise to this modal disanalogy:

> T12.   I can here and now choose whether to see events that occur now or then (or later than now).
> S12.   I can now and here choose whether to see objects that exist here or there (or in front of here).

in which "choose" distributes over the disjunction: I can choose p or q is short for I can choose p and I can choose q. Again, stiff necks are irrelevant.

(ii) Because visual perception is selective among places but not times, there will be a selectivity in the use of spatial indexical terms that is lacking for temporal indexical terms. We will confine ourselves to the "primary use" of an indexical term, i.e., one in which it does not pick up its reference by falling within the scope of some other referring term. A primary use of "this place" is spatially selective whereas a primary use of "this time" is not.

> T13.   I can choose whether my primary use here and now of "this time" denotes now or then (or a time later than now).
> S13.   I can choose whether my primary use now and here of "this place" denotes here or there (or a place in front of here).

This modal disanalogy, cast in the formal mode, results from a difference in the rules of use for these indexical terms. The rules of use for "this place" specify that the denotatum of a tokening of it is the place ostended by the speaker. (Remember that I can point to the place I occupy.) No such act of ostending enters into determining the denotatum of a tokening of "this time." To be sure, I can choose when to token "this time," but given that I token it at the time I do I have no choice but to refer to that time. Herein I am requiring that the time at which a temporal indexical term is used be kept constant when we ask counter-factual questions about its referent. This could be called the principle of "contextual constancy."

It might come as a surprise, but exactly the same sort of disanalogy holds between the rules for the primary use of "here" and "now." *Pace* what was tentatively granted above, a token of "here" need not denote the place at which it is tokened, thereby giving rise to this modal disanalogy:

> T14.   A primary use of "now" must denote the time at which it is tokened.[9]
> S14.   A primary use of "here" must denote the place at which it is tokened.

A counter-example to S14 is my saying "Place the piano here," as I point to some place in front of me.

It might be countered that S14 becomes necessary when restricted to a "naked" use of "here," i.e., a use in which there is no accompanying ostensive act of pointing, gesturing, or staring. This must be granted; however, this restriction to a naked use gives rise to a different modal disanalogy.

> T15.   I can choose whether or not to use "now" nakedly.
> S15.   I can choose whether or not to use "here" nakedly.

Whereas, admittedly, S15 is necessary, T15 is not, since, as T13 has shown, a use of "now" or "this time" cannot involve an act of ostending.[10] Therefore, every primary use of "here," including the naked one, involves selection of some sort, unlike the primary use of "now."

(iii) Not only is our past–present–future perspective, unlike our here–there one, non-selective in regard to perception and reference, it also is so in regard to our power of locomotion. We can move about in space at will but not time, thus the reason for it making sense to say "Come here" but not "Come now," assuming it is only the locomotive sense that is relevant. We can return to the same place but not the same time, which yields this modal disanalogy:

S16.   I can exist here both now and at some time, t_2, later than now, and there at some time, t_1, temporally between now and t_2.
T16.   I can exist now both here and at some place, P_2, in front of here, and then at some place, P_1, spatially between here and P_2.

This modal disanalogy is a consequence of the conceptual truth that a material object can occupy the same place at different times but not the same time at different places.

S17.   I can exist here both now and then.
T17.   I can exist now both here and there.

A philosopher of the likes of Richard Taylor would not accept these as genuine modal disanalogies. He would claim that a physical object is composed of both spatial and temporal parts. Thus, he would claim that both S16 and T16 are necessary truths; just as I can exist both here and there by having different spatial parts of myself occupy these two places I can exist here both now and then by having different temporal parts of myself happen at these two times.

He is wrong, however, in his claim that physical objects, as contrasted with events, have temporal as well as spatial parts. When a man has his legs amputated, as did Ronald Reagan in an old movie, he can ask "Where's the rest of me?", for he is referring to some of his former spatial parts. But he cannot claim to be incomplete now because some of his "temporal parts," i.e., events in his history, are not happening now. If my view of someone is obstructed so that I see only his back, I say that I see only a part of him, but I do not say this if I do not see some events in his past and future history. I would say that I see only part of his *history* rather than part of the *man*.

It might be replied that while we do not at present speak of a physical object's temporal parts, this might not be due to it being conceptually absurd to do so but simply because we have not yet had the proper contingent occasion to do so. It might be that the reason why we do not now speak of temporal parts is that an object's parts are connected with its sortal nature, and so far it has proven advantageous for the purpose of devising intellectually satisfying scientific systems of classification and successfully interacting with our environment to define the sortal or essential nature of objects solely in terms of how their spatial parts are concatenated. Think of the periodic table of elements in this connection. There are, however, conceivable circumstances in which it would no longer prove advantageous to define an object's essence exclusively in spatial terms; how it fills time, its history, would then be at least partially determinative of its nature. In fact, this is already the case in some areas of sub-atomic physics. It is part of the definition of a certain kind of mesons that they have a half-life of a certain duration. In such cases in which the definition of an object's essence makes demands upon its history it might be appropriate to talk of an object's temporal as well as its spatial parts. Since our present spatially-biased system of definitions of essences or sortal natures is revisable in this manner, it is doubtful that S16–T16 and S17–T17 are genuine modal disanalogies.

The reply to this is that this essay is a study in descriptive rather than revisionary metaphysics. The concern is with how we actually do conceive and talk about the world. No doubt, if we were radically to revise our empirical beliefs, this would occasion a conceptual revolution, such as is envisioned in the preceding response. How we play the language-games we do is a different question than why we do. A proper answer to the latter is not given by a description of linguistic rules but by an account of why the world rewards those who play them.

Fortunately, there are locomotive-based modal disanalogies that do not rest on an object's having only spatial parts. Because I can choose to move in any spatial direction but cannot backwardly cause something to happen, there is this modal disanalogy:

S18.   I can choose here and now whether my use of "here" later than now denotes a place in front of or to the rear of here.
T18.   I can choose now and here whether my use of "now" in front of here denotes a time later or earlier than now.

Other modal disanalogies that have the same conceptual underpinnings are:

S19.   I can choose here and now whether to occupy here later than now.
T19.   I can choose now and here whether to occupy now in front of here.

and

S20.   I can choose here and now to occupy here at all times between now and five minutes later than now.
T20.   I can choose now and here to occupy now at all places between here and five feet in front of here.

The reason for these two modal disanalogies is that I can now choose to bring something about neither in the past nor the present. Whether I now occupy both here and certain places in front of here, by having different spatial parts of me occupy them, can be caused only by past events, such as an earlier decision of mine to overeat to that I would occupy these places now.

Shared-perspectives disanalogies

To complete my account of the objectivity-based modal disanalogies between our spatial and temporal indexical perspectives it remains to consider the other component of our concept of objectivity – that of being common to or shared by different observers. There is a sense in which both spatial and temporal indexical facts are objective. It is open to public verification both that some place is here and that some time is now, as well as that some event occurs here and that some event occurs now. The disanalogy I seek is implicated in the nature of the agreement in judgment or the unanimity test for verifying such facts. Because it is a necessary truth that

> S21. Two observers who exist now at different places can both see what happens here now.

but false, and necessarily false at that, given my above convention for the use of "now," that

> T21. Two observers who exist here at different times can both see what happens now here.

it follows that our here–there perspective is perceptually transcendable in a way in which our past–present–future one is not. Whereas only observers who exist now can directly verify or see what occurs now, observers who do not exist here can directly verify or see what occurs here. This is a variation on the T10–S10 modal disanalogy. Thus, while it is necessarily true that

> T22. Observers who can directly verify (see) what occurs now share the same temporal indexical perspective, i.e., they both exist now.

it is not necessarily true that

> S22. Observers who can directly verify (see) what occurs here share the same spatial indexical perspective, i.e., they both exist here.

Often observers who do not occupy here can have a better view of what is here than do those who are here.

Thus, our agreement in judgment or unanimity test for objectivity, which, I might add, is only one of the relevant tests for objectivity, shows a modal disanalogy between now and here in regard to their being shared by or common to the *relevant* observers. The relevant observers for directly verifying or seeing what occurs now must share the same temporal indexical perspective but not the same spatial indexical perspective; they must all exist now but needn't all exist here. This is why it seemed less chauvinistic to say that there is no time like the present rather than there is no place like here. Even if, *per impossible*, we could converse with Plato via some mysterious telephone connection, his testimony as to what he then perceives would be irrelevant for the purpose of determining what is happening now. Our unanimity test, therefore, presupposes a shared or common now among the relevant observers but not a common here. And given that one mark of the objective is to be shared or common, if follows that our past–present–future perspective is objective in a way in which our here–there one is not. And when this modal disanalogy is conjoined with the non-selectivity modal disanalogy between these two kinds of indexical perspectives, there results a powerful conceptual case for now but not here being objective. These modal disanalogies are the cash that underlies our common-sense beliefs and feelings about being prisoners of time but not space, being spatially but not temporally free and rangy, and the like. There is no need, thank God, to appeal to the doctrine of temporal becoming to explain and justify them.

Conclusion

What connection, if any, is there between the agency-based axiological modal disanalogies and the various objectivity-based modal disanalogies? One would hope that there is a deep connection, and, fortunately, this hope is not disappointed. That our temporal but not our spatial indexical perspectives are objective gives an ontological grounding to an agent having axiological biases in favor of the future but not any spatial direction from here. If the past–present–future perspective were to be non-objective, an agent's axiological biases in favor of the future would be merely subjective. There would be a serious and depressing bifurcation between agents and nature. The value-preferences of agents would be based on a mistaken view of reality in which how things are taken to be by agents is not how they really or objectively are. If I am right, this is not the case. The irreducibly tensed perspective of an agent as someone whose major concern is "What should I **now** do so as to create future value?" also is nature's own perspective.

Notes

1   I am fully aware that in making use of modal notions I am imposing on the good will of many readers. For those who are willing to countenance such notions, I give them license to fill in their own favorite account of modality in terms of linguistic rules, platonic forms, possible worlds, metaphysical necessities, and the like; while for those who view the modal distinction between necessity and contingency as an untenable dualism, I leave them free to reinterpret my talk about necessity in a Quinean way concerning

how deeply embedded or central in our web of belief a given proposition is. For the latter my project is to show that there are truths about time whose spatial analogues are not as deeply embedded or central in our web of belief.

2   For a defense of this see chapter 5 of my *The Language of Time* (London: Routledge & Kegan Paul, 1968).

3   The agent-causation in S5 must be of the simultaneous sort, such as figures in the laws of classical physics, for otherwise some temporal component of T5 would fail to get translated in S5.

4   I am assuming that an agent cannot perform a so-called "supertask," consisting in the performance of an infinite number of distinct acts in a finite time by performing each task in half of the time of its immediate predecessor.

5   *Reasons and Persons* (Oxford: Oxford University Press, 1984), pp. 176–7.

6   *The Will to Believe and Other Popular Essays in Philosophy* (Cambridge, MA: Harvard University Press, 1979), p. 67.

7   It is worth pointing out that what an agent prefers from a tensed perspective might differ from what she prefers from a tenseless one. If an agent existing now has a choice between suffering one unit of pain tomorrow or eight units of pain yesterday, she will prefer to have already suffered eight units of pain yesterday rather than one unit of pain tomorrow; but if this same agent adopts a tenseless Myth of Ur perspective on her life and is given the choice between suffering one unit of pain at t_9 or eight units of pain at t_7, she will prefer to suffer one unit of pain at t_9 rather than eight units of pain at t_7. Assume, as is possible, that tomorrow is t_9 and yesterday is t_8. In this case her tensed preferences conflict with her tenseless ones. This result should not surprise us, for we know that coreferring expressions that differ in sense are not intersubstitutable *salva veritate* within the scope of the verb "prefer," since it creates a non-extensional context. Thus, even though t_7 = yesterday and t_9 = tomorrow, these coreferring expressions, given that they differ in sense, are not intersubstitutable *salva veritate* within the scope of "prefer."

8   This might be challenged by appeal to the doctrine of the specious present according to which each pulse of perceptual experience has a sensory content comprised of successive events, thereby enabling us to perceive a succession of events in a single pulse of experience. This has the consequence that when I see an arm rise I really am seeing a Hindu-type god, and thus am seeing not a temporal succession but a concatenation of coexistent arms, and that when I hear the final note of a melody I am hearing a chord. (If Mozart had an auditory specious present of 30 minutes, being able to hear an entire symphony all at once, he must have had some horrible headaches.) For a fuller account see my book *The Divided Self of William James* (New York: Cambridge University Press, 1999).

9   Sean Gallagher has shown that there are some surface counter-examples to this, e.g., "Now he has won" and "Now he will do it." But these are stylistic variants respectively for "He has just won" and "He will do it shortly."

10 It is interesting to note that there are some analogous ways in which we can choose the context for our use of spatial and temporal indexical terms. For example, for both types of indexes, one can adopt the rule of having their referent determined either *quoad* the place or time of the tokening, as is usual, or *quoad* the place or time of the perception of the tokening.

Bibliography

Richard M. Gale, ed. (1967). *The Philosophy of Time*. New York: Anchor Doubleday.
Robin Le Poidevin, ed. (1998). *Questions of Time and Tense*. Oxford: Clarendon Press.
J. J. C. Smart, ed. (1964). *Problems of Space and Time*. New York: The Macmillan Co.

Each of these volumes contains valuable bibliographies, along with helpful introductions by the editors, that will give the student ample background to appreciate my essay.

Chapter 5

A Thomist Metaphysics

John J. Haldane

Since the modern world began in the sixteenth century, nobody's system of philosophy has corresponded to everybody's sense of reality; to what if left to themselves, common men would call common sense ... the Thomist philosophy is nearer than most philosophies to the mind of the man in the street. (Chesterton, 1933, pp. 172–3)

Introduction

Every philosophical system has a view about the nature and scope of philosophy itself. For that reason and because of the particular need to distinguish the present essay from others that might appear under this title, I begin with a brief explanation of the expression "a thomist metaphysics."

Metaphysics is concerned with the nature of reality as it may be comprehended in the most general terms. It is a small step from this to the claim that metaphysics investigates not just how things are as a matter of contingent fact, but how they must and how they may be. This concern with what is essential, and hence with what is necessary and what is possible, arises from the aim of describing and understanding the nature of reality as such.

The various sciences are focused on and defined by classes of empirical objects and features. Metaphysicians, by contrast, are concerned with the natures of substance, causality, and time *per se*. In investigating these and other aspects of reality they are also enquiring into something yet more extensive, namely the nature and modes of existence. In the language of classical metaphysics, of which thomism is a part, they are concerned with *being in general* (*ens commune*).

Works of reference often use the terms "thomist" and "thomistic" as equivalents to characterize something as pertaining to the thought of the medieval philosopher–theologian Thomas Aquinas (1224/5–74). Metaphysical themes recur throughout his copious writings including theological presentations and commentaries on works of Aristotle and others. But there are only two treatises on metaphysics as such: *On the Principles of Nature* (*De principiis naturae*) and *On Being and Essence* (*De ente et essentia*). The latter is by far the more important and is required reading for anyone wishing to know about Aquinean philosophy.[1] Both texts were composed while Aquinas was still a student (before 1256) and are among his earliest writings; both are short, and both set out in analytical fashion the basic elements of his neo-Aristotelian position. Although his metaphysical views matured in later life they did not change significantly.

Where it is clear that the work of Aquinas himself is at issue the use of "thomist" and "thomistic" is unproblematic; but their application is often extended to cover a multitude of thinkers influenced by and ideas deriving from Aquinas, and in this there is potential for confusion.[2] First, there is the issue of how close to the original the intendedly faithful interpretations of Aquinas may be. Second, is the fact that some who have been inspired by Aquinas have knowingly developed his thought along lines different to those which most disinterested commentators would take to be authentically Aquinean. As might be imagined this has given rise to some controversy. Particularly since the revival of interest in Aquinas marked in 1879 by the encyclical of Pope Leo XIII, *Aeterni Patris*, there have been several movements which have sought accommodation between aspects of Aquinas's thought and more recent philosophical systems such as those of Descartes and Kant. The best known of these syntheses is "transcendental thomism" which tried to reinterpret Aquinas in terms of demands imposed by Kantian critical philosophy (see McCool, 1994). And of late the expression "analytical thomism" has been used to describe approaches combining methods and interests characteristic of Anglo-American analytical philosophy with ideas and doctrines drawn from Aquinas (see Haldane, 1998b).

Here, however, I am not primarily concerned with historical exegesis, nor with the attempt to adjudicate between competing interpretations of Aquinas's own thought. These are exercises in what I shall just term "Thomistic" interpretation (capitalizing "T" to make the link with the person of Thomas himself). My purpose is rather to set out the main elements of a philosophical view that is inspired by Aquinas and which I believe is both coherent and credible. I use the term "thomism" (the lower case "t" registering the non-exegetical emphasis) to indicate the project of practicing philosophy along lines suggested by Aquinas's main ideas and methods. Since there is no unified thomist school I speak only of "*a* thomist metaphysics" and not of "thomist metaphysics" as such.[3]

Aquinas, Aristotle, and Descriptive Metaphysics

Anyone who knows anything about Aquinas knows that he effected an extraordinary synthesis between Aristotelian philosophy and Christian theology, and that he is honored as one of the greatest thinkers of the Roman Catholic Church: Leo's encyclical describes him as "the chief master among all the scholastic doctors." In the eyes of some, these few facts alone provide grounds for suspicion if not dismissal. Unsurprisingly, atheists will suspect that where any philosophy can be extracted from Thomas's theology it will be compromised by doctrinal commitments. But religious believers, and even his co-religionists, have at times been hostile to the Aquinean synthesis. In 1277, three years after his death and in the city where he had studied and taught, Bishop Tempier of Paris denounced a series of Thomistic propositions, though without mentioning Aquinas by name; and in the same year Archbishop Kilwardby of Canterbury issued a similar condemnation in Oxford. These were but two expressions of contemporary hostility to Aristotelianism, which was regarded as dangerously naturalistic. The broader religious opposition, meanwhile, comes from those who regard Aquinas, and thomism generally, as seeking to put reason in the place of faith.

It would go beyond the scope of this essay to debate the second criticism. I shall only say that those who make it tend to be hostile to philosophy *per se*. This then raises the question of why the good and wise God in whose image they believe themselves to have been created, should have fashioned us with the power of speculative reason. So far as their hostility to Aristotelian naturalism is concerned Aquinas's contemporaries had reason to be suspicious; for hitherto it had seemed that the only metaphysics congenial to Christian doctrines was some form of neo-Platonism. Furthermore, they had evidence in the teachings of radical Aristotelians of the period (such as Siger of Brabant) that on one interpretation this alternative Greek philosophy was indeed at odds with Christian belief. Part of the genius of Aquinas was to do as much as anyone ever has done to show that this is not so (which is not to say that there are no points of difference between thomistic and Aristotelian metaphysics).

The dominant form of neo-Platonism in medieval Christian thought was Augustineanism. It is little wonder that the Platonic tradition should have seemed agreeable to the early Church Fathers, for it is not difficult to map Christian beliefs and practices into central elements of neo-Platonism. Most fundamentally, just as the Christian distinguishes between the physical cosmos and the eternal kingdom of God, so Plato and his followers distinguish between the material world and the timeless and unchanging realm of immaterial forms. Similarly, Christians commonly distinguish between body and soul and look forward to a life after death in which the blessed will enjoy forever the sight of God; while Platonists contrast the mortal frame and the immortal mind that will ascend to eternal vision of the forms. Supreme among these forms is that of the One whose principal aspects are those of truth, beauty and goodness; a trinity-in-unity ready-made to assist Christians struggling with the idea that God is three persons in one divinity. The lesser Platonic forms, including those corresponding to natures experienced in the empirical world, became the ideas out of which God created the world. Even Christian mysticism found its rational warrant in the idea that the most noble experiences consist in inexpressible encounters with transcendental realities.

Aristotle came into his own as a philosopher through his rejection of the fundamental tenets of Platonism and through his provision of a more naturalistic and less dualistic world view. It is hardly surprising, therefore, that the enthusiasm for Aristotelianism shown by Aquinas and by his teachers Peter of Ireland and Albert the Great was viewed with suspicion by the Augustinean masters of the thirteenth century. Even so, it is a serious mistake, still perpetrated today, to represent Aristotle as if he were some sort of scientific materialist.

In one of the classics of analytical philosophy, *Individuals: an essay in descriptive metaphysics*, Peter Strawson explains his subtitle by distinguishing between two types of philosophy, writing that "descriptive metaphysics is content to describe the actual structure of our thought about the world, [while] revisionary metaphysics is concerned to produce a better structure" (Strawson, 1959: p. 9). He goes on to point out that few if any actual metaphysicians have been wholly of one or other sort, but that broadly speaking Leibniz and Berkeley are revisionary while Aristotle and Kant are descriptive. In these terms Aquinas's thought and thomist metaphysics are fundamentally "descriptive," notwithstanding that they are at odds with the materialism and scientism which some contemporary philosophers proclaim as enlightened common sense. The words of G. K. Chesterton quoted at the outset of this essay were written in an earlier era and in a non-academic idiom but they capture well the proximity of Aquinas's descriptive metaphysics to "the actual structure of our thought about the world" (and the distance from it of those of Leibniz, Berkeley, and Hegel).

Substance and Accident

We proceed from what is evident in experience and in reflection upon it. What these teach are the all pervasive facts of identity and difference. On the one hand the world exhibits plurality and flux, on the other it manifests sameness and continuity. As I look into the garden I see a variety of plants and animals. Keeping watch across the seasons I observe the shedding of leaves and the appearance of buds; the passing away of one thing and the coming to be of another. Though considerable, this variety is nothing compared to what I might record were I to keep a general inventory of observed identity and difference, continuity and change.

To make descriptive and explanatory sense of this we need to identify principles of composition, organization, identity, and distinctness. The bushes grow and their foliage changes color, but this is not a case of the substitution of one set of objects by another. Over a period of time the matter of the plants and animals is replaced through processes of nutrition and metabolism, but the individuals in question survive this replacement – indeed they would not live were it not to occur. The blades of grass on the lawn seem qualitatively identical to one another, yet each is numerically distinct; so too with the ants crawling around on the path.

The first distinction to be drawn is between particular things and the properties they possess. The second is a distinction within the latter grouping between those properties which are essential and those which are contingent, i.e., which may be acquired or lost without the thing that has them thereby changing its identity or ceasing to exist. Following Aristotle and Aquinas let us refer to what may be predicated of a particular as "a form" and note that forms may either be constitutive of (or in some way express) the very nature of a thing; or else they may be wholly contingent properties of it. Reflection on the variety of forms suggests a range of basic classes into which they fall. Aquinas adopts Aristotle's identification of ten such categories. I may say of Molly, for example, that she is a cat (*substance*), that she is small (*quantity*), friendly (*quality*), younger than our other cat Salem (*relation*), lying by the fire (*place*), alive during the turn of the millennium (*time*), covered in fur (*vesture*), resting on her side (*posture*), purring (*action*) and being warmed (*passion*). Of these ten kinds of predication one tells me *what* Molly is or to what kind she belongs, and the other nine say *how* she is or what modifications she is undergoing. The first is a predication in the category of *substance*, the others predications of *accidents* or features. Typically this distinction in predications is marked by a difference in their logical forms: we say that Molly *is* a kind of substance (*a is a K*) and that she *exhibits* or *has* a certain feature (*a is f*). Thus "substance" may refer either to a *kind* of basic existent, as referred to by a sortal term such as "gold," "water," "cat," "man," etc.; or else to an instance of such a kind: a nugget of gold, a drop of water, a cat, a man.

Use of the term "accident" may risk confusion. While all substantial predications attribute something essential which is identified in a "scientific" definition of the thing's nature, not all non-substantial predications identify features which subjects possess only as a matter of pure contingency, merely "by accident." While being warm and being warmed are each non-substantial predications the latter is contingent in a sense in which the former is not. Molly's being warm naturally follows from the facts of her physiology, that is why there is an intelligible connection between warmth and life. Accordingly we must distinguish "proper accidents" (*propria*), namely those qualities which are naturally related to and hence express a certain kind of essence as properties of it. The fact that a thing has the *propria* it does is due to its substantial nature from which they follow as "proper" effects. I will return to this later when discussing causality.

In thomist metaphysics the principal point of the substance–accident distinction is to mark a difference between things and attributes of things, and to indicate an order of ontological priority between them. It is of the nature of attributes to inhere in substances, but substances do not inhere in attributes or in anything else. Her warmth is a modification of Molly; but Molly is not a modification of any more basic subject that might then be said to bear her as she bears the property of being warm. Predication comes to a halt with substances, and without substances there could be no other predication. Another way of putting the point is by saying that while accidents exist, theirs is a secondary and dependent mode of existence while the being of substances is primary in the order of nature.

Here it is necessary to consider cases where it may be held that accidents occur in the absence of substances of the type in which they normally inhere. For Aquinas's co-religionists this issue arises with some urgency given the Catholic doctrine of eucharistic transubstantiation. Lest this should seem a matter of no philosophical interest it is worth emphasizing that theological problems often raise metaphysical questions in particularly acute forms; exploration of which can show the scope, and often the need for refinement, in one's philosophical theses, even if one does not share the religious assumptions.

The doctrine of transubstantiation holds that "by the consecration of the bread and wine there takes place a change of the whole substance of the bread into the substance of the body of Christ and of the whole substance of the wine into the substance of his blood" with only the appearances (accidents) of bread and wine remaining. Although this doctrine long predates Aquinas, its authoritative statement by the Council of Trent in 1551, from which I have quoted, draws heavily on his treatment of it in the *Summa Theologiae*.[4] There are two issues here depending upon whether one holds that the appearances of bread and wine are annexed to the substances of Christ's body and blood; or that they exist wholly detached, "floating in the air," as it were. First, does it make sense to suppose that an accident can exist apart from the sort of substance of which it is a natural feature? Second, is it compatible with the very idea of accidents that they should occur apart from any substance at all?

Not even the most ardent believers in the real presence of Christ in the eucharistic elements suppose that this could be anything other than miraculous, or that the change is empirically evident. As early as the fourth century St. Ambrose had advised "be convinced that this is not what nature has formed, but by the blessing nature itself has changed," and Aquinas writes that the fact of transubstantiation "cannot be apprehended but only believed by faith." The question, therefore, is not one of natural feasibility but of metaphysical intelligibility. Communion wine has a characteristic alcoholic odor, is typically sweet tasting, and is intoxicating. The doctrine of transubstantiation has it that after the consecration these and other accidents persist though the elements have changed completely from bread and wine. It is not that the latter have simply been annihilated and that new substances have been created where they previously existed; rather there has been a change of substance. What was wine and is now held to be the blood of Christ smells of alcohol, tastes sweet, and if taken in sufficient quantity induces intoxication, but according to the doctrine no wine at all is present. Aquinas would have us say that there is the smell of wine but no wine, the taste of wine but no wine, and the potency of wine but no wine; yet this seems to violate the doctrine that accidents inhere in (and generally arise from) the substances to which they belong.

The sort of account that Aquinas offers of the causal connections between a substance and the proper accidents that inhere in it would suggest that the relationship between having the power to intoxicate and being an alcoholic substance is a non-contingent one.[5] Even so the modality is that of natural causality, which is weaker than either logical or metaphysical necessity.[6] So while it may be a miracle that the power of intoxication should be found co-present with something non-alcoholic – the blood of Christ – this is not in fact incompatible with the claim that proper accidents *naturally* inhere in their proper substances. What are called for are disambiguations of expressions such as "the smell of wine" between interpretations which presume the presence and causality of wine and ones which do not. It is indeed a mystery that the smell, color and intoxicating power of wine should be conjoined with something that neither is wine nor would, according to its own natural causality, smell, look or taste like wine. But while the disassociation from the one substance and association with the other may be wholly unnatural and metaphysically exceptional, they are not, so far as I can see, unintelligible.[7]

I took care, however, to express myself in terms that are compatible first, with the claim that, post-consecration, the accidents of bread and wine inhere in the body and blood of Christ, and second, with the distinct claim that while they are "associated" or "conjoined" with the sacred substances they are not inherent as accidents of them. Aquinas himself avows the second option on the grounds that Christ does not exhibit the appearances of bread and wine. The course he opts for is the more radical. It involves the idea of accidents not only not inhering in their proper substances but not inhering in *any* substances at all; and this apparently runs counter to what he says elsewhere when he writes that "the things which are signified by the names of accidents would not exist if they did not exist in a thing."[8]

In the eucharistic case the suggestion is that the accidents remain where they previously existed but without subsequent reattachment, continuing to be individuated only by time and place. This is understood to be a miracle, but there are apparent examples of substanceless-accidents outwith the theological sphere. Consider statements such as "it's bright," "it's hot," and "it's noisy," said in relation to the environment generally. Being bright, being hot and being noisy are accidents, but what do they qualify? Often there will be identifiable substance-sources of the features in question, such as a light, a fire, or a siren, and one may then rephrase the statements so as to make reference to these. But that is not guaranteed. So far as the nature of light, heat or noise are concerned they could just be "in the air," but it would be straining things to insist that they are then accidents of air as a substance.

In this case and in that of the eucharist one could abandon the requirement of accident-inherence, but that would seem to involve withdrawing a central plank of the general metaphysical scheme. An alternative is to take up Aquinas's observation that the accidents of bread and wine are individuated by "dimensive quantity" and introduce a category of "quasi-substances": the sections of space–time in which the accidents are located. In the case of the consecrated host, for example, one might say that in the time and place where the bread was (and where it would still be, had it continued to exist) there now inhere characteristics miraculously co-instantiated. Admittedly, in the non-praeternatural cases of brightness, heat, and noise the relevant characteristics doubtless flow from other properties of those regions, such as the movements of molecules within them. However, this is a difference in the particular causality and not in the basic structure of subject and accident. In addition, Aquinas's own claim that accidents would not exist if they did not inhere in a thing, is compatible with the possibility that, exceptionally, the role of a "thing" (*ens*) may be discharged directly by that which is indirectly implied by the existence of material substances, namely particular quantities of space–time.[9]

All of this requires a refinement in the thesis about the general character of accidents. I said it is of their nature to inhere in substances, and that accidents exist in a secondary manner whereas substances exist in themselves. This now has to be understood as saying that accidents are the *kinds of things* that are fitted to inhere in substances and are not ontologically basic, and *not* that necessarily every accident inheres in a fully-fledged substance.

One might wonder what the content of this claim could be other than to say that sometimes it is like this and at other times not. But that reaction overlooks an important general feature of the holistic metaphysics with which I am concerned, namely, the belief that not every connection is either contingent or logically necessary. By way of analogy consider the Wittgensteinean understanding of a criterion, whereby if *a* is a criterion of *b* then it is *a priori* that *a*'s existence provides good evidence for that of *b*, even though it is not logically sufficient for it. Applied to the present case we might say that the relations between the existence of accidents and that of a substance in which they inhere is criterial, such that while there can be accidents in the absence of proper substances it is *a priori* that this could not be so generally, and indeed that necessarily the occasions on which it may be so are exceptional.

Form, Matter, and Identity

When we identify what something is, then either explicitly or implicitly we advert to its *nature*, the principal determinant of which is its *substantial form*. This is done directly in saying that Aquinas is a [hu]man, and indirectly by saying he is a theologian. Assuming there are no non-human theologians, to say that a particular theologian died in 1274 is to say that a particular human being did. Substantial forms are the fundamental principles of specific identity and organization. It is in virtue of possessing such a form that an individual thing has the nature it does, whether it be that of a man, a cat, or a cube. In the case of these and all other material substances, however, nature is more than form, since while it belongs to their natures to be physical objects, matter is not part of their formal principles of organization.

By way of analogy think of a design for a house. For this to be implemented there needs to be matter, and it is part of the nature of the resulting structure that it has physical properties. The design may even specify the use of certain kinds of building materials; and so it may even be part of the essence of a certain kind of house that it is built of limestone and oak. It is not in general part of the nature of a material substance, however, that it has the *particular* matter that it does – *these* stones and *this* wood. In the case of living organisms that is not so, or else any material change would amount to the ceasing to be of one substance and the coming to be of another. And even in the case of artefacts we do not in general suppose that, by themselves, erosion and replacement amount to a change of substance, either of kind or of number. In being repaired a house does not cease to be a house and nor (ordinarily) does it become a different one. This said, there is an issue of just how extensive material change can be if a substance is to remain one and the same entity. In art (and for that matter in architectural) conservation, for example, there is a lively debate about the extent to which restoration poses a threat to the identity of an artefact. Clearly successive restorations of a painting do not change its kind – it is still a painting – but there may come a point at which it is doubtful whether it is still *the same* painting.

The current metaphysics provides a clue to how this and similar questions about the persistence of substantial identity through material change might be answered. In Aristotelian and thomist metaphysics, "substances," properly speaking, are only ever natural entities possessed of intrinsic principles of organization, which in the case of living substances are also principles of movement from within (*ab intrinseco*). However, by extension we may regard artefacts as secondary substances in as much as they too are "kinded" and possessed of some nature – be it one imposed by a designer or a user. In the thomist scheme empirical substances are entities comprised of two aspects: (a) a structuring principle, and (b) matter in which this is realized. The first is the form; the second is what Aquinas, following Aristotle, terms "prime" or "first matter" (*materia prima*), and what I propose to call "matter-in-general." At this level of analysis, form and matter are to be understood as metaphysical principles not empirical components. They are not objects of experience but abstractions grounded in the reality of particular natures and actual quantities of stuff. The idea of matter-in-general is arrived at by recognizing that there can be change not just with regard to accidents, but change of one substance into another. When cells divide, when compounds are transformed in a chemical reaction, or when Molly drinks a saucer of water, we recognize that one thing has turned into, or become part of another.

Often in change of this sort we can identify a quantity of some particular material that persists in some new combination. That need not always be so, however. Hence it would be a mistake to conclude from the use of the expression "one thing" that there is a third, and more fundamental, common substance underlying such changes: e.g., some particular object that is first one cell and then several, or some kind of empirical super-element that is first one compound and then another, or some stuff that is first water and then cat. Rather, what we are recognizing in the analysis of substantial change is the fact that one aspect of reality is the natural potential for the successive reception of structuring substantial principles. Prime matter is not any kind of stuff but the empirical condition for the existence of material particulars.

To insist that it is not itself any specific kind of material is not to say that it is immaterial, let alone that it is nothing at all; and this is one reason for following Aquinas in speaking of matter-in-general as "potentiality," meaning by this the very broadest empirical potentiality. "Nothing" is the absence of anything, *a fortiori* of material potentiality. Here there is a difference from Descartes whose notion of matter is that of pure spatial extension. Unlike Cartesian metaphysics, the thomist view does not try to reduce the formal aspect of a substance to its "material" properties of shape, size, divisibility, position, and motion. Put another way, Descartes has a restricted idea of the potentialities of matter which is such that it is impossible that these should account for non-geometrical aspects of substances.[10] The contrasting thomist idea of prime matter is best understood, I suggest, as a theoretical concept identifying whatever it is that is the fundamental ground of the empirical instantiation of substantial and accidental forms. This may be space–time, conceived of not as a pure recepticle but as the counterpart to structuring natures, and as restricted to the instantiation of these. The range of this restriction is not specifiable independently of identifying what substantial and other forms are realized, but that range constitutes the potentiality of prime matter.

In contrast to the idea of matter-in-general stands that of secondary matter (*materia secunda*). This is the stuff of particular kinds that we are familiar with and which chemists analyze. Notice, however, that there is a further ambiguity here, since we may think of such stuff in two ways: on the one hand we may be concerned with specific kinds of stuff, e.g., paper, metal, bone, etc., and on the other we may be considering particular quantities of these, actual heaps or pieces. Here again I follow Aquinas and refer to these as "undesignated matter" and as "designated matter" (*materia signata*), respectively; the rationale being that one can mark or point to the latter but not so the former. By the same token, it is undesignated and not signified matter that is included in the essential definition of a kind of material substance, as when one says that Man is comprised of flesh, blood, and bones (meaning not "this flesh," "this blood" etc.).[11]

Change, then, may be of two sorts, accidental and substantial. In the first case a substance persists through modifications of its attributes; in the second it is destroyed and replaced by another substance or an aggregate of these, as when an organism dies and decomposes into a heap of chemical compounds. In some cases of substantial change what results is the emergence of a substance(s) that was contained virtually within a prior substance, as, for example, in the separation out of an element that was hitherto wholly integrated within a perfect mixture or blend. Ultimately, however, the very possibility of substantial change rests upon the existence of the empirical potentiality that is matter-in-general.

The subject of accidental change, by contrast, is substance, which is to say a quantity of designated matter (*materia signata quantitate*) organized according to some substantial form. While it is part of the nature of such a substance to exist materially, what is required for its continued existence and *ipso facto* its identity over time is not the particular quantity of matter but the persistence of the particular organizing form. Accordingly, questions about the identity conditions for substantial particulars devolve to questions about the nature of the substantial form in question. Imagine the case of a clay cube. In virtue of its form this has six, equal area, square faces and twelve, equal length, edges. This "formula" is empirically realized in a particular quantity of secondary matter. Now suppose that this matter is in process of being systematically replaced. If this is a continuous process such that at no time is the form of the cube destroyed – say by the balance of input and output being lost and it growing or diminishing in height to be a rectangular cuboid – then it remains one and the same substance.

So far as the identity of a painting is concerned, therefore, what is at issue is the question of what constitutes its particular form and what the material conditions of the persistence of this form may be. Western art history attaches great importance to the preservation of the original artist's marks but that is a cultural preoccupation not shared in other places and at other times (such as in the modern orient or in pre-modern Europe). Metaphysically speaking, what matters is material continuity, inasmuch as this is a necessary complement to the preservation of one and the same individualized substantial form. I see no *metaphysical* reason, therefore, to deny that a work all of whose original matter has been replaced through a process of continuous restoration is not one and the same painting. If this sounds odd it is because of our understandable aesthetic concern with the achievement of the original artist. The oddness diminishes as one thinks not of "great works" but of folk-art murals on the gable-ends of houses, produced and refreshed by many hands over many years. In such cases it is not so obvious that different paint implies a different painting.

For Aristotle and Aquinas, and for this thomist metaphysics, the paradigm substances are not artefacts such as clay cubes, or paintings; or chemical elements or compounds such as gold and water, but living organisms. Unlike the former these are dynamically organized and their forms are responsible not just for the disposition of their designated matter but also for their vital operations. The shrubs outside my window alter their appearance as spring arrives, as it gives way to summer and as summer itself passes by. Having emerged from buds the blossoms fade and shrivel, the leaves become fewer and darker in color and the soft wood hardens. Occasionally, however, through disease or through extremes of temperature a shrub dies. In the first example the changes are accidental and follow from the nature of the substance and its interaction with the environment, in the second the change is substantial involving the ceasing to be of the particular nature. This again is the difference between modification and destruction. What it is for an organism to die is for it to lose its principle of organization and activity. So long as a plant or animal is alive a certain aggregation of chemicals is organized structurally and functionally within an overall dynamic unity; once that unity is lost so too is the substance.

Individuation

Earlier I remarked that experience and reflection teach the reality of identity and difference, plurality and flux. Thus far I have dealt with identity and difference so far as these relate to particular substances and the changes they may undergo. There remains the question of unity and diversity within the range of substances. The view from my window reveals a variety of flora and fauna, with difference (and sameness) featuring at distinct levels. Two organisms may differ generically, specifically, and/or numerically: we may distinguish between cats and dogs, as kinds of animals; between European wild cats (*felis sylvestris*) and domestic cats (*felis catus*), as kinds of cats; and between Molly and Salem as individual cats within the same species. Individuation, therefore, may be *generic, specific* or *numerical*. If we ask what makes things different, the answer may be *substantial form* as this features in the definition of the essence of a kind, or *matter* as this is adverted to in identifying an individual.

Given what was said earlier it should be clear that the matter which serves as the principle of individuation of substantial particulars is designated secondary matter (*materia signata quantitate*). In other words, Molly and Salem differ not in respect of their specific natures but in virtue of the fact that those natures are enmattered in different quantities of empirical stuff. One might be tempted to think that numerical difference is attributable to accidental forms; after all two cats will differ in color, size, and location. However, these accidental differences supervene upon the fact that they are two distinct quantities of matter. It is a mere contingency that there are such differences in size and color, and there is certainly no incoherence in the idea that two cats may be qualitatively identical in these respects. As regards difference of location, it is true that two substances of the same kind cannot be in the same space at the same time, but that is because quantitative matter is its primary and proper occupant. Aquinas, who thinks of space as absolute, writes that "bodies fill and are measured by the extent of the places they occupy."[12] One might be mindful, though, of the idea that locations are defined by the relations between things. These two possibilities need not be in conflict, for in general it may be a mistake to suppose that one or other of *things* or *locations* must always have individuative priority (see Strawson, 1959, pp. 36–8). We may, I think, hold that (designated quantitative) *matter* and (dimensive) *place* are co-relative notions. In any event, individuation is secured by matter even if it is also secured by spatiotemporal location (as in the earlier example of the eucharist).

An oft noted corollary of this general view of individuation, as it is held by Aquinas, is the claim that since angels are spiritual substances they cannot be individuated materially and so cannot be diversified within a species. Angelic individuation occurs at the specific level, hence Michael and Gabriel differ not as Peter and Paul, or as Molly and Salem, but as distinct species within a common genus.

It may be added that, to the extent that the notion applies where there can be no plurality, God is "individuated" by his necessary uniqueness and is beyond species and genus. He belongs to no natural nor praeternatural kind.

Substance, Causality, and Science

We can come to know the nature or quiddity (the "what-it-is-ness") of a thing only by attending to and reflecting on its qualities or accidental forms. In this respect substantial form is not itself immediately observable as a sensible feature alongside color, shape or location. However, it is especially important to appreciate that this is not at all equivalent to saying, as Locke and others have done, that substance is an unknowable and unchanging substratum enshrouded in perceptible accidents. It is not as if in looking across the room all I can know is that there is a certain combination of colors, textures and sounds gathered at a particular location, and that the claim that the *cat* is there is a speculative inference from this, or a hypothesis about some unobservable and theoretical common cause of these features. What I see is a substance (Molly) with certain qualities some of which express its essential nature and others of which are extrinsic to this. However, whereas seeing the color of her coat is a matter of sensory perception, seeing that the coat is of fur and that the fur is that of a cat involves understanding. In this respect judgments about the existence and nature of substances are always acts of intellection and not of mere sense-perception.

As Molly grew from a kitten to a cat different accidents were predicable of her but it would be wrong to say that it was the accidents that changed and not Molly herself. She changed in respect of certain of her qualities. As she grew heavier, for example, a succession of weight properties was predicable of her but none of these accidents was itself modified. The properties of being one pound or one kilogram cannot become those of being two pounds or two kilograms; but a substance can and does change in passing from one weight to the other. As I emphasized earlier, the relation between a substance and its accidents is an intimate one. Substances themselves change through the acquisition and loss of properties, and they are known in and through their (proper) accidents.

These facts are important in understanding thomist philosophy of natural science and its contrast with that of classical empiricism. According to the latter there are no non-contingent relations given in experience. Nothing implies or suggests anything else, save in the psychological sense that on the basis of some kind of association we find ourselves expecting one thing given the presence of another. On this view the most we could ever have reason to assert about the structure of nature are observed regularities. The thomist perspective is quite different and it provides a basis for regarding the material world as intrinsically intelligible – indeed as operating in an orderly way according to something analogous to reason. Proper accidents flow from the nature of a substance as from an organised source of activity; organic change is not just a matter of successive differences but is generally developmental; and substances influence others, through the accidents of each, in ways that may conform to regularities but which are not reducible to them. To summarize in a slogan, the one thing that "a thomist metaphysics" is not, and indeed that to which it is implacably opposed, is the similarly sounding "atomist metaphysics."

Among the areas in which the contrast is most marked is that of causality. Modern discussions of this have been dominated by the Humean orthodoxy that causality is not encountered in experience, and that the conception of it is analyzable in terms of other observed factors or imposed ideas. Hume's account of our concept of a causal relation is that it is a compound of three elements: ideas of spatial contiguity, temporal succession, and necessary connection. Whereas in the cases of the first two the matching of these ideas to experiences is unproblematic, there is, Hume presumes, no perceptual warrant for the idea of a necessary connection between events, such that given the first the second had to follow, and that had not the first occurred the second would not have happened. This being the case he offers a psychological substitute, namely that succession and contiguity of types of objects found conjoined in our experience are such as to determine the mind to form the idea of one object or event upon the occasion of observing (or forming the idea of) the other object or event.

There are several problems with this as a positive analysis of the concept of causality. It disallows action at a distance, simultaneity of cause and effect, singular (non-law like) efficacy, and types of "making to be" other than efficient causality. Even so it has been deeply influential. So much so that when philosophers have rejected aspects of Hume's view they have then tended to reconstruct some analogue of it in terms of necessary and sufficient conditions holding between types of events. The depth of Hume's influence is due perhaps to the acceptance of his negative claim that causality itself is not observed and that we can have no experience of necessary connections.

The thomist response is partly concessive and partly critical. It is true that we do not observe causality as such, just as we do not observe matter in general or substantial form *per se*. As in the latter cases, causality is a metaphysical principle and not an empirical phenomenon. However, just as we may observe designated secondary matter, and see particular substances in seeing their properties, so we may also see causality at work in observing cases of activity and reactivity. Elizabeth Anscombe, the most powerful modern critic of Hume (and a philosopher influenced by her reading of Aristotle and Aquinas), points out that many of our words represent causal concepts which are commonly applied in observation or in hypotheses about the sources of certain events (Anscombe, 1981). Thus I may observe that Molly *purred, rolled over, scratched the wall, sniffed the air*, and also conjecture that she has *caught a chill*, and that her figure does not betoken *pregnancy*. All such concepts are causal and in applying them correctly we express causal knowledge.

Furthermore, concepts of natural substances and of artefacts often embody references to characteristic activities or to causal dispositions. Obvious examples are acid, seed, rain, siren, radio, and light bulb; but it is true more generally that a mastery of substance concepts involves an understanding of how they may act or react. Under various conditions, some of which we may be able to specify but of which there is no complete list, cats typically (but not necessarily) meow, purr, wash themselves, walk, and so on. What this suggests is that contrary to Hume's atomistic epistemology in which no impressions "ever give us the least intimation of anything beyond" (Hume, 1978, p. 189), we may properly infer the (presumptive) existence of one thing from that of another. In addition there are other forms of causality than that in which one event brings about another. Aquinas follows Aristotle in specifying four kinds of cause which may be cited in explanations of why things are as they are: *formal* (form), *material* (matter), *efficient* (agency), and *final* (purpose). I would go further and say that there are as many kinds of causality as there are distinct kinds of true "because" statements.[13]

Thus, while it may not be the case that the relations between substances, accidents, and events are necessary ones, it does not follow that they are wholly contingent in the sense Hume intends, and it may even be that sometimes they are necessitating. Ironically, therefore, whereas Hume's stance is dogmatic and exclusionary, the thomist one recognizes that there is non-contingency in nature but is also open to the possibility that some relations are wholly contingent and that some may be naturally and even metaphysically necessary.

From the thomist perspective, enquiry into nature looks very different. For one thing, this view begins to make sense of actual scientific practice and shows it to be philosophically defensible, which it hardly is on the Humean account. In Aquinas and in the writings of other scholastic-Aristotelians one finds various versions of the slogan "acting follows upon being" (*agere sequitur esse*). Earlier I referred to the nature of a substance. In Aquinas this idea of a nature is explicitly linked to the notion of activity: the former being responsible for the latter, which is (naturally) expressive of its source. As a principle of action "from within" (*ab intrinseco*), substantial form constitutes *a nature*; as scientifically definable it is described as an *essence*.

To understand this correctly we need to distinguish *nominal* and *real* definitions. Aristotle and Aquinas did just this, so did Locke (from whom the current terminology derives); and in recent times Putnam (Putnam, 1975) and Kripke (Kripke, 1980) have done so again. A nominal definition provides an account of how a word is used in terms of standard, non-theoretical criteria for its application. A real definition, by contrast, purports to describe the essential constitution of what is referred to. Sometimes these two kinds of definition serve to pick out the same range of entities, but at other times they are divergent, as, for example, in cases where the usual non-theoretical criteria may be absent. Water is typically the clear, colorless, potable liquid found in rivers and lakes; but it is conceivable that in some environment a liquid satisfying that nominal description should fail to be water, i.e., the chemical compound hydrogen oxide (H_2O). Again it is easily imaginable that under certain conditions H_2O is neither colorless, potable nor liquid. For most everyday purposes the nominal definition serves, but scientists, and others for whom real natures matter, are concerned with whether specimen quantities satisfy the real definition, that is whether they really are *water*.

While Locke adopted this distinction from the scholastics, he did not at the same time take from them the conviction that real science, the science of real definitions, was possible. That was in part because of his view that substance was an inaccessible substratum; but his empiricism also disposed him to think that essence must be unobservable. Aquinas sees no such theoretical obstacles to the formation of real-essence definitions. At the same time, though, he is not unduly optimistic about our arriving at them. There are various reasons for his reserve. First, while proper accidents are criterial with respect to the substances in which they inhere we cannot tell straight off which accidents are proper to a substance and which are more contingently related to it. Second, even where accidents do express the nature of their subject, for example in the case of activity that follows from the primary causal powers of a substance, these accidents may be inhibited or transformed by other factors (causes) in the substance or in the environment. The contemporary literature on dispositions is full of examples which create difficulties for analyses of causal powers (see Martin, 1994 and Lewis, 1997), but something of these problems has always been evident to those involved in scientific investigation. Add human limitations, and it is understandable, if a surprise to those unfamiliar with his writings, to find Aquinas saying that enquiry into essence must proceed via accidents; and that generally we do not get very far towards an adequate definition of essence though that is the proper goal of the search.

One reason why such epistemic modesty may seem surprising is that in the historical Aristotelian–Thomistic scheme a science is an axiomatic system in which statements about particulars are logically derived from a fully comprehensive set of essential definitions. On that view it can seem that, strictly, one does not know anything until one knows everything, and that knowledge proper must always be of real essences. This is somewhat in keeping with the noble intellectualism of Plato and is in contrast to the dominant note in contemporary philosophy which is to maintain that knowledge is not an "all-or-nothing" state. Aquinas, however, was quite aware of this and deals with the matter in the way I have described: indicating that a certain (perhaps idealized) state of information defines the proper goal of enquiry, while allowing that movement along the way to it constitutes cognition to the extent that enquiry is oriented towards, and approximates to this goal.

Here we see an instance of the famous Aquinean doctrine of analogy, according to which, terms may have both principal and secondary, related but non-identical senses. Again this is a development of something in Aristotle: the idea of "controlled equivocation." For Aquinas, all metaphysical terms (and I would add, all central expressions of philosophical analysis) are analogical. The question which an account of analogy needs to answer, however, is not that of whether analogical predication is possible (it obviously is) but rather of what, in a given case, is the ground of it: both what the primary use may be, and also what licenses the secondary ones. This is an area in which much more work needs to be done by thomists and others (though McInerny, 1996, and Ross, 1981 are both valuable). Here, however, it is enough to say that the use of the term "knowledge" for something less than a secure grasp of essences rests on an analogy of proportion.[14]

Individuals, Universals, and Abstraction

The idea that fully fledged knowledge of the natural order may be organized into a deductive system is at best an ideal. It does, though, raise another matter of some importance. In Aristotle's *Posterior Analytics* and in Aquinas's *Commentary*, where this conception of scientific knowledge is under discussion, the point is made that while deduction (from axioms) proceeds from universals, induction (*inductione*) starts from particulars. Aquinas then goes on to add that without induction it is impossible to investigate universals. This raises the question of how we might hope to get from the observation of particular substances to conclusions about general essences. Talk of "induction" in this context may well mislead, since to modern ears it is bound to raise the specter of Hume's inductive skepticism. Hume's rejection of the possibility of knowledge of non-contingent relations in nature expressed itself famously in the claim that "after the observation of the frequent or constant conjunction of objects, we have no reason to draw any inference concerning any object beyond those of which we have had experience" (Hume, 1978, p. 139). This has seemed to many to refute the idea that enumerative induction could be a form of warranted inference to universal claims. But this is not what Aquinas has in mind in talking about induction as a route to knowledge of general essence.

Thus far I have deployed, but not made explicit, a distinction between substantial forms as immanent constitutive principles (of particular individual substances), and substantial forms as general kinds. That is to say we may distinguish between the catness-of-Molly, or the catness-of-Salem, and Catness as such. The former are numerically distinct individual entities (individualized forms), the latter is a universal. In antiquity, in the middle ages, and again in our time, there have been extensive debates about the reality and status of common natures. Here I follow Aquinas and maintain a position between the view that everything that exists is individual, and the opinion that universals exist as such outside the mind. This *via media* holds that distinct substances may yet possess formally identical (though numerically diverse) natures: the *fness-of-a*, the *fness-of-b*, etc., and that these are the basis for the formation of a universal entity *Fness* which really exists as a universal species – but only as abstracted in the intellect. An implication of this view is that the old question "are natures plural or single?" rests on the false presupposition that the answer must be exclusively one or the other. Instead we may say that it is both: natures are many in things and one in the mind; but that as such, i.e., until a context has been specified, they are neither.

Universality is only to be found in the intellect, but general species are nonetheless real: they are formed by abstraction from a plurality of formally identical natures existing in materially individuated substances. Thus, for Aquinas, *inductione* is not a process of collecting singulars and positing claims about further cases; but is the intellectual activity of abstractive induction: fashioning a universal on the basis of particulars. This is not the occasion to defend this view (for that, see Haldane, 2000); but one will not begin to see merit in it unless one also adopts a non-Cartesian standpoint on the issue of knowledge. For Aquinas, and the thomism I subscribe to, the idea that we begin with the burden of skepticism and must forever be justifying ourselves is a misconception based on a quite false assumption about the nature of knowledge. Thought begins in the world and then has the task of enquiring into the metaphysical conditions of its own possibility. The question for epistemology is not whether we know anything but rather, given what we do know, how does cognition work? Abstractive induction and non-contingency in nature are part of the answer to that latter question.

Mind and Soul

The individualization of form in nature (*in esse naturale*) is due to the fact of its enmatterment. Given that form features universally in thought (*in esse intentionale*) we may conclude that "there" it does not exist under material conditions. Recalling that acting follows upon being, we may then be drawn to the idea that the subject of intellectual acts cannot itself be a material substance. So arises the issue of the immateriality of the human soul and the possibility of life after death. In general terms, soul is the principle of organization of a living substance. That being so, one might suppose that the substantial form of a human individual is no more capable of existing apart from enmatterment than is the substantial form of a cube of clay. It might be different, however, if the form were the subject acts that were not exercised through its embodiment, which were not operations of its materially individuated parts. If intellection is indeed an immaterial power then it may be that the human soul transcends the quantity of matter which it informs.

This is brief and speculative but rather than try to make the case I wish simply to address a standard objection to a thomistic view of the possibility of postmortem existence. Aquinas himself maintains, with good reason, that even if an intellectual agent survives the dissolution of the living human substance it would not be a human person. He writes of this imagined remnant "I am not my soul" (*anima mea non est ego*) and goes on to say that the possibility of human life depends upon embodiment. Hence all hopes for future existence must be directed towards the promise betokened by the example of Christ, and discussed by St. Paul, of bodily resurrection.[15] Apart from any question of theological credibility there stands the challenge that the suggestion of (temporary) disembodiment implies a dualism at odds with the anti-Cartesianism characteristic of Aristotle and Aquinas. It is indeed the case that thomists have been given to a certain smugness in their attitude toward classical dualism while failing adequately to address the point that what they favor seems not much different from it. This said, there may be logical space between the view that persons are wholly constituted independently of their association with bodies, and the view that the only substances that could serve as the bearers of psychological properties are materially individuated substances.

For want of an existing term let me introduce the expression "residual substance" to introduce the idea of a something to which are transferred certain powers hitherto possessed and exercised by a more extensive and more potent substance. One way of conceiving of this is in terms of the relationship touched on earlier between an actual substance and a virtual one contained within it. Imagine the case of a perfect (i.e., idealized) compound of elements a/b such that the constituents are not independently identifiable. The point to bear in mind in this example is that unlike the case of chemical components the constituents do not ordinarily occur outside the context of their interactive union in a/b. So a, for example, does not enjoy actual existence qua a in the compound state. There its existence is virtual; that is to say, while it is correct to claim that the behavior of a/b is in part a result of the contribution of a, the powers of the compound are not a linear combination of the powers of their parts.[16]

Now the question is whether in the case that a/b ceases to exist certain of its powers might be transferred to a, which, though hitherto merely virtual, might now emerge as actual. To fix this idea think of compound pigment colors such as brown, and the claim that red, say, exists virtually but not actually in this compound. What that means is that, certain conditions obtaining, the brown pigment might be destroyed but red pigment is precipitated out. Might this provide a model for the postmortem existence of a subject of abstract thought?

In order for it to do so it is necessary that the residual powers transferred from a/b to a do not depend essentially for their possession or exercise on the contribution of b. What was proposed earlier was this: that there is at least one power of the living human being, that of abstract thought (and any other powers which may be subservient to it), which is not necessarily exercised through any part of the body, i.e., it has no bodily organ. That being supposed it cannot be objected that such a power could not be exercised by some precipitated non-physical substance because it requires a material embodiment. So if thought is an immaterial activity exercised ante-mortem through the operation of a/b there is no contradiction involved in supposing that it might continue postmortem but transferred from the hitherto actual substance a/b to the hitherto merely virtual but then actual substance a. However, a is to this extent a secondary and restricted bearer and miracles obliging it will be better when a's residual activity is returned to the more extensive subject a/b. Though this is not at all Aquinas's way of dealing with the issue it lends itself to the plaintive refrain that *anima mea* (a) *non est ego* (a/b) and to the view that the possibility of complete (a/b) life depends upon the re-creation of **a**/**b** via the restoration of **b**. Needless to say that re-creation of the *status quo ante* is not something that is possible in the natural order of things. But as in the case of the eucharist there may be general philosophical insights to be gained by thinking about theologically inspired examples.

Essence, Existence, and God

This brings me finally to the subject which readers may best associate with an Aquinean or thomistic metaphysics, namely the attempt to argue from general facts about the existence and nature of the world to the existence of a creator God. Familiarly, these cosmological and teleological proofs argue from contingency or order (understood as natural regularity or as beneficial functioning) to the existence of a first cause of existence or of design. Such arguments begin, as in Aquinas's "five ways" (*quinque viae*), with observation of some fact or facts taken to be generally evident in experience. Introducing the first way, Thomas writes of how "it is certain, and evident to our senses, that in the world some things are in process of change." Presenting the second he writes that "in the world of sensible things we find there is an order of efficient causes." Introducing the third he says that "we find in nature things that are possible to be and not to be." Presenting the fourth, he notes that "among beings there are some more and some less good, true, noble, and the like." Finally, in giving the fifth way he writes of how "we see that things which lack knowledge, such as natural bodies, act for an end."[17]

It is clear that in every case Aquinas is appealing to experience of the world as a mind-independent reality. It is worth noting, however, that some and perhaps all of the arguments he gives can be reconstructed even if that realist assumption were unwarranted – and even if it were false. Suppose, for example, that there were no external world, or that it lacked the structure our concepts appear to attribute to it, or that all we ever have access to are our own thoughts. It would still be possible to pursue the *via prima* given that there is change in respect of these last, with one idea or impression being succeeded by another. Similarly, differences in modality and in degree of excellence are to be found within thought itself; as I believe are differences in causality and in teleology. Admittedly, however, these last claims are more controversial than are their counterparts concerning what is found in the extra-mental world. Nonetheless, the general point holds good, which is that the traditional arguments can be worked on the basis of idealism as well as of realism.

This generally unremarked fact is relevant to assessing the scope and power of an argument which has some claim to be Thomas's most original contribution to the search for theistic proofs, but which does not feature in the *quinque viae*. In his *Commentary on the Sentences* Aquinas presents three arguments for the existence of God. The first is teleological (being concerned with order in the universe); the second is cosmological (concerning change and becoming); and the third might be termed "ontological" – not because it is akin to Anselm's conceptual argument but in as much as it arises from the idea that existence is something additional to nature. Every object (*ens*) is both a *something*, of such and such a nature, and an *existent*.[18] Although these aspects are not distinct entities (either substances or accidents), nonetheless they are real and are related to one another as potentiality and actuality. That is to say a nature constitutes a kind of possibility (of there being a such and such) of which existence is an actualization. There are two possibilities arising from this distinction. First, the existence of a being might be implied by, and hence be dependent upon its nature. Second, essence and existence might be metaphysically distinct. In the latter case the being or actuality of an entity is not self-accounting but calls for explanation from beyond the thing itself. Generalized, the question becomes that of how it is possible that entities whose essences do not imply their existence nevertheless are actual. The answer can only be that they participate in being through the action of some prior actuality which is the efficient cause of their *esse*. The impending regress can only terminate in an actuality that is self-subsistent: something of which, uniquely, its existence belongs to its nature – and this is God.

That momentous conclusion is voiced repeatedly in the *Summa Theologiae* and elsewhere in Aquinas's writings in the form "and this we call God" (*et hoc dicimus Deum*). It would certainly be true to say that whatever the starting point of Aquinas's metaphysical investigations they reach a natural conclusion in the idea that the next stage in the movement towards truth is not via the practice of philosophy but through theology or the "sacred science of God." Though I am sympathetic to this conclusion (Smart and Haldane, 1996), even to prepare for that movement, let alone to embark upon it, really would be to go beyond the bounds of the present essay.

Notes

1 Both are contained in Aquinas 1993, pp. 67–80, and pp. 90–113, and in Aquinas 1998, pp. 18–29 and 30–49. Future references to the *Summa Theologiae* are to the translations in the edition of the *English Dominican Fathers*, London: Washbourne, 1912.

2 For an account of the history of thomism, its reception and development see Haldane, 1998a and 1999a.

3 For accounts of just how great the difference in interpretations of Aquinas's central metaphysical ideas can be see McCool, 1994, ch. 1 and epilogue; and Knasas, 2000.

4 *Summa Theologiae*, III, q. 75.

5 *Summa Theologiae*, Ia, q. 77, a. 6, ad. 2.

6 For an account of the various forms of necessity see Kripke, 1980.

7 For contrary views see Kenny, 1980, and Dummett, 1987.

8 *Commentary on the metaphysics of Aristotle*, Book VII, lectio 1.

9   I say "exceptionally" because one may reasonably suppose that the individuation of space and time is not independent of that of regular substances, and that as centers of activity the latter enjoy ontological primacy.

10 Descartes writes as follows: "there is nothing in the whole of nature . . . which is incapable of being deductively explained on the basis of these self same principles [the shape, size, position and motion of particles of matter]." *Principles of Philosophy*, Pt. IV, art. 187 in Descartes, 1985.

11 In *De ente et essentia*, II, 5, Aquinas says that if the individual Socrates could be defined then the definition would include reference to particular quantities of matter, "this particular flesh and this particular bone," but these can only be pointed to and are not part of the general description of the nature of Socrates, which is the definition of man as such.

12 *Summa Theologiae*, Ia, q. 8, a. 2.

13 For some discussion of this see Putnam, 1999.

14 For Aquinas's account of the route between univocality and equivocality see *Summa Theologiae* Ia, q. 13, a 1–6 in Aquinas, 1993, pp. 214–30.

15 Aquinas, *Commentary of St. Paul's Letter to the Corinthians*, in Aquinas, 1993.

16 One might be disposed to say that the powers of the whole are thus "emergent." But if "thus" is meant to suggest some form of explanation it is liable to be spurious. Like the idea of supervenience that of emergence has been grasped at by those hoping to reconcile non-reducible, non-physical characteristics with substance physicalism. Some of the difficulties attending this attempt are discussed in Haldane, 1999b, and a proposed form of emergentist physicalism is discussed in Haldane, 1996.

17 *Summa Theologiae* Ia, q. 2, a. 3, *responsio*.

18 For contrasting analytical discussions on Aquinas's doctrine of the distinction between essence and existence see Geach, 1961, and Kenny, 1980.

References

Anscombe, G. E. M. (1981). "Causality and determination," in Anscombe, *Metaphysics and the Philosophy of Mind: collected philosophical papers, vol. 2*. Oxford: Blackwell.

Aquinas, T. (1993). *Aquinas, Selected Philosophical Writings* (T. McDermott, trans. and ed.). Oxford: Oxford University Press.

Aquinas, T. (1998). *Thomas Aquinas: selected writings* (R. McInerny, trans.). London: Penguin Books.

Chesterton, G. K. T. (1933). *St. Thomas Aquinas*. London: Hodder and Stoughton. (For an account of the history of thomism, its reception and development, see Haldane [1998a] and [1999b].)

Descartes (1985). J. Cottingham, R. Stoothoff, and D. Murdoch (eds.). *Philosophical Writings of Descartes*. Cambridge: Cambridge University Press, 2 vols.

Dummett, M. (1987). "The intelligibility of eucharistic doctrine," in W. J. Abraham and S. W. Holtzer (eds.), *The Rationality of Religious Belief*. Oxford: Oxford University Press.

Geach, P. (1961). "Aquinas," in E. Anscombe and P. Geach, *Three Philosophers*. Oxford: Blackwell.

Haldane, J. (1996). "The mystery of emergence." *Proceedings of the Aristotelian Society*, Vol. XCVI, pp. 261–7.

Haldane, J. (1998a). "Thomism," in E. Craig (ed.), *Routledge Encyclopedia of Philosophy*. London: Routledge. Vol. 9, pp. 380–8.

Haldane, J. (1998b) (ed.). "Analytical Thomism," *The Monist*, 81.

Haldane, J. (1999a). "Thomism and the future of catholic philosophy," *New Blackfriars*, 80, 158–71 (this is a special issue bearing the same title as the essay and containing twelve responses from Timothy Chappell, Dagfinn Follesdal, Bas van Frassen, John Greco, Bonnie Kent, Christopher Martin, Ralph McInerny, Hayden Ramsay, Nicholas Rescher, Thomas Sullivan, Charles Taylor, and Linda Zagzebski).

Haldane, J. (1999b). "A return to form in the philosophy of mind," in D. Oderberg (ed.), *Form and Matter: themes in contemporary metaphysics*. Oxford: Blackwell.

Haldane, J. (2000). "Insight, inference and intellection," in M. Baur (ed.), *Insight and Inference. Proceedings of the American Catholic Philosophical Association*, Vol. 73, pp. 31–45.

Hume, D. (1978). *A Treatise of Human Nature*, ed. L. A. Selby-Bigge and P. H. Nidditch. Oxford: Oxford University Press.

Kenny, A. (1980). *Aquinas*. Oxford: Oxford University Press.

Knasas, J. F. X. (2000). "Whither the neo-Thomist revival?" *Logos*, 3, pp. 121–49.

Kripke, S. (1980). *Naming and Necessity*. Oxford: Blackwell.

Lewis, D. (1997). "Finkish dispositions." *Philosophical Quarterly*, 47, pp. 143–58.

McCool, G. (1994). *The Neo-Thomists*. New York: Marquette University Press.

McInerny, R. (1996). *Aquinas and Analogy*. Washington, DC: Catholic University of America Press.

Martin, C. B. (1994). "Dispositions and conditionals." *Philosophical Quarterly*, 44, pp. 1–8.

Putnam, H. (1975). "The meaning of 'meaning,' " in H. Putnam, *Mind, Language and Reality*. Cambridge: Cambridge University Press.

Putnam, H. (1999). *The Threefold Cord*. New York: Columbia University Press.

Quine, W. V. O. (1969). *Ontological Relativity and Other Essays*. New York: Columbia University Press.

Ross, J. (1981). *Portraying Analogy*. Cambridge: Cambridge University Press.

Smart, J. J. C. (1989). *Our Place in the Universe*. Oxford: Blackwell.

Smart, J. J. C. and Haldane, J. J. (1996). *Atheism and Theism*. Oxford: Balckwell.

Suggested Further Reading

Copleston, F. C. (1975). *Thomas Aquinas*. London: Penguin Books.

Davies, B. (1993). *The Thought of Thomas Aquinas*. Oxford: Clarendon Press.

Kenny, A. (1993). *Aquinas on Mind*. London: Routledge.

Martin, C. (ed.) (1988). *The Philosophy of Thomas Aquinas: introductory readings*. London: Routledge.

Martin, C. (1997). *Thomas Aquinas: God and understanding*. Edinburgh: Edinburgh University Press.

Wippel, J. (1993). "Metaphysics," in N. Kretzmann and E. Stump (eds.), *The Cambridge Companion to Aquinas*. Cambridge: Cambridge University Press, pp. 85–127.

Chapter 6

The Concept of Ontological Category: A New Approach

Lorenz B. Puntel

Preliminaries

If we are to make sense of the world, we have to recognize from the outset that it is a highly differentiated and structured whole. Toward this end many philosophers, beginning with Aristotle, have made use of the concept of a category. It is not the aim of this essay to give a comprehensive treatment of this topic, something that would not be possible in the limited space available. Instead, the attempt will be made to bring into bold relief the categorial structure of ordinary language, which will be found to be that of a substance-property sort. It then will be argued that the concept of a substance, along with that of an abstract property or universal, is not acceptable. An effort will be made to create a new language that will not be committed to a substance-property ontology or any sort of dualism between the concrete and the abstract, that is, between items that are locatable within the spatial and/or temporal world and those that are not.

Philosophers are in agreement that categories are fundamental classifications that frame the way in which we think and talk about the world. But philosophers disagree as to how to understand the phrase, "our ways of thinking and talking about the world." If one takes the clause "about the world" as having priority in the order of understanding and explanation, that is, as being that clause which determines how the other clause "our ways of thinking and talking" must be interpreted, then categories will emerge as having an ontological status, for they will mark different kinds of items or entities *in the world* as being the most fundamental structures *of the world*. The category of *substance*, beginning with Aristotle, has usually been taken to be the primary or most fundamental one.

But if we understand "our ways of thinking and talking about the world" in the inverse order by taking the clause "our ways of thinking and talking" as prior, categories will be understood as the most fundamental concepts we can avail ourselves of and/or our most general ways of using language. Kant's a priori categories gave priority to the clause "our ways of thinking," whereas the analytical philosophy performed a "linguistic turn" according to which the categories (often called "conceptual schemes") are to be understood on the basis of the priority of "our ways of talking (about the world)." The aim of the present essay is to develop a theory of "ontological category" in which these two approaches are shown to be two sides of the same coin.

The essay divides into three sections. In section 1 the most important conceptions about ontological categories in contemporary philosophy will be presented in a sketchy way and submitted to a concise critique. The purpose of section 1 is to motivate the reader to engage in the pursuit of a significantly different approach to this topic. In section 2 this new approach will be worked out. The general strategy can be delineated as follows: It will be shown that the semantics presupposed by the "substance ontologies" is a compositional semantics, i.e., a semantics based on the acceptance of the Compositionality Principle, as will be explained at the end of section 1. This principle will be shown to have unacceptable ontological implications, so it should be abandoned. A semantics based on another principle, the Principle of Sentential Compositionality (or Context Principle), is then developed. The new approach to the concept of ontological category is what results when one develops a non-compositional ontology. As for those contemporary theories of ontological categories that reject the idea of a "substance" (the so-called "bundle theories") it will be briefly shown that they are defective in not being developed on the basis of a conspicuous semantics. Section 3 contains some concluding remarks.

1   The Highly Problematic Status of the Category of Substance

(1) In contemporary philosophy the "concept of substance" has at least *three* different senses. The *first* holds that substance is a *substratum* in which properties (and relations) subsist or inhere. Thus, substratum is supposed to be an entity distinct from another entity, the attribute (property and/or relation), since the concrete particular or individual is taken to be constituted by those two entities. This substratum has rightly been called a "bare particular," since it is devoid of all attributes. There are numerous conceptual problems with this conception of a bare particular. (See Denkel, 2000, for a good account of these problems.) Shortly, the root problem of this concept, along with that of a universal, which is what a bare particular is supposed to instantiate, will be presented.

A *second* tendency rejects the idea of a bare particular, but not the idea of a subject. The key concept introduced by those authors who favor this approach is that of *kind* in order to explain what they understand by a substance or concrete particular. M. Loux, for instance, asserts:

> What a concrete particular is, on this view, is simply an instance of its proper kind; and Aristotelians argue that to be an instance of a kind is simply to exhibit the form

of being that is the kind. Since that form of being is irreducibly unified, the things that exhibit it are themselves irreducibly unified entities, things that cannot be construed as constructions out of more basic entities. (Loux, 1998, p. 121)

The idea of a subject, though, is not entirely rejected by those authors. They claim that the substances or concrete particulars themselves are the subjects for all the attributes associated with them; but they hasten to say that one should distinguish between attributes that are *essential* to their bearers and others that are merely *accidental* to them. In the second case the particular, as the bearer of an attribute, is understood as a subject whose essence or core does not necessarily include that attribute; but according to those authors, in the first case a necessary inclusion of attributes must be recognized, it being the case that the substance or the concrete particular is also the subject for a kind. M. Loux explains this view by means of an example:

Socrates is also the subject for the kind *human being*. Socrates and not some constituent in him is the thing that is human; but the kind *human being* is what marks out Socrates as *what* he is, so in this case our subject is not something with an identity independent of the universal for which it is subject. Take the *man* away from Socrates and there is nothing left that could be a subject for anything. (Ibid., p. 120)

There can be no doubt that the proponents of this view make a considerable effort to eliminate the obscurity of the notion of *substratum*. But fundamental doubts remain as to whether this has really been accomplished. What does it mean to say that a concrete particular is "simply an instance of its proper kind"? If the concrete particular is simply identified with its proper kind, the concept of instantiation ceases to be an explanatory one. But if it is said that "our subject is not something with an identity independent of the universal for which it is subject," then it is hard to understand what this means. For how can an item x be a subject for a universal U if x's identity is not independent of U? Perhaps one could say that in this case one has to do with a "limiting case" of the concept of instantiation. But in philosophy, limiting cases of that sort are problematic concepts; they are in general indicative of the need to introduce another, more suitable "conceptual scheme" in order to articulate the intuition one wants to express.

A *third* tendency eschews the concept of *substratum* (and subject) and introduces instead the feature of *independence* as the "criterion" of substance (see especially Hoffman and Rosenkrantz, 1994, ch. 4; Lowe, 1998, ch. 6). This approach is found in Descartes, Spinoza, and others. It holds a substance to be independent, because it is capable of existing all by itself. Many divergent understandings of the concept of independence have been proposed. The main problem with this view is that *independence* is only a necessary but not a sufficient condition for being a substance. Having independence is only an external aspect, not the internal structure of a substance.

(2) Ontological theories that do not accept the traditional idea of substance explain concrete particulars (and every kind of complex entity) as bundles of some kind of entities. Such theories are in general called *bundle theories*. Instead of the expression "bundle" other expressions are used as well, for instance, "configuration," "collection," "cluster," and the like. In the present paper the expression "configuration" will be used whenever the author is referring to his own position. But there are very divergent bundle theories according, first, to the kind of entities that are taken to constitute a bundle and, second, to the more exact sense that is associated with the expression "bundle."

Three main versions are especially worth mentioning. The *first* version, called *trope theory*, is a radically revisionary theory that not only rejects the idea of substratum and subject but also, and above all, calls into question the concept of *universal*. Philosophers who hold this theory accept a (new) entity or category they call *trope*[1] and characterize it as an *abstract particular* or as a particularized or concretized property (and relation). According to this view, tropes are the fundamental elements of being from which all else can be constructed; more exactly, tropes are considered the sole fundamental category and the complete ontology built on tropes is understood as a one-category ontology. A concrete particular or an individual is explained as a bundle of tropes: the entity traditionally called "universal" is reinterpreted as a collection of tropes bundled together by the relation of resemblance (see Williams, 1953, Campbell, 1990).

This conception represents an interesting new development as regards the concept of ontological category. But it faces many and deep difficulties that have been pointed out by many authors (see, among others, Simons, 1994; Daly, 1994). As the author of the present essay sees it, the most salient difficulty lies in the fact that trope theory did not succeed in making clear how it can dispense with the relation of *instantiation* (see especially Daly, 1994, pp. 250–60), a relation that presupposes the very concept of universals that the trope theory pretends to reject. This difficulty is apparent even in the terminology used by trope theorists, when they say, for instance, that tropes are "abstract particulars," "particularized properties (and relations)" or even "instances of properties (and relations)."

This difficulty in its turn is rooted in what one should take to be the systematic deficiency of trope theory: although this theory relies on a valuable intuition, it entirely lacks the semantics needed to express this right intuition. Trope theory maintains the kind of semantics that in one respect is a function of traditional substance ontology and in another respect gives rise to a new ontology, as will be shown in section 2. Trope theorists simply take the entity *trope* as the referent of expressions like "Napoleon's posture" and the like. But they do not ask what kind of ontology is presupposed or implied by the other expressions of natural or ordinary language. The old concepts of universals and particulars are not eliminated. In order to carry out a genuine revision of the substance ontology the linguistic or semantic framework presupposed by this ontology must be examined in the first place. The new approach to be propounded in the present essay can be seen as the result of the attempt of systematically developing what the author assumes to be the right intuition underlying the trope theory. But the new approach introduces a completely new terminology derived from a new semantics and also rejects other basic assumptions and claims made by trope theorists.

A *second* version takes concrete particulars to be *bundles of qualities* tied together by the relation of compresence. Finally, a *third* version considers concrete particulars to be bundles of immanent universals, i.e., universals that "by contrast with Platonic universals, are as fully present in space and time as their bearers" (O'Leary-Hawthorne and Cover, 1998, p. 205).[2] Universals so understood are according to this version the sole fundamental constituents of the world.

It should also be noted that some authors admit tropes without considering them to be items or elements bundled together in the sense of the bundle theory; according to those authors tropes, instead of universals, are combined with a substratum in order to constitute a concrete particular. Another theory, called the *nuclear theory*, develops a two-stage approach: The first stage is understood as a tight bundle of tropes that form the essential kernel or *nucleus* or essential nature of the concrete particular; the second stage is built up from further non-essential tropes which may be replaced without the nucleus ceasing to exist. This second stage is dependent on the nucleus as its bearer. "The nucleus is thus itself a tight bundle that serves as the substratum to the looser bundle of accidental tropes, and accounts for their all being together" (Simons, 1994, p. 568). This version does not, therefore, reject entirely a substratum; it only dispenses with an ultimate substratum.

(3) Now for the promised presentation of the *root problem* with all traditional, as well as revisionary, conceptions of substance. All of the other problems derive from the root problem, but space does not permit this to be shown here. The root problem concerns the *semantico-ontological framework* presupposed by all aforementioned conceptions of substance This is the framework that is characteristic of so-called "natural" or "ordinary" languages of the Indo-European tradition. The syntax and semantics of those languages and the "ontology of substance" are two sides of one coin. To be more precise, one should speak of the semantico-ontological framework worked out and accepted by a vast majority of philosophers using natural language and theorizing about it. Natural language "as such," i.e., as existing independently of a philosophical understanding of it, should be kept distinguished from the natural language as used, interpreted and theoretized by philosophers. Moreover, as a matter of fact, there are many different philosophical understandings of natural language. But in this essay the expression "natural language" will be used in the sense of "first order predicate language." This well-known formulation expresses a well-defined *philosophical* view of natural language.

In order to work out *the root problem* in question let us look once again at the theories of substance that were briefly described above. We have first to make explicit two features of the semantico-ontological framework underlying those theories. (i) Even if other ontological categories than the category of substance are introduced and accepted (for instance, event, process, and so on), a more fundamental semantico-ontological categorial framework is still presupposed by all those theories: the "diadic" framework *subject-universals* or *subject-attributes* (attributes being properties and/or relations). This categorial framework constitutes the fundamental level as regards all other categories, being, therefore, presupposed by those categories. This claim relies on the undeniable fact that the other onto-logical categories (like events, processes etc.) are explained as entities that have properties and stand in relations to other entities. This becomes manifest by the fact that those categories are articulated in the syntactico-semantical framework of first order predicate language. In its standard interpretation this language possesses exactly the semantical structure that corresponds to the diadic framework of subject-universals (attributes).

(ii) The semantics of first order predicate language relies fundamentally and entirely on the *Principle of Compositionality*, that as applied to sentences is as follows:

(PSCP) The meaning (or semantic value) of a sentence is a function of the meanings (or semantic values) of its subsentential components.

According to this principle, at least a relative independence of the semantic values of the subsentential components is admitted. Thus, the singular term has its own referent, the *denotatum*; the predicate – at least in a realistic semantics – has its own *designatum*, the attribute. The referent or denotatum of the singular term (and/or proper name) is generally and unspecifiedly called "object" in analytic philosophy. But since this entity is determined by being attributed properties and relations, it plays undoubtedly the role of the old category of substance under-stood as being constituted by a subject (substratum) and universals.

The root problem can now be formulated as the problem posed by predication on the level of first order predicate language. The most fundamental and simple shape of predication of this kind is "Fa," i.e., the assignment of the attribute "F" to the item "a" (in quantified form, $(\exists x)(Fx)$). A subject (substratum!) "a" or (the value of the bound variable) "x" is presupposed all the way down. The problem is this: Such an entity is not intelligible, since *ex hypothesi* or by supposition it has to be the presupposed item for attributing or predicating every kind of universals or attributes, i.e., properties and relations), as well as every other kind of entity that is attributable to them or statable about them, for instance "states of affairs" and/or "facts." But then the question arises as to what this presupposed entity is. If *all* the attributes (properties and relations) and every kind of other entities like states of affairs and/or facts are taken away from it, it seems that nothing remains. Since the entity in question (the "subject") is presupposed by every case of pred-ication, it is not itself determinate at all. But then the same question reemerges as to what it is? Such an entity is not intelligible and thus should be rejected.

The attempts to rescue the idea of such a subject have been unsuccessful, since they rely on the assumption that the 'a' or 'x' is a subject that in some sense is already determinate. But if so, in what sense? *Ex hypothesi*, this alleged "determinateness" of the subject must be predicated of this very subject; but then in order to be meaningful the predication must presuppose a subject as an entity that is not (yet) determinate. The assumption misses the point, since it must be explained under what presuppositions this allegedly determinate character of "a" or "x" comes about or makes sense; in other words: what should be explained is the *ontological constitution* of such a subject.

A new ontology must be devised to replace this substance ontology. This requires the construction of a new semantics. *Ex hypothesi*, the new semantics must avoid the problems and difficulties that result from the fundamental tenets and presuppositions of the semantics of natural languages. How can such a new semantics and ontology be constructed?

2   A New Approach: Prime State of Affairs ("Pristate") as the Only Ontological Category at the Fundamental Level

The following is a brief sketch of this new semantics and ontology.

(1) In order to avoid the subject–predicate structure of (atomic) sentences a language must be devised that is devoid of the singular terms (proper names) and predicates that are responsible for the substance ontology of natural or ordinary Indo-European languages.

This idea, though, is not entirely unprecedented in the philosophical literature. Quine had developed an interesting technique for eliminating singular terms in order to cope with the problem posed by the fact that many singular terms (for instance, "Pegasus") fail to have real-life referents. Other authors claimed that predicates are altogether dispensable. Prior to Quine, Russell had devised a logico-semantic procedure for clarifying the ambiguities and perplexities of phenomena like definite descriptions. Such logico-semantic devices are the result of deciding to significantly transform the philosophical understanding of natural language. To be sure, this does not mean that we should stop using natural languages so far as their syntax is concerned, i.e., we are not prohibited to continue to build subject–predicate sentences. Rather, the transformation of the language at stake is to be understood with respect to the semantics and the ontology of that language. This transformation involves translation and/or reinterpretation.

Quine does not understand his technique of elimination of singular terms as having a significant semantic and ontological import. On the contrary, he stresses that "the objects stay on as values of the variables though the singular terms be swept away" (Quine, 1960, p. 192, note 1). In this respect, the approach being pursued in this essay radically diverges from Quine's position. Let me explain. For Quine elimination of singular terms is only a logico-semantic device whose application aims at clarifying the problem posed by the fact that some singular terms, like "Pegasus," lack existent referents. The technique consists essentially in maneuvering singular terms into a standard position "= a," which, taken as a whole, is a predicate or general term; but general terms are not affected by the problems singular terms give rise to. It is worth quoting Quine's detailed explanation:

> The equation 'x = a' is reparsed in effect as a predication 'x = a' where '= a' is the verb, the 'F' of 'Fx'. Or look at it as follows. What was in words 'x is Socrates' and in symbols 'x = Socrates' is now in words still 'x is Socrates', but the 'is' ceases to be treated as a separate relative term '='. The 'is' is now treated as a copula which, as in 'is mortal' and 'is a man', serves merely to give a general term the form of a verb and so suit it to predicative position. 'Socrates' becomes a general term that is true of just one object, but general in being treated henceforward as grammatically admissible in predicative position and not in positions suitable for variables. It comes to play the role of the 'F' of 'Fa' and ceases to play that of the 'a'. (Ibid., §37, p. 179)

What Quine is concerned with is regimentation of scientific language by means of first order standard predicate logic, which he takes to be "the adopted form, for better or worse, of scientific theory" (Quine, 1985, p. 170). And he thinks that predicate logic "gains the required strength through reification" (ibid.). Sentences not fitting the features of first order predicate language Quine considers as sentences without any referential import; indeed, he thinks we utter such sentences "without meaning to refer to any object" (ibid., p. 169). He shows this by working out the semantics and ontology of an "observation sentence," such as:

A white cat is facing a dog and bristling.

Quine distinguishes two "rephrasings" of this sentence. The first is a non-referential one: it has the effect "to mask its [i.e., the sentence's] referential function" (ibid.). According to Quine the non-referential rephrasing amounts to saying in the sensible presence of a cat "It's catting" and to parsing the whole sentence thus:

It's catting whitely, bristlingly, and dogwardly.

Plainly, if one maintains that the world is populated by objects, i.e., subjects/substances, having properties and standing in relations to other objects (subjects/substances), this first rephrasing is undoubtedly non-referential. Quine seems to take it as obvious that the world is featured this way. Thus, without the slightest hesitancy, he sticks to what might be called the "dogma of objectual or substance ontology."[3]

In perfect accordance with that ontological preconception, he presents a second rephrasing that aims at articulating reference; this is obtained by regimenting "the sentence to fit predicate logic, which is the chosen mold of our scientific theory" (ibid.):

(∃x)(x is a cat and x is white and x is bristling and x is dogward).

Quine's technique for eliminating singular terms turns out to be a purely logico-semantic device without any significant ontological import. Instead of considering the "old" objects as the denotata of the singular terms, they are taken as the values of bound (first order) variables. In a fundamental ontological perspective nothing really has changed: Quine's logico-semantic device maintains the old "substantialist" ontological stance. It is very important for the purpose of the present essay to thoroughly clarify this issue, since the new semantico-ontological framework being proposed parts company with Quine at exactly this point. All the way down Quine presupposes an *x* as a subject. Without this presupposition Quine's technique and his logico-semantic device(s) would not work. In other words, the reason why he rejects the rephrasing according to the form "It Socratizes . . ." is clear: this rephrasing does not contain a subject *x*. This shows that Quine sticks with an ontology of objects, of substances, and, thus, also of subjects/substrata.[4]

In order to locate the approach being pursued in this essay within contemporary philosophy, another philosopher is worth mentioning. In his efforts to work out what he calls descriptive metaphysics P. F. Strawson envisages the foundation of a grammatical theory conceived of in terms of "the notion" or "of the basic framework of substantiation + complementary predication" (Strawson, 1974, pp. 127, 135). By this he means a language-type whose sentences are of the subject–predicate form. But at the same time he envisions the possibility of a language "without particulars," containing only "feature-placing sentences" like the following: "Now it is raining," "Snow is falling," "There is water here." Such a language eliminates "particulars," i.e., the referents of singular terms as the "subjects" of the sentences of the subject–predicate form.

Strawson's concept of "feature-placing sentences" is ambiguous in several respects. First, as the examples above show, some of his "feature-placing sentences" contain "stuff terms," like "snow," "water," and the like. But such sentences clearly possess the subject–predicate structure. Second, Strawson endeavors to show that the feature-placing sentences "present no very strong resistance to assimilation in our substantiating grammar" (ibid., p. 136). In order to do that he proposes a "broadening" of his framework of substantiation and complementary predication by introducing the "generalization of the subject" whose first step removes

> the restriction on subject-phrases to the function of i.i. [i.e., identified individual] substantiation by representing the latter as a special case of substantiation in general. The next step is to remove the restriction on subject-phrases to the function of substantiation by representing the latter as a special case of a more general function still – which we might provisionally name *subjection-in-general*. (Ibid., p. 125)

Third, in so doing Strawson never abandons the fundamental idea of a subject with the complementary idea of a feature (a universal) that determines it. His "generalization of the subject" yields particulars according to the substantialistic framework, the only difference from the traditional view being the fact that this procedure leads to the distinction between "ordinary particulars" and "particulars of a kind."

Strawson never calls into question the concept of subject. He ignores what has been called above (section 1) the *root problem* of the substantialist semantico-ontological framework.

(2) If we do not only pay attention to isolated questions and topics, but proceed systematically, then we must ask on what principle(s) the new semantics should be based. From what has been shown above it follows that PSCP should not be accepted. But there is an alternative to PSCP: the *Principle of Sentential Contextuality* (PSCT) (often called *Context Principle*) that was first formulated by Frege in 1884. In one of his formulations the principle reads:

(PSCT) "Only in the context of a sentence do words have any meaning." (Frege, 1884/1953, §62)

(Because of the ambiguities of the expression "meaning" it is preferable to say instead "semantic value.") But Frege clearly holds PSCP also in his subsequent writings. There is much controversy as to the exact meaning Frege attached to PSCT and whether he continued to hold it together with PSCP. Many contemporary analytic philosophers hold PSCT, often using different labels like "(the principle of) the semantic primacy of sentences" (Quine, 1981, p. 20). And, in general, they defend the view that both principles are perfectly compatible. In so doing, those authors presuppose what might be called a *weak version* of PSCT (hereafter: W-PSCT). According to one understanding of such a weak version each subsentential constituent has its own "meaning" or "semantic value" only insofar it contributes to the meaning or semantic value of the sentence as a whole. But this leaves all semantic and ontological matters as they were: no fundamental change in semantics and ontology is required or induced.

In order to develop a new semantic and ontological approach another understanding or version of PSCT is required. This version may be dubbed the *Strong Version* of PSCT (hereafter: S-PSCT). Three features must be put forward in order to characterize S-PSCT:

(i)   S-PSCT is incompatible with PSCP.
(ii) Singular terms and predicates are radically eliminated from sentences with respect to their semantical status. The resulting sentences will be called *prime sentences*, i.e., sentences of the form: "It greens," "It rains," "It milks," "Mamma" (taken as the abbreviation of a sentence), and the like. In (philosophical) English one would adequately say: "It's F-ing," "It F-s," and the like. (But "being F" won't do, since this expression designates a property (according to a realist view of properties), an entity that requires another entity, a subject/substratum, of which it is predicated.)
(iii) Every syntactically well-formed and semantically meaningful descriptive prime sentence in accordance with (i) and (ii), i.e., every *prime sentence*,

has (or expresses) an *informational content* which may be called *prime state of affairs*, or, for short, *pristate*. In one important respect this entity is what in a first order predicate language is in general taken to be the *designatum* of a *predicate*; to be sure, the "old" predicates are not contained in the reinterpreted language *as predicates*, since predicates as such have been eliminated. But the "expressive role" played by those expressions that in first order predicate languages are considered "predicates" reappears or is maintained in the "new" language in the guise of a prime sentence whose general form is "It F-s." For short, a prime state of affairs is the informational content we grasp by using the expression "F" in "It F-s."

This attempt to replace our ordinary or natural language by a new language, possessed by a superior semantics and ontology, might seem to be a self-defeating exercise, since it must employ the language that is to be replaced in the construction of the replacing language. It is as if one must climb a ladder and then throw it away when the top has been reached. But it can be done, as is evidenced by the creation of scientific languages out of ordinary language. (Even mystics seem to succeed in employing ordinary language in constructing a language that portrays a view of reality that is at radical variance with that of ordinary language.) The first stage in the revisionary quest being propounded in this essay is to present arguments, in ordinary language, primarily the *root problem* objection (see section 1), to motivate the construction of a new language by making us unhappy with the commitment of ordinary language to a substance-attribute ontology. The second stage involves the actual construction of the new and improved language. The following gives a recipe, in ordinary language, for constructing a *prime sentence* (and thereby a *pristate*) out of an ordinary subject–predicate one by a process of *substraction*.

Begin with the ordinary subject–predicate sentence "S is F (or Fs)." The informational content that is expressed by this sentence is that some substance, S, instantiates the abstract attribute or universal *being F* (or *being an F-ing*). Next, *substract* the substance S from this information content. What are you left with? It cannot be the abstract universal. The reason is that a universal is conceptually tied to a substance in the sense that an abstract universal must admit of the conceptual possibility of being instantiated by a substance, even if no substances actually exist. Thus, if the concept of a substance is an impossible one, as has been contended by the root objection, then so is the concept of an abstract universal. What you are left with, therefore, is not the abstract property of *being F* (or *being an F-ing*) but a state (occurrence, event or process) of F (or F-ing), without there being any substance that is the subject of or participant in this state or event.

As to the *singular terms* (and proper names) and the predicates proper, it has been already shown that they are to be eliminated as regards their semantical status. But it is not required that they be eliminated from the syntactic dimension of language. As syntactic items they can stand, provided that they be semantically reinterpreted.

There are *two* ways of carrying out and of expressing such a reinterpretation. *One way* is to take singular terms (and proper names) as *abbreviations* of a large number of *prime sentences*, or more exactly, as abbreviations of the prime sentences that express those pristates which, as will be shown, constitute what we are used to calling "individuals" ("concrete particulars," "things," and "objects"). Predicates proper (in the syntactical sense) in turn should be understood as short for a prime sentence expressing a pristate (and eventually a prifact) belonging to a configuration of pristates. The *other way* of formulating the reinterpretation is to introduce an (unusual, artificial) sentence expressing a *complex pristate*, i.e., a *configuration of pristates*. Applying the profoundly modified form of Quine's technique worked out above, this would issue in a sentence of the form: "It Socratizes philosophically." "It Socratizes" is a complex prime sentence that expresses a complex pristate (prifact). The adverb "philosophically" in turn must be taken as an abbreviation of the prime sentence "It philosophizes" that expresses the corresponding single pristate.

This example illustrates the intended semantical reinterpretation. The sentence "Socrates is a philosopher" is of the syntactical subject–predicate form. One of the possible semi-formal analyses of the reinterpretation of this sentence according to the semantics and ontology sketched in this paper would be:

> There is an x such that x is ("is" in the sense of: "is to be conceived of semantically and ontologically as") the configuration S of pristates $p_1, p_2, \ldots, p_r$ and there is a pristate p_i such that p_i is the prime state of affairs expressed by the prime sentence "It's philosophizing" and p_i is a component constituent of S.

(3) At this point the approach being pursued clearly turns in the ontological direction. The entity we dubbed pristate or ustate is what a descriptive prime sentence expresses. According to the semantics so far sketched, prime sentences are the only linguistic expressions hooking on (or endowed with a connection to) the world. From that it follows that the ontological dimension within the framework chosen can be clarified only on that basis. To be sure, the step from the semantical to the ontological dimension must be explicitly considered and explained. In a compositional semantics this step is seen as a two-tiered step: first as the *reference relation* to the world, this relation being taken as a semantical feature of singular terms (and, depending on further assumptions, predicates); second as the *feature of truth* being attributed to the compositionally understood sentences (and to the propositions or states of affairs they express).

But according to the *non-compositional semantics* being pursued here the only kind of semantical "reference (to the world)," if one decides to maintain this expression, is a feature only of sentences, more exactly of prime sentences. And this reference relation of the sentences to the ontological dimension turns out to be also a two-tier mode of directedness toward the ontological dimension, but a very different one: first, the (prime) sentence *expresses* a (prime) state of affairs; second, the prime state of affairs *obtains* or *is true*.

The decisive step to ontology is made by explaining what it means to say that a pristate *obtains* or *is true*. This is a very central issue known as the topic of the theory of truth; but it cannot be adequately tackled in this essay (see Puntel, 1999 and 2001). Suffice it to claim here without argument that the explanation which best fits in with the general coherence of the approach being developed is to say that an *obtaining* or a *true pristate* is simply a *prime fact* (or, for short, *prifact*), whereby "is" here is to be taken as the "is" of identity. This is the main claim made by the so-called Identity Theory of Truth (see Baldwin, 1991, Puntel, 1999 and 2001). Frege famously asked the question "What is a fact?" and his answer was: "A fact is a thought that is true" (Frege, 1967, p. 35). The identity between a (prime) state of affairs and a fact can be seen as a limiting case of the correspondence relation (see Baldwin, 1991, p. 36; Brandom, 1994, p. 330).

It should be remarked that the expression "prime fact (prifact)" is not an adequate one because it has almost exclusively empirical connotations. But according to the conception propounded here this category does not designate only something exclusively empirical; rather, it pervades all domains of being and knowledge, empirical as well as non-empirical ones. It would be more fitting to introduce another suitable expression. Still, it may be interesting to point out that the expression "fact" in contemporary philosophy is at least sometimes used in a very broad, even in an all-pervasive sense to mean something like *factor*. This is the case when this expression is employed in formulations like "logical facts," "mathematical facts," and so on. Clearly, in such formulations "fact" does not mean something empirical. For lack of a more suitable expression, "fact (prifact)" will be used.

(4) The semantical framework just outlined leads to a significant conclusion: the only (kind of) entities admissible are pristates (and, taking the fully determinate status of pristates into account, prifacts; for short, in general only the expression "pristate" will be used). In other words: pristates are not only one ontological category among others, they are *the only ontological category at the very fundamental level*. If the sketched semantical framework is accepted, the ensuing ontology is a *one-category ontology* (see Campbell, 1990).[5]

But it would be wrong to infer from this claim that the world is something like the totality of isolated atomic and undifferentiated (one-kind) pristates (prifacts). Indeed, admitting only one ontological category on the fundamental level does not prevent one from recognizing three central specifications of this category. According to the concept of ontological category worked out in this paper it is possible to devise a highly differentiated and detailed categorial ontology by explaining all "ontological data or phenomena" first as being (or belonging to) subspecies or different kinds of the only fundamental ontological category pristate; second by reducing (certain) kinds of pristates to other kinds of pristates; third by showing that "simple" pristates are members of some configuration (of subspecies) of pristates, it being the case that the configuration in turn is also a pristate, to be sure a complex one. Of course, this systematization of a categorial ontology on the basis of the fundamental category of pristate is a huge task that cannot be adequately dealt with in this paper. But some hints at how it should be conceived of and carried out may be in place here. We turn now to each of those specifications in more detail.

(4.1) As to the first specification, we should start from the claim that the category of pristate (and prifact) is all-pervasive, being the only ontological category at the fundamental level. But then the question arises as to whether this category is able to do justice to the large variety of ontological phenomena which the theories of categories examined in section 1 intend to capture. Most of the listed categories cannot be integrated in the conception being developed here for the simple reason that they are the direct result of some unexamined semantico-ontological framework lacking sufficient intelligibility; among such categories is to be reckoned, apart from substance, for instance property (relation). But what about "categories" like event and process? (Incidentally, it should be remarked that, surprisingly, most "tables of categories" being proposed and defended in contemporary philosophy do not even mention "process.") Such "categories" do not seem to be simply the result of a prefabricated linguistic framework; rather, they seem to betoken something ontological that does not fit well into the natural linguistic framework whose central category is substance.

Let us first observe that there are no "universal" and/or "particular" pristates, if "particular" is understood as "particularized" since this presupposes acceptance of a universal. This is a direct consequence of the semantico-ontological position held in this essay. Pristates are what they are, as it were, "originally": they are single entities, not being the result of an "instantiation," an "exemplification," an "individuation," and the like. Within the semantico-ontological framework questions about "instantiation," "exemplification," "individuation" and the like simply do not arise, since the presupposition underlying those questions, namely acceptance of universals, has no place in the framework. If the expression "particular (entity)" is taken in the just described sense of "single entity," then pristates can be called "prime particulars."

On the purely descriptive level one can easily distinguish different kinds of pristates. For instance, the following distinctions between kinds of pristates suggest themselves: abstract pristates and concrete pristates (but there is a serious problem as to the exact or at least unambiguous understanding of the terms "abstract" and "concrete"); uni-configurational pristates: pristates occurring in one configuration in such a way that they do not connect this configuration with other configurations (i.e., properties as reinterpreted) and pluri-configurational or connective pristates: pristates that connect the configuration they occur in to other configurations (i.e., relations as reinterpreted, for instance causal pristates); static pristates and dynamic pristates (i.e., events, processes etc.); on a more determinate ontological level: pristates constituting space and time, physical pristates, biological pristates, mental pristates, social pristates; on an even more problematic ontological level: moral pristates, aesthetic pristates; furthermore: linguistic pristates (syntactical, semantical, pragmatic pristates); ideal pristates like concepts, all kinds of formal structures (rules), sets, theories, etc.

If all the entities mentioned are considered kinds of the unique category of pristates, then the further question arises as to whether they can be classified in a systematic way. This is a quite different problem, a huge and highly difficult enterprise. A systematic classification of all (and even of very fundamental) kinds of pristates can only succeed as the result of a systematically developed ontology. There is much theoretical work to do before it can be said that this task has been even partially fulfilled. But to effectively tackle this task it is of utmost importance to take into account and to clarify from the outset two central questions or topics that will be dubbed the *reductionism question* and the *configuration question*.

(4.2) The reductionism question arises out of considerations about different levels of analysis whereby at least two such levels, a *surface level* and a *deep structure level*, must be recognized. Surface level analyses are in general pure descriptions of a phenomenon, of the meaning of an expression, of a concept, and the like, as it presents itself or appears without (or before) having been submitted to an exact scrutiny of its inner constitution. Deep structure level analyses, on the other hand, are the result of a detailed scrutiny that goes beyond the level of pure appearance or self-presentation. But surface structure and deep structure are not necessarily mutually exclusive; they only should not be confused, i.e., the one should not be taken as simply being identical with the other. The concept of reduction has the function of systematically avoiding such a confusion, or to put it in positive terms: the concept of reduction articulates the relationship between surface structure level and deep structure level. To be sure, concerning the surface structure level it clearly has a negative connotation: it means that the entities located at this level must be either removed or radically reinterpreted.

Kinds of pristates as described above are different kinds at the surface structure level. A conspicuous ontology has to articulate the kinds of perspicuous pristates we arrive at after applying the concept and the procedure of reduction to the aforementioned kinds of pristates. It is no exaggeration to say that this issue pervades all areas of philosophy. Let us illustrate the point by giving an example. One may attempt to consider what was called, above, mental pristates as not being genuine ontological pristates by reducing them, say, to physical pristates. In the terminology being used in this essay this is the thesis held by reductive physicalism (or identity theory) in the Philosophy of Mind.

(4.3) The third specification concerns the fundamental topic of configuration(s) of pristates. This topic must be addressed by considering three questions.

(4.3.1) The first question is motivated by an insight regarding a special form of reductionism: Are not some or many or even most pristates mentioned above in reality not simple entities, i.e., pristates in the narrow sense, but complex entities, i.e., configurations (bundles) of pristates, in disguise? This is an extremely important question. If we set aside terminological questions for a moment, examples of reductions of seemingly simple entities to compound or complex entities – configurations of some sort – are in abundance in the history of philosophy and science. Perhaps the most famous example is the history of the concept of *atom*: as the word connotes, an atom is an indivisible (simple) entity. But progress of science made manifest that what science for a long time took to be an atom in the strong sense turned out to be in reality a compound entity. (That notwithstanding, science and philosophy continue to use the expression "atom" to designate the kind of compound entity originally taken as being an "atom" proper.) During many hundreds of years water was considered an "element," a simple, non-compound entity. Today nobody doubts that water is H_2O: a molecule of water is a configuration of two hydrogen atoms and an oxygen atom, each of the two hydrogen atoms being linked by a chemical bond to the oxygen atom.

One can hardly deny that some among the entities mentioned above as being pristates on the surface structure level, especially event and process, are in reality, considered at the deep structure level, not just simple entities, but very complex entities, in our terminology: configurations of many significantly different kinds of pristates. Take as an example of an event the death of a horse and as an example of a process the evolution of a human being. Such examples show that death and evolution are highly complex or compound entities; in other words, they are configurations of many variegated pristates. (4.3.2) Those considerations give rise to a second question regarding the idea of configuration: How is this concept and this entity to be characterized?

The problem is a notorious one for all versions of the so-called bundle theories. Despite the difficulties posed by the theories opposed to the bundle theories, many philosophers refrain from holding a version of the bundle theory because they do not know how to conceive of the concept of a bundle or configuration in such a way that our intuitions concerning individuals, especially human persons, are matched. On the other hand, the arguments against all theories of substance seem to carry such a weight that it is preferable to hold some version of a bundle or configuration theory even if the concept of bundle/configuration has not yet been satisfactorily clarified.

Let us only observe in this context that several philosophers have attempted to clarify the concept of bundle/configuration, among other things having recourse to formal tools like mereology, set theory and even mathematical topology, often combining those formal tools in order to explain this concept (see, for instance, Simons, 1994; Bacon, 1995; Mormann, 1995). But it should be remarked that those attempts suffer from the fact that the character of the entities taken to build up a bundle or configuration remain in the dark. Some authors admit universals, others reject universals and introduce instead "tropes" ("abstract particulars"), again others simply speak of "qualities," and so on. Since the concept of a bundle or configuration makes explicit the connections between the items in the bundle or configuration, it is obvious that the clarification of the concept depends fundamentally on the question of what kinds of items are admitted. The main motivation for developing the new approach propounded in this essay lies precisely in the insight that the first systematic step to be undertaken by a conspicuous ontology must be the systematic clarification of the question as to what kind of entities should be admitted.

(4.3.3) Finally, the third question as regards the concept of configuration is this: What is the place of the concept of a bundle/configuration in a systematic ontology? This question arises from the fact that up to this point a central topic has not been dealt with (and has not even been mentioned).

To begin with, the exposition so far presented conveys the impression that the conception envisaged is to be considered a kind of semantical and ontological atomism. The categorial structure of the world arrived at seems to be at last in the spirit of the logical atomism provided only that instead of "logical" one says "semantico-ontological." Was it not intended to claim that the world is built up from entities belonging only to one category, called pristates (prifacts), even if this category is understood as being diversified in many different kinds? Are those simple pristates and kinds of pristates not the least atoms from which the world is built up? And is it not a stringent consequence of this "atomistic" basis that con-nections between pristates can be only purely external (non-essential) connections of a clearly secondary or derivative sort? This point concerns both the connections between numerically distinct simple pristates constituting a single complex bundle or configuration and the connections between different bundles or configurations. Does this not seem to be a perfect form of *ontological atomism* based on pristates (prifacts)?

The answer is: not necessarily. The impression that the propounded new approach to the concept of ontological category leads to some version of onto-logical atomism is due to the fact that the presentation of the semantico-ontological framework had to be restricted to working out only some aspects of the envisaged semantico-ontological conception. And it cannot be denied that on the basis only of those aspects some version of ontological atomism cannot be written off. But a completely different view ensues from a comprehensive elabor-ation of the semantico-ontological framework sketched above: a *holistic* one. This claim will be explained in the remainder of this essay.

First of all, a configuration of pristates belongs to the same semantico-ontological category that has been called "pristate" ("prifact"): a configuration of pristates is also a pristate, to be sure a complex one. This is exactly analogous to the well-known logico-sentential (or logico-propositional) fact that a conjunction of sentences (propositions) is also a sentence (a proposition), to be sure a complex one.

The expression "prime" has been introduced to characterize the very specific new sense that must be attached to the expressions "sentence" and "state of affairs." "Prime" does not mean "atomic," "simple" (i.e., non-complex); rather it means that no "subject" (singular term, proper name, and the like) occurs as a semantically relevant factor in the sentence and that, consequently, the state of affairs expressed by such a sentence does not contain something like a "subject," a "substance" in the sense of an entity x having properties F and/or standing in relation(s) to other "substances" (often simply called "objects"). To put it in positive terms: "prime" is used to characterize sentences/states of affairs of the form "It F-s." From that meaning attached to "prime" it follows that prime sentences and prime states of affairs ("pristates" and "prifacts") can be simple (atomic, non-complex) prime sentences/pristates as well as configurations thereof, i.e., complex prime sentences and complex pristates (prifacts).

Without developing a systematic ontology in all details it is difficult or perhaps even impossible to give examples of absolutely (ultimately) irreducible simple ("atomic" in the strong sense) pristates. As was done above, one can give examples of "simple" pristates according to a given (accepted or used) determinate semantico-ontological framework. For instance, within the natural-linguistic framework a spot of color would be considered a simple (atomic) pristate; but things change completely if we locate a "spot of color" within a scientific framework.

Traditional Christian (pre-Kantian) metaphysics held that the mind or the soul is a simple immaterial (spiritual) entity. Let us suppose that a philosopher who accepts the ontological framework propounded in this essay is prepared to endorse the claim that the mind is an immaterial entity. He would, then, have to say that the mind is not a substance but a pristate (prifact). Would he have to say further that the mind is a simple (a non-complex) pristate? It is not difficult to show that the concept of simplicity presupposed by the "old" metaphysics in this case turns out to be highly problematic. Indeed, Christian pre-Kantian metaphysics had admitted that the soul or the mind has two "essential faculties": intelligence and will. How does this square with the claim that soul or mind is a simple entity? It becomes apparent that this metaphysics had a very superficial and inadequate concept of simplicity: the concept was defined only in a negative and partial way, namely, as indivisible, whereby divisibility was taken to be the characteristic of an entity having material parts or components. But material components are not in the least the only kind of "components" that can be conceived of. Therefore, if one holds that the mind is an immaterial entity and if in accordance with the conception sketched in this essay one characterizes it as being a pristate (prifact), it does not follow that it is a simple pristate: rather, it is a configuration of a certain kind of (immaterial) pristates (prifacts).

As to the other kind of pristates, the *complex* ones, i.e., a configuration of pristates, it is not difficult to find examples. One telling example was examined above: "Socrates is a philosopher." The name "Socrates" can be taken as the abbreviation of a high number of prime sentences each expressing a single pristate; the single pristates, taken together, constitute a complex pristate, a configuration of pristates. Or one can introduce a new, artificial sentence: "It Socratizes philosophically" (see above (2)). This second way of expressing the reinterpretation is more congenial to the conception defended in this essay, since it articulates explicitly the configuration as a whole.

Having noted that pristates (prifacts) can be simple or complex, we can attempt to give an answer to the third question mentioned above, the question as to what systematic place one should attribute to each of those kinds of pristates, especially to complex pristates, i.e., to configurations of pristates. An adequate treatment of this question goes far beyond what can be dealt with in this essay. More exactly, the question is this: should the complex pristates be considered as built up from simple pristates in the way traditional logical (and ontological) atomism characterized complex entities of every kind and in all domains? Or should complex pristates, i.e., configurations of pristates, be seen in a holistic perspective as being the very central systematic "points" or "places" constituting connections between the pristates?

A final consideration will be presented in order to show that a holistic conception should be favored. The proposed approach to a new conception of the concept of ontological category relies fundamentally on semantic considerations. But how should a systematic semantics, a systematic philosophy of language, be conceived of? The holistic perspective seems to be essential to this project. It was shown that sentences are the central semantic units according to the Strong Version of the Principle of Sentential Contextuality. But sentences do not occur in isolation; they constitute the whole we call language. It seems that this insight can be taken seriously only if a further, more comprehensive principle is introduced, the Principle of Holistic Contextuality:

> (PHCT) Only in the context of language as a whole do sentences have semantic values.

But if an atomistic conception of language is rejected, then this has important consequences for the ontology ensuing from the non-atomistic semantics. The idea of configuration would turn out to be absolutely central both in the area of semantics and in the area of ontology. But this topic cannot be developed in this essay in more detail.

3   Concluding Remarks

The purpose of this essay has been to work out the concept of ontological category from a new approach. The most salient contemporary positions in this area have been sketchily presented and submitted to a concise critique. The new approach emerged from what this critique brought to the fore: a new ontology should be considered the result of taking seriously the insight that ontology and semantics are two sides of one coin. Accordingly, in order to avoid the difficulties affecting the substance ontology and its many forms the semantics underlying the substance ontology based on the Compositionality Principle should be given up in favor of a new semantics relying upon the Principle of Semantical Contextuality. This new semantics yields a new ontology whose only category at the fundamental level is the category of prime state of affairs (pristate) or, on the ontological level proper, the category of prime fact (prifact).

This result is only the very first step in the development of a new comprehensive ontology. In the last part of the essay some hints at some of the most important questions the new ontology has to tackle have been given. Still, the propounded conception so far remains very sketchy and very abstract. Many central topics have not been even mentioned, for instance the central topic of space and time. A great deal of philosophical work of many sorts remains to be done. But without first having worked out the fundamentals, a new ontology is not worth pursuing since it will rely on unclarified basic assumptions.

The reader sympathetic to the new approach delineated in this essay is asked to look into the literature about the trope theory (see especially Campbell, 1990; Bacon, 1995; Mormann, 1995). As regards the general perspective and many important specific topics, this ontology comes closest to the new ontology envisaged in the present essay.

Notes

1 This expression has been introduced by Williams (1953).
2 O'Leary-Hawthorne and Cover call their theory "the Bundle Theory of substance" (1998, p. 205). Those authors simply take the expression "substance" as synonymous with "concrete particular" or "individual." It should be remarked that this terminology is ambiguous, to say the least.
3 The expression "objectual" is employed by Quine to characterize a reading or interpretation of the quantifiers ("objectual reading" in opposition to "substitutional reading").
4 It should, however, be remarked that in other passages of his writings Quine sketches a twofold revision or reinterpretation of ontology (see Quine, 1981, ch. 1). This gives rise to the question whether (and how) such a revision squares with the ontology framed on the basis of *reification*.
5 In order to make precise the conception just delineated several questions should be addressed, especially the question: What are the identity conditions for introducing the entity dubbed "pristate" (and "prifact")? The author accepts Quine's claim that there is no entity without identity and thus it behooves him to spell out adequate criteria of identity for this entity in virtue of which it can be picked out, reidentified, and counted. Space limitations preclude his doing so in this chapter.

References

Bacon, J. (1995). *Universals and Property Instances. The Alphabet of Being*. Oxford: Blackwell.
Baldwin, Th. (1991). "The Identity Theory of Truth," *Mind*, 100, pp. 35–52.
Brandom, R. B. (1994). *Making It Explicit. Reasoning, Representing, and Discursive Commitment*. Cambridge, MA and London: Harvard University Press.
Campbell, K. (1990). *Abstract Particulars*. Oxford: Blackwell.

Daly, Ch. (1994). "Tropes." *Proceedings of the Aristotelian Society.* New Series 94, pp. 253–61.

Denkel, A. (2000). "The Refutation of Substrata," *Philosophy and Phenomenological Research,* 60, pp. 431–9.

Frege, G. (1884/1953). *The Foundations of Arithmetic* [*Die Grundalgen der Arithmetik,* 1884]. Trans. J. L. Austin, 2nd ed. Oxford: Blackwell.

Frege, G. (1967). "The Thought," in P. Strawson (ed.), *Philosophical Logic.* Oxford: Oxford University Press, pp. 17–38.

Hoffman, J., and Rosenkrantz, G. S. (1994). *Substance Among Other Categories.* Cambridge: Cambridge University Press.

Loux, M. J. (1998). *Metaphysics. A Contemporary Introduction.* London and New York: Routledge.

Lowe, E. J. (1998). *The Possibility of Metaphysics. Substance, Identity, and Time.* Oxford: Clarendon Press.

Mormann, Th. (1995). "Trope Sheaves. A Topological Ontology of Tropes," *Logic and Logical Philosophy,* 3, pp. 129–50.

O'Leary-Hawthorne, J., and Cover, J. A. (1998). "A World of Universals," *Philosophical Studies,* 91, pp. 205–19.

Puntel, L. B. (1999). "The 'Identity Theory of Truth': Semantic and Ontological Aspects," in *Rationality, Realism, Revision,* ed. J. Nida-Rümelin. Berlin and New York: de Gruyter, pp. 351–8.

Puntel, L. B. (2001). "Truth, Sentential Non-Compositionality, and Ontology," *Synthese,* 126, pp. 221–59.

Quine, W. V. O. (1960). *Word and Object.* Cambridge, MA: The MIT Press.

Quine, W. V. O. (1981). *Theories and Things.* Cambridge, MA: Harvard University Press.

Quine, W. V. O. (1985). "Events and Reification," in E. LePore and B. P. McLaughlin (eds.), *Actions and Events. Perspectives on the Philosophy of Donald Davidson.* Oxford: Blackwell, pp. 162–71.

Simons, P. (1994). "Particulars in Particular Clothing: Three Trope Theories of Substance," *Philosophy and Phenomenological Research,* 54, pp. 553–75.

Strawson, P. F. (1974). *Subject and Predicate in Logic and Grammar.* London: Methuen.

Williams, D. C. (1953). "On the Elements of Being," *Review of Metaphysics,* 7, pp. 13–18, 171–92.

Chapter 7

Universals and Predication

Bruce Aune

Theories of universals, the supposed referents of general terms,[1] fall into three basic classes, which I shall call P-theories, A-theories, and T-theories. The theory featured in Plato's *Republic* is an example of a P-theory; the theory commonly ascribed to Aristotle is an A-theory; and the "trope" theories expounded by Donald Williams and Keith Campbell are T-theories. (If the reader associates "P" with Plato, "A" with Aristotle, and "T" with trope, my exposition will be easier to follow.) T-theories and A-theories are more commonly held today than P-theories, but they involve a serious error about predication, which P-theories easily avoid. In this essay I shall support the claim that T- and A-theories involve this error, and I shall develop and defend a P-theory that avoids it.

A-theories, T-theories, and P-theories

Although I introduced the expression "A-theory" by reference to Aristotle, I could just as well have referred to D. M. Armstrong, for his theory is a striking contemporary instance of the sort of theory I have in mind. According to him, a universal is an absolutely determinate feature (a quality or relation) that may exist at many different places at the same time; it is a "repeatable" entity. The basic reason he gives for thinking that such repeatables exist is that different particulars have what appears to be the same nature and that this sameness of nature cannot be explained away.[2] There is such a thing as identity of nature, he says, and this nature, which can be present in two things, is a universal.[3] The sameness of nature Armstrong speaks of here may be partial rather than complete, for a red ball and a red book may have something in common too. Normally, a general predicate is applicable to a thing because of some universal the thing possesses; but if two things are truly described by the same predicate, say "colored," the color-universal possessed by one may be very different from the color-universal possessed by the other: one may be green while the other is red.

A T-theory differs from an A-theory in denying that any attribute possessed by one particular is (or could be) identical to an attribute possessed by another particular; for a T-theorist, universals are nonrepeatable entities: each one of them is uniquely instantiated, a unique attribute-instance. Such instances may be more or less similar, however. If two objects, x and y, are both $scarlet_{29}$, the $scarlet_{29}$ of x is an exact duplicate of the $scarlet_{29}$ of y; if x is $scarlet_{29}$ and y is $scarlet_{16}$, the scarlet of x is very similar to the scarlet of y, but not a duplicate of it.

A P-theory differs from A- and T-theories in denying that universals are literally present in the spatio-temporal world. According to a P-theory, an elementary statement, judgment, or belief "a is F" is true just when the referent of "a" (the subject) *falls under* (or bears some comparable "relation" to) a P-universal that is associated with the predicate "is F." The predicate "is F" need not be held to denote the associated P-universal, and the P-universal need not be a Platonic Form which particulars imitate or partake of. On the contrary, the P-universal might be describable as some kind of intensional object, something we can mentally take account of in deciding whether a predicate is or is not applicable to a particular object. The universals of the P-theory I shall recommend might, in fact, be best described by the word "concept," though "concept" will have to be used in a specially clarified sense.

Problems with A-theories and T-theories

In expounding his trope theory, Keith Campbell began by identifying a key difficulty of Armstrong's A-theory, that of comprehending how anything could enjoy the "unrestricted" reality that an A-theorist assigns to a universal, a reality neither diminished nor augmented by diminishing or augmenting the reality of its instances.[4] I am not sure that this is a genuine difficulty in an A-theory; the basic difficulty I see in such a theory is that it is either inconsistent in what it requires to be explained or obfuscating in the explanation it offers. These unsatisfactory alternatives ultimately arise from an erroneous view of predication, but they can be grasped most easily by reference to two problems the theory creates, one about particulars and one about universals.

The problem about particulars can be brought out as follows. There are two alternatives concerning particulars available to A-theorists. According to one, particulars are simply complexes of A-universals; according to the other, particulars are something in addition to the A-universals they possess. The first alternative is not plausible by contemporary standards.[5] It is rejected by leading A-theorists – Armstrong rejects it, for example[6] – and it is vulnerable to an objection that I shall develop later in connection with T-theories.[7] I shall therefore pass over it now and consider the second alternative – that particulars are something in addition to the A-universals that they possess. The difficulty with this alternative is that it renders particulars unnecessarily mysterious. Particulars become mysterious on this alternative because the nature of a thing, according to A-theories, is constituted by the universals it possesses, but the particular is distinct from those universals. As a result of this, a particular is distinct from its nature – distinct not just in the sense of being not identical with it but in the sense of being something in addition to it. John Locke famously described such distinct particulars as "things I know not what," mere *substrata* that support qualities or provide a subject in which qualities can inhere.[8] He acknowledged that he has no clear and distinct idea of such things, and A-theorists who regard particulars as ultimately "bare" subjects ("bare particulars")[9] describe them in an equally mysterious way.

Armstrong, an A-theorist who accepts the second alternative, thinks that these problematic descriptions can be avoided by distinguishing two conceptions of a particular, one thick and one thin. According to the thick conception, a particular is a "thin" thing along with its qualities: If the thin thing is **a** and **S** is the conjunction of **a**'s qualities, the thick particular is the state of affairs, **a**-having-**S**.[10] According to the thin conception, a particular – in this case, **a** – can be thought of in abstraction from the state of affairs in which it figures; so conceived, it can be thought of as distinct from the properties **S**. Armstrong concedes that, thought of this way, the thing **a** is "perhaps . . . in a way" a bare particular: "it is the mere thisness of a thing as a Scotist would put it"; it "can have no properties. It is a bare principle of numerical difference."[11] Although Armstrong allows that non-spatio-temporal particulars are imaginable, he nevertheless suggests that the particularity "or thisness" of a particular might in fact be identifiable (owing to the nonexistence of immaterial things) with a "total-position" in space–time. The attributes of such positions, their shape and size, are of course universals, he says; but two different total positions may yet be two, he thinks, even though they have the same attributes.[12]

It seems to me that Armstrong's thinly conceived particulars, and therefore the thickly conceived ones of which they are constituents, are every bit as mysterious, ultimately, as Locke's "things I know not what." It is, of course, possible (epistemically speaking) that Armstrong's thin conception of a particular is not really required for a defensible A-theory denying that particulars are complexes of universals. Roderick Chisholm, who spoke of a thing's properties in a way that suggested he held an A-theory himself, said that the following assertions are "simply a muddle":

1   If we distinguish between a thing and its properties, then we must say that the thing is a "bare particular" that doesn't have any properties.
2   One is tempted to regard "This is red" as a subject–predicate proposition, but if one does so, one finds that "this" becomes a substance, an unknown subject in which predicates can inhere. . . .[13]

Chisholm did little to explain why these assertions are muddles other than observing that the idea of a self (a self being a particular) is "the idea of an x such that x loves or hates and such that x feels cold or x feels warm, and so forth."[14] Evidently he was confident that the x he speaks of here is not a bare particular because it is patently not characterless but warm, cold, a lover or hater, and so on.

The claim that something that is warm or cold or wet or dry cannot be a bare particular is perfectly acceptable to me, but then I do not hold an A-theory. Those who do, conceive of properties in a particular way, and they also assume an analysis of predication that makes a mystery of something otherwise not mysterious at all. They take properties to be entities that are "possessed" by particulars but distinguishable from them. When a particular, **a**, is said to be **F** – blue, say – the A-theorist adopting the first alternative construes the claim as affirming that a universal, **u**, is present to **a** but distinguishable not only from it but from the entire "bundle" (or sum) of universals **a** possesses. Although **a** can be known as the possessor of **u** and whatever other universals it may possess, its nature as something distinct from those universals cannot be known because any predicate or concept that one might use to characterize (or cognize) its nature is said (by the A-theorist) to refer to some other universal that is distinct from it or any part of it. So the intrinsic character of **a** remains mysterious according to the theory.

I said earlier that A-theories also create a problem about universals. The problem is this. According to A-theories, if we are to explain why a general term is truly applicable to a thing, we must ultimately acknowledge the presence in it of some A-universal.[15] But A-universals can perform this explanatory role only if they differ from one another: the A-universal whose presence in **x** explains why "blue" is applicable to **x** must differ from the A-universal whose presence in **y** explains why "red" is applicable to **y**. Similarly, the A-universal whose presence in **z** explains why the absolutely determinate predicate "scarlet$_{29}$" (assuming it to be such) applies to it must be the same as the universal that explains why this predicate is applicable to some **w** ≠ **z**. But if universals can differ or be identical in this way, they must have natures that differ or are identical; and differing natures must have features that distinguish them. Since A-theorists assume that things possess features (are thus and so) only if they have appropriate A-universals, such A-universals must be their constituents in just the way that the A-universals of particulars are their constituents. As in the case of particulars, a distinction will have to be drawn between the A-universals and their constituents, and the A-universals will end up with the characterless "thisness" that Armstrong attributes to particulars. Since the constituents comprising the nature of a universal must be distinguishable from one another, they too must have different natures, and this means that they will possess constituents in turn. There can be no end to this on A-theorist assumptions: every universal will be like an infinitely complex system of Chinese boxes, one within another and each containing its own peculiar "thisness." This consequence strikes me as incredible.

Armstrong does not accept this criticism of his theory. When I brought it to his attention in the mid-eighties, he replied that although a fully determinate shade of white, W_{57}, will be different from every other universal, the relevant differences may only be "numerical."[16] I find this suggestion unintelligible and certainly at odds with the assumptions about predication implicit in his A-theory. If particulars x and y could not have distinct natures without having attributes (that is, A-universals) that distinguish them, how could two universals be distinct things without having attributes (that is, A-universals) that distinguish them? A-theorists attribute universals to particulars on general grounds – they want to explain the similarities and differences that are recorded by the application of predicates. We may not have an infinity of predicates that we customarily apply to universals, but that fact is irrelevant to the metaphysical explanation of the similarities and differences that must exist between them if they are to do the explanatory work that A-theorists attribute to them. If u_1 and u_2 are distinct objects with explanatory potential, there must be some F that u_1 has but that u_2 does not have – and so on without end.

On the face of it, T-theories (trope theories) do not face the problems I have attributed to A-theories. According to them, particulars are not ultimately mysterious subjects of predication but "bundles" of tropes. But tropes differ from one another in spite of the similarities that may exist among them. They cannot differ or be similar, however, without having definite natures – and this means (given the assumptions of the theory) having distinguishing attributes. If a trope theory is consistent in all its presuppositions, a thing's ostensible attributes are actually its constituents: "a is F" implies that a particular **F-ness** is part of **a**. Consequently, if a T-theory is consistent in this way, it must allow that every trope consists of further tropes – and so on without end. Since unanalyzable particularity can be no more allowable for tropes than for ordinary particulars, every identifiable thing will decompose into a bundle of other things, and no bundle will have an irreducible core. (An analogous consequence will hold for A-theories that regard particulars as complexes of A-universals; this is the objection that applies to "the first alternative" that I did not discuss when I considered A-theories.)[17]

Adopting a defensive strategy similar to one naturally adopted by A-theorists, T-theorists might argue that tropes can resemble and differ without having similar or contrasting components – that their resemblances and differences can be ultimate facts about them. But an exactly parallel argument could be used to argue that particulars can resemble and differ without having tropal constituents: their resemblances and differences can be ultimate facts about them. The latter claim is no less credible than the former. In fact, it is far more credible, all things considered: it does not have the bizarre consequences of a consistently developed trope theory.

Predication

When David Lewis, in his important paper "New Work for a Theory of Universals," criticized Armstrong's main argument for universals, he insisted that predication should be acknowledged as "primitive," as not requiring any analysis, least of all the sort of analysis that Armstrong was tacitly requiring.[18] When you attempt to explain why a thing **a** is **G** by introducing some constituent **u** in **a**, whether A-type or T-type, you are always left with an unexplained datum of the same structure: **u** is **F**. This way of putting the point is closely related to mine; I have simply tried to show what happens when predication is consistently analyzed according to the pattern assumed by an A- or T-theory.[19]

Although I would not attempt to analyze predication, I don't want to say that I accept it as primitive and let it go at that. The fact that shrewd philosophers constantly provide (or assume) unacceptable analyses of it makes it important to offer some clarification of it – to say enough to help readers resist the tendency to offer an analysis. I also want to say enough to discourage a philosopher from saying, as Armstrong did, that if I say that a dog is barking but "deny the metaphysical reality of properties and relations" I am committed, against my will, to the view that the world consists of "truly bare particulars."[20]

To clarify the basic nature of predication as I understand it, it is helpful to consider what is fundamentally accomplished by elementary English sentences having a predicative function. The following examples illustrate the simplest forms that A-theorists make use of in developing their views; they are also employed by T-theorists, but I shall ignore the latter in this context.

(1)   Socrates is wise.
(2)   Alcibiades laughed.
(3)   Plato admired Socrates.

In (1) the predicate contains a linking verb conjoined to an adjective, a construction that A-theorists interpret as relating a subject to a repeatable universal. In (2) the predicate is a mere verb, which is less plausibly interpreted by the subject-R-*Fness* paradigm; and in (3) the entire sentence must be transformed to accord smoothly with A-theorist preconceptions: it must assume the form of "The ordered pair <Plato, Socrates> R *admires*."

In contrast to the A-theorist, I take the predicate of (1) to be a unit, one by means of which the person denoted by the subject is described as wise. The predicate does not denote (or pick out) a repeatable component that is attached to this subject; it applies directly to the subject itself, telling us what *the subject* is like. Since a wise person is not a characterless "this" but a wise thing, the predicate of (1) gives no support to the inferences Chisholm regarded as muddled. The same is true of the predicate in (2). Here a simple verb is predicated of a subject: Alcibiades is described as having laughed at some time. If, using the sentence, I describe Alcibiades this way, I cannot reasonably allow that I have described a "bare" particular, for I have described Alcibiades as having laughed, and nothing ultimately characterless can do a thing like that. Sentence (3) is similar to (1) and (2) in describing something, but it describes two people rather than one: it describes Plato in relation to Socrates. It does not identify anything other than Plato and

Socrates, and there is no justification for representing its logical structure in the contrived way suggested above.

What I have just said no doubt needs elaboration, for the reasoning supporting the postulation of A-universals is very deeply entrenched in the thought of many philosophers. The key consideration is that the predicates in sentences like (1) and (2) directly apply to the things picked out by their subjects; they do not apply to some further items that their subjects may possess. If I say that a fire plug is red, the only thing I am talking about is the fire plug; I am not talking about something that it "has." Anyone who is familiar with red things and understands English will know what I am in effect saying about the plug: *It* is a red thing. Red things resemble one another with respect to color, but one should not suppose that this resemblance consists in a common component, an A-universal. The A-theorist Armstrong actually denies that there are generic universals: he claims that repeatable determinate whites (for instance, yellowish white$_{25}$ and greenish white$_{14}$) color-resemble without exemplifying a higher-order whiteness, and a T-theorist would claim that corresponding tropes would color-resemble without containing a common white. I avoid the exotic but make a parallel claim: white things (bed-sheets, writing paper) and red things (fire engines, balloons) color-resemble one another without containing any common metaphysical element. If you are familiar with fire engines and can speak English, you will know what I mean in speaking of a red balloon. You will not have to be familiar with any metaphysical entities, particular or general, that supposedly inhere in certain balloons and fire engines.

Armstrong has argued that one cannot avoid postulating A-universals by speaking of color-resemblance or shape-resemblance, because these resemblances are merely "respects" in which objects resemble and differ, and such respects require explanation by reference to A-universals. Armstrong's argument is unconvincing, however. When we learn to apply a color vocabulary to the objects around us, we learn to classify *them*, the objects, as more or less similar in color; and we readily learn to classify things as more or less similar in respect to other possible descriptions: for instance, in respect to being round or square. ("Is this as round as that?" we may ask.) What is redder or more round or squarer than another thing are *particulars*; it is they that we are comparing, not some abstract component that they have; and it is *they* that resemble and differ in respect of their color or shape, and not their supposed abstract components. When we apply predicates, simple or compound, to particulars, we describe *those particulars* (we say what *they* are like). We do the same when we speak of how *they* resemble one another.

It is useless for an A-theorist or T-theorist to reply, "Why do you emphasize that we describe particulars? We don't deny this. We simply insist that particulars are truly described as thus and so because they possess qualities, though we disagree about whether those qualities are repeatable or particular." The reply is useless because it assumes that true predication is invariably explained or justified by reference to items *other than* the particulars that are described.[21] Yet these other items can do the intended work (of explaining or justifying) only if *they* have

natures of their own. If *having a nature* is invariably assumed to involve some kind
of relation to a higher-order object that must itself have a nature of its own, a
single predication is never fully understandable: it must always be understood (or
tacitly analyzed) in relation to something further, which must be understood in
the same way – and so on without end. If a predication is ever fully understandable – and it usually is – some predication must be understandable in its own terms,
without reference to further objects. I contend that "x is round" and "x is scarlet"
are acceptable examples of predications understandable in this way.

Thus far I have been speaking of *describing* objects. When we *classify* them, we
commonly employ a form of predication importantly distinguishable from the
forms involved in (1), (2), and (3). This additional form is illustrated by (4):

(4)   Gorgias is a sophist.

From a logical point of view, this sentence is actually ambiguous. On one reading
it recalls Aristotle's examples of "things said of a subject that are not present in a
subject."[22] Read this way, the sentence serves to classify its subject in relation to
other things. Today, we commonly represent such a classification by specifying a
class to which the subject is related. If the subject is an individual, we say it *is a
member* of the relevant class, as in "Gorgias is a member of the class of sophists";
if the subject is itself a class, we often say it is *included in* a class," as in "Humans
are mortals." These set-theoretical readings of the copula are not the only relevant readings, because neither is appropriate for its occurrence in the formula
"g ∈ {x: x is a sophist}," which may be read "g is a member of the set of x's
such that x is a sophist." The "x is a sophist" here calls for a reading that Frege
would have represented by the now-familiar notation "Sx": the object x falls
under the concept **S**.

Advantages of P-theories

This last example brings me to the subject of P-theories of universals, for Frege's
concepts are special cases of such universals.[23] As I understand them, P-theories
are significantly different from A-theories and T-theories. One merit of all of P-
theories is that they do not attempt to analyze predication. They specify a condition that must be satisfied if certain predications are true, but they do not imply
that *every* predication – least of all one to the effect that a thing falls under a
concept – must satisfy a similar condition.[24] Thus, to be a human being, Socrates
must fall under the concept *human being*, but to do this, *he* must satisfy the conditions for being human; he does have to be related to some further object, which
falls under a further concept, as A- and T-theories stubbornly suppose.[25]

Although theories of classes (or sets) are not usually considered theories of
universals, classes can also be considered P-universals in my sense of the term. The

relation between classes and their members is naturally expressed in English by "is a" – as in "Gorgias is a sophist" – words that can also be used to express the relation between a thing and a concept or Form that it falls under. I have said that one merit of a P-theory is that it does not attempt to analyze predication, but whether a given P-theory is actually acceptable obviously depends on how it conceives its P-universals, how it conceives the relation between P-universals and particulars, and many other things. I want to say something about these matters now.

Instead of speaking of universals, most philosophers now speak of properties, relations being n-place properties. Those who speak freely of properties generally suppose that the predicate "property" picks out a definite or determinate class of objects. I have long regarded this supposition as erroneous, and I am glad to see that the same view has recently been expressed by a philosopher of David Lewis's distinction. When he introduced his own unusual conception of a property in *On the Plurality of Worlds*, Lewis remarked:

> It is not as if we have fixed once and for all, in some perfectly definite and unequivocal way, on the things we call "the properties," so that we are now ready to enter into the debate about such questions as . . . whether two of them are necessarily coextensive. . . . The conception [of a property] is in considerable disarray. It comes in many versions, differing in a number of ways. The question worth asking is: which entities, if any, among those we should believe in, can occupy which versions of the property role.[26]

Lewis claims that sets of *possibilia* are right for one version of the property role. I myself am not entirely happy with sets of *possibilia* as Lewis understands them, for I am reluctant to acknowledge *possibilia* as primitive entities. For this and other reasons, I want to develop another conception of P-universals. It may or may not be able to do the work of Lewis's sets, but there is some work it can do very well.

The conception I want to recommend takes P-universals to be concepts. The word "concept" in current usage (even in current philosophical usage) is just as indefinite and equivocal as the word "property," but it has connotations that make it suitable for the work I have in mind. Judging from an observation by Elizabeth Anscombe, the terminology of objects falling under concepts is not unusual in everyday German. She reported that Michael Dummett once saw in a Münster railway station a notice beginning "All objects that fall under the concept *hand-luggage* . . ." (*Alle Gegenstände, die unter den Begriff Handgepäck fallen* . . .). This anecdote reminds us that we commonly classify things by "concepts" that are humanly-invented and rest on conventions that may have significance only for special groups. *Hand-luggage* is such a concept, and so are *personal effects, engagement ring, American citizen, slave-driver, mule, venetian blind, reptile,*[27] *flotsam, jetsam, retriever, pointer, barber, typewriter, zipper, computer, computer-programmer, disk jockey,* and *play-boy* – this list can be extended *ad libitum*. It is true that things in nature fall under these concepts, but it is absurd to suppose that these concepts are "eternal entities" that define the structure of reality, as

Plato's Forms were supposed to do. They all have histories, and they came into existence as the result of numerous contingencies.

Another important feature of the concepts we use to classify objects is that they – or the words that "express" them – are vague. A vague word, as I understand it, is one that clearly applies to some actual or imaginable things, that clearly fails to apply to some such things, and that neither clearly applies nor clearly fails to apply to other such things. *Bald* and *tall* are standard examples of vague words, but in fact every generic color word is vague, and so are most of the words we use in everyday life. Consider such words as *sarcastic, sardonic, frivolous, trivial, flimsy, superficial, paltry, petty, trifling, lucky, unimportant, yuppie, dismal, morose, severe, zaney, dour, carefree, windy, brisk, sparse* – again, the list can be continued almost endlessly. Although such words can perfectly well express vague concepts or ideas, they cannot stand for definite properties or items in reality, because nothing definite or determinate is connoted by them.

One might suppose that a word like *bald* could be construed to apply in a strict sense to people whose head is utterly hairless and to apply to people with some hair only in a loose and popular sense. But the word is not really used this way; and an analogous claim holds for vague words generally. Take the word "sarcastic," which is familiar to every adult speaker of English and is used with confidence even by high school students. No adult or adolescent has any doubt about its application to some people and some things they say. Some people are clearly sarcastic either generally or on some occasions; some people clearly are not; and a great many people exhibit behavior that is not clearly classifiable either way. In spite of the confidence with which "sarcastic" is commonly used, it is a very difficult word to define or even clarify by synonyms. Its etymology is very illuminating, however. It derives from the Greek σαρκάζω (sarcazô), which Liddell and Scott define as "to rend of flesh like dogs."[28] As this derivation indicates, "sarcastic" was originally metaphorical. The metaphor is very tenuous today, but we still think of a sarcastic remark as one that is wounding, hurtful (and a sarcastic person as someone prone to making such remarks). Since we have encountered many clear cases of sarcasm and non-sarcasm, we have the ability to recognize such cases when we see them; but we are constantly presented with borderline cases that we cannot confidently classify either way. *Most of our vocabulary is like this.* Our words commonly involve metaphors – compare *inspire, inspiration; expire, expiration; understand, understanding* – and their meaning is rarely precise or determinate.

A vague word does not specify an ordinary class of objects because it is not applicable to a definite totality of things. So-called fuzzy classes do not require definite totalities, and it is sometimes suggested that they can serve as the semantic correlates of vague predicates.[29] Fuzzy classes do not simply have members; they have members in various degrees. A particular fuzzy set is defined by a function f_A that assigns to every object x in the relevant domain A a number $f_A(x)$ between 0 and 1 inclusively that represents x's degree of membership in A. If a vague predicate clearly applies to an object a, $f_A(a) = 1$; if the predicate clearly fails to apply to an object b, $f_A(b) = 0$; and if the predicate applies to c in a less decisive way, s's degree of membership in **A** falls somewhere in the interval between 0 and 1, say 0.6.

Although it is often useful to think of vague predicates as associated with fuzzy sets, thinking of them this way involves a significant idealization, for vague predicates are generally too vague to be associated with a function assigning definite degrees of membership in the relevant class. Such membership degrees correspond to the degrees to which predicates are applicable to objects, and as matters stand one cannot rightly specify a degree to which a vague predicate ("bald," say) is applicable to every object. (Jones may be a bit on the bald side, but we cannot realistically say that there is a precise degree to which he is bald: the notion of being bald is simply not that determinate.) The significance of this fact for theories of properties or universals is that there is nothing in the world – no unitary class or thing – corresponding to vague predicates that is sufficiently determinate to be the A- or T-universal (the "property") that such predicates supposedly represent. By contrast, the concepts expressed by such predicates are just as vague, intuitively speaking, as the predicates themselves. The phenomenon of vagueness therefore poses no evident problems for a P-theory.

A New Look at Some Old Examples

Analytic philosophers attracted to A-theories often support their views by reflecting on statements such as the following:

(5) Honesty is a virtue.
(6) Red is a color.
(7) Napoleon had all the qualities of a great general.

Statements (5) and (6) here appear to be obvious truths, and if (7) is not true, a corresponding statement is no doubt true for some other outstanding personage – Caesar, Hannibal, or perhaps Rommel or McCarthur. Yet these truths seem to concern qualities, ostensible A-universals. If no analysis of them compatible with a rejection of A-universals is possible (the claim is), a theory of A-universals is *prima facie* acceptable and should be accepted if no preferable alternative can be found.

In view of what I have argued in the last section, (5), (6), and (7) – even if obviously true – do not actually support an A-theory: the principal words they contain – "red," "virtue," "honesty," "great general" – are patently vague, and vague words are very poor candidates for denoters of A-universals. Since the statements are general and not restricted to the particular qualities of this or that particular, they lend no obvious support to a trope theory either. Might they accord with a P-theory, one that takes P-universals to be concepts? The fact that they contain vague words and are universal in import is not at odds with the assumptions of a P-theory. Could one plausibly read them as saying something about concepts or as being explicable in relation to such things?

I think (5) and (6) can be plausibly interpreted by reference to a P-theory of concepts, but (7) is best understood as involving only the kind of predication that does not introduce universals at all. Since the development of a theory of concepts is the last item on my agenda, I shall dispose of (7) first. It is really not very complicated.

If we use schematic or "dummy" predicates as Quine often does,[30] we can express (7) without actually referring to qualities, by (8):

(8) If all great generals are F, Napoleon is F.

A dummy predicate stands in place of ordinary predicates; (8) is understood to be true just in case all substitution instances of (8) are true, a substitution instance being a well-formed sentence of English exactly like (8) except for having a predicate in place of the dummy predicate "F." An equivalent rendering of (7) would dispense with a dummy predicate in favor of a variable bound by a substitutional quantifier. The use of substitutional quantifiers has been criticized in recent years, but not effectively. There is really nothing wrong with substitutional quantification if the language to which it is applied is appropriately regimented – as it should always be understood as being when formal devices are employed.[31]

The formulas (5) and (6) are so similar in logical structure that it might seem a waste of time to discuss both, but they actually raise slightly different problems. Anti-Platonists might be content to analyze (6) as "Anything red is colored," but a parallel analysis for (7) is clearly untenable, since "Anyone honest is virtuous" fails for honest people who lack other virtues – wisdom or courage, for instance. The fact that these analyses clearly fail for one case is good evidence that they fail for both, (5) and (6) pretty clearly have the same logical structure. A different approach to both is therefore in order.

What are Concepts?

Earlier, I said that (6) and (7) could plausibly be interpreted by reference to a theory of concepts. To provide such an interpretation, I must first explain what I shall understand by concepts. Analytic philosophers constantly speak of concepts and their analysis, but they rarely explain what they conceive concepts to be. As I noted, there is no definite and unequivocal sense in which the word is normally used in philosophy. There is general agreement in limited respects – for example, it is commonly presumed that concepts are associated with general words: A person who understands the adjective "red" is said to have the concept of red, and this same concept is said to be possessed by someone who understands a word synonymous with "red." If we accept this presumption, we can say that the concept *red* is something associated with "red" and its counterparts in other languages. The question is, "What is the 'something' and how is it associated with the relevant words?"

One way of answering the question is suggested by the observation that a person who uses the word "red" in speaking or thinking would generally be held to be *employing* the concept *red*. The same concept would be employed by a French person who uses "rouge." Now, if "rouge" is a good translation of "red," the words are used in formally analogous ways: Speakers of French apply "rouge" to objects that speakers of English would describe as red, and each would relate their word to other words of their language in a way that is parallel, formally speaking, to the usage of the other. Thus, the French would use "rouge" in relation to "bleu" in basically the way that we use "red" in relation to "blue." It is convenient to have a general term by which to classify words that are functional counterparts in this way. Such a term was supplied years ago by Wilfrid Sellars; he constructed it by means of his dot-quotes: any expression that is a functional counterpart to "red" can be described as a *red*.[32] (I use asterisks where Sellars uses dot-quotes.) If we use Sellars' terminology, we can say that the concept *red* is something that is common and peculiar to *red*s.

D. M. Armstrong once said that the task of giving an account of "the" type-token distinction is a "compulsory question on the [philosopher's] examination paper."[33] A plausible way of relating *red*s to the concept *red* is to say that the latter is the type of which the former are tokens. Saying this requires that one come to terms with *a* type-token distinction (their may be more than one), but it accords with the common assumption that if you understand and use "red," you have and employ the concept *red*, and that if you understand and employ "rouge," you have and employ the same concept.

When we think of types, we often describe them in ways appropriate to tokens. This tendency is perhaps evident in Plato's practice of describing particulars as imperfect imitations of perfect Forms,[34] but it stands out in Hilaire Belloc's amusing lines:

> The llama is a woolly sort of fleecy hairy goat,
> With an indolent expression and an undulating throat.[35]

It is obvious that what is said of the type here is properly predicated of the tokens, for only particular llamas are fleecy hairy goats with indolent expressions and undulating throats. Surely no abstract object is hairy and has an indolent expression! Wilfrid Sellars devoted a lot of attention to expressions such as "the llama"; he called them *distributive singular terms* (or *DSTs*) and said that statements containing them are definitionally equivalent to statements about concrete things. In his view a statement of the form "The llama is f" can be paraphrased as "Llamas are f."[36] His view is very plausible, I think, for "The llama is a woolly sort of fleecy hairy goat" seems to be about actual llamas. Doubts have been raised about whether the view is actually true, however; and I want to say something about these doubts before proceeding with the subject of concepts. They are clearly pertinent to the view I wish to defend.

Some Problems about DSTs

The doubts in question were directed to a claim by Nelson Goodman, who viewed types pretty much as Sellars did. Goodman had said that a statement ostensibly about types, "'Paris' consists of five letters," is short for "Every 'Paris'-inscription consists of five letter-inscriptions."[37] Linda Wetzel has recently objected to Goodman's claim on two principal grounds.[38] The first was that the statement ostensibly about the type "Paris" is true but the alleged equivalent is actually false: Many "Paris"-inscriptions are misspelled, damaged, or contain typos, and as a result do not contain five letter-inscriptions. Wetzel's point is a general one: what is true of the type is not correspondingly true of all tokens: "the species *Ursus horribilis* can be characterized as ferocious," she says, "even if some members of the species are timid" (p. 363). The second ground was that there may be truths about types in the absence of any tokens of those types. Many sentences of English have never been uttered or written down; and while there may be tokens of formulas Φ and Ψ, there may be no tokens of their conjunction, although the conjunction-type unquestionably exists. (This last objection, as I have formulated it, obviously needs some development to provide a counterexample to Goodman's claim, but I shall give that later. It does clearly conflict, however, with the idea that statements about types are short for statements about tokens.)

Wetzel's first objection is clearly right: tokens often fail to live up to the type. This fact does not require one to reject the suggested analysis, however; it merely requires an obvious amendment.[39] Ostensible type-statements seem to involve idealizations: "the" llama has the traits of typical examples of the species, not unusual examples that have been shaved, burned, starved, or beaten. An analogous point holds for words and letters. The type "Paris" has the traits of undamaged, unblemished, well-formed tokens. To save the analysis, we therefore adjust the domain of quantification relevant to the tokens. "'Paris' consists of five letters" is thus short for a qualified statement about inscriptions: "Every well-formed 'Paris'-inscription (every good example) consists of five letter-inscriptions."

Goodman actually eludes Wetzel's second objection by the way he formulates his view. His claim about ostensible types is actually restricted to inscriptions: it is any "'Paris' consists of five letters"-*inscription* that is supposed to be short for "Every 'Paris'-inscription consists of five letter-inscriptions." Since every "'Paris' consists of five letters"-*inscription* contains a "Paris"-inscription containing five letter-inscriptions, there can be no problem *for Goodman* of not having enough tokens to vindicate his analysis. A problem apparently remains, however, for a claim I think he ought to accept. He ought to agree that there are sentences of English that have never been tokened and never will be tokened, and that there are falsehoods about these sentences (these sentence-types) that correspond to vacuous truths about the untokened tokens. Consider the following nonsense that can be kicked away like Wittgenstein's ladder once the relevant point is grasped: "Sentence type Φ contains one hundred and twenty words" is false (because it contains a hundred and twenty-one words) but "$\forall t(t$ is a Φ-inscription $\supset t$ contains 121 word-inscriptions)" is vacuously true (because $\sim\exists t(t$ a Φ-inscription)).

Goodman has a solution to this last problem, however. It is owing to his calculus of individuals. According to his sum axiom, the sum of any two individuals is an individual, no matter how scattered those individuals may be.[40] As the result of this axiom, Goodman would say that if there are inscriptions of Φ, Ψ, and "&," an inscription that is the conjunction of Φ and Ψ also exists. This solution seems acceptable to me, but if one is unwilling to make use of it, one could equally say (as I have earlier) that a token of every sentence of English can be found in any token of the alphabet: to find it one simply has to go through the alphabet in the right way.[41]

More about Concepts

My concern here is concepts, not sentence-types and sentence-tokens; so I shall say no more about Goodman's views of word-types and word-tokens. The hypothesis I am considering is that what is ostensibly true of concepts reduces to what is true of certain tokens, specifically certain general terms. The idea seems reasonable in view of some standard assumptions about concepts: Jacques has the concept *snow* iff he understands some general term, perhaps "neige," that is a *snow*; Jacques and Tom have a common concept iff they understand general terms that are functional counterparts; and I have a concept that is applicable to snow iff I have a general term that is applicable to it.

Since I am using Sellars' dot-quotes to create special predicates applicable to tokens that are functional counterparts, I should emphasize that Sellars applied these predicates to mental tokens as well as physical ones. He did this because he was convinced that we can think what we can say and that we can do so without saying anything to ourselves, in the way we mentally say something when we silently recite a poem to ourselves. If, without uttering anything, we think "That snow is yellow," we are employing concepts of snow and of something yellow, and doing this requires that certain elements of our thought do the functional work of "snow" and "yellow." These elements are reasonably described as *snow*s and *yellow*s even though they differ from audible *snow*s and *yellow*s in material (that is, nonfunctional) respects.

One more point about concepts. Could a concept exist at a time if no tokens "expressing" it existed at that time or any time before it? Since I believe that concepts are plainly created by human beings (some evolve in human speech; some are created deliberately), I want to say no. But surely a concept could still exist if everyone were asleep and no tokens of it were written down anywhere. This sounds right. One could, of course, say (as I did earlier) that every sentence of English can be found in any instance of the English alphabet, but it seems reasonable to concede that a given concept could exist if everyone were asleep and no English letter-tokens existed at all. For the concept to exist under such conditions, I would maintain, however, that it must be "present in potentiality," as Aristotle would say: people must have instances of it in their verbal repertoire, so that they can bring it to mind if they want to. (If they have actually lost it, it is gone and can exist only if it is recreated.) This last contention requires a further qualification to the definitional schema for concept DSTs: the *A* is F just when every typical *A* is F *and* there are *A*s in someone's verbal repertoire. The last clause need not actually appear on the right-hand side of the formula if it is allowed that it is implied by the left-hand side. I think the implication should be allowed because we would not speak of *the llama* if there were no llamas. I think we would speak of *the unicorn* only in a mythological context. If someone spoke of *the unicorn* in an ordinary context, we would probably say "What do you mean, *the* unicorn? There aren't any, you know."[42]

I have now said enough about concepts to return to the problem sentences (5) and (6) – namely, "Honesty is a virtue" and "Red is a color." If the term "honesty," owing to vagueness and other things, must represent a concept rather than an A-universal, then the predicate in "Honesty is a virtue" must be appropriate to such a concept. Intuitively speaking, the idea must be that *honesty* is a *virtue concept*. Sentence (5) is thus reconstructed, according to the P-theory I am recommending, by a kind of semantic ascent. As thus reconstructed, (5) is not equivalent to an assertion about mere words; it is equivalent to an assertion about items (words or thought-fragments) that are *honest*s and virtue-predicates. Since both terms of (5) are implicitly general, its copula has the sense of "are": All (typical) *honest*s are virtue-predicates. A similar analysis is appropriate for (6): All *red*s are color-predicates. A predicate in the sense in point here is simply something that plays the role of (that is, functions as) a predicate.[43]

The Plausibility of the P-theory

The treatment just given of (5) and (6) may seem excessively contrived, but it gives the right results, fitting together nicely with the arguments of preceding sections. We obviously have a concept of honesty; and when we apply it to Tom and Sally (or say, in a Fregean moment, that they "fall under" it) we are describing *them*, saying that *they* are honest: we are not talking about an object that is separable from human beings.[44] We may apply the same concept to other people, too; if we are right about them and also right about Tom and Sally, they are all relevantly similar. We know what an honest person is like, and if we are pressed into trying to describe honesty, we either talk about our concept or we end up describing someone behaving honestly – just as John Locke's blind man, trying to say what scarlet is like, ends up describing something that is as bright and strident as he knows the sound of a trumpet is. (What is thus bright and strident is a visible thing, not an abstract entity "possessed" by visible things.)

Since the predicate "is honest," like the predicates "is virtuous" and "is wise," is vague, a treatment of "honesty" that construes it as referring to a concept has additional merit – as is a treatment that declares concepts to be human inventions. The advantages increase when concepts are construed as reducible to predicates. Predicates are vague or nonvague, and they are also human creations belonging to contingently existing languages. As for the application of concepts to reality, this can be explained by means of the application (or denotation) of predicates. Concepts "apply to" objects just when things "fall under" them; and if "the (concept) honesty applies to x's" can be understood as equivalent to "all *honest*s denote x's," the notion of a thing "falling under" a concept will be explicable in relation to *denotes*, a concept relating fragments of utterances or inscriptions to linguistic norms (or dispositions) and associated natural objects. Since norms or dispositions relate utterances and inscriptions to natural objects in naturalistically understandable ways, the P-theory I have been sketching lacks the other-worldly mystery of the Platonic original. It accords nicely with the naturalistic view of the world that is becoming common in analytic philosophy.[45]

Acknowledgment

I thank Jean-Paul Vessel and Jonathan Schaffer for helpful comments on an earlier version of the chapter.

Notes

1   I speak loosely of universals here. The term is best applied to the objects of A-theories or P-theories, but T-theories provide an alternative account of what general terms supposedly denote, and it is convenient to have a word that applies to the supposed objects of all such theories. My choice of "universal" seems well-suited for this limited purpose.

2   D. M. Armstrong, *Nominalism and Realism* (Cambridge: Cambridge University Press, 1978), p. xiii.

3   Armstrong says, "If two things have the very same property, then that property is, in some sense, 'in' each of them," ibid., p. 108.

4   Keith Campbell, "The Metaphysics of Abstract Particulars," in D. H. Mellor and Alex Oliver, eds., *Properties* (Oxford: Oxford University Press, 1997), pp. 125–39.

5   I have criticized it in Bruce Aune, *Metaphysics: the Elements* (Minneapolis: University of Minnesota Press, 1985), pp. 48f.

6   See Armstrong, *Nominalism and Realism*, pp. 89–101.

7   See below.

8   John Locke, *An Essay Concerning Human Understanding*, ed. G. A. Fraser, vol. 1 (Oxford: Clarendon Press, 1984), p. 392.

9   See Edwin Allaire, "Bare Particulars," *Philosophical Studies*, 16 (1963).

10 D. M. Armstrong, "[Reply] To Aune," in Radu J. Bogden, ed., *D. M. Armstrong* (Dordrecht: Reidel, 1984), p. 254.

11 Ibid.

12 Ibid.

13 R. M. Chisholm, *Person and Object* (London: Allen & Unwin, 1976), pp. 43f. Chisholm says the first argument "seems" to have been offered by Edwin Allaire in "Bare Particulars"; he quotes the second argument from Bertrand Russell, *An Inquiry Into Meaning and Truth* (London: Allen & Unwin, 1948), p. 97.

14 Chisholm, *Person and Object*, p. 39.

15 In "To Aune," Armstrong expresses a cautious attitude to this principle, saying "It may be that some such principle is true" (p. 252); but in discussing the view that he calls Predicate Nominalism, he raises the question, "In virtue of what do these general terms apply to the things that they apply to?" implying that a satisfactory answer will have to refer to universals. See *Nominalism and Realism*, p. 19.

16 Armstrong, "[Reply] To Aune," p. 252.

17 See earlier.

18 David Lewis, "New Work for a Theory of Universals," *Australasian Journal of Philosophy*, 61/4 (December 1983), pp. 343–77; reprinted in *Properties*, pp. 188–227. (Lewis's remarks about predication occur on pp. 197–201.) I interpret Lewis's claim that predication should be acknowledged as primitive as equivalent to the claim that a predication to the effect that a thing a is F may be incapapable of any ontologically more revealing paraphrase. I say "may" rather than "is" because some predications do admit of such paraphrases. "$\exists x(x$ is a brother of Tom or x is a sister of Tom)" may be a revealing paraphrase of "Tom is a sibling."

19 Actually, I made essentially the same point as Lewis both in *Metaphysics: the Elements*, p. 44, and in "Armstrong on Universals and Particulars," where I said "Whatever the ultimate entities of the world may be, a proposition of the form 'a is F' must be true of them without implying the existence of further, more elementary entities. If universals did exist, they themselves would be describable by propositions of this form; but the proponent of universals would not insist that such propositions could be true only if entites of a further sort exist. To parody Wittgenstein, Predication has to come to an end somewhere" (Bogden, *D. M. Armstrong*, p. 167).

20 Ibid., p. 254.

21 This claim would not be made by my colleague Jonathan Shaffer, who postulates tropes only to account for the causal properties (or interactions) of empirical objects: he does not suppose that a trope corresponds to every true predication. In opposition to his view, I say that the special tropes he recognizes are excess baggage, for a thing's causal interactions are adequately explainable by reference to its own empirical character: a window shatters, for example, because *it* is brittle and struck by a sufficiently heavy object. The same principle applies to the interactions of micro-entities: they behave as they do because of what *they* are like. No special tropes are needed.

22 Aristotle, Categories, 1a20–25.

23 See Gottlob Frege, "On Concept and Object," trans. P. T. Geach, in P. T. Geach and Max Black, eds., *Translations from the Philosophical Writings of Gottlob Frege* (Oxford: Blackwell, 1952), pp. 42–55.

24   That is, they do not require that "a falls under the concept C" is true only if a falls
     under the concept *falls under the concept* C – as "a swims" is supposed to be true only
     if a falls under the concept *swims*.

25   There are, of course, certain cases in which a thing satisfies the conditions for being F
     only if it is related to a further thing: to be a brother one must be suitably related to
     another person. The point is simply that there is no general requirement to this effect.

26   David Lewis, *On the Plurality of Worlds* (Oxford: Blackwell, 1986), p. 55.

27   The word "reptile" is apparently now obsolete for the purposes of zoological classifi-
     cation. According to Gribben and Cherfas, zoological species are now classified (at
     least among influential groups) partly by reference to DNA and histological proper-
     ties, and animals formerly classified as reptiles are often quite dissimilar in these
     respects, turtles sharing more DNA with chickens than with snakes. See John Gribben
     and Jeremy Cherfas, *The Monkey Puzzle* (New York: McGraw-Hill, 1983), p. 93.

28   *A Lexicon Abridged from Liddell and Scott's Greek–English Lexicon* (Oxford: Claren-
     don Press, 1984), p. 630.

29   See Paul Kay and Chad K. McDaniel, "Linguistic Significance of Meanings of Basic
     Color Terms," in Alex Byrne and David R. Hilbert, eds., *Readings on Color*, vol. 2
     (Cambridge, MA: MIT Press, 1997), pp. 411–14.

30   See W. V. O. Quine, *Set Theory and Its Logic* (Cambridge, MA: Harvard University
     Press, 1969), pp. 9f.

31   See Saul Kripke, "Is There a Problem about Substitutional Quantification?" in Gareth
     Evans and John McDowell, eds., *Truth and Meaning* (Oxford: Clarendon Press,
     1976), pp. 325–419. More recently, the use of substitutional quantification has been
     criticized in certain contexts by Peter van Inwagen and James Tomberlin: they obtain
     false conclusions from true premises by introducing expressions that would tacitly
     be excluded by a thoughtful user of the device. It is well known that standard logical
     axioms are easily falsified if schematic letters are replaced by unintended substituends
     such as "This statement is false," but the class of such substituends is not explicitly
     identified when logic is informally used. The same is true for the informal use of sub-
     stitutional quantifiers. See Peter van Inwagen, "Why I Don't Understand Substitu-
     tional Quantification," *Philosophical Studies*, 39 (1981), 281–5, and James Tomberlin,
     "Belief, Nominalism, and Quantification," in J. Tomberlin, ed., *Philosophical Perspec-
     tives*, vol. 4 (Atascadero, CA: Ridgeview, 1990), pp. 573–9.

32   See Wilfrid Sellars, "Abstract Entities," *Review of Metaphysics*, 16 (1963), reprinted in
     W. Sellars, *Philosophical Perspectives* (Springfield, IL: Charles Thomas, 1967), pp.
     229–69.

33   *Nominalism and Realism*, p. 17.

34   As in *Republic*, 597a.

35   Hilaire Belloc, "The Llama," in H. Belloc, *Complete Verse* (London: Duckworth,
     1970), p. 245.

36   See "Abstract Entities," and also W. Sellars, *Naturalism and Ontology* (Atascadero,
     CA: Ridgeview, 1979), pp. 89–99. For a general discussion of the logic of DSTs, see
     C. H. Langford, "The Institutional Use of 'The'," *Philosophy and Phenomenological
     Research*, X (1949), pp. 115–20.

37   Nelson Goodman, *The Structure of Appearance*, second edn. (Indianapolis: Bobbs-
     Merrill, 1966), pp. 360ff.

38   Linda Wetzel, "The Trouble with Nominalism," *Philosophical Studies*, 98 (2000),
     pp. 361–70.

39   Frege noted this in "On Concept and Object"; he said that "The horse is a four-legged animal" is "probably best regarded" as expressing a universal judgment, say "All properly constituted horses are four-legged animals"; see Frege, p. 45.

40   See *Structure of Appearance*, p. 51.

41   I expressed this view in my book, *Metaphysics: The Elements*, p. 66.

42   What about the assertion "The passenger pigeon is extinct"? It seems to me that in this context "the passenger pigeon" is not a DST but the name of a species. Individual pigeons are not extinct; the species is: it has no instances.

43   As my qualification is intended to indicate, speaking of a predicate *playing a role* does not "commit one to the irreducible reality of roles," for "functions as a predicate" merely describes a predicate in the way "is red" or "acts foolish" describes a thing or a person.

44   If we want to retain the word "property" in espousing a P-theory, we may easily do so by employing the schema, *x* has the property of being *F* just when *x* falls under (or satisfies) the concept of being *F*. If we adopt this theoretically limited usage for "property," which does not take the word to denote irreducible objects distinct from particulars, we can say that a bald man has the property of being bald or sarcastic even though we insist that the only things vague in the world are words or concepts. Our talk of properties will be a mere *façon de parler*, having no ontological significance.

45   My treatment of a P-theory featuring concepts is indebted to Wilfrid Sellars's "naturalistic" treatment of abstract objects in *Naturalism and Ontology*, but it is considerably less ambitious: my account is restricted to a theory of P-universals, not abstract objects generally. What I say here is actually consistent with a realist view of classes, species, and numbers.

Chapter 8

Composition as a Fiction

Gideon Rosen and Cian Dorr

1 A Question about Composition

Let R be a region of otherwise empty space containing three simple particles, A, B, and C.

Region R

Question: How many objects – entities, things – are contained in R? Ignore the empty space. Our question might better be put, "How many *material* objects does R contain?" Let's stipulate that A, B, and C are metaphysical atoms: absolutely simple entities with no parts whatsoever besides themselves. So you don't have to worry about counting a particle's top half and bottom half as different objects. Perhaps they are "point-particles," with no length, width or breadth. Perhaps they are extended in space without possessing spatial parts (if that is possible). Never mind. We stipulate that A, B, and C are perfectly simple. We also stipulate that they are connected as follows. A and B are stuck together in such a way that when a force is applied to one of them, they move together "as a unit." Moreover, the two of them together exhibit behavior that neither would exhibit on its own – perhaps they emit a certain sound, or glow in the dark – whereas C is effectively independent of the others. Now then, How many material objects are contained in R?

2   Some Answers

The most natural answer is probably *four*: the atoms A, B and C, and the dyadic
"molecule" A + B. Naïve common sense apparently has it that small things sometimes come together to form larger things. Common sense does not deliver an
explicit rule or principle governing composition. But it does have firm opinions
about particular cases. The particles in a chemical atom, the cells in your body, the
cards in a house of cards, the stars and planets in the Milky Way galaxy: – by commonsensical standards these are all cases in which several things compose a single
thing. The connection between A and B in our example is meant to be an example
of the sort of relation that suffices for composition by commonsensical standards,
whereas A and C are supposed to be so completely loose and separate as to compose
nothing (or at any rate, nothing worth mentioning) by those same standards.

Common sense about composition is opposed on both sides by distinctively
philosophical approaches to the topic. Certain highly restrictive theories of composition claim that common sense is much too liberal. In his closely argued book
Material Beings, Peter van Inwagen defends the view that several things compose
a single thing only when their activity constitutes the life of an organism.[1] On this
view, the cells in your body – or perhaps better, the elementary particles in your
body – do indeed compose a single thing, namely you. But when the chemist says
that three quarks together make a proton, or when the cosmologist says that billions of stars and planets and specks of interstellar dust together make up the Milky
Way, or when the voice of common sense says that twenty cards make up a house
of cards – what they say is false, strictly speaking. There are no protons or galaxies
or houses of cards. There are rather billions of simple particles arranged proton-
wise and galaxy-wise and house-of-cards-wise. The most radical view of this sort
is compositional nihilism, according to which there is no such thing as a composite entity. On this view, it is probable that you do not exist. You just might be
an absolutely simple Cartesian soul. But if not – if the only objects in your vicinity are material objects – then strictly speaking, there is no such thing as you. There
are rather many simple things arranged "person-wise" and engaged in various collective activities. Since you are not any one of these particles, and since there are
no other candidates, the compositional nihilist maintains that strictly speaking, you
do not exist.[2] (Which is not to say that he is chauvinistic; he says the same about
himself.) In any case, compositional nihilism and van Inwagen's "organicism"
reject the natural answer to our question. They say that there are only three things
in R, and in particular that the alleged complex A + B does not exist.

Nihilism and organicism are minority opinions. But the commonsensical answer
to our question is equally at odds with the most widely accepted philosophical
theory of parts and wholes, according to which there exist exactly seven things in
R: three atoms: A, B and C, and four composite entities; the mereological aggregates or fusions A + B, B + C, A + C and A + B + C. The theory in question is
classical mereology: an axiomatic theory of the part/whole relation developed by
Stanislaw Lesniewski in the 1920s, and since adopted widely, most notably by

Nelson Goodman, W. V. Quine and David Lewis.[3] It will be useful in what follows to have the theory in front of us.

The language of the theory is a first-order language supplemented with devices for plural reference and quantification.[4] It contains one primitive relation symbol, "... is a part of ...," which is to be understood in the usual way. Other mereological notions are defined in terms of "part". For example,

X is a **proper part** of Y $=_{df}$ X is a part of Y and X ≠ Y.
X is an **atom** $=_{df}$ X has no proper parts.
X and Y **overlap** $=_{df}$ Some object Z is a part of X and a part of Y.
X and Y are **disjoint** $=_{df}$ X and Y do not overlap.
X is **pure atomless gunk** $=_{df}$ No atom is a part of X.
The Fs **compose** X (X is a **fusion** of the Fs) $=_{df}$ Every F is a part of X, and every part of X overlaps an F.

The theory itself has four axioms:

Reflexivity: Everything is part of itself.
Transitivity: If A is part of B and B is part of C then A is part of C.
Unrestricted Composition: Whenever there are some things, there is at least one thing that they compose.
Uniqueness of Composition: Whenever there are some things, there is at most one thing that they compose.

In this essay we focus on Unrestricted Composition and certain alternatives to it. It may be useful, however, to say a word about the other axioms.

Reflexivity is little more than a terminological stipulation. If it sounds wrong to say that Fred is a part of himself, you can always interpret the technical mereological term "is a part of" to mean "is a part of or is identical to."

Transitivity may seem obvious, but consider:

Fred is part of the conga line, and Fred's spleen is part of Fred. But Fred's spleen is not part of the conga line.[5]

This sort of difficulty is not decisive, however. No doubt it sounds peculiar to say that Fred's internal organs are parts of a dance formation. But think again about the conga line. What sort of thing might it be? According to one natural answer, it is a large physical object made of people, snaking its way around the dance floor – an animated organic sculpture. It has a front half and a back half, but also a top half (made of heads and torsos) and a bottom half (made of legs and feet). Once you think of the line in this way – as a single, spatially extended physical object – it becomes plausible that the parts of its salient parts are also parts of it. Fred's legs and feet are clearly part of the line. And if his legs are in, why not his spleen? In any case, we shall assume transitivity in all that follows.[6]

Uniqueness of Composition is sometimes called the principle of extensionality. It says, in effect, that composite objects are numerically identical (one and the same) whenever they have all of their proper parts in common: "No difference without a difference maker," as the saying goes. And this should not be obvious. As we are normally inclined to think, two sentences can be made out of just the same words; two tunes can made out of just the same notes, and so on.[7] These examples suggest that things may differ without differing in constituency, so long as they differ in the arrangement of their constituents. Here is another example, this time involving concrete objects. On Monday, Jones takes some bricks and builds a castle. He lets it be for a while, and then takes it apart, leaving the bricks in a heap. Years later he takes the very same bricks and builds a statue of Lesniewski. On the face of it, the castle and the statue are not identical. The castle no longer exists when the statue comes to be. But they are made of just the same bricks, and therefore (plausibly) just the same parts.

This sort of problem for Uniqueness can be evaded in several ways. According to Goodman, the time at which a thing exists counts as a non-physical part of it.[8] On this bizarre view, the castle and the statue clearly differ in constituency, since only the castle contains Monday as a part. According to Quine and Lewis, on the other hand, the "bricks" that make the castle are distinct from the "bricks" that make the statue. On this view, temporally extended physical objects (such as bricks) are made of short-lived temporal parts or stages. The castle is not the fusion of the bricks simpliciter. It is a fusion of the Monday-bricks, the temporally restricted stages of the bricks that exist only on Monday, whereas the statue is made of an altogether distinct array of stages. Both solutions are workable, but neither is obviously correct. Uniqueness of composition is thus a bit of philosophical theory. It is not commonsensical; it requires substantive defense.

Many of the "intuitive" objections to mereology depend on Uniqueness. For instance, the full theory entails that composition is automatic: Whenever the parts exist, the one and only whole composed of them exists as well. And this means that short of creating a brand new atom *ex nihilo*, there is no such thing as genuine creation, bringing a new thing into being. What we call "creation" – of a painting, or a person – is really a matter of modifying the shape of an object that would have existed anyway. And that is a surprise. Nonetheless, we shall have nothing more to say about Uniqueness, and we shall not presuppose it in our discussion of mereology. Our focus will be the principle of Unrestricted Composition. This is the principle that generates the scattered aggregates A + C, B + C and A + B + C in our example, and hence the divergence from what we have (perhaps tendentiously) labeled common sense.

3   How Shall We Decide?

Our question was, "How many objects exist in R?" Compositional nihilism says "three"; "Common sense" says "four"; and classical mereology says "seven."

These are not the only possibilities, but let's ignore the others.[9] The answers appear to conflict, in which case only one can be correct. So which is it? And more importantly, how shall we decide?

The question is neither straightforwardly empirical nor straightforwardly conceptual. Each proposal is formally consistent – there are no "paradoxes of mereology."[10] Could the meaning of "part" be such as to render one of the proposals *analytically* inconsistent? The mereological nihilist's proposal, at least, is analytically consistent. For it is analytically consistent that no two material objects overlap spatially – no analysis of "part" could reveal an inconsistency in this claim! – and mereological nihilism follows from this claim, assuming that every object must overlap spatially with any of its parts.

It is conceivable that there exists a compelling analytic definition of "part" which, when substituted for the word in one of the competing principles of composition (other than nihilism), yields a contradiction or some other patent absurdity. But until someone provides such a definition, the presumption must be that there is none, for the parties to the dispute appear to speak the language well enough. We shall therefore assume that the debate cannot be resolved by conceptual analysis.

Nor can it be resolved by straightforward empirical means. Let R be located in the midst of our finest laboratory. The question is whether A and B (or A and C) together compose a single thing. Can you tell just by looking? That is hard to believe. Those who disagree with you – the nihilist and the mereologist, let us say – have eyes in their heads that work every bit as well as yours. On the basis of observation, they arrive at divergent answers. And that suggests that this is one of those cases in which observation is inevitably so "theory-laden" that a neutral observational standpoint is unavailable.[11] And if observation will not help, neither will experiment. Prod the particles gently: A and B stick together; C drifts off on its own. But you knew that would happen, so the result is uninformative. Wheel out your stethoscope, your electron microscope, your MRI, your Geiger counter. Dip the particles in acid; freeze them in liquid helium. Who knows what will happen? Our description of the case does not say. And yet it seems perfectly clear that experiments of this sort are beside the point. Our competing hypotheses are not testable in this sense. If the question is to be resolved, it must be resolved by other means.

4 Common Sense and Unrestricted Composition

Consider first the status of the principle of Unrestricted Composition. Since the most natural, most commonsensical count of objects in R failed to mention the scattered aggregates, A + C, etc., there is a sense in which the principle is "counter-intuitive" or "revisionary". And it might be thought that this by itself counts as a reason to reject it. The *appeal to common sense* – to what we find it natural to believe, to what we regard as settled before we come to philosophy – plays a central role in antiskeptical epistemology in other areas. Consider two competing hypotheses about ordinary experience: the commonsensical hypothesis that sense experience is a reliable source of information about the external world, and the skeptical hypothesis that everyday experience is systematically delusory. Like the dispute over composition, this skeptical dispute is neither straightforwardly empirical nor straightforwardly conceptual. But it is not unresolvable. Philosophers differ as to why the skeptical hypothesis should be rejected. But according to one account it is precisely its eccentricity that rules it out. The transition from "where we are now" to the skeptical alternative would involve rejecting nearly everything we take for granted. The skeptic gives us no positive reason to make this transition. There is no sense in which his view is clearly "superior" to the normal one. And so it is said: a principle of conservatism governs rational change in belief. If Unrestricted Composition (or Nihilism or some other restrictive principle) is at odds with settled opinion – and if there is nothing compelling to be said in favor of revision – then it is reasonable for us to reject it despite its consistency and its adequacy to the phenomena.

We shall not attempt to assess the appeal to common sense as an antiskeptical strategy in other areas. Whatever its merits as a response to (say) Cartesian skepticism, it cannot help us to rule out Unrestricted Composition. As Reid pointed out, common sense is invincibly persuaded that the external world exists. When the skeptical alternative is presented, it is *manifestly* incompatible with what we take for granted. It strikes us as absolutely ridiculous given what we think we know. The typical response to Unrestricted Composition is rather different. It is true that our first thought about R's inventory omits the scattered sums. But when the mereologist asks, "Are you sure you haven't forgotten something? What about A + C?" etc., the commonsensical response is not, "What are you talking about? There is no such thing!" It is rather much more equivocal.[12] It may even take the form: "Well, if you count *that* as a thing, then I suppose there must be seven things in R after all."

According to the mereologist we can always explain away the intuitive counter-examples to unrestricted composition in this way. Ordinary discourse, he will say, proceeds with a vague restriction to "unified" objects in place. If an object fails to display a certain degree of integrity or "thinginess" – if its parts don't tend to move together; if it does not contrast with its surroundings – then we tend to ignore it. We don't count it when we tally up the number of "things" with a given feature. Suppose someone puts a 2 lb. cannonball and a feather on the table and asks, "How many objects weighing more than one pound are there in front of you?" Your first thought is "one." But the mereologist will suggest that you are ignoring countless things: the top $\frac{2}{3}$ of the cannonball; the bottom $\frac{2}{3}$; the ball plus the feather, etc. None of these things is sufficiently "thingy" to feature as an object of concern or attention in any normal context. But to say that X is properly ignored for certain purposes is not to say that X does not exist.

Contrast the mereologist's attempt to call your attention to these inconsequential items with the demonologist's attempt to call your attention to the invisible 2 lb. imp perched on top of the cannon ball. You are not inclined to say, "Well, if you count that as a thing, then I guess there must be more 1 lb. objects than I supposed." No, the demonologist strikes us as straightforwardly deluded: he sees things that aren't there. The mereologist strikes us, by contrast, as pointlessly observant. The objects she bothers about may not be worth bothering about. But that is not to say that they do not exist.

The mereologist explains the seeming oddness of her view by appealing to a vague restriction governing ordinary discourse about material objects. This appeal is not ad hoc. It corresponds to something real in the "phenomenology" of our encounter with the mereologist. For this reason, the appeal to common sense is unpersuasive in this context. Common sense may not bother with heterogeneous mereological fusions, but upon reflection, it is not robustly committed to their non-existence. At best, it is committed to the view that the scattered objects of mereology, if they exist, are for the most part not worth mentioning. But that is something the mereologist may well accept.

5   Common Sense and Compositional Nihilism

The appeal to common sense may not exclude Unrestricted Composition. But doesn't it at least exclude compositional nihilism and the other highly restrictive views we have mentioned? These views deny the existence of composite entities whose existence common sense appears to affirm with utter confidence. They say: "You may think that there is such a thing as the molecule A + B. You may think the bricks compose a house; that the trees compose a forest; that the bits of ink and paper compose a book. But strictly speaking you are mistaken. There is no such thing as a house; there is no such thing as a brick. So when you claim that there are ten houses on your street, six of which are made of bricks, you are wrong." Is not this view, at least, so profoundly at odds with common sense that we can dismiss it in the same spirit in which we dismiss the more familiar skeptical hypotheses?

Even this is not so clear. Common sense as we have construed it claims that A and B together make up a further thing. The compositional nihilist denies this. But of course he doesn't deny that A and B are stuck together, that together they exhibit behavior that neither would exhibit on its own, that together they contrast with their surroundings, and so on. In short, he denies the existence of the molecule but agrees that there are some things arranged "molecule-wise." And he will say the same about bricks and houses and the rest. Strictly speaking, there is no such thing as a brick or a house; but there are some things – God knows how many – arranged brick-wise and some other things arranged house-wise. This arrangement is not merely a matter of disposition in space. For some things to be arranged house-wise they must cohere; they must collectively possess a certain mass, a certain shape, and so on. If we put some things arranged house-wise on the corner, they would look and feel and act just like a house, whether or not they constituted a single thing.

So consider two claims:

(1)   There is a house on the corner.
(2)   There are some things arranged house-wise on the corner.

These claims are distinct. The nihilist asserts (2) but denies (1), whereas common sense affirms (1) without conscious reservation. Now, there are many cases in which we do not strictly believe what we say. We exaggerate or oversimplify. We speak metaphorically or elliptically. And when we do, we are not committed to believing the proposition expressed by the sentence we utter. In most of these cases, if we interrupt the speaker and demand, "Is what you just said strictly true?" he will say, "No. I was just exaggerating (or what have you)." In conceding that common sense affirms (1) *without conscious reservation*, we are conceding that our claim about the house is not plausibly assimilated to non-literal speech. We do not think of (1) as a rough and ready shorthand, a way of conveying, if somewhat misleadingly, the sober truth expressed by (2). Let us not deny then that common sense is committed to the existence of composite objects of various sorts, and that it is therefore incompatible with compositional nihilism. The question is how deep this commitment runs and what sort of authority it should be accorded.

The first thing to note is that common sense has never given (2) a moment's thought. It takes some effort to get someone to see a difference between (1) and (2). (That's why it is implausible to attribute to common sense the thought that (1) is simply shorthand for (2).) But once we bring the contrast into focus we can ask, "Now that you see the difference, is it really so obvious that the bricks compose a single thing? Can you point to something in the perceptual scene which indicates, not just that the bricks are arranged house-wise on the corner, but that, in addition, composition has taken place in this case?" If the answer is "no," or "I'm not so sure," as we think it ought to be, then we find ourselves in the following situation. *Un*reflective common sense comes down squarely on the side of (1). But upon reflection it emerges that in taking this stance, common sense is excluding an alternative without having considered it, an alternative which, so far as we have yet been able to see, is undetectably different from the preferred alternative, and which, upon reflection, common sense hesitates to exclude. To insist upon the epistemic authority of ordinary, everyday common sense in this context is to lapse into an unappealing dogmatism. Naïve common sense may be forgiven for unreflective acquiescence in a theory of composition incompatible with nihilism. But it would be a mistake for us – having raised the question explicitly – to defer to an authority which has never considered the matter and which delivers no decisive verdict when the question is put directly.

6 Compositional Nihilism and the Self

There is a striking argument for the conclusion that even if some very restrictive theory of composition is true, at least compositional nihilism is not true. It runs as follows:

1 I exist.
2 If I exist, I have proper parts.
3 Therefore, there is at least one composite object.[13]

There is no doubt that the premises of this argument are very compelling and plausible, that their denial initially strikes us as absurd. But this is true of the conclusion as well. If the argument is to get us anywhere, it can't be just another version of the appeal to common sense. Our confidence in the premises must be less prone to being undermined when we consider scenarios in which compositional nihilism is true, than our confidence in the existence of houses and bricks.

In the case of the first premise, there is a relevant difference between your belief that you exist and the belief that some other composite object exists. An important part of the compositional nihilist's strategy for undermining your belief in galaxies and tables and molecules and even other people is the observation that things would *seem* the same way to you whether or not those composite things existed, provided that the atoms continued to be arranged in the same way. This is hard to deny when other composite things are in question. But when your own existence is challenged, you might well respond: "Indeed, no one *else* would be able to tell the difference if my atoms were arranged as they are even though I didn't exist. But *I* can tell the difference. If I did not exist, things would not seem any way at all *to me*. My own existence is immediately evident, for while I can doubt that things really are the way they seem to me, I cannot doubt that things do seem that way to me." The thought is compelling. But the compositional nihilist has a response: "You don't exist; but the things you used to think of yourself as doing get done all the same. Certain atoms *jointly* think those thoughts, dream those dreams, and so forth. Things seem the way they do to those atoms jointly, but not to any single thing."

Does the compositional nihilist's story make any sense? If we admit that it does, it will be hard to maintain our former degree of confidence in our own existence. Whatever I might do to convince myself that I exist, it is possible that some atoms might collectively do – but when those atoms collectively think "I exist," they express a falsehood. Would you not at least start to get worried if you found out somehow that most of the thinking at the actual world was done collectively by atoms rather than individually by composite entities? If so, we are back to discussing the probability of the compositional nihilists' hypothesis. Thus, if you want to maintain your right to be completely confident that you exist, there is considerable pressure on you to declare that the compositional nihilist's story is conceptually incoherent.[14] You must maintain that thinking, or desiring, or feeling, or seeming to, is not the sort of thing that several things could do collectively. It is not clear to us how this view could be argued for; and in any case, until it has been argued for, compositional nihilism remains an option.

7   The Appeal to Science

The appeal to common sense is only one gambit in antiskeptical dialectics. Another approach, and perhaps the most significant from our point of view, is what might be called *the appeal to science*. Just to vary the example, consider the following hypotheses:

(1)   The physical universe is roughly 11 billion years old.
(2)   The physical universe was created by an impish deity 500 years ago with all the traces of an extensive past in place.

As before, neither hypothesis is self-contradictory and there is no crucial experiment to tell between them. And yet we think we have compelling grounds for accepting (1) rather than (2). In this case, however, the grounds come not from "common sense," but from astrophysics. There is no clear consensus as to how this fact is to be understood. But let us begin with the following rough caricature. The sciences embody a practice for distinguishing between more or less "acceptable" theories. Some theories are better at explaining the data. Some are more faithful – they make fewer or less extreme mistakes in prediction or retrodiction; and among equally faithful theories, some are simpler, more compelling, more tractable, more easily reconciled with settled doctrine in other fields, and so on. The appeal to science then exploits a general epistemological principle which may be framed very roughly as follows:

(*)   It is rational – rationally permissible, and perhaps even rationally obligatory – to believe the best, most acceptable scientific theory, and in particular to believe in the real existence of the objects that exist according to that theory.

The old earth hypothesis – (1) above – is clearly more acceptable by astrophysical standards than the trumped up alternative (2). That is why – so the story goes – we have reason to believe that (1) is true.

How does this bear on our question about composition? Just as there is little doubt that common sense bears a commitment to run-of-the-mill composite entities, there is little doubt that the best, most acceptable scientific theories that we have posit the existence of composite things at every scale: nucleons are made of quarks; atoms are made of nucleons and electrons. . . . Galaxies are made of stars and planets and interstellar debris. According to astrophysics, there is even such an entity as the universe itself, which is roughly eleven billion years old. Given (*), it follows that it is rational to believe that composite objects exist, and so to reject nihilism, organicism, and any other restrictive principle of composition.

One way to resist this argument is to reject the appeal to science altogether. It is sometimes said that we should regard even the best modern science as a useful fiction with no distinctive claim on our belief. On this view, the fact that modern chemistry makes reference to composite objects provides us with no reason what-soever to believe that such things exist. But let us set this radical antiscientism to one side.[15] Let us assume that the best modern science is a genuine source of infor-mation about its subject matter. Still, it is clear upon reflection that (*) is not quite right: the injunction to believe the best, most acceptable scientific theory requires qualification along several dimensions, and these qualifications bear directly on the appeal to science in the case that interests us.

There are several contexts in which it would clearly be a mistake to believe the most acceptable extant scientific account of the phenomena, and in particular to believe in (all of) the objects it posits.

(A) *Sometimes the best theory is known to be false.* General relativity (GR) is the best available theory of gravitation. It is more fully developed and better confirmed than any rival, and cosmologists routinely take it for granted in their calculations. Nonetheless it is incompatible with an even more successful theory of the other forces: quantum field theory. Given this, it would be unreasonable to believe the theory as it stands. It is one thing to say that something roughly like GR must be correct, or that GR must be the "classical limit" of any convincing successor theory. Perhaps these opinions are licensed by the success of GR in its domain. But it is another thing altogether to say that we have reason to believe the theory in its present form. If (*) implies this strong conclusion, it is unacceptable.

(B) *Sometimes the best available theory is not good enough.* There are several theories about the origins of life. Some posit rudimentary systems of self-reproducing nucleic acids; others posit proteins that catalyze their own duplica-tion. One such theory – the RNA world hypothesis[16] – is widely held to be super-ior to the others. And given this, it obviously makes excellent sense for scientists to elaborate this theory, to seek confirmation of it, to attempt to reproduce the mechanism that it posits and so on. But at this stage even the best theory is too sketchy and too speculative to merit significant credence by scientific standards. The prevailing attitude seems to be, "This is a promising line of research, but the theory faces formidable difficulties."[17] Under the circumstances it would be a bizarre scientism to insist that we are obliged to believe it nonetheless, simply because it is more promising than the alternatives.

(C) *Sometimes the best theory is not significantly better than its nearest rival.* Prior to the discovery of the microwave background radiation in 1964, there were two competing cosmological accounts of the Hubble expansion: the big bang theory, according to which all of space–time is expanding from a singularity of infinite density, and the steady state theory, according to which new matter is constantly created and in such a way as to maintain a constant mean density in a universe of constant size. Both approaches had proponents, and each theory had its difficulties. Let us suppose that by the early 1960s, the big bang hypothesis was the better hypothesis overall. Still, the theory was not significantly better than its most serious rival. And given this, it is clear that a commitment to science did not require that one repose any significant confidence in it at the time. It was clearly permissible and perhaps even required to say rather: "We don't know what explains the Hubble expansion. We have two competing theories. One is better than the other, but we cannot rule either one out. The marginal superiority of the big bang theory at this stage does not constitute scientific grounds for believing that it is correct." Insofar as (*) is incompatible with this sensible posture, it is unacceptable.

(D) *Sometimes the best theory employs what are known to be simplifying assumptions or devices of convenience.* With a small number of speculative exceptions, every developed theory of physical processes assumes the continuity of physical space and time. Without this assumption, the mathematical apparatus of the calculus is inapplicable. The assumption of a continuum is thus for all intents and purposes practically indispensable in modern physics. (*) therefore suggests that we have reason from science to believe that space–time is continuous. But is this right? Penelope Maddy has argued persuasively that the very fact that this hypothesis is forced upon us by considerations of mathematical convenience counts against the claim that the continuity of space–time is well supported by recent physics.[18] The hypothesis has not been tested; indeed it is unclear how it could be tested. Alternatives have not been explored in detail; certainly none has been developed with anything like the generality of the standard approach. In light of all this it is not unreasonable to suggest that the continuity of space and time is to be regarded as a working assumption which may turn out to be an idealization, and not, therefore, as a settled result.

We acknowledge that, without exception, the best available theories make extensive reference to composite things. Simple-minded application of (*) would then mean that we reject compositional nihilism. But we have seen that (*) should not be applied simple-mindedly. The last two reservations are especially relevant in the present context. We do not suggest that working scientists themselves regard the appeal to composite entities as a matter of convenience, in the sense in which some regard the appeal to the continuity of space–time in this light. And we do not suggest that extant theories exist side by side with near rivals that manage to do without composition. But once the possibility of doing without composition has been drawn to our attention, it does not require any great expertise in science for us to introduce new theories which differ from the old ones in being neutral on questions of composition. A team of scientifically-inclined compositional nihilists would have no trouble with the job.

There is a canonical way of eliminating the mereological commitments of almost any theory.[19] The method is to rewrite the theory in such a way that singulars are replaced with plurals throughout. For example, the current best theory in chemistry might be full of talk about molecules allegedly being composed of atoms. The new, mereologically neutral theory will be constructed from the old one by:

(i)   replacing every occurrence of "there is something which" with "there are some things which"
(ii) replacing every occurrence of "for every thing" with "whenever there are some things"
(iii) replacing every occurrence of "is part of" with "are among" (the *x*s are among the *y*s iff whenever something is one of the *x*s, it is one of the *y*s)
(iv) replacing every occurrence of "is identical to" with "are the same things as" (the *x*s are the same things as the *y*s iff for any thing, it is one of the *x*s iff it is one of the *y*s)
(v)   replacing every singular predicate in the theory with a new plural predicate. Thus "is a molecule" is replaced by "are arranged molecule-wise," "has mass M" is replaced by "have mass M," "is located one nanometer away from" is replaced by "are located one nanometer away from."[20, 21]

A new theory constructed according to this method will not be *logically* entailed by the old theory upon which it was based, since it will contain predicates that did not occur in the old theory ("are arranged molecule-wise," "have mass M," and so forth). But it is very plausible that the meanings of these new predicates are systematically related to the meanings of the predicates of the old theory in such a way that the old theory *analytically* entails the new theory. It's part of the meaning of "are arranged molecule-wise" that atoms which in fact compose a molecule are *ipso facto* arranged molecule-wise. This doesn't depend on the assumption that the predicates of the new theory orthographically contain the corresponding predicates of the old theory. If we had written the new theory using nothing but arbitrary predicate-letters, the meanings of these predicate-letters would still have been fixed in such a way that if the old theory was in fact true, the new theory could not have failed to be true.

   This method is not guaranteed to work – sometimes the new theory one gets by applying (i)–(v) is not entailed by the old theory, or is even contradictory – but for currently accepted scientific theories it works perfectly well.[22] In these cases, since the old theory analytically entails the new one, the new theory cannot be less credible, or less well confirmed, than the old one.[23] Anyone who thinks that science somehow gives us reason to believe in composite objects must therefore maintain that by scientific standards, the old theory is *almost* as well-supported as the new one, so that if we were sure that the new theory were true, we should be almost as sure that the old theory, with all its mereological commitments, was true as well.

   What grounds could there be for believing the stronger, old theory rather than the new one? Given that we are justified in thinking that there are things arranged star-wise, solar-system-wise, and galaxy-wise, what further scientific considerations can be cited in support of the further conclusion that there are stars, solar systems, and galaxies?

To give a really satisfying answer to this question, one would have to point to some piece of *data* that was better explained by the old theory than by the new one. Initially, nothing seems easier: Ordinary science explains why unsupported bricks fall towards the earth, why ice cubes melt, why bombs explode; whereas, far from explaining these things, mereologically neutral science doesn't even commit itself on the question of whether there are such things as bricks, the earth, ice cubes, and bombs. But if we help ourselves to descriptions of the data in terms of composite things, the appeal to science will have turned out to be nothing more than a disguised version of the appeal to common sense. To vindicate the claim that there is some distinctively *scientific* reason to believe some claim about composition, one must describe the data in neutral terms so as not to "beg the question" against the neutralist; we must speak of things arranged brick-wise falling towards things arranged planet-wise, things arranged ice-cube-wise melting, things arranged bomb-wise exploding. When this is done, it is hard to see how the old theory's explanation of the data can be better than that given by the new, mereologically uncommitted theory.

In the absence of a really satisfying answer to the question, we must appeal to "tie-breaking" considerations like simplicity and the rest. Now there can be no doubt that in most cases the old theory is more familiar, more convenient to use, more perspicuous, and so on. But as we have seen, it is not at all obvious that these virtues by themselves ever count by scientific standards as reason for belief. For our judgments about relative simplicity of theories to have clear weight in justifying belief, we must abstract away, to some extent, from merely practical considerations. There is some question whether this abstraction needs to be total: maybe the Martians have scientific theories which are empirically equivalent to ours but which are so alien to our ways of thinking that we can be justified in disbelieving them on those grounds alone. The mereologically uncommitted substitutes for our current scientific theories are not like that, however. They are well within our grasp; we could talk that way if we wanted to, although it would be awkward and time-consuming. They preserve all of the structural features of the theories they are based on, so that scientists themselves (with their lax standards for theory individuation) are liable to treat them as notational variants of a single theory. Given all this, it would be dogmatic scientism at its worst to suggest that science as we find it requires us to believe in the real existence of composite entities.

As we have said, the algorithm described in steps (i)–(v) does not always succeed in producing a mereologically uncommitted weakening of a theory. In certain cases it generates a contradiction. This happens when the original theory entails the falsehood of one or more of the axioms of mereology; it also happens when the original theory entails the existence of atomless gunk.[24] What happens if our current best scientific theory of something or other is like this? Does the appeal to science then justify us in having some substantive view about composition?

We doubt it. First, consider what a theory would have to be like to conflict with mereology. One way for a theory to put itself at odds with mereology is for it to be the conjunction of some ordinary scientific theory with some tendentious independent claims about composition. We can find a mereologically uncommitted rival to such a theory just by dropping the additional claims, and then applying the algorithm as before. The task becomes somewhat more difficult when the mereological presuppositions of the theory are more tightly woven into the science. For example, we can imagine a version of physical theory in which the question "How many other things have exactly the same parts as a given object?" – a question whose answer is always "None," according to mereology – plays an important role in predicting the behavior of that object. Say that X is bad if and only if it has exactly the same parts as another object. Then there might be a law according to which bad things repel one another while attracting things that are not bad. The strategy for eliminating the mereological presuppositions from theories like these is clear: We replace mereological predicates with new predicates. For example, instead of speaking of "the number of other objects which have exactly the same parts as x," we can just speak of "the P-number of x," leaving it open what something's having a given P-number might amount to. We can then apply the algorithm to the revised theory.

The only theories we can think of which contradict the axioms of mereology are trumped-up and artificial. By contrast, it is possible to develop natural, unified scientific theories that entail the existence of gunk. Initially it might seem that a physics of gunk would have to be very unlike any theory of physics that has been seriously entertained since the seventeenth century. For all of our theories, since then, have used a geometric framework that is most naturally interpreted as a way of talking about certain *point-sized* entities.[25] But Whitehead showed how the believer in gunk can give an alternative interpretation of the framework, using nested sequences of pieces of gunk as surrogates for point-sized things.[26]

Nevertheless, it is hard to see how a gunk-postulating theory could ever be decisively superior to its mereologically uncommitted rivals from a scientific point of view. Given a gunk-postulating theory consistent with the axioms of mereology, it is not hard to come up with a new, gunk-free theory modeled after it, by adding some extra things ("points") not posited by the original theory. The gunk-free theory will of course not entail the gunk-positing one, but if we do the construction correctly it will entail that the gunk-positing theory comes out true when all quantifiers are restricted to things other than the points.[27] Having generated a gunk-free theory in this way, we can then apply the algorithm to generate a mereologically uncommitted theory which is equivalent to the original gunk-positing theory for all scientific purposes. This theory will not be entailed by the original theory. But it seems sure to be a strong competitor, and it is doubtful that any properly scientific considerations could favor the gunk-positing theory over the mereologically uncommitted one.[28]

Of course we cannot predict what the future will bring. It is conceivable that science will someday provide grounds for believing, with Anaxagoras, that "neither is there a smallest part of what is small, but there is always a smaller."[29] Our point is not that these issues are absolutely, in principle, immune to resolution on scientific grounds. It is rather to stress that even given the widespread commitment to composite things in extant science, compositional nihilism remains on the table.

8 Problem or Pseudoproblem?

The true principle of composition – whatever it may be – is neither analytic nor straightforwardly empirical. If it is knowable at all, it must therefore be a synthetic a priori proposition, and a non-evident one at that. We do not deny the existence of such principles. It may be – it *may* be – that the truths of mathematics, the truths of ethics, the principles of metaphysics, and the like must be accorded such a status. Our case for agnosticism about composition does not depend on the rejection of synthetic knowledge a priori. It is rather the upshot of having canvassed the main sources of grounds or evidence and come up wanting. In other domains in which substantive a priori knowledge appears to be possible, one ultimately comes upon principles which, though clearly synthetic, nonetheless strike us as obvious or indisputable, perhaps on pain of incoherence. These underived principles need not be obvious. It is not a platitude that "whatever looks luminous does not look gray."[30] But on reflection, the claim "strikes us" as clearly correct, and this fact plays a central role in the account of what (if anything) justified its acceptance.

In our opinion, there is nothing analogous in the case of principles of composition. Upon reflection, unrestricted composition is a contender; but so are certain more restricted principles, perhaps including nihilism. Close your eyes and think through the alternatives. Some will strike you as more "plausible" – but that is the appeal to common sense, which we have rejected. None will strike you as evident, as indisputable on pain of incoherence, or so we say. The choice is a choice among coherent alternatives. And for the present we see no basis on which it might be made.

Now some philosophers are profoundly impatient with this sort of question. The will say – or try to say – that the appearance of an epistemological impasse is based on a mistake. The most straightforward version of this gambit proceeds as follows:

Take the two extreme alternatives, nihilism and universalism. On the face of it these seem like different, incompatible theories. They appear to disagree, for example, about the number of objects in R. But this appearance is misleading. The two parties employ distinct "conceptions" of an object. When they make seemingly incompatible claims of the form "There are *n* objects in R," in effect, they mean different things by their words. Nonetheless, any description of the world framed in terms of one account can be translated into a description framed in terms of the other *without remainder*. And when these translations are borne in mind it turns out that the two sides do not really disagree at all. Consider the following exchanges:

First exchange:
Nihilist: I don't believe in composition. There are only three objects in R; there is no such thing as a house or a brick, only atoms arranged house-wise and brick-wise, and so on.

Universalist: I agree completely, but from my point of view, you have expressed yourself misleadingly. I see from what you say that your quantifiers are restricted. When you say "There are only three objects in R," what you mean is expressed in my language by the sentence "Considering only the atoms, there are only three things in R." When you say that there are no houses, etc., what you mean is that considering only the atoms, there are no houses, etc. In general, when you say "For all x..." or "For some x...," what you really mean is "For all x, if x is an atom..." or "For some x, x is an atom and..." Your quantifiers are thus restricted, whereas mine are wide open, ranging over everything there is. In order for me to say in my language what you say in yours, I must make the restriction to atoms explicit. But when I do, I agree wholeheartedly with what you say.

Second exchange:
Universalist: I believe in unrestricted composition. Given n atoms, there exist $2^n - 1$ objects altogether. So there are seven things in R. There is an object composed of your head and my body, etc.

Nihilist: I agree completely, although from my point of view you have expressed yourself misleadingly. I see from what you say that your quantifiers always fall within the scope of a tacit operator. When you say that there are really seven objects in R, what you say is better expressed in my language by the claim that *if unrestricted composition were true and the atoms were arranged just as they are, there would be seven objects in R*. When you say that there exists a scattered object composed of your head and my body, you mean that such a thing exists, *according to the mereological fiction*. In general, when you assert a sentence S, what you say is better expressed in my language by the sentence "So far as the atoms are concerned, things are as if S were true." You routinely speak from within a tacit fiction. You convey information about the configuration of atoms in actuality indirectly by speaking counterfactually about how things would be if there were composite things. I speak directly, without a detour through fiction. In order for me to say in your language what you say in yours, I must make this fiction or hypothesis explicit. But when I do, I agree wholeheartedly with what you say.

If either of these proposals were correct, the dispute would be merely verbal: Both sides could be right. In an interesting variation on this suggestion, Hilary

Putnam has proposed that since the crucial claims of synonymy are indeterminate in truth-value, there is no fact of the matter as to whether the two parties disagree.[31] Against this, we maintain that the translations in question clearly fail to preserve meaning. To be sure, they may be adequate translations for certain purposes. The disputants might well want to *pretend* that their respective translations are correct, so as to enable them to talk about other things without always being distracted by their disagreements about mereological matters. But this kind of pretence must be distinguished from a serious interpretation of another person's opinions. This is made vividly apparent when we imagine the following continuations of the dialogues:

First exchange, continued

Nihilist: Who are you to tell me that my quantifiers are restricted? When I say that composite things do not exist, I mean that among all of the things there are, with no restrictions or qualifications (pound table, stamp foot) there is no such thing as a composite object. You yourself have been known to say "There are composite objects" in expressing your view. Focus your mind on the claim you made by using these words: it is the negation of *that very claim* that I mean to express when I say "There are no composite objects."

Second exchange, continued

Universalist: Who are you to tell me that my claims are prefixed by a tacit operator? When I say that there exist seven objects in R, I am not talking about what would have been the case if some far-fetched conjecture were correct; I am not talking about what is so according to some false story. I am speaking strictly and literally and without ellipsis. My view is that in the actual world – forget about the others – the principle of unrestricted composition obtains. You yourself have been known to say "There exist some things which compose nothing." Focus your mind on the claim you made by using these words. It is the negation of *that very claim* that I mean to express when I say that whenever there are some things, there is something they compose.

The availability of these responses rules out the idea that the dispute must be merely verbal. If the universalist and the nihilist respond in these ways, then we have no option but to take them at their words.

What To Do?

We thus have no choice but to regard the dispute as genuine. And yet it is quite unclear how it is to be resolved. We have not shown that there is no straight solution. In particular we have not shown that considerations of philosophical theory cannot do the trick. Principles of composition may not be self-evident; but they do interact with other principles in metaphysics, and it may be that the only satisfying systematic account of problems in other areas – problems of identity over time, problems about causation, or problems in the theory of universals, for example – are consistent with only one (or only some) principle(s) of composition. We cannot hope to survey every possible argument of this form. Let us suppose, however, that at this stage in our reflections, we find ourselves at an impasse. Let us suppose that we do not know what to think. This raises a practical question. What should we do? How should we speak? What attitude should we take towards those aspects of science and common sense which appear to make claims about composition?

In some areas the agnostic's predicament is less than urgent. If you have no opinion about the age of the earth or the extinction of the dinosaurs, then you should not pretend you do. If someone asks you what you think, you should say, "I don't know," and you should not assert any statement which entails a position on these topics. When it comes to principles of composition, however, this sort of abstention is not an option. To refrain from *talking* about composite things is to refrain from talking altogether, at least if one is constrained to speak ordinary English. And this is not just a point about outward speech. We have no way to think about the world we live in, whether for practical purposes or for more purely intellectual ones, without invoking composite things of various sorts. You are hungry and you wonder whether there's an apple in the fridge; so you do your best to remember whether you saw one there last time you looked. If you doubt whether apples exist strictly speaking, then you are not in a position to ask this question much less to answer it by normal means. But if you can't think about what to eat, you're in trouble. What to do?

Here's our advice. There are two sorts of attitudes one can adopt to the settled claims of common sense and science – the claims one is prepared simply to affirm without reservation, whether in conversation or in one's own practical thinking. One can regard these claims as strictly and literally true: that is the default option. But one can also regard them as in one way or another apt or adequate, where aptness and adequacy fall short of truth. Perhaps the clearest everyday examples of this phenomenon occur in figurative speech. I may express my disgust with my unpleasant neighbor by saying (or thinking) "Fred is the most hideous man alive" without believing that my claim is strictly true. Another example, perhaps more pertinent for our purposes, is everyday discourse about the content of a fiction. When you ask me what happened in the film, I may answer by saying, "A young woman in New York gave birth to the Antichrist." Now I don't believe that this sentence, taken literally, expresses a truth. But that doesn't matter, because when I uttered it I was expressing a different belief, a belief about what happened in the film. I wasn't committing myself to the literal truth of the sentence. I was committing myself, rather, to its truth *in the movie*.[32]

As we have suggested, we do not ordinarily maintain conscious reservations of this sort about what we say concerning parts and wholes. When the chemist says that a water molecule is made of two atoms of hydrogen and one of oxygen, he does not take himself to be speaking figuratively. If you ask him whether his claim is meant to express the sober truth, he may well say, "Yes, of course; this is serious business." Nonetheless, apprised of the considerations we have rehearsed in this essay, he may be inclined to back off from his confident claim about composition. If he is canny he may say, "I'm not sure whether what I said is strictly true. But what I am sure of is this: what I said was *true on the assumption that composite things such as molecules exist.*"

There are in fact many different statuses short of strict and literal truth which one might claim for sentences about composite objects whose strict and literal truth is cast in doubt. One such status is that of *atomistic adequacy*. Roughly, we can say that a sentence is **atomistically adequate** iff it is true, or would be true if the facts about composition were different but all else were just as it actually is. If precision is desired, it can be supplied using "possible worlds" talk: a sentence is atomistically adequate iff it is true at some world that is *atomistically equivalent* to the actual world; two worlds are **atomistically equivalent** iff they share a *mereological closure*; the **mereological closure** of a world *w* is a world where everything that exists at *w* exists and is exactly as it is at *w*, and there also exist just enough extra things to make the principle of universal composition true.[33]

Atomistic adequacy is a particularly undemanding status. A sentence and its negation can both be atomistically adequate: this will be true whenever S says that certain things compose something. There are many more demanding statuses which lack this feature. For example, there is *truth according to the fiction that composition is universal.* This can be thought of as equivalent to truth at the mereological closure of the actual world. Likewise, for any other theory of composition, we can speak according to the fiction that that theory is the correct one. A sentence is true according to the fiction that *T* is the correct theory of composition iff it is true at all the worlds which are atomistically equivalent to the actual world, and at which *T* is true.[34]

We can explicitly disavow commitment to the literal truth of sentences about composite objects. We can prefix a sentence like "Water molecules are composed of hydrogen and oxygen atoms" with an operator like "On the assumption that composite things exist . . . ," or "It is atomistically adequate that . . . ," or "Doubts about the existence of composite entities aside. . . ." But of course it would be tedious to speak in this way at any length, just as it would be tedious to keep saying "in the movie, this" and "in the movie, that" when discussing a film. The solution is to adopt a general policy of committing oneself only to the atomistic adequacy (or truth according to some theory of composition) of what one says or thinks. One may begin to regulate one's speech and explicit verbalized thought, not by what one takes to be strictly true, but rather by what one takes to be true on the hypothesis or assumption that one or another principle of composition is correct. This principle need not be a fully worked out theory of composition. It might even be the vague principle that several things compose a single thing when they are sufficiently "unified" or "connected." The vague principle is objectionable if construed as a serious theoretical claim. It seems to entail the deeply obscure doctrine that it is a vague matter how many things there are.[35] But there is no comparable obstacle to employing the vague principle as a fiction that guides our thought and talk.

There is no doubt that this is a feasible policy. Consider the mariner who knows full well that Copernicus was right. When he is navigating he speaks and thinks in Ptolemaic terms. In the midst of a storm, when things are urgent, he may have no conscious reservations about what he says or thinks. Nonetheless, when he says "If Venus has crossed the moon, we're off course" he is not committed to its truth. His official view, his genuine view, is that Copernicus was right and that his Ptolemaic remark is a useful fiction.

It is possible to regard the idea of composition as a fiction to live by. We speak as if composite things were ubiquitous. But we need not, in so speaking, take on a commitment to this hypothesis. We may take a light-hearted stance toward our discourse about composition. So far as we can see, there is nothing unreasonable in this policy. It is, after all, merely a retreat to a weaker set of commitments than is usual, and again, so far as we can see, nothing of scientific or practical importance is thereby lost.

Is anything lost? That remains to be seen. We have already mentioned that for certain philosophical purposes, it may turn out to matter whether composite things in fact exist. It is plausible, however, that at present, no such consideration decides the question. If you agree, then our fictionalist agnosticism should seem like an attractive option. We have no serious alternative but to speak as if we knew a great deal about when several things compose a single thing. But on reflection, it is hard to see how we could have such knowledge. Would it be better to know? Of course it would. But in the meantime we need an alternative to the bad faith that comes from pretending to know in "daily life" what one does not know in philosophy. The fictionalist stance we have described is designed to serve this purpose. The ambitious metaphysician will not be satisfied. She wants to know how things stand simply for the sake of knowing. We do not disparage this ambition – far from it. But until it can be realized, fictionalism strikes us as preferable to dogmatic acquiescence in "common sense" or in the sciences.

Notes

1   Peter van Inwagen, *Material Beings* (Cornell University Press, 1990).
2   Is this a coherent view? See below, §6.
3   For an English translation of Lesniewski's work on mereology, see "On the Foundations of Mathematics," *Topoi*, 2 (1983). See also Goodman and Leonard, "The Calculus of Individuals and its Uses," *Journal of Symbolic Logic*, 5 (1940); Eberle, *Nominalistic Systems* (D. Reidel, 1970); Lewis, *Parts of Classes* (Blackwell, 1990), §3.4; and for an extensive discussion, P. Simons, *Parts: A Study in Ontology* (Oxford, 1987).
4   This innovation in its modern form is due to Lewis, *Parts of Classes*.
5   Thanks to Mark Johnston for the example.
6   There are other ways to think of the conga line. One might, for example, think of it as an *event* or *state of affairs* of a certain kind, towards which Fred is related, not as a

part, but rather as a *participant*. The "participation" relation has not been widely studied. But it is not implausible that it will fail to be transitive.

7   The claim concerns sentences and tunes considered as *types*. The sentence *tokens* "John loves Phil" and "Phil loves John" are made of distinct bits of ink. But the sentences themselves are not made of ink at all. If it makes sense to say that they are made of anything, they are made of words, and on the face of it, the very same words.

8   Goodman, *The Structure of Appearance* (Harvard, 1951), ch. 2.

9   One of us favors the answer "At least eight": Three atoms, four mereological fusions, and the genuine molecule AB. What's the difference between the mereological fusion A + B and the genuine molecule AB? They occupy just the same space, and exhibit just the same manifest behavior. Nonetheless, they differ modally. The genuine molecule would not have existed if A and B had never been connected to one another. The fusion, by contrast, would have existed even if A and B had been at opposite ends of the universe.

10 The commonsense account has not been formulated as an explicit principle, so the claim of formal consistency does not apply. But there is no doubt that the commonsensical description of R is logically consistent.

11 This is not to say that you cannot see composite things. If A + B exists, you may see it when you look at it. The point is rather that in this case, given the background of theoretical disagreement, seeing X is not sufficient for knowing that X exists.

12 Strictly speaking, of course there is no such thing as *the* commonsense response. The point is that someone who responded in this way would not strike us as odd or bizarre. In this sense, the response is at least compatible with a commonsense view of the matter.

13 This statement of the argument is due to van Inwagen, *Material Beings*, p. 73.

14 This is the attitude taken by van Inwagen, *Material Beings*.

15 Cf. van Fraassen, "'World' is not a Count Noun," *Noûs*, 29 (1995).

16 Gilbert, "The RNA World," *Nature*, 319 (1986), p. 618.

17 Orgel, "The Origin of Life on the Earth," *Scientific American*, October 1994, pp. 77–83.

18 Maddy, *Naturalism in Mathematics* (Oxford, 1997), ch. 2, §6.

19 The main ideas are implicit in van Inwagen, *Material Beings*.

20 Understand all these plural expressions in such a way that there is nothing contradictory in claiming that there are some things such that there is only one of them. So it may be compatible with our new chemical theory that atoms are single things – that is, whenever there are some things arranged atom-wise, there is always necessarily only one of them. By contrast, since it followed from the old theory that most molecules have more than one part, it will follow from the new theory that mostly, when there are some things arranged molecule-wise, there are more than one of them.

21 What do we do if the old theory contained *plural* quantifiers? It seems that in that case we will need to introduce "pluplural" quantifiers in the new theory, quantifiers which stand to plural quantifiers just as plural quantifiers stand to singular ones (see Allen Hazen, "Relations in Lewis's framework without atoms," *Analysis*, 57, 1997). Ordinary language doesn't contain any clear examples of such quantifiers, though it does, arguably, contain "pluplural" referring expressions ("the Beatles and the Stones" might be an example, on one of its disambiguations). Some philosophers have claimed not to understand such quantifiers. Others have claimed to be able to understand them only as disguised quantifiers over sets. The question of what implications this view, or

the related view that *plural* quantifiers are only intelligible as quantifiers over sets, would have for our proposal is too deeply embedded in the philosophy of mathematics for us to address here. In any case, few extant theories in science seem to make any essential use of plural quantifiers.

22   This assumes that the theory in question is formulated in such a way that predications having the form "x is part of y" are made *tenselessly*. If the theory uses the notion of tensed parthood – so that "x is part of y at t" can be true without "x is part of y at t" being true, a more elaborate version of the algorithm needs to be used, since of course "the xs are among the ys" is not the sort of thing that can be true at one time and not at another. The more elaborate version of the algorithm introduces a new four-place predicate taking two plural expressions and two times as arguments to do the work done in the old theory by identity through time. The new translation of "x is F at t" is "there exist a t and some ys such that R (the xs, t, the ys, t') and the ys are arranged F-wise at t'."

23   This echoes an argument of van Fraassen's. See, for example, "Empiricism in the Philosophy of Science," in Churchland and Hooker, eds., *Images of Science* (Chicago, 1995), p. 294.

24   If the algorithm does not generate a contradiction, it may still fail to geneate a theory entailed by the original theory. For example, applying the algorithm to the theory "Either there are some things that compose two different things, or there are no stars" gives us something logically equivalent to "there are no things that are arranged starwise," plainly not a consequence of the original theory. In general, the algorithm runs into trouble when the theory we start with is one according to which the non-mereological facts – those to which even the new theory generated by the algorithm is sensitive – depend somehow on mereological facts which contradict the axioms of gunkless mereology. For the algorithm to be successful, each possible world at which the original theory is true must be *atomistically equivalent* to a world at which the original theory is true, the axioms of mereology are true, and there is no gunk.

25   Couldn't there be a point-sized piece of gunk? Perhaps: but why would anyone believe in such things?

26   Whitehead, "The Method of Extensive Abstraction," chapter 4 in *The Concept of Nature* (Cambridge University Press, 1920).

27   This is a consequence of Stone's Representation Theorem for Boolean algebras (see Hazen, *Relations in Lewis's Framework*, p. 246).

28   Sometimes an inductive argument in support of the gunk hypothesis is suggested (e.g., by Ted Sider, "Van Inwagen and the Possibility of Gunk," *Analysis*, 53 (1993): 285–9, p. 286). Macroscopic things turned out to be composed of molecules. Molecules turned out to be composed of atoms. Atoms turned out to be composed of protons, neutrons and electrons. Protons turned out to be composed of quarks. Given this history, isn't it somewhat likely that everything is composed of some other, smaller things? The problem with this argument, in a context where we are trying to decide among theories of composition, is that the mereological nihilist does not accept its premises. According to the nihilist, it did not turn out that molecules were composed of atoms; rather, it turned out that molecules didn't exist. Plainly there is no force in an inductive argument for the conclusion that nothing at all exists!

29   In Kirk, Raven and Schofield, eds., *The Presocratic Philosophers*, 2nd edn. (Cambridge University Press, 1983), p. 360. Cited in Sider, *Van Inwagen and the Possibility of Gunk*.

30   Wittgenstein, *Remarks on Color*, G. E. M. Anscombe, trans. (University of California Press, 1977), p. 7.

31   Putnam, "Truth and Convention," in *Realism with a Human Face* (Harvard, 1990).

32   Given that the sentence isn't literally true, but is true in the movie, is it true *simpliciter* in the context in which it was uttered? Is the case one in which a false sentence is used to express or convey true beliefs, or is it one in which contextual factors allow a sentence to be true without being *strictly* or *literally* true? We adopt no view about which of these accounts is correct, or even whether there is a genuine issue between the two.

33   There are two ways to understand the claim that a sentence is true at a given world. We can consider the proposition that is actually expressed by the sentence, and ask whether *it* is true at the world; alternatively, we can consider the truth of the proposition that would be expressed by the sentence at the world in question. The answer will be the same when the world in question is like the actual world as far as the propositions expressed by sentences are concerned. How should we understand the notion of truth at a world as it occurs in our definition of atomistic adequacy? Perhaps the second way is better. For if compositional nihilism or any other restrictive theory of composition is true, many of the proper names and demonstratives which we normally take to have referents are actually denotationless. If so, according to an influential tradition in the philosophy of language, simple sentences that contain these names either express no propositions at all, or express necessarily false propositions. To get the result that "Mars is a planet" is atomistically adequate even if there are no planets, we need to take account of the fact that "Mars" *would* have had a referent if certain particles arranged planet-wise had composed something.

34   This account of the semantics of "according to the fiction" is too simple to be quite right. It breaks down when there is no world atomistically equivalent to the actual world at which the relevant theory of composition is true. This will happen, for example, if the actual world contains counterexamples to Uniqueness of Composition and the theory is classical mereology. It will also happen if the actual world contains gunk and the theory is compositional nihilism or some other restrictive theory. A more sophisticated sort of semantics would be required to settle what to say in such cases.

35   See Lewis, *On the Plurality of Worlds* (Blackwell, 1986), pp. 212–13.

Chapter 9

What Do We Refer to When We Say "I"?

Peter van Inwagen

I will begin by asking you to consider certain words and phrases whose meanings are obviously closely related – closely enough that you will see what I mean if I say that these words constitute a family: 'soul', 'self', 'person', 'ego', 'I' (used as if it were a common noun, as when Descartes refers to 'this I'), 'mind' (used with the implication that the things it refers to are *objects*, substances in the metaphysical sense of 'substance'). I think you will agree that the meanings of these words are indeed closely related. Perhaps you will also agree that it is not always entirely clear what these words do mean, or how their meanings are related. Questions about the meanings of and the relations between the meanings of the words in this family are, in my view, best framed in terms of their relations to 'I' – the first-person singular pronoun, that is, not the pseudo-noun. Thus, for example, we can explain the difference between St. Thomas's and Descartes' use of 'mind' and 'soul' (*mens* and *anima*) by pointing out that Thomas did not think that when he used the word 'I' (or 'ego' or whatever) he referred to his mind or his soul, and Descartes thought that when he used the word 'I' he referred to both his mind and his soul. Or here is an autobiographical example: whenever I hear present-day philosophers going on about "selves" – asserting, perhaps that modern neurobiology has exploded the old myth of the self or that the self is a social construct or that Descartes was mistaken in thinking that a sharp boundary could be drawn between self and world – the first thing that I always ask these philosophers is whether, when I use the word 'I' I refer, or at least am attempting to refer, to one of these "selves" (my own, of course). After all, if there are selves and if, when I use the word 'I' I refer to something, it would seem that it must be my Self I refer to.[1] Or if there is such a thing as my Self, and I do *not* refer to it when I use the word 'I', how could it be correct to call this thing my Self? It is not I, it is rather something numerically distinct from me, and how can something that is not I be properly called my Self? Or, if the philosophers I am talking to are of the party that holds that selves are myths, I ask them whether their position is that they do not exist – for if they exist, then, of course, each time one of them uses the word

'I', that use refers to something, and what could that referent be but the self of the speaker? These questions may seem to some to be trivial quibbles on my part, but they are no such thing. They confront the philosophers who talk of selves with a dilemma I have never seen satisfactorily resolved. If they say, "Yes, that's just what your Self is (or that's just what it would be if there were such a thing): what you refer to when you say 'I'," then their theses almost invariably turn out to be nonsense or obviously false or so obviously true that it is hard to think why anyone would bother stating them. (Modern neurobiology has obviously not shown that there are no such things as you and I.) Or, if they say, "No, that's not what your Self is – your Self is not you but something numerically distinct from you; it is [or 'is supposed to be'] something you *have*; it's not what you *are*," then they are never able to give any real explanation of what they mean by 'self': their attempts at explanation turn out to be so much semantical arm-waving.

Well, then, what *do* we refer to when we say 'I'? I am sorry to say that there seem to be nine possibilities. I begin with this one:

(1)   We refer to nothing.

Many philosophers have endorsed this position. The endorsements are mostly of two sorts: the old-fashioned "Humean" sort, or the more modern "Wittgensteinian" sort.[2] Hume, or so I interpret him, held that there is just nothing *there* for the word 'I' to refer to. If there were, we should be able to find it in introspection, and we find no suitable referent for the word when we enter most intimately into what we call *ourselves*. What we find in introspection are impressions and ideas that would be qualities of the referent of 'I' if it had one; but since (we find) there is nothing "in there" to be the referent of the word, there are only the impressions and ideas, free-floating qualities that inhere in no underlying substance. One who took the general Humean line might of course say that the word 'I' referred to some *collection* of these qualities, but collections of ideas aren't really suitable candidates for the referent of 'I' (or so it might be argued) because it is part of the meaning of the word 'I' that its referent is something that persists through changes of qualities, and that is just what collections of qualities don't do. The Wittgensteinian view, most clearly stated in Elizabeth Anscombe's well-known essay "The First Person,"[3] is that it is not the function of the word 'I' to refer; the word is thus unlike "the present king of France," which is in the denoting business but is a failure at it; rather, the word, despite the fact that it can be the subject of a verb or (usually in its objective-case guise, 'me') the object of a verb, is not in the denoting business at all. Thus, for Hume, the word 'I' refers to nothing in the way 'the present king of France' refers to nothing; for Professor Anscombe, the word 'I' refers to nothing in a way more like the way in which 'if' and 'however' refer to nothing.[4]

The remaining eight possibilities – all, of course, cases of "We refer to something' – are generated by the possible ways of picking one each from the pairs 'transitory'/'lasting', 'enduring'/'temporally extended',[5] and 'material'/ 'immaterial'. ('Physical' and 'natural' might be alternative readings for 'material'.) They are:

(2)   We refer to something transitory and enduring and material.
(3)   We refer to something transitory and enduring and immaterial.
(4)   We refer to something lasting and enduring and material.
(5)   We refer to something lasting and enduring and immaterial.
(6)   We refer to something transitory and temporally extended and material.
(7)   We refer to something transitory and temporally extended and immaterial.
(8)   We refer to something lasting and temporally extended and material.
(9)   We refer to something lasting and temporally extended and immaterial.

The most common answers to the question "What do we refer to when we say 'I'?" are special cases of the general possibilities I have labeled (4), (5), (6), and (8). Some examples would be:

(4)   Many materialists, those who accept an "endurantist" or "three-dimensionalist" theory of identity across time.

(5)   Most idealists (Berkeleyan, not Absolute) and dualists. (All or almost all idealists and dualists are endurantists; it may be that Jonathan Edwards was a dualist and a "temporal extentionalist" – a lonely exemplar of possibility (9).)

(6)   Many materialists, those who accept a "perdurantist" or "four-dimensionalist" theory of identity across time and who hold that an utterance of the word 'I' at the time t denotes a "time-slice" of the utterer, the slice taken at the time t. (These are the philosophers who hold that phrases like 'Peter -now' and 'Peter-at-noon-yesterday' are denoting phrases and that they denote numerically distinct objects, objects related by "gen-identity" rather than identity.)[6]

(8)   Many materialists, those who accept a "perdurantist" or "four-dimensionalist" theory of identity across time and who hold that an utterance of the word 'I' at the time t does not denote the time-slice of the utterer taken at the time t, but denotes rather the "whole four-dimensional individual," the mereological sum of all the time-slices related to t-slice by gen-identity.

My purpose in this essay is not to endorse any one of these positions – I am in fact an adherent of (4) – but to try to show something that seems to me to be important about the two very popular positions (4) and (5): they cannot be coherently combined with the psychological-continuity theory of personal identity. I will argue for the following two conclusions: that any materialist who accepts a psychological-continuity theory of personal identity must accept not (4) but (8); that any immaterialist (any dualist or idealist) who accepts a psychological-

continuity theory of personal identity must accept not (5) but (9). The proponent of a psychological-continuity theory of personal identity, in other words, must
be a perdurantist (or temporal extensionalist) and not an endurantist.

Let us begin by considering a dualist who accepts a psychological-continuity
theory of personal identity. Let us consider John Locke. Locke believes that when
I utter the word 'I', I refer to my soul, to an immaterial substance. He also accepts
– as untold generations of philosophy students have been informed in one of the
first philosophy lectures they have attended – a "memory" criterion of personal
identity.[7] (A memory criterion of personal identity is, of course, a species of
psychological-continuity criterion of personal identity.) Now suppose that in 1990
all my memories were obliterated – that my soul became once more the *tabula
rasa* that, in Locke's view, she was at the beginning of her existence. And let us
suppose that experience immediately began once more to "write" on the tablet of
my soul, or rather the soul that was mine before 1990, and that presently, owing
to this influx of useful information, this soul once more became capable of ratio-
cination and (being still properly connected with the vocal apparatus that had once
been mine) speech. Then she, or the man whose soul she is, is once more capable
of producing meaningful utterances of the word 'I' and, when she does produce
them, they refer to the soul that once was, but is no longer, mine. Let us distinguish "pre-traumatic utterances of 'I' that proceeded from *this* vocal apparatus"
and "post-traumatic utterances of 'I' that proceed from *this* vocal apparatus" – the
"trauma" being the conversion in 1990 of what was till then my soul to a *tabula
rasa*. And let us give the soul that was mine till 1990 the proper name 'Anima'.
It is clear that Locke's philosophy of personal identity entails all three of the following propositions:

> The referent of the pre-traumatic utterances of 'I' that proceeded from this
> vocal apparatus = Anima

> Anima = the referent of the post-traumatic utterances of 'I' that proceed from
> this vocal apparatus

> The referent of the pre-traumatic utterances of 'I' that proceeded from this
> vocal apparatus ≠ the referent of the post-traumatic utterances of 'I' that
> proceed from this vocal apparatus.

(The third proposition is entailed by the memory criterion of personal identity; if
this proposition were false, then the post-traumatic utterer of 'I' could say, and
say truly, "I existed before the trauma" – and this he cannot do if the memory
criterion is correct, since, by definition, he has no memories of anything that preceded the trauma.) But to assert all three of these propositions is obviously to fall
into logical incoherency, for they together constitute a violation of the principle
of the transitivity of identity – and hence, a violation of the principle of the indiscernibility of identicals, of which the transitivity of identity is an immediate consequence. And how does Locke fall into this incoherency? Obviously as a result

of accepting the memory criterion of personal identity, for it is that principle that has the consequence that the person (myself) who called Anima 'I' before 1990 is not the person who later called Anima 'I'.

If this argument is too complicated for your taste, here is a simpler one. Suppose that when I utter the word 'I' I refer to Anima. Then I *am* Anima – for the same reason that if, when I utter "the largest structure in Egypt" I refer to the Great Pyramid, then the largest structure in Egypt *is* the Great Pyramid. That is how reference works. And if I am Anima, then I am logically stuck with being Anima – and Anima is logically stuck with being me, for the plain reason that a thing and itself cannot go their separate ways. And, therefore, Anima is always going to be me (as long as she exists, anyway) no matter what happens to her. If all her memories are obliterated, that will no doubt be a grave misfortune for her, or for the man whose soul she is, but it won't turn her into something or someone else. The thing about logical truisms is, there is just no way round them, and the following is a logical truism: no misfortune, however grave, can turn someone into someone else, for nothing can turn someone into someone else. But the memory criterion of personal identity has the consequence that Anima can be me at one time and someone else at a later time.

The logical incoherency of Locke's position has nothing in particular to do with his belief that when one uses that word 'I', one refers to an immaterial soul. Plenty of materialists have fallen into exactly the same incoherency. If the materialists are right, and if, when I use the word 'I' I refer to something, then I refer to something material – for the only alternative is that I refer to something immaterial, and if I referred to something immaterial, there would *be* something immaterial and materialism would be false. But plenty of materialists believe in the conceptual (if not the technological) possibility of a certain sort of "bodily transfer," and it is these materialists who have fallen into the same incoherency as Locke. Sydney Shoemaker is a good example of a materialist who believes in the possibility of this sort of bodily transfer, or at least takes its possibility very seriously.[8] Shoemaker, although he is a materialist, holds that it is possible for a person to "change bodies" – or at least he holds that there are good reasons to think that bodily transfer is possible, even if these reasons are not absolutely conclusive. And he does not think that changing bodies requires a "brain transplant" or any other procedure that involves moving matter from one human body to another. In his view, it is entirely plausible to suppose that (even if it is not self-evident that) a transfer of the information contained in my brain to a suitably prepared "bland" brain in another human body would suffice for my acquiring a new body – at least if my "original" brain is destroyed or turned into a "blank" in the process. (In the sequel, I will for convenience's sake write as if Shoemaker accepted without qualification the possibility of bodily transfer simply in virtue of a flow of information.)

If we use the common noun 'person' for those things that are referred to by uses of the personal pronouns ('I', in particular), Shoemaker's position is that it is possible for a person (a material thing) to change bodies; Locke's position was that it was possible for a person (an immaterial thing) to change souls. An argument exactly parallel to the argument I used to show that Locke's position was incoherent can be used to show that Shoemaker's position is incoherent.[9] Here is the simple version. Let 'Hylas' be the material thing I refer to when I use the word 'I'. (There must be such a thing if I refer to something when I use the word 'I' and if – as the materialist contends – everything is material. That's logic, as Tweedledee said.) Then I *am* Hylas – for the same reason that if when I utter "the tallest structure in Paris" I refer to the Eiffel Tower, then the tallest structure in Paris *is* the Eiffel Tower. That is how reference works. And if I am Hylas, then I am logically stuck with being Hylas – and Hylas is logically stuck with being me, for the plain reason that a thing and itself cannot go their separate ways. And, therefore, Hylas is always going to be me (as long as he exists, anyway) no matter what happens to him. If all Hylas's memories – *my* memories – are obliterated and their informational content somehow transferred to and caused to be embodied in some appropriately structured but numerically distinct material thing *x*, that will not cause Hylas to become *x*. The thing about logical truisms is, there is just no way round them, and the following is a logical truism: no transfer of information, however perfect, can turn a thing and another thing into a thing and itself, for nothing can turn a thing and another thing into a thing and itself. (Hylas and *x* are a thing and another thing; if Hylas became *x*, Hylas and *x* would be a thing and itself: that is, there would be only one of them. Identity is, after all, identity; it is what it is, and not some other relation.) Bodily transfer by a flow of information is therefore impossible.

It is important to note that in this argument 'Hylas' does not necessarily refer to what is commonly called 'my body' – to a "whole" human organism. Rather, 'Hylas' refers to *whatever* material thing it is that I am. Other possible candidates – other than what is commonly called my body – for the referent of 'Hylas' would be: my brain and central nervous system (which Sellars has called the "core person"), my brain, whichever of my cerebral hemispheres it is that controls my use of language and thus is the source of all those occurrences of the word 'I' that you have been exposed to in this essay (this is the position of Roland Puccetti), my cerebral cortex (commonly supposed to be the seat of conscious experience), my pineal gland (so might Descartes have said in the unlikely event of his conversion to materialism), and a tiny material particle that, although it is probably located somewhere in my brain, has so far eluded the observations of brain-physiologists (R. M. Chisholm once held this view[10]). This argument, therefore, does not assume that the materialist is committed to the premise that I am identical with what is commonly called my body; it assumes only that the materialist – the materialist who does not deny that I and other persons exist – is committed to the thesis that I am identical with *some* material thing. I said that my conclusion was that bodily transfer (in virtue of a flow of information) was impossible. But this way of formulating my conclusion captures its whole content only if – on the assumption that human persons are material things – one's "body" is whatever material thing one is identical with. On this understanding of the word 'body', if I am my pineal gland, then my body is a small pine-cone-shaped outgrowth of my forebrain, and not the whole human organism inside which this little structure makes its home.

Shoemaker has recently tried to show that my argument for the conclusion that (given the assumptions I have made) a person cannot change bodies simply in virtue of a flow of information is mistaken.[11] The mistake, he says, consists in my supposing that those who believe in the real existence of persons – who believe that when one uses the pronoun 'I' one really does refer to something – are committed thereby to the position that persons are *individual substances*, that they are what he calls "(relatively) autonomous self-perpetuators," things that persist through time (at least largely) in virtue of ongoing internal processes or "immanent causation." Consider, by way of contrast, the Privy Council of an autocratic monarch, a body whose continued existence and whose membership at a given time depend on and only on the decree of the monarch. If the Privy Council really exists, it is a good example of a thing that is *not* an autonomous self-perpetuator, since its continued existence and its membership at a time depend entirely on things outside itself.[12] (It is thus unlike a private club, which can gain new members only by the actions of those who are already its members.) And, if we are materialists and believe the Privy Council really exists, we must believe that the Privy Council is a material thing. Suppose that Elizabeth – our autocratic monarch – declares to the Privy Council, assembled in London at noon, January 1, 1590, "I'm giving *you* all the sack. I hereby appoint the following persons to this council." She proceeds to recite the names of ten men all of whom happen to be in York at the moment. Then the Privy Council is translated instantly to York. Despite its being a material object, it manages this translation without ever occupying any point in space between London and York. This translation, it will be noted, does not require even a transfer of information. If we supposed, however, that a person could become a member of the Privy Council only by accepting the offer of an appointment to it, a transfer of information from London to York would be necessary for the translation; but *only* a transfer of information would be necessary, and even in 1590 it was possible to transfer information from London to York without causing any material thing to move from one city to the other. Thus, if Shoemaker is right, there is no *logical* barrier to the translation of a material thing from one place to another simply in virtue of a transfer of information between the places. All that is necessary is that the translated material thing *not* be a substance, an autonomous self-perpetuator, a thing whose identity across time depends on immanent causation.

That the instantaneous translation from London to York of a material thing is a feature of our imaginary case follows simply from the premises that the Privy Council really exists, that *it* is at one moment in London and a moment later in York, and that everything is material. And, Shoemaker argues, since we have strong intuitions that favor the thesis that a perfect transfer of the information in one brain to another brain would (at least under certain conditions) be "person-preserving" – and, more generally, strong intuitions that favor a psychological-continuity criterion of personal identity – we have a strong motivation for

believing that a person can change bodies merely in virtue of a transfer of information from one body to the other. (Locke, of course, could offer essentially the
same argument for the conclusion that we have a strong motivation for believing
that a properly conducted transfer of information from one soul to another would
result in a person's changing souls, and that this belief faces no logical difficulties.)

Does the "Privy Council" example show that it is possible for a material thing
to change places simply in virtue of a flow of information between those places?
I think we can see that it does not if we ask ourselves this question: What material object is the Privy Council? There are, we know, twenty men (men, we are
assuming, are material objects), ten in London and ten in York, who, at various
moments, in some sense make up or constitute the Privy Council. But what is this
"making up" or "constitution"? What relation do these men bear to the Privy
Council? I can't see any relation for this relation to be but that of part to whole.
That is: if τ is the moment of the supposed translation of the Privy Council from
London to York (noon, January 1, 1590), then, immediately before τ the Privy
Council is the mereological sum of ten men in London, and immediately after τ
the Privy Council is the mereological sum of ten men – ten *other* men – in York.
(Mereological summation is defined as follows:

x is a mereological sum of the ys at t = df

At t, all the ys are parts of x, and everything that is a part of x at t then overlaps [shares a part with] one of the ys.

The mereological sum of the ys at t is the unique object that is a mereological sum
of the ys at t.)

One might object that it is a rather naive social ontology that identifies a social
entity like a council, team, corporation, or sect with the mereological sum of its
members. And I would agree: that is to say, I would agree that it is a rather naive
social ontology that maintains that (given that individual human beings are material objects) a social entity is a material object. No doubt it is a much more
plausible thesis that a social entity is some sort of "logical construct." (To say that
General Motors is a logical construct is to say either that 'General Motors' does
not denote anything and that the true sentences in which this term occurs can be
paraphrased as sentences in which it does not occur, or else to say that General
Motors is some sort of set or other abstract object.) But it is essential to the point
of the example that the Privy Council be a material object, and if it is a material
object, there doesn't seem to be any material object for it to be but the mereological sum of its members. If the example is to provide a case of a material object
that is translated from London to York simply in virtue of a flow of information,
then the following must be true: before τ the Privy Council is the mereological
sum of ten men in London, and after τ it is the mereological sum of ten men in
York.

Now suppose that immediately before τ, someone in London had said, "See
those ten men there? I hereby name their mereological sum 'Londinium'." And

suppose that immediately after τ, someone in York had said, "See those ten men there? I hereby name their mereological sum 'Eboracum'." Can it be that Londinium *was* Eboracum? – that 'Londinium' and 'Eboracum' are two names for one thing? If the Privy Council example is to be an example of a material object changing its position simply in virtue of a flow of information between two places, this will have to be the case. Here is a consecutive account of the sequence of events in our story. Londinium was sitting there in London. Elizabeth spoke a few words. Londinium instantly lost all its proper parts and, without having moved, found itself in York with a new set of proper parts – whereupon someone conferred the new name 'Eboracum' on it. And some other strange things may have happened as well. Consider the ten men in York. If, immediately before τ, they had a mereological sum, this object was either annihilated at τ or at least changed some of its parts – it was immediately after τ composed of some five of the ten men who had composed it a moment before, or it was composed of the parts that had a moment before composed York Minster, or something of that general sort. And let's not forget the ten men in London. If immediately after τ they had a mereological sum, either this object was created *ex nihilo* at τ, or else it had before τ a different set of parts, some or all of which it instantly discarded as a necessary concomitant of becoming the mereological sum of those ten men. (I have been assuming that for any *x*s, those *x*s have at most one mereological sum at a given time. Other assumptions are possible – possible in the sense that they are not ruled out by the definition of a mereological sum. Suppose that just before τ, each set of ten men had six mereological sums. Perhaps only one of them, whichever one it was that was the Privy Council, was translated: after the translation, the ten men in London had only five mereological sums and the ten men in York had seven.) And, remember, all these things happened because an irascible queen spoke a few words. If she hadn't said, "I'm giving *you* all the sack. I hereby appoint the following persons to this council . . . ," Londinium would have remained in London and would have continued to be composed of the same ten men.

That this could happen looks to me like an excellent candidate for an incoherent thesis. I concede that I can't derive a formal contradiction from it without introducing a premise that some might dispute. (Any of the following three premises would do: that an object can't instantaneously lose all its proper parts and continue to exist; that if certain objects have a mereological sum at two different times, then their sum at the one time is identical with their sum at the other; that the identity of the mereological sum of a given set of objects can't be determined by a decree, even a royal one.) But, I would ask, is the thesis that Londinium changed position instantaneously a better candidate for ontological coherency than the following thesis: The Prime Minister changed position instantaneously when "he" switched from being John Major to being Tony Blair? Given that Privy Councils are mereological sums of their members, isn't *this* what Elizabeth's decree would cause to happen: Londinium stays in London and continues to be the sum of the same ten men; Eboracum was in York before the decree

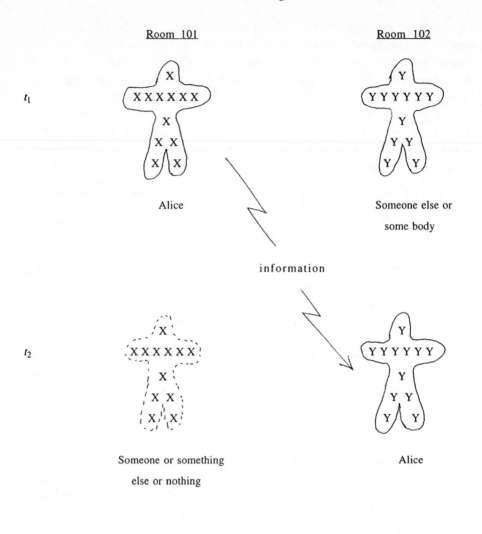

Figure 9.1

and remains in York and continues to be the sum of the same ten men; the title "the Privy Council" is transferred from Londinium to Eboracum?

We can apply essentially the same argument "directly" to Shoemaker-style body-changes. (This application of the argument is illustrated in figure 9.1.)

Suppose we intend to "transfer" our friend Alice "to another body." If Alice really exists and is a material thing, she is now (at t_1) the mereological sum of certain atoms. Here is what would have to take place if we successfully transferred her to another body. The atoms whose sum she is are now in Room 101. (They are represented by Xs in figure 9.1.) Certain *other* atoms (represented by Ys), atoms to be found in Room 102, compose (now, at t_1) some other human being or some human body other than hers. Information and nothing else passes from Room

101 to Room 102 (or "nothing else" besides whatever must, of metaphysical necessity, move from Room 101 to Room 102 if information flows in that way). Solely in virtue of this flow of information, the object that had been the mereological sum of the atoms in Room 101 becomes (at t_2, almost immediately after t_1) the mereological sum of the atoms in Room 102. The atoms that *had* composed that object, the atoms in Room 101, either cease to have a mereological sum or immediately acquire a new mereological sum, and the object that had been the mereological sum of the atoms in Room 102 is no longer the mereological sum of those atoms – either it is destroyed or it becomes the mereological sum of some other atoms.[13] (In the diagram, a solid outline around a group of atoms represents those atoms as having a mereological sum. A dotted outline around a group of atoms represents our declining to take a stand on whether those atoms have a mereological sum.) Well, you can say this and I can't catch you in a formal contradiction – unless I help myself to some premises that you might want to reject. But can you really suppose that your position is coherent? Isn't *this* what would really happen when the machinery was put into operation: Alice stays in Room 101 – or else she is destroyed, depending on what is done with the atoms in Room 101 – and some unfortunate woman in Room 102 is turned into a psychological duplicate of Alice? That is, wouldn't things happen in the way illustrated by *this* diagram (figure 9.2)?

Shoemaker's position is therefore incoherent. At least it has some very odd consequences, consequences that seem to *me* to be incoherent. We may ask Shoemaker to respond to the following dilemma. Consider the story of Alice. In this story, either some material thing that was in Room 101 when the story began was in Room 102 when the story ended, or else no material thing that was in Room 101 when the story began was in Room 102 when the story ended. In the latter case, materialism is false, since Alice was in Room 101 when the story began and in Room 102 when the story ended. But if we say that some material thing that was in Room 101 when the story opened was in Room 102 at the close of the story, we seem to have endorsed the possibility of a kind of "movement" comparable to the movement of the Prime Minister when he changed from being Major to being Blair – which is at the very least an excellent candidate for incoherency.

Now it might be objected that the above arguments, even if they are completely successful, show only that Position (4) is inconsistent with the possibility of bodily transfer (*sc.*, by flow of information) and not, as promised, with the psychological-continuity theory of personal identity; for we have not shown that the psychological-continuity theory entails the possibility of bodily transfer. Here I will simply assume that it would be at least very odd for the proponent of the psychological-continuity theory to reject the possibility of bodily transfer: why *couldn't* the psychological states tokened in one body be continuous with those tokened in another body?[14]

But if you are a friend of body-change operations, do not despair. One can have body-change operations if one does not make the assumption that persons endure

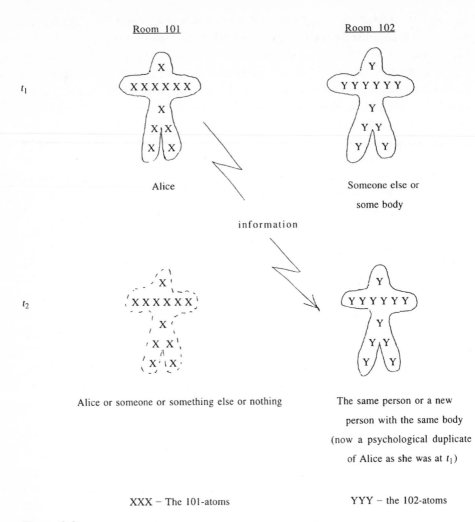

Figure 9.2

through time – that is, if one is willing to make the assumption that persons are extended in time. This is the position of David Lewis, who has applied it to questions about the nature of the human person and the identity of the person across time with his usual technical perfection.[15] The essential trick is this:

> Material objects are four-dimensional things, things extended in time as well as in space: what we normally think of as cases of objects that "endure through time" are actually cases of objects that are extended in time. Any two such four-dimensional objects have a mereological sum that is itself a four-dimensional object. Certain four-dimensional objects count as persons. A four-dimensional object is a person if it is a maximal aggregate of person-stages – a person-stage being a four-dimensional object that would be a person if it existed "all by itself." Leave aside the question of the meaning and purpose of the qualification "maximal." A mereological sum of person-

stages is an "aggregate" if the stages are psychologically continuous with one another in the right sort of way.

Given this view, the outcome of a successful "bodily transfer" between Room 101 and Room 102 may be described as follows. Alice is, like all of us, a four-dimensional object, a maximal aggregate of person-stages. Unlike most of us, however, she is not a spatially continuous four-dimensional object. She is, rather, the sum of two individually spatially continuous aggregates of person-stages that are not spatially connected with each other. The earlier of the two ends in Room 101, and the later begins in Room 102 almost immediately afterwards. Despite the fact that these two aggregates are not spatially connected, they are (owing to the operations of the "bodily transfer machine") psychologically connected, and in the right sort of way for the two aggregates together to form a maximal aggregate of person-stages – that is, a single person.

But to accept the theory of personal identity on which this story is based is to reject position (4) in favor of position (8) – or, if one is a dualist like Locke, to reject (5) in favor of (9): to become a temporal extentionalist. (And it is not simply to become a temporal extentionalist with respect to persons, but with respect to everything temporal. After all, it could hardly be that although *some* material objects, persons, are extended in time, all other material objects endure through time.)

My conclusion is that (4), (5), (8), and (9) are all at least initially viable theories of the nature of the referent of 'I'. Nevertheless, anyone who accepts the possibility of bodily transfer – anyone, in fact, who accepts any sort of psychological-continuity theory of identity across time – cannot accept (4) or (5). That philosopher must become a temporal extentionalist.

Notes

1 Whenever I follow a possessive pronoun like 'my' or 'your' by the word 'self', I will capitalize 'Self' – just to make it clear to the reader that I am not writing 'myself' or 'yourself'.

2 According to Hume and the Wittgensteinians, 'I' refers to nothing because of considerations peculiar to the self or the first person. Other philosophers would endorse this position as a consequence of some very general metaphysical view, one that entails that *all* those things that are normally thought of as individual things are in some sense unreal: Parmenides, Spinoza, the Absolute Idealists, the adherents of certain Eastern religions, Bertrand Russell (at some points in his career), Peter Unger (at some points in his career).

3 G. E. M. Anscombe, *Metaphysics and the Philosophy of Mind: Collected Philosophical Papers, Volume II* (Minneapolis: University of Minnesota Press, 1981), pp. 21–36.

4 This comparison is mine and not Anscombe's. It has an important weakness: 'if' and 'however' do not occur in nominal positions, and thus no one is even tempted to regard them as having referents.

5   An enduring object is one that, well, "endures through time"; a temporally extended object is one that is extended in time in a way analogous to the way in which ordinary material objects are extended in space. In an earlier version of this essay, I used the terms 'three-dimensional' and 'four-dimensional' instead of 'enduring' and 'temporally extended'. Richard Swinburne pointed out to me that applying the former pair of terms to an immaterial soul implies that the soul is extended in space, which can hardly be an accurate representation of the views of those who believe in immaterial souls. This was, as Jonathan Bennett likes to say, a fair cop.

6   At least these philosophers hold that the referents of utterances of 'I' are four-dimensional objects if they admit that these referents have to have *some* extension in time, to be "time-slices" that, like slices of bread, have some thickness. It is hard to see how the utterance of an indexical word like 'I' could pick out a time-slice of zero temporal extent – just as it is hard to see how an utterance of 'here' could pick out a dimensionless point in space.

7   Paul Helm has suggested to me that Locke did not hold a "memory criterion of personal identity" – he held rather that the deliverances of memory constitute the primary evidence that we appeal to when questions of personal identity are in dispute. I am willing to grant that there are passages in Locke that support this interpretation; but Locke does sometimes at least talk as if memory *constituted* personal identity. The famous §10 of the chapter "Of Identity and Diversity" the *Essay* is introduced with the rubric '*Consciousness makes personal identity*' and it contains the sentence, "For it being the same consciousness that makes a man be himself to himself, personal identity depends on that only, whether it be annexed only to one individual substance, or can be continued in a succession of several substances." (See also §13 *passim*.) And so Locke has been interpreted by Reid and many other critics. But I have no wish to engage in a controversy about what Locke meant. Let the references to Locke in the present essay be read as references to "the Locke of the textbooks," a possibly historical, possibly fictional, but certainly important figure.

8   The following brief summary of Shoemaker's views is based on his well-known debate with Richard Swinburne on dualism and personal identity. See Sydney Shoemaker and Richard Swinburne, *Personal Identity* (Oxford: Basil Blackwell, 1984), pp. 108–10.

9   The argument that follows is a version of an argument I first presented in my essay "Materialism and the Psychological-Continuity Account of Personal Identity," *Philosophical Perspectives*, Vol. 11: *Mind, Causation, and World* (1997), pp. 305–19. This essay is reprinted in *Ontology, Identity and Modality: Essays in Metaphysics* (a collection of some of my essays on metaphysics), forthcoming from Cambridge University Press.

The argument for the incoherency of Locke's theory of personal identity set out earlier in the present essay is an adaptation of this argument.

10   Dean Zimmerman has tried to persuade me that Chisholm never actually *held* this view. Well, if he did not hold it, he at any rate (to borrow a phrase of Plantinga's) entertained it with a considerable degree of hospitality.

11   S. Shoemaker, "Self and Substance," *Philosophical Perspectives*, Vol. 11: *Mind, Causation, and World* (1997), pp. 283–304. See particularly pp. 300–1.

12   The "Privy Council" example is not Shoemaker's. It is suggested by his list of examples of things that are not autonomous self-perpetuators: "baseball teams, corporations, religious sects." I have used the Privy Council as an example because it might be argued that teams, corporations, and sects incorporate at least some immanent causation.

13   Or this is what would have to happen if, for any *xs*, those *xs* have at most one mereological sum at a time. If a given set of objects can simultaneously have more than one mereological sum, the following might be what happens. Before the transfer of information, both the 101-atoms and the 102-atoms have six mereological sums. One of them, the one that is Alice, is translated from one room to the other, and then the 101-atoms have five sums and the 102-atoms have seven sums.

14   For a discussion of the relation between bodily transfer and psychological continuity, see "Materialism and the Psychological-Continuity Account of Personal Identity," pp. 315–18.

15   See his "Survival and Identity," in David Lewis, *Philosophical Papers, Volume I* (New York: Oxford University Press, 1983), pp. 55–73. The paper was originally published in Amélie O. Rorty (ed.), *The Identities of Persons* (Berkeley: University of California Press, 1976).

Chapter 10

Personal Identity: The Non-Branching Form of "What Matters"

Jennifer E. Whiting

The traditional problem of personal identity is an instance of a general problem about what makes it the case that an object existing at one time is identical to an object existing at some other time. But it is so special an instance that it demands its own chapter here. Its special character is due largely to the fact that persons view their own existence and persistence over time from two different points of view.

We view ourselves "from the outside" just as we view any other animal: we measure ourselves in various ways, notice ourselves doing things we do not understand and form explanatory hypotheses about why we do them, etc. If this were the only way we viewed ourselves, we would probably be content to treat our own identity over time the way we treat the identity not simply of other animals but of material objects in general: as an instance of causal and spatiotemporal continuity under a substance sortal (i.e., common noun, like "man" or "dog", that *sorts* things according the fundamental kinds to which they belong). We would say that I now am identical to the 1986 author of "Friends and Future Selves" because there is a spatiotemporal path (involving no fission or fusion) from the human animal I now am back to the human animal that authored that paper such that there is at every point along that path a human animal whose states have evolved causally from those of the human animal immediately preceding it. Assuming that there is no fission or fusion, there is really only one persisting animal here whose later states are (unlike for example the states of a shadow) largely a function of *its* earlier states and how (given that it was in those states) *it* responded to any external influences to which it was subjected.

What tempts us away from this Aristotelian or "animalist" account of our own persistence is the fact that we *also* view ourselves "from the inside." We – apparently unlike other animals – have experiential memories of particular past experiences, compare our present experiences qualitatively to past ones, reflect on the evolution of our present beliefs, imagine what it will be like to do various things we intend to do, etc. In viewing ourselves this way, we form a conception of ourselves as psychological subjects that can think, experience, and act in different times and places. It then begins to seem possible – especially if like the meditating Descartes we bracket our agency and focus on our subjectivity – that we should someday find ourselves thinking, experiencing, and perhaps even acting, in *different* bodies. Such thoughts do not require Cartesian dualism: a materialist can imagine that she – the *psychological* subject she is – is transferred from one human body to another by means of a brain or cerebrum transplant. The advantage of imagining cerebrum transplants is that they are supposed to leave the brain stem controlling the rudimentary biological functions of the original animal more or less as usual, thus presenting a vivid case in which a psychological subject seems to part company with its animal.

Locke's seminal move – which set the problem as we know it – was to take a continuous *psychological* life to be necessary for the persistence of a *person* in something like the way a continuous *biological* life is necessary for the persistence of an *animal*, and then to run parallel arguments against identifying persons either with Aristotelian animals or with Cartesian souls (Locke, 1975). Just as the persistence of a mere (even human) animal lacking the relevant sort of psychological life is not sufficient for the persistence of the sort of psychological subject he takes a person to be, so too (Locke thinks) the persistence of a bare Cartesian soul lacking the relevant sort of psychological life is *not sufficient* for the persistence of the relevant sort of psychological subject: in order for a *person* to persist from t1 to t2 there must be at every point between t1 and t2 a (unique) psychological subject whose states have evolved causally from those of the (unique) psychological subject immediately preceding it (uniqueness ruling out fission and fusion). Similarly, just as the persistence of a mere animal is not necessary for the persistence of a person (since we can imagine a psychological subject being transferred from one animal body to another), so too (Locke thinks) the persistence of a bare Cartesian soul is *not necessary* for the persistence of a person (since we can imagine a psychological subject persisting throughout changes in the immaterial souls that constitute it in something like the way an animal persists throughout changes in the material particles that constitute it, a continuous train of thought being had by a succession of immaterial souls in something like the way a relay is run by a succession of runners). The naturalness of illustrating continuity of consciousness by means of a process different portions of which might occur in different animals or souls at different times raises a question about the nature of Lockean persons. There are two main possibilities here, each representing actual developments of Locke's basic view.

The first – which I call "Lockean dualism" – is to treat persons as substances distinct from the animals with which they coincide. This differs from Cartesian dualism in allowing (though not requiring) that a person be a purely material substance, one constituted at any given time by the same matter as the animal with which it coincides at that time (leaving open the possibility that it might coincide with different animals at different times). I use "substance" here not as early modern philosophers tend to do, to refer to something simple and indivisible like an immaterial soul or an indivisible particle, but rather in an Aristotelian way: a substance is a *basic explanatory entity* whose existence, behavior, and persistence over time are not reducible to the existence, behavior, and persistence over time of other things (such as the material particles or stuffs of which they are composed). To treat persons as substances in this sense is to be a *non-reductionist* about *persons* in the way Aristotle is a non-reductionist about *animals*.

Aristotle thinks that an animal is a substance whose existence, behavior, and persistence over time cannot be explained simply in terms of the materials of which it is composed: we must introduce talk of the formal or functional capacities that make an animal the kind of thing it is, capacities for the distinctive modes of locomotion, perception, et cetera characteristic of its animal kind. This requires talk of *animal* capacities *as such*. And while Aristotle (1993) speaks of the relevant capacities as capacities of *soul*, his talk of souls is not intended to imply anything like Cartesian dualism. In fact, the point of his hylomorphic view – according to which the soul stands to the body as form [*morphê*] to matter [*hulê*] – is largely to avoid such dualism: he regards most if not all capacities of soul as *essentially embodied*. Aristotle's hylomorphism thus serves as a potential model for a materialist version of non-reductionism about persons and their persistence over time. Even if we cannot explain the existence, behavior, and persistence of a person from the "bottom up" in terms of the materials of which it is composed, we may be able to explain its existence, behavior, and persistence from the "top down" in terms of the formal and functional capacities in virtue of which a person exists and persists over time – capacities for the distinctive modes of psychological activity characteristic of *persons as such*. One point of adopting a "top down" functional approach is to explain the persistence of persons throughout changes in the matter of which they are composed without having to introduce immaterial souls. As long as the existence and persistence of the formal and functional capacities in virtue of which a person exists do not depend on any non-material entities or stuffs, the result will be a materialist version of non-reductionism about persons like that of Sydney Shoemaker, whose functionalist account of the sorts of mental states in terms of which persons are defined is motivated largely by his commitment to materialism. On Shoemaker's non-reductionist view, persons and animals are different *kinds* of things, each with their own distinctive conditions of existence and persistence over time, a person being composed at any given time of the same matter as the animal with which it is associated at that time.

The second way of understanding Lockean persons avoids Lockean dualism by treating being-a-person (or being-a-particular-person) as a *mere attribute* of any animal said to be a person. This sort of view is *reductionist* in the sense in which Derek Parfit now uses that label: it reduces the existence and persistence of a person to the existence and persistence of an animal body (or a series of such bodies) having certain properties. And it treats "person" as a phase-sortal – i.e., as a common noun, like "senator" or "adolescent", that may refer to a substance only during certain phases of its existence. There are different versions of this sort of view corresponding to different kinds of attributes and phase-sortals.

One is the sort of "practical not metaphysical" view some see in Locke's talk of "Person" as a "forensick term." Such views treat being-a-person as a matter of having a certain social status (like being a legal minor) and being-a-particular-person as a matter occupying a particular social position involving entitlements and obligations, a social position that can (like being heir to a throne) be occupied by different human animals at different times ("Person X" functioning like "Crown Prince"). But this is a bad way to read Locke or to develop his view. For there is an important difference between continuity of status or office and what Locke calls "continuity of consciousness." Continuity of status or position is primarily a function of social facts external to the occupants of the status or position, whereas continuity of consciousness is primarily a function of psychological states and their relationships to one another. And it is pretty clear that Locke does *not* take sameness of person to be primarily a function of external social facts. For he grants that our Laws – because it is difficult for courts to establish a defendant's continuity of consciousness or lack thereof with the actual offender – typically *treat* sameness of animal *as if* it were sufficient for sameness of person. But he does *not* think that this fact about how our Laws operate *makes it the case* that sameness of animal *is* sufficient for sameness of person. He suggests that *we* may make mistakes here but that *God* will make no such mistakes come Judgment Day, when B will be punished for crimes A committed if and only if B's consciousness is continuous with A's in the sense that B remembers (or has the capacity to remember) A's crime [*Essay* II. XXVII. 22].

Locke would thus reject a "practical not metaphysical" account of personhood. He aims to capture our intuitive notion of a psychological subject that persists over time in something like the way that a material object persists over time – a subject whose later states evolve causally from its earlier ones, the later states including memories of experiences had in the earlier states, and intentions that have evolved from the intentions formed in earlier states. And he takes continuity of consciousness to play the same role in the persistence of a psychological subject that continuity of biological life plays in the persistence of an animal: it is the metaphysical glue, so to speak, that binds later psychological states to earlier ones in a way such that they are states of one and the same persisting subject. But this threatens to lead to Lockean dualism unless the requisite relations among the psychological states can be treated *as mere attributes* of the animals whose psychological states they seem to be. This is the sort of view towards which Parfit has gravitated. Parfit (1999) reduces the existence of a person to "the existence of a body, and the occurrence of various interrelated mental processes and events". And he treats the persistence of a person over time primarily as a function of the continuity of such mental (or psychological) processes and events. The main difference between such reductionism and Lockean dualism is that such reductionism treats bodies or animals as the basic subjects of the relevant psychological states and relations, whereas Lockean dualism attributes these states and relations to psychological subjects distinct from the animals with which they coincide.

The differences between Parfit's reductionist way of developing Locke's basic view and Shoemaker's non-reductionist way are often overlooked because of their shared commitments to two theses: first, that personal identity consists in non-branching psychological continuity, and second that identity is not "what matters." My aim here is to expose some differences between these two ways of developing Locke's basic view, especially with respect to the second claim, which is intended primarily as a claim about what *should* matter to us (*not* about what *in fact* matters to us).

'Identity' is used here in what is sometimes called the "strict numerical sense": it refers to an equivalence relation that is distinguished from other equivalence relations (i.e., from other relations that are also reflexive, symmetrical, and transitive) by its conformity to the Indiscernability of Identicals (according to which *if a* is identical to *b*, then everything truly predicable of *a* is truly predicable of *b* and vice versa). Personal identity in this sense has traditionally been supposed to matter in two important ways. It has been supposed first, that there is a special "prudential" sort of concern that a person can *rationally* have *only* for her "strict numerical" self; and second, that a person is responsible *only* for actions that she *herself* performed. Our everyday practices of planning for our futures, and of assigning merit and responsibility, are thus supposed to assume the importance of personal identity in the "strict numerical sense." If (as on Humean and Buddhist views) there is no such identity, then our everyday practices seem to be jeopardized.

This helps to explain why metaphysicians like David Lewis are willing to say counterintuitive things in order to protect our right to speak of personal identity in this sense. Lewis (1976) claims that in imaginary cases of personal fission, there were two people there all along, even before the fission (when they were always in the same place at the same time, thinking the same thoughts, etc.). Lewis thinks we need to say this in order to be able to say that each of the fission-products is identical in the "strict numerical sense" to its pre-fission self, which he seems to think is required if we are to say (as he thinks we should) that persons anticipating fission *should* have "prudential" concern for their fission-products.

This characteristically modern obsession with "strict numerical identity" – an obsession not found in Aristotle – seems to me to stem from various factors, including early modern interest in resurrection, social practices and institutions predicated on belief in such identity, and the phenomenology of first-person experience. But the important questions for those who do not believe in resurrection and who recognize the contingency of social practices are whether the phenomenology of first-person experience presupposes strict numerical identity and if so how. My primary aim is to argue that the non-reductionist way of developing Locke's view allows us to recognize the importance of "strict numerical identity" without letting it dominate the metaphysical picture: the dominant questions (to which questions of identity are, however, *relevant*) are questions about the causal and functional relations in virtue of which persons exist in the first place. The non-reductionist view thus allows us to put concerns about "strict numerical identity" in their place, assigning them neither too much nor too little importance.

I

Parfit's argument that "identity is not what matters" involves an imaginary case of fission designed to be as "naturalistic" as possible (1984, ch. 12).

(1)   First, assume (as any neo-Lockean must) that where a Prince's cerebrum is transplanted into a Cobbler's body – with the result that the "product" has all or most of the Prince's memories, beliefs, and character-traits – the "product" is to be identified with the Prince. Parfit uses "identical" twins, but it is enough if the Cobbler's body is *sufficiently like* the Prince's original body that the transplant does not lead to any gross disruption of psychological continuity. So suppose the disruption is no greater than we find in severe injuries involving for example paralysis or loss of limbs.

(2)   Now recall that many actual stroke-victims suffer the loss of function of one of their cerebral hemispheres, and that there is often *enough psychological continuity* between the post-stroke person and the pre-stroke person that neo-Lockeans would say that the post-stroke person is the *same person* as the pre-stroke person.

(3)   Finally, imagine a person each of whose cerebral hemispheres is the locus of enough psychological continuity that a neo-Lockean would grant that *she* could survive the loss of functioning of either cerebral hemisphere, and that she could do so even if the functioning hemisphere were transplanted into another (sufficiently similar) body. Imagine also that her two hemispheres are *equipollent*: each is the locus of exactly the same kind and degree of psychological continuity as the other. Then, keeping in mind actual split-brain phenomena, imagine that *each* of her hemispheres is removed and transplanted into a body qualitatively indistinguishable from the body into which the other is transplanted, the bodies being sufficiently like her original body that there is minimal disruption of psychological continuity. There are now two persons, each of whom stands to the original person, O, in exactly the same relations of psychological continuity (and physical discontinuity) as the other. Let's call them "Lefty" and "Righty" (each with reference to the hemisphere she inherits). Now ask: which (if either) is *identical* to O?

Parfit (with whom Shoemaker agrees) answers as follows:

(4)   Assuming that O had no immaterial soul that might have gone either with Lefty or with Righty, we know not which, there seems to be no *metaphysical* ground for identifying one rather than the other with O. For each stands in exactly the

same relations of psychological continuity and physical discontinuity to O. So we must conclude *either* that *both* are identical to O *or* that *neither* is. But saying that *both* are identical to O, however we interpret that, has unacceptable consequences. On one interpretation, the claim is *distributive*: it is that *each by itself* is identical to O. But that requires us either to respect the transitivity of identity by identifying L and R with one another or to deny the transitivity of identity. And neither of these options seems acceptable. On another interpretation, the claim is *collective*: it is that the *two together* constitute one person, a person with "two bodies and a divided mind". But that would fly in the face of our ordinary concept of person, since each "half-witted" body could be sent her own separate way, without knowledge of the other, to live a complete life with no direct causal relations to the other. Since, then, identifying *both* with O requires us either radically to revise our concept of person or to violate (or deny) the transitivity of identity, it seems that we must (in the absence of immaterial souls that determine identity) conclude that *neither* is strictly *identical* to O, though each is *psychologically continuous* with her.

Fission cases have played important roles in arguments both for and against Lockean views. They were originally introduced by Bernard Williams (1970a) to support a common objection to Lockean views – namely, that psychological continuity (because it is susceptible to branching or "duplication") is not of the right *logical form* to constitute identity. For identity is *necessarily one–one*: although two distinct subjects may each be *psychologically continuous* with a single subject, no two distinct subjects can each be *identical* to one subject. So psychological continuity is *not sufficient* for personal *identity*.

Fission cases have also been used in answering Butler's original objection to Locke. Butler (1736) objected that Locke's view is *circular* because it presupposes what it seeks to explain: P_{t2} can remember P_{t1}'s experiences *only if* P_{t2}'s are strictly *identical* to P_{t1}. So P_{t2}'s memory of P_{t1}'s experiences (or P_{t2}'s capacity to remember P_{t1}'s experiences) cannot be what *makes* P_{t2} identical to P_{t1}. The same objection can be applied to other components of psychological continuity, such as intention-connectedness: a person can intend to perform *only* the actions of her "strict numerical" self. This objection is a problem, however, only for Lockeans who mean to give either a *reductive analysis* of personal identity (i.e., an analysis not itself mentioning such identity) or an *epistemological criterion* that allows us to determine whether or not P_{t2} is the same person as P_{t1} without already knowing that (as we would have to know in order to know whether or not P_{t2} *really* remembered P_{t1}'s experiences). And it is not obvious that Locke means to do either of these things. Nor is it obvious that neo-Lockeans must do so. But many neo-Lockeans *have* wanted to give reductive analyses, and Shoemaker suggests a strategy (adopted by Parfit) for doing so.

Shoemaker (1970) concedes that it is part of our *concept* of memory that the subject who remembers an experience must be *identical* to the subject who originally had the experience. He then articulates an alternative concept that does *not* presuppose such identity. The clearest way to motivate this alternative is to think of L's and R's apparent memories of O's pre-fission experiences. Assuming that these apparent memories are *caused in approximately the same way* that ordinary memories are caused – that is, by memory traces preserved in the brain – we can refer to the generic causal process as "quasi-memory": a subject quasi-remembers an experience if she has an apparent memory of that experience which is caused "in the right way" by the experience itself. This condition is satisfied both by ordinary memories and by the apparent memories of L and R. So *quasi-memory* forms a genus that includes both *ordinary memories* (in which the remembering subject *is* identical to the subject of the original experience) and *mere quasi-memories* (in which the remembering subject is *not* identical to the subject of the original experience). Shoemaker (1984) thus suggests that Lockeans who aim to give a reductive analysis can avoid the circularity objection by defining personal identity in terms of quasi-memory, which does *not* presuppose identity. Parfit makes similar moves with other components of psychological continuity, such as intention-connectedness. His basic idea is to take psychological continuity to consist in these *generic* relations, which do *not* presuppose identity.

Shoemaker's response to the circularity objection renders the duplication objection even more pressing. For if the relations that constitute psychological continuity do not presuppose identity, it becomes more difficult to see how the psychological continuity of P_{t2} with P_{t1} *could* secure the identity of P_{t2} with P_{t1}. But Shoemaker and Parfit find in (2) resources for answering the duplication objection. For they take (2) to show that, if one of the attempted transplants fails and only the left-branch (or only the right-branch) survives, then the survivor would *be* O (i.e., strictly *identical* to O). This does not, as sometimes objected, require them to deny the necessity of identity by saying of any *one* thing that *it* is identical to O though *it* would not have been had the other branch survived. For they can – as Shoemaker (1984) suggests – treat "Lefty" and "Righty" as descriptive terms like "the 43rd President", which refers to different individuals in different possible worlds depending on (among other things) whether or not they count "dimpled" ballots. On this account, O survives in the strict numerical sense in those worlds in which only the left transplant (or only the right transplant) succeeds. In worlds where *both* transplants succeed, O is replaced by two numerically distinct individuals, "Lefty" and "Righty" referring in those worlds to new individuals distinct from those to which they refer in worlds in which only the left (or only the right) transplant succeeds.

Shoemaker and Parfit thus answer the duplication objection by supplementing Locke's basic psychological criterion with a non-branching clause, which secures the logical form required for identity. For *non-branching* continuity is *logically* one–one. On their view, P_{t2} is *identical* to P_{t1} if and only if (a) P_{t2} is psychologically continuous with P_{t1} (psychological continuity now being defined in terms of *generic* relations like quasi-memory, quasi-intention, etc.) and (b) P_{t2} has no simultaneous "competitor" that is equally psychologically continuous with P_{t1}. On this view personal identity *just is* non-branching psychological continuity (Shoemaker, 1970, 1984; Parfit, 1971, 1984).

The non-branching criterion is controversial for various reasons, especially insofar as it makes Lefty's identity (as distinct from "what matters") depend on an "extrinsic" factor (namely, whether or not Righty also exists). But not everyone is troubled by this. For, as Robert Nozick (1981) argues, we often take the identity of things to depend on extrinsic factors. But we cannot enter this controversy here.

Imagine now that Parfit – who accepts that non-branching psychological criterion – has been kidnapped and told that he will soon undergo the sort of fission described above. The possible outcomes are: (A) the operation fails completely and he dies an ordinary death; (B) the operation is only partly successful and only one offshoot survives; and (C) the operation is entirely successful and there result two people, Lefty and Righty, each equally continuous psychologically with OP (original Parfit). What should OP's attitudes towards these outcomes be? OP believes that *he* will not survive in the "strict numerical sense" *unless* there results *only one* subject psychologically continuous with him. Should he – as Swinburne (1973–4) suggests – bribe the kidnapper's assistant to ensure that at most one offshoot results? Parfit thinks not. He argues (1984, ch. 13) as follows.

In the world where the operation is only partly successful and (for example) the left offshoot alone exists, *OP* will survive in the "strict numerical sense" *as* the left offshoot: the left offshoot's existence will involve everything that a case of ordinary survival involves (including everything that "matters") *because* its existence *constitutes* a case of ordinary survival. But in the world where the operation is fully successful and both offshoots exist, the relation between OP and the left offshoot, considered *in itself* and with reference only to its *intrinsic* features, will be *no different* from the relation that obtains between OP and the left offshoot in the world where *only* the left offshoot exists. So in the world where both offshoots exist, the relation between OP and the left offshoot, considered *in itself* and with reference only to its *intrinsic* features, involves everything that is involved in a case of ordinary survival (including everything that "matters"): the only difference is that in this world the right offshoot's relation to OP *also* involves everything involved in a case of ordinary survival. So in the world where the operation is fully successful, OP will have what he has in ordinary survival (including everything that "matters") *twice over*. And, as Parfit asks, "how can a double success be a failure?"

Parfit (1971, 1984) takes this argument to show that identity is not what matters primarily in our survival. For insofar as OP would regard the existence of either L or R *alone* as sufficient for his survival in the "strict numerical sense," OP *should* regard the case in which he is succeeded by *both* as a case in which he has *twice over* what he has in ordinary survival. Parfit thus suggests that we distinguish a person's "survival" from her "identity" over time, "survival" being a generic relation that stands to "unique survival" (*with* identity) and "mere survival" (*without* identity) as "quasi-memory" stands to "ordinary memory" (which *presupposes* identity) and "mere quasi-memory" (which does *not* presuppose identity). His idea is that what we have in fission cases (i.e., survival) is *essentially* the same as what we have in non-fission cases (i.e., survival), and that the "mere" survival we have in fission cases differs *only accidentally* from the "unique" survival we have in non-fission cases. For the same *intrinsic* relations obtain between O and R, *whatever* relations do or do not obtain between O and L. If L proves in the end to be strictly identical to O, that will be a matter of *extrinsic* facts about O's relations or lack thereof to *other* entities besides L. But *what matters* is the *intrinsic* relations.

Parfit's argument is I think largely responsible for the increasingly popular distinction between metaphysical and practical accounts of personal identity. Marya Schechtman (1996), for example, suggests that we reorient discussions of personal identity away from the traditional metaphysical problem about identity in the "strict numerical sense" and focus instead on the popular notion of personal identity that psychologists have in mind when they speak of "identity crises," the notion Schechtman takes to be involved in prudential concern and attributions of responsibility. And Eric Olson (1997) proposes to divide the labor here, leaving questions about personal identity in what he calls the "practical sense" to ethicists while metaphysicians like himself seek to provide a metaphysical account of personal identity in what he calls the "numerical sense." Though Schechtman and Olson are interested in what they take to be different questions, they agree in taking the questions to be distinct. But this seems to me a mistake.

I take this mistake to be due largely to two factors: first, the widespread assumption that the primary (perhaps the only) metaphysical question here is the question about "strict numerical identity"; and second, Parfit's reductionist development of Locke's basic view, which emphasizes the subjectivity of persons at the expense of their agency. We can best appreciate this if we examine some fundamental differences between Parfit's reductionist way of developing Locke's view and the non-reductionist way suggested by Shoemaker. For the non-reductionist way reveals an alternative: we can assign primary metaphysical significance to the causal and functional relations in virtue of which persons exist in the first place. Considerations of "strict numerical identity" will matter here. But they will not matter in quite the way they have traditionally been supposed to matter.

II

The importance Shoemaker attaches to "strict numerical identity" stems from his commitment to a functionalist account of mental states. According to this account, "what constitutes a mental state or event as being of a particular kind (e.g., an experience or a belief having a certain content) is its being so related to a larger system to which it belongs as to be apt to play a certain "causal role" in the workings of that system" (Shoemaker, 1985). Moreover, the larger system is one whose nature can be understood only in terms of operations that play out over time – i.e., only in terms of how *its* being in certain states at one time tends, given certain inputs, to cause *it* to be in other states at other times. The definition of any given mental state is thus a complex and holistic affair involving both synchronic and diachronic relations to other states of the *same system*.

For example, the belief that it is likely to rain today can be caused in various ways and it tends in conjunction with other simultaneous states or dispositions of the system to which it belongs to have certain behavioral and mental effects: it may lead one to go to the launderette where one can use dryers, or to believe that farmers will suffer financially this year. But the belief that it is likely to rain today will function this way only if it is part of *the same system* with various other states, such as (1) a *desire* to do laundry today, (2) a *belief* that there are dryers at the launderette but none at home, (3) a *standing concern* for farmers, connected with (4) a *disposition to notice* their plight, etc. And the relevant systems are typically taken to be *persons*. *Your* belief that it is likely to rain today will *not* interact with *my* desire to do laundry to lead either of us to go to the launderette (unless of course you communicate your belief to me with the result that I come to have the "same" belief). But *my* belief that it is likely to rain today *will* tend to interact with *my* desire to do laundry so as to produce a trip on *my* part to the launderette: indeed the tendency of these states to interact in these ways is part of what *makes* them states of the same person.

What distinguishes this conception of a psychological subject from a Cartesian one is that there is *not* some fact of the matter, *independent* of the causal-cum-functional relations involved, that makes it the case that these states are states of one and the same personal system. On the Cartesian view, the relevant states are states of the same person simply in virtue of being states of the same soul, whether or not these states tend to interact in the relevant ways. But on Shoemaker's functionalist view the states' tendencies to interact in the relevant ways are what *constitute* their *being* states of the same system. So questions about the causal and functional relations among these states involve questions about the identity of the systems of which they are states: if the states in question tend to interact in the relevant ways, then they tend ipso facto to be states of one and the same system. I say "*tend* ipso facto" here so as to allow for the possibility (discussed below) that there may be deviant cases in which such states interact in the relevant ways but are not *ipso facto* states of the same system.

There is limited room here for the beliefs and desires of one and the same person to fail to interact in the normal ways, as in repression and self-deception. But if a human body houses two "subsystems" of belief and desire whose elements are radically insulated from one another in ways such that the elements of one subsystem tend neither to cause nor to be caused by elements of the other, it becomes natural to speak (as some do in cases of "multiple personality") of two persons sharing a single body. One can of course seek to unify the elements of different "personalities" by arguing that it is *possible* for them to be integrated and that it is this possibility (which is presumably a function of their sharing something like the same body) that makes them "copersonal" (i.e., states of numerically the same person). But to the extent that this possibility is supposed to be a function of the independent fact that these "personalities" share the same body, appealing to it threatens to lead away from a Lockean view towards an Aristotelian view in which bodies play the role played in the Cartesian view by souls. So Lockeans should seek to unify these elements by appealing instead to the motivated (and to that extent functionally integrated) nature of their apparent isolation from one another.

The crucial point is that we cannot give an account of the functional relations among the relevant states without giving an account of the copersonality relation; nor can we give an account of the copersonality relation without an account of the functional relations among the relevant states. The functionalist view is in this sense *non-reductionist*: we cannot give an account of personal identity except in terms of the sorts of psychological states and relations among those states characteristic of *persons*, and we cannot give an adequate account of *these* states and relations without introducing considerations of "strict numerical identity." This allows us to say both (1) that we have subjects in the first place only if we have ordinary relations of memory and intention (which are both phenomenologically and in fact "identity-involving") and (2) that these relations provide the context in which there might be "deviant" relations sufficiently like the ordinary ones for us to view them as belonging to the same "quasi" genus.

Consider one's genetic relationship to one's offspring, a relation typically taken to "matter" specially. *If* we take this relationship to matter specially, then we are likely to have genetic concepts of *Mother* and *Father* that lead us to introduce modifiers like "adoptive" or "birth" in referring to subjects who play the social roles typically played by those who stand in the relevant genetic relationship to a child. We are also likely to have derivative concepts such as those of (genetic) *Grandmother, Sibling, Aunt, Cousin*, etc. All of these genetic relationships (as distinct from the social roles associated with them) exist whether or not we recognize them as such or associate them with any distinctive social roles. But the genetic relationship between parent and child is primary. It is *causally* primary insofar as the other relations exist because of it: if people did not reproduce more or less as they do, none of these relations (as distinct from the social relations founded on them) would exist. And it is *conceptually* primary in the sense that the other relationships are *defined* in terms of it: because Harriet, Emily and I have the same parents, they are my sisters and their children are my nieces. It is taking this primary relationship to matter that typically leads to our taking these other relationships to matter. Harriet's and Emily's children carry some of the same genetic material (inherited from our parents) that my own children would, so I can view their children as standing to me in a relationship *like* that in which my own children would stand to me. So if I thought that the genetic relations were what mattered primarily, I would view myself as having similar reasons to care for their children as I have to care for my own: I would regard myself as a kind of "quasi-parent" to my nieces.

The non-reductionist view affords this "egocentric" structure. For various reasons, both evolutionary and cultural, we typically care about our own future selves and take our relationships to them to "matter" specially. Only *we* remember their past experiences and actions – and anticipate their future ones – "from the inside." But if we suddenly found ourselves undergoing fission at not too frequent intervals, we would be likely both to experience and to conceptualize our relationships to our pre-fission predecessors and our post-fission successors in something like the way we experience and conceptualize our relationships to our own "strict numerical" past and future selves: we would seem phenomenologically to remember and to anticipate *their* experiences and actions, and we would probably conceptualize our relationships to them in something like the way we conceptualize our relationships to our "strict numerical" selves. We would develop concepts like that of quasi-memory. But memory would be both causally and conceptually primary: mere quasi-memories would be possible *only because* there were (for a sufficient time) subjects who had genuine memories. So the concept of quasi-memory – even if it could be described generically – would always be derivative from the concept of ordinary memory.

It is important here that fission not occur too often, since we would not in that case have persisting subjects with the sorts of mental states characteristic of persons. How often would be too often is an open question. Every 5 minutes is clearly too often, but what about every 5 months? Suppose that 5 or 10 years was the *average life span* of a "personal subject" (which "comes to be" either in the ordinary way or by the fission of an existing subject and "ceases to be" either in the ordinary way or by itself undergoing fission). And suppose that we could no more know when fission would occur than we now know when death will occur, so that we go on acting more or less as if it will not – at least not too soon. In this scenario, something like ordinary memory and anticipation would still hold *within* the boundaries set by fission, and it would be in virtue of *their* holding *within* these boundaries that we would allow that something *like* them could hold *across* such boundaries. The point is that we need – in order for there to *be* personal subjects in the first place – for there to be psychological states related to one another in the ways that copersonal states are typically related to one another: it must *generally* be the case that subjects *remember* experiences and actions (at least in their relatively recent pasts) and *anticipate* experiences and actions (at least in the relatively near future). For it is only in that case that we have subjects who can then be said to branch and so to stand to numerically distinct subjects in relationships *like* the relationships in which they stand to their past and future selves when branching does not occur. So memory and anticipation – to which considerations of "strict numerical identity" *are* relevant – are both causally and conceptually primary. But it does not follow from this that such identity matters in the way it has traditionally been supposed to matter.

The "egocentric" view allows us to say that *once* we *are* personal subjects (which presupposes *some* copersonal relations among psychological states) we can *then* stand to other such subjects in relations sufficiently *like* those in which we stand to our "strict numerical" selves for our concern for these other subjects to be very *like* (both in its causes and in its justification) the sort of concern we typically have for our "strict numerical" selves. This view is *egocentric* insofar as the relevant sort of concern grows out of – and can only exist in the context of – the existence of personal subjects who persist, numerically one and the same, at least for a time. But such concern need not presuppose the "strict numerical identity" of its subject and object in the traditional sense that such identity is *always* required in order for such concern to be *justified*. The justification of such concern may presuppose only that the object be related to the subject in ways sufficiently *like* the ways in which the objects of prudential concern are *typically* related to the subject of such concern. For we can take concern for one's fission-products to stand to concern for one's "strict numerical" self in something like the way that concern for one's genetic nieces and nephews is often taken to stand to concern for one's own offspring.

<h1 style="text-align:center">III</h1>

The non-reductionist development of Locke's view differs significantly from Parfit's reductionist development of it. Parfit (1999) seeks to reduce the existence and persistence of a person to a body (or series of bodies) and various psychological processes and events standing in certain relations to one another, all of which he thinks can be described in impersonal terms (i.e., without any talk of persons or their identity over time). His view is primarily a "bottom up" compositional view according to which many of the psychological processes and events that, suitably related, constitute a particular person *need not* have been so related. So we *need not* – as on the "top down" functionalist view – introduce talk of persons or their identity over time in order to characterize the psychological processes and events in terms of which persons and their persistence are primarily defined.

There are two common objections to Parfit's impersonal reduction: first, that the relations in which a person's identity over time is supposed to consist *cannot* be described in impersonal terms because these relations *necessarily* include *first-person* thoughts and relations (such as those involved in memory) that *presuppose* the identity of the person whose identity they are supposed to constitute; and second, that there cannot be thoughts without thinkers or experiences without subjects, nor the sort of thoughts and experiences characteristic of *persons* without *personal* thinkers and subjects. Parfit's response is roughly the same in each case: he think that each objection is an artifact of the objector's commitment to a conceptual scheme that one *need not* adopt.

Let's focus on the first objection, since we can in examining Parfit's response to it discern his response to the second. The idea here is that there is no *personal* thinker or subject unless there are *first-person* thoughts and relations of the sort involved in memory and intention. Parfit's response is to deny that the life of a person requires the thinking of I-thoughts. Parfit (1999) claims that we can coherently imagine thinkers who could understand the facts to which a Reductionist account appeals [e.g., the existence of thoughts and experiences standing in certain relations to one another], even though they did not have the concept of a person, or the wider concept of a subject of experiences.

Parfit claims that we can imagine thinking subjects whose lives contain the sorts of events (i.e., thoughts and experiences), and the sorts of relations among these events, that *in fact* constitute the existence and persistence of persons, even though these subjects do *not* think of themselves as persons nor even as thinkers or subjects.

In shifting from *our* conception of the lives of such subjects to their *own* conception of these lives, Parfit is in part replying to the second objection. He is conceding that *we*, given *our* conceptual scheme, *could not* think of the thoughts and experiences of such subjects without ascribing them to thinkers and subjects, but arguing that it is nevertheless possible that there should be *other* thinkers whose conceptual scheme was such that *they* did *not* take thoughts and experiences to be conceptually so-tied to thinkers and subjects. It is partly, he thinks, because of the way *we* think and talk that *we* reject the idea that there can be thoughts without thinkers or experiences without subjects: given what we *mean* by "thinker" and "subject", it is a *conceptual* (but world-involving) truth that there are no thoughts without thinkers or experiences without subjects. But we *need not* think and talk this way, in which case we would simply fail to recognize some genuine (or thought-independent) truths that our actual conceptual scheme allows us to recognize. Parfit (in unpublished work) compares this to a case in which some thinkers lack the concept of a hand, and so the concept of a handshake, even though they have concepts of palms, fingers and thumbs, and knowingly put their palms, fingers and thumbs together in the ways and circumstances in which we put our hands together when we shake hands. He thinks it is *true* – given the conjunction of *the way the world is* and *what we mean by "hand" and "handshake"* – that these people have hands and perform handshakes; it's just that they fail to recognize these truths which our richer conceptual scheme allows us to recognize.

Parfit (1999) explains the sorts of thinkers we are supposed to imagine as follows:

> Apart from their having no concept of a subject, and the consequences of that fact, their conceptual scheme would be like ours. Thus they would have concepts of persisting objects, such as stones or trees, and among such objects they would include their bodies. And they would have concepts of connected sequences of thoughts, experiences, and acts, each of which is closely related to, or occurs in, one such body. [Parfit should I think add "or a sequence of such bodies."] *But they would have no concept of themselves as the thinkers of these thoughts, or as the agents of these acts. And they would regard their experiences as occurring, rather than as being had.*

Parfit then suggests that different sorts of indexical thoughts could play for these thinkers the practical roles played for us by first-person thoughts:

In place of the pronoun "I," these beings might have a special use of "*this*" which referred to the sequence in which this use of "*this*" occurred. Where one of us would say "I saw the Great Fire," one of them would say "*This* included a seeing of the fire" . . . They might also have a special use of "*here*," so that, instead of "I am angry," they would say "Anger has arisen *here*." In the mind of our imagined mountaineer, a few connected thoughts might be as follows: "Was it wisely decided *here* to make an attempt on this summit? Since a storm is coming, *this* may not have another chance. Should *this* include a crossing of that ridge of ice? The pain of the wind against *this* face hardly matters with a view like that."

These subjects are supposed to be as much like us as possible, compatible with their operating with an "impersonal" conceptual scheme: whereas *we* think of ourselves as subjects and ascribe thoughts and experiences to ourselves and to other subjects like us, *they* do not think of themselves or others as subjects. They think simply in terms of thoughts and experiences being connected in impersonally specifiable ways to demonstratively identifiable thoughts and experiences. It is true, according to Parfit, that the existence of thoughts and experiences that are connected in the ways their thoughts and experiences are connected is sufficient – given what we *mean* by "person" and "subject" – for the existence of persons or subjects. It is just that these thinkers, lacking the relevant concepts, fail to realize that persons or subjects of experience are what they *in fact* are.

Parfit thinks that the differences between ourselves and such thinkers are primarily differences in *what can be thought and said* by those operating the different schemes, *not* differences in *what exists* given the operation of the different schemes. He realizes that the *character* of our thoughts and experiences can be affected by what we think and say about them, so that our thoughts and experiences might to some extent differ from the thoughts and experiences of creatures who operated with the impersonal scheme. But he thinks that *their* thoughts and experiences would still be essentially the same *sorts* of things as *ours*. And he thinks that these subjects – though they might differ somewhat *in character* from us – would still be essentially the same *sorts* of subjects as we are. The two schemes describe the *same realities* (i.e., persons), but our personal scheme makes it possible for us to think and say *additional* things about those realities, things we could not think or say if we operated only with the impersonal scheme. The important point, according to Parfit, is that thinkers who thought of their own existence only in the terms afforded by the impersonal scheme would not differ in fundamental *kind* from thinkers who thought of their existence in the additional terms afforded by the personal scheme: he suggests that the differences between them and us are like the differences between humans who happen to have children and humans who do not.

Here, however, Parfit seems to me not fully appreciative of the extent to which our thinking of ourselves in the ways that Locke takes persons to think of themselves – i.e., as subjects that think and act in different times and places – plays both causal and constitutive roles in our *being* such subjects. Locke would I think deny that human animals who operated only with Parfit's impersonal scheme are *persons*. Although such animals might have the instinctive sorts of concern with their own relatively immediate pleasures and pains that non-rational animals have, and might thus be able to act in ways that non-rational animals act, they would lack the sort of self-conceptions required in order to engage in the sorts of action that Locke takes to be distinctive of persons: they would not *be* agents who impute past actions to *themselves* and make plans for their *own* futures in ways such that it makes *sense* to punish them for past actions or to encourage them to undertake long-term "personal" projects.

The point here is that coming to have I-thoughts that are systematically connected in certain ways contributes *causally* to coming to be a person, while continuing to have I-thoughts that are systematically connected in the relevant ways contributes *constitutively* to one's being and continuing to be a person. By "systematic connections" I mean for example the sort of connections involved when thinking first "I was F at t1" and then "I was G at t2" leads one to conclude "first I was F then I was G" and perhaps also to think about how my being F at t1 might have contributed, given my circumstances between t1 to t2, to my being G at t2; and then perhaps, if being G is something of which I disapprove (e.g., being violent), to think about how I might avoid the move to being G in future circumstances in which I find myself being F (e.g., being angry). Taking such connections among I-thoughts to be *constitutive* of a person's existence, and thus of her persistence over time, seems to me the basic Lockean move: it is what makes it plausible to reject the idea that a person's identity over time consists primarily in the persistence of some independently existing substance, such as a Cartesian soul or an Aristotelian animal.

The fundamental idea behind this constitutive move is that the kinds of *thought* a subject is capable of having can play a role in the kind of *subject* it *is*. But this is not a simple, "thinking makes it so" mechanism. For the kind of subject in question comes to be *pari passu* with the relevant kinds of thought. The ways in which a human animal comes to think of itself as itself, the same thing thinking and acting in different times and places, play a complicated and partly constitutive (but not therefore non-causal) role in making it the *kind* of subject it *is* – namely, a person. Moreover, it is not just *thoughts* that play this role. A subject's *concerns* also play a causal-cum-constitutive role in making it the *kind* of subject it is: just as a subject who had no special concern for me would not *be* my friend, so too a subject who had no special concern for its own future states would not *be* a person (Whiting, 1986). Locke repeatedly invokes such concern in his account of personal identity.

> *Self* is that conscious thinking thing . . . which is sensible, or conscious of Pleasure and Pain, capable of Happiness or Misery, **and so is concern'd** for it *self*, as far as that consciousness extends. [*Essay* II. XXVII. 17]

> *Person*, as I take it, is the name for this *self*. Where-ever a Man finds, what he calls *himself*, there I think another may say is the same *Person*. It is a Forensick Term appro-

priating Actions and their Merit; and so belongs only to intelligent Agents capable of a Law, and Happiness and Misery. This **personality extends it** *self* **beyond present Existence to what is past, only by consciousness, whereby it becomes concerned and accountable, owns and imputes to it** *self* **past Actions** just upon the same ground, and for the same reason, that it does the present. [*Essay* II. XXVII. 26]

These passages suggest that Locke is not interested (as Parfit is) in continuity of consciousness simply *as such*. Consciousness figures here as the *basis* of the sort of concern and accountability that are presupposed in forensic contexts. Locke's view is *not* that persons are conscious thinking things that *happen also* to be concerned about the hedonic quality of their experiences and *moreover* accountable for their actions. What we have here is a *holistic package* whose components are functionally related to one another: consciousness in a normally embodied creature is (among other things) consciousness of pleasure and pain, the very essence of which engage their subject's *concern* in ways that lead their subject to *act* so as to increase the pleasures and diminish the pains of which it is *conscious*, and *consciousness* of such action and its basis in the subject's *concern* leads the subject to *impute such action to itself* in a way that renders intelligible the forensic practices of holding oneself and other such subjects *responsible* for their actions. The relevant sort of consciousness must extend beyond the specious present. Only creatures whose consciousness is temporally extended in ways that involve memory of past experiences and actions and anticipation of future ones will be susceptible to the sort of influence wielded by (for example) the institution of non-temporally-immediate punishment. So memory plays an essential role here. But neither memory alone nor even temporally extended consciousness alone would constitute a person: for that we need the sort of self-referential concern about the quality of the subject's own experiences that leads the subject to act in ways that produce in the subject *a sense of itself as an agent*.

The point here is that the relevant sort of continuity – without which the relevant sort of subject would not exist in the first place – is what affords its subjects the very sense of themselves as temporally extended agents that enables them to *be* accountable for their actions and so for them to *be* agents in the relevant sense. This is why Locke refuses to identify Persons either with immaterial Thinking Substances (which are not *agents* of the relevant sort) or with Organisms (even human ones). For even human Organisms can fail to achieve – or be irreversibly deprived of – the relevant sort of agency. Continuity of consciousness functions here much as continuity of life functions in the existence of an animal: just as there would be no persisting animal without continuity of the life functions that enable the animal to engage in the activities characteristic of its kind, so too there would be no temporally extended self-reflexive agent without continuity of the sort of consciousness that enables a person to engage in the sorts of activities characteristic of persons. But continuity of consciousness is only part of the holistic package that constitutes the existence of a person: self-referential concern and the tendency to impute actions to oneself are also necessary.

This non-reductionist reading of Locke's basic view permits but does not require the sort of dualism of person and animal that Locke himself seems to accept. For it is open to us first to build the capacities associated with being a person into our account of the capacities distinctive of human (and perhaps other) animals in something like the way Aristotle does in referring to human animals as essentially rational and political animals, and then to follow Aristotle's "top-down" approach to individuation according to which an animal goes where the capacities in terms of which it is defined go. This will require us to say what John McDowell (1997) thinks Locke should have said about his Prince–Cobbler case – namely, that the human animal follows the person: the thing with the Prince's consciousness and the Cobbler's body is not only the same *person* – but also the same *animal* – as the original Prince.

The non-reductionist reading also enables us to see what is potentially misleading about Parfit's claim that identity is not "what matters." Consider the analogy between identity and the exclusive relation of monogamous marriage: just as there are *logical* laws that must be satisfied if x is to be identical to y, so too there are *positive* laws that must be satisfied if x is to be married to y. In the marriage case, we tend to treat the satisfaction of the relevant laws as a purely *formal* matter, independent of the quality of the relationship between the legal relata. This means not only that x and y can stand in the *formal* relationship of marriage without standing to one another in the relationships of care and commitment that are supposed to *matter* in a marriage, but also that x and y can stand to one another in the relationships of care and commitment that are supposed to *matter* in a marriage without standing to one another in the *formal* relationship of marriage. In this case, it makes perfect sense to say "marriage is not what matters" and everyone knows what this means.

But this is not a good model for the egocentric version of the claim that "identity is not what matters" afforded by the non-reductionist development of Locke's view. For part of the point of adopting a psychological criterion is to *build* the relationships that matter *into* personal identity – i.e., to say that personal identity (when we have it) is *constituted* by the relationships that *matter*. Lockean views are plausible precisely because persons are *essentially* subjects to whom things *matter* (which is why some people have far more trouble with the idea that computers might be persons than with the idea that non-human animals might be). It is thus an important feature of the Lockean view that, although we can sometimes have what matters without personal identity, we can never have *personal* identity without what matters: for *personal* identity *just is* the non-branching instantiation of the psychological relations that *matter*.

Someone might take an analogous view about marriage: she might say, as she walks out on her legal spouse, "this is no marriage." And we would know what she means – namely, that what *really* makes something a marriage is the relationships of care and commitment that are part of the *point* of a marriage. She could go different ways here. She could say that standing in these relationships is *sufficient* for being truly married. Or she could say that standing in these relationships is simply a *necessary* condition for being truly married, and that standing in the relevant legal relation is *also* required. But even if she goes the latter way, the importance she attaches to standing in the legal relation will be significantly reduced, perhaps even to the extent that she begins to question whether it really matters at all. That, I think, is roughly how Parfit's views about the importance of identity have evolved. He began by viewing the sort of psychological continuity that matters as *constitutive* of personal identity and thus as *necessary* for it. Then, upon examining fission cases and seeing that one could have psychological continuity without thereby satisfying the formal conditions for identity, he began to question whether satisfying the formal conditions ever matters at all. In doing so, he overlooked the way in which (as the non-reductionist view maintains) there must be *some* copersonal relations among psychological states in order for there to be any personal subjects, to whom things *matter*, in the first place.

The advantage of the egocentric version of non-reductionism recommended here is that it allows us to recognize the importance of the copersonality relation without however having to say that prudential concern and attributions of responsibility always presuppose "strict numerical identity" in the traditional sense that such identity is always required to justify any particular case of prudential concern or attribution of responsibility. Personal identity *itself* matters because the existence of *persons* matters; without some copersonal relations there would not even *be* persons, capable of the sorts of relationships and long-term projects whose existence arguably involves distinctive kinds of value fundamentally different in kind from those involved in the merely hedonic states and activities of non-personal subjects. But *once* we have such subjects, it is *then* possible for the sort of relations that typically hold between the states of one and the same personal subject to hold between the states of numerically distinct personal subjects, as in cases of fission. On this view, personal identity *just is* the *non-branching form of what matters*.

IV

I want to conclude by considering briefly an important objection to this view. John Campbell (1992) objects that the psychological relations in which we stand to our fission products are *not like* the relations in which we stand to our "strict numerical" selves because our relations to the former lack the normative dimension characteristic of our relations to the latter. Campbell focuses on the way in which genuine memory tends not only to *cause* the belief that one *oneself* had the remembered experience but also to *warrant* that belief, whereas mere quasi-memory tends simply to *cause* such a belief *without* providing any warrant for it.

The problem with Campbell's objection is that he focuses narrowly on the admittedly important but limited portion of psychological continuity involving first-person experiential memory. If we take a more comprehensive view of psychological continuity, paying attention *both* to the normative dimensions of such continuity afforded by allowing the causal relations among psychological states to include "rationalizing" relations *and* to the way in which first-person thoughts are embedded in a larger and primarily world-directed network, then we should not be tempted by Campbell's argument.

Suppose that I undergo the sort of fission described above and that each of the products knows what has happened. Each as a matter of causal fact inherits from me countless beliefs about the world and attitudes towards it, as well as apparent memories of my pre-fission experiences etc. Consider first their *general* beliefs and attitudes. How *should* Lefty (or Righty) regard her tendency to hold these beliefs and attitudes? Assume for now that she has not yet encountered the sort of counterevidence exposure to which normally warrants (but often fails to cause) changes in one's beliefs and attitudes. *Should* Lefty reason that however much *she* feels impelled by the causal mechanisms to hold these beliefs and attitudes, they were nevertheless formed by a numerically *distinct* subject so that she has no more *warrant* for holding them than she has for holding the beliefs and attitudes of any other third party? She should throw them all out and start from scratch?

Of course not. To the extent that *my* general beliefs and attitudes immediately prior to fission were warranted by *my* previous experiences, *her* general beliefs and attitudes immediately after fission will be warranted by those very experiences in spite of the fact that she is numerically distinct from their original subject. If *my* pre-fission tendency to believe that that dogs that cringe a certain way tend to bite was warranted by *my* exposure to the evidence, then *her* tendency to believe this will be warranted by *my* exposure to the evidence. And if *my* pre-fission tendency not to trust men who constantly profess their feminist sensibilities was warranted by *my* experience, then *her* similar tendency will be warranted by *my* experience. She has of course a standing obligation to remain open to the need to revise these beliefs and attitudes in light of new experiences and exposure to new evidence, but so do *I* in the case where I do *not* undergo fission: this does not distinguish *her* normative relations to *my* past experience and the counterevidence from the normative relations *I* would have had to *my* past experience had I never suffered fission. So her relation to my past experience is generally speaking similar – both causally and normatively – to the relation that my future self would have had to my past experience had I never suffered fission.

Campbell will object that first-person experiential beliefs and attitudes are central to the sort of psychological continuity that Lockeans take to constitute a person's identity over time and that I have changed the subject by focusing on the preservation of *general* beliefs and attitudes. Here, however, we must remember that our first-person beliefs and attitudes do not operate in a vacuum, but are inferentially integrated with our world-directed beliefs and attitudes, including evaluative ones. Suppose that prior to fission, I come to have the following sorts of beliefs and attitudes, capable of the sort of "impersonal" expression given here: "Martin Luther King's method of non-violent resistance is admirable"; "Mrs.

Whiting is an exemplary mother"; "Leon is someone whose advice is to be trusted." I will also of course come to have other, more self-referential attitudes such as "*I* have an important commitment to Tom," "*I* should care for Mom the way she cared for *me*," etc. Now consider my fission products. Each will tend to have the same sorts of beliefs and attitudes as I had immediately prior to fission. How then would each – and more importantly how *should* each – regard these beliefs and attitudes?

Each would and I think *should* in the absence of new evidence continue to have the beliefs and attitudes capable of the sort of impersonal expression exemplified above. For it was exposure to the evidence about for example the value of King's method of non-violence or the wisdom of Leon's advice that justified her prede-cessor's beliefs (if they were justified) about these things. But what about her *self-referential* beliefs and attitudes?

Here again she needs to keep the right sort of *outward* focus. Consider my rela-tionships with my friends and loved ones. To the extent my relationships, however they came about, tend to be sustained by my appreciation of my *friends* and *loved ones* and concern for *their* well-being, it is psychologically implausible to suppose that my fission-product will be tempted to abandon the concern she tends to have for my friends and loved ones by reasoning: "That was *her*, this is *me*. Why should *I* care about *her* friends and loved ones?" She is likely for self-interested reasons to seek the company of those whose company I enjoyed immediately before the fission. And she is likely for other-directed reasons to express concern for the well-being of those the appreciation of whom and concern for whom she has "inher-ited" from me. This would be true even in intimate relationships such as marriage. I can imagine my fission-products thinking as follows:

> "Tom is such a great guy, so warm and caring, and so much fun. He's really per-ceptive and has a wicked sense of humor, though he only lets people really close to him see any of this. Aren't I *lucky* to have inherited this relationship with him? But wait. My competitor has also inherited the same relationship . . ."

At this point, one might expect my fission-products to think about slaying the competition, and the fission-products of some persons would no doubt think that way. There is room here for considerable variation in actual attitudes and I do not intend to generalize from my own (perhaps idealized) case. My aim is only to establish its *coherence*. The point is that a fission-product who inherited a genuine appreciation of and concern for *Tom*, even if she was tempted by such thoughts, would at least struggle – or *should* at least struggle – to deal with them in ways expressive of genuine concern for *Tom*. She should – and I submit could – think the following sorts of thoughts:

> "Gosh, this must be difficult for *Tom*. Given how kind and loyal he is, he will surely find it impossible to prefer one of us to the other, knowing how much pain and suf-fering that would cause the other. [A sigh of relief.] But one of 'me' was hard enough

for him to handle. How could he bear to deal with two? Maybe I'd better talk to
her – I'm sure she'd feel the same way – to see if we can come to some sort of agreement about how to share him."

Her next step might be to start talking to the competition – and of course to Tom
– about how things could be worked out so as to respect the interests and preferences of the relevant parties. It may be that they would all agree that sharing
Tom would (given their actual personalities) be too difficult, and that they would
agree to go their separate ways. And if this is what Tom wants, they should – out
of consideration for *him* – agree to this.

We can allow here that my fission-products would tend to have apparent
memories involving illusions – that they would have mere quasi-memories that
presented themselves as genuine memories of their *own* experiences – and that
they would (at least initially) tend on the basis of these apparent memories to form
false first-person beliefs about what they *themselves* had experienced and done. This
tendency might recede with time, as they became more accustomed to checking
the tendency to slide directly from apparent memories to first-person beliefs about
their own pasts. But if the fission-products are to amass genuine memories of their
own post-fission experiences and to rely in acting both on their own genuine
memories and on their mere quasi-memories – as I think they should – then we
cannot assume that this tendency will disappear altogether.

The important point though is that the illusory aspects of these beliefs need
not in general interfere with the ability of these beliefs and attitudes to stand in
functional relations like those characteristic of genuine first-person attitudes – relations not only to behavioral outputs but also to privileged sorts of input. To the
extent that genuine memory allows one to know on the basis of something other
than observation things about one's own past, their mere quasi-memories could
be viewed as allowing them to know on the basis of something other than observation things about the pasts of their *predecessors*. We should not assimilate the
sort of relation involved here to ordinary observation for the simple reason that
a fission-product would have a kind of knowledge "from the inside" of how her
predecessor once thought and felt. But her knowledge of how her predecessor
thought and felt, while it might rest on some inferences involving knowledge that
(and of when) fission occurred, would *not* be based on inferences from the sorts
of things a third person might observe "from the outside" (such as actions or a
blush on the cheek). So a fission-product's "first-personal" thoughts – while they
might involve some degree of illusion – can nevertheless stand in the same sorts
of relations as their non-illusory counterparts both to action and to the special
sorts of access we have to our own pasts. They might for example play the same
sort of role in psychotherapy as their non-illusory counterparts. If *we* did not
start with *genuine* memories, our fission-products could not have mere quasi-
memories. But given that we *do* start with genuine memories, our fission-
products *can* have mere quasi-memories that play for them the same *sorts* of roles

– not only in *causing* their present thoughts and actions but also in *warranting* their present thoughts and actions – that memories play for us.

Annotated Bibliography

There has been much good work on this topic in recent years and my bibliography is of necessity selective. But I have tried to cite – in addition to the works to which I explicitly refer – the most important of the relevant works I have not had the space to discuss. After listing general introductory works, I list the remaining works more or less in the order in which the issues they treat appear in my text. I would also like to acknowledge here my profound indebtedness to the written work of David Wiggins, and to years of dialogue (both written and unwritten) with Richard Gale, John McDowell, Dick Moran, Derek Parfit, and Sydney Shoemaker.

The best introduction to this topic (in terms of both clarity and sophistication) is:

Perry, John (1978) *A Dialogue on Personal Identity and Immortality* (Indianapolis: Hackett).

Perry has also collected useful historical and contemporary classics (including many to which I refer) in:

Perry, John ed. (1975) *Personal Identity* (Berkeley and Los Angeles: University of California Press).

Another collection with important contemporary essays is:

Rorty, Amélie ed. (1976) *The Identities of Persons* (Berkeley: University of California Press).

A somewhat more challenging introduction, presenting the best recent defense of a "dualist" (or "Cartesian") account of personal identity (by Richard Swinburne) and of a "materialist" account (by Sydney Shoemaker), is:

Shoemaker, Sydney and Swinburne, Richard (1984) *Personal Identity* (Oxford: Basil Blackwell). (All references to Shoemaker [1984] are to Shoemaker's contribution to this volume.)

Although most contemporary participants in this debate assume that Descartes identifies a person simply with an immaterial soul, there is an interesting defense of the claim that he identifies a person with a "substantial union" of such a soul and a human body, in:

Baier, Annette (1981) "Cartesian Persons," *Philosophia*, 10 (1981), pp. 169–88; reprinted in A. Baier, *Postures of the Mind* (Minneapolis: University of Minnesota Press, 1985).

Baier discusses Descartes' views in connection with a classic that I have regretfully neglected here:

Peter Strawson (1959) *Individuals: An Essay in Descriptive Metaphysics* (London: Methuen).

Another good introduction, containing more on the historical background, is:

Noonan, Harold (1989) *Personal Identity* (London: Routledge).

For general discussions of diachronic identity as involving spatio-temporal continuity under a substance (as opposed to a phase) sortal, see:

Wiggins, David (1967) *Identity and Spatio-Temporal Continuity* (Oxford: Blackwell Publishers).
Wiggins, David (1980) *Sameness and Substance* (Cambridge, MA: Harvard University Press).

For defenses of the "animalist" view, see:

Snowdon, Paul (1990) "Persons, Animals, and Ourselves," in *The Person and the Human Mind*, edited by C. Gill (Oxford: Clarendon Press).
Snowdon, Paul (1991) "Personal Identity and Brain Transplants," in *Human Beings*, edited by D. Cockburn (Cambridge: Cambridge University Press), pp. 109–26.
Snowdon, Paul (1995) "Persons, Animals, and Bodies," in *The Body and the Self*, edited by J. L. Bermúdez, A. Marcel, and N. Eilan (Cambridge, MA: MIT Press), pp. 71–86.
Olson, Eric (1997) *The Human Animal: Personal Identity without Psychology* (Oxford: Oxford University Press).

Talk of the "animalist" view has generally replaced talk of the "bodily" view, originally defended by Bernard Williams in several papers reprinted in his *Problems of the Self* (Cambridge: Cambridge University Press, 1973), most notably:

Williams, Bernard (1970a) "Are Persons Bodies?" in *The Philosophy of the Body*, edited by S. Spicker (Chicago: Quadrant Books), pp. 137–56.
Williams, Bernard (1970b) "The Self and the Future," *Philosophical Review*, 79, pp. 161–80.

I discuss Williams (1970b) in a way relevant to the "egocentric" view recommended here, in:

Whiting, Jennifer (1999) "Back to 'The Self and the Future'," *Philosophical Topics*, pp. 441–77. (This issue of *Philosophical Topics* is a special issue devoted to the Philosophy of Sydney Shoemaker, whose views on personal identity are discussed in several other papers in this volume, most notably Parfit [1999].)

For and about Locke's views, see:

Locke, John (1975) *An Essay Concerning Human Understanding*, edited by P. H. Nidditch (Oxford: Clarendon Press). (Nidditch's edition is based on Locke's fourth edition, published in 1700, which contains significant changes on the issue of personal identity from the first edition, published in 1689. In fact, Locke's account of personal identity – which appears in Book II, Chapter XXVII (reprinted in Perry, 1975) – first appeared in the second edition, published in 1694.
Mackie, John (1976) *Problems from Locke* (Oxford: Clarendon Press).
Ayers, Michael (1991) *Locke, Volume II: Ontology* (London: Routledge).

For and about Aristotle's views, see:

Aristotle (1993) *De Anima: Books II and III with passages from Book I*, translated with introduction and notes by D. W. Hamlyn, with a report on recent work by C. Shields (Oxford: Clarendon Press).
Williams, Bernard (1986) "Hylomorphism," *Oxford Studies in Ancient Philosophy*, IV, pp. 189–99.

Nussbaum, M. and A. Rorty eds. (1992) *Essays on Aristotle's De Anima* (Oxford: Clarendon Press). See especially the essays by Nussbaum and Putnam, Cohen, and Whiting.

For an interesting attribution of "hylomorphism" to Descartes, see:

Hoffman, Paul (1986) "The Unity of Descartes's Man," *The Philosophical Review*, 95, pp. 339–70.

For a general discussion of "non-reductionist materialism" see:

Boyd, Richard (1980) "Materialism without Reductionism," in *Readings in Philosophical Psychology: Volume I*, edited by Ned Block (Cambridge, MA: MIT Press).

For an unabashed version of what I call "Lockean dualism" see:

Shoemaker, Sydney (1999) "Self, Body, and Coincidence," *Proceedings of the Aristotelian Society*, Supplementary Volume 43, pp. 286–307.

For the development of Parfit's views, see:

Parfit, Derek (1971) "Personal Identity," *Philosophical Review*, 80, pp. 3–27; reprinted in Perry (1978).
Parfit, Derek (1984) *Reasons and Persons* (Oxford: Clarendon Press); reprinted with minor changes in 1985 and 1987. Parfit's views on personal identity are presented in Part III of this magisterial work.
Parfit, Derek (1999) "Experiences, Subjects, and Conceptual Schemes," *Philosophical Topics*, 26, pp. 217–70.

For Swinburne's suggestion about the fission-example, see:

Swinburne, Richard (1973–4) "Personal Identity," *Proceedings of the Aristotelian Society*, 74, pp. 231–48.

Shoemaker has over the years developed the most sophisticated version of Locke's "psychological continuity" theory. But his views are both complex and changing subtly over time, being consistently "reductionist" in the sense that they do not require the existence of any non-material stuffs or entities, but becoming progressively less "reductionist" in the sense that he has become increasingly sympathetic to the idea that we can give an account of a particular person's existence over time in "weak reductionist" terms that do not presuppose the identity of that *particular* person. Shoemaker's non-reductionist tendencies are clearest in two papers reprinted in his *Identity, Cause, and Mind* (Cambridge: Cambridge University Press):

Shoemaker, Sydney (1970) "Persons and Their Pasts," *American Philosophical Quarterly*, 7, pp. 269–85.
Shoemaker, Sydney (1979) "Identities, Properties, and Causality," *Midwest Studies in Philosophy*, 4, pp. 321–42.

Shoemaker's increasingly reductionist tendencies are most evident in section 7 of his contribution to Shoemaker and Swinburne (cited above), but one should keep in mind the objections he expresses to Parfit's "reductionism" in:

Shoemaker, Sydney (1985) "Critical Notice of *Reasons and Persons*," *Mind*, 94, pp. 443–53; a slightly abridged version is reprinted as "Parfit on Identity" in *Reading Parfit*, edited by J. Dancy (1997) (Oxford: Blackwell Publishers). (Note: Dancy's volume contains several other important papers on Parfit's account of personal identity, most notably for present purposes, Mark Johnston's "Human Concerns without Superlative Selves.")

The complexity of Shoemaker's view – and the best summary of his current position – can be found in:

Shoemaker, Sydney (1997) "Self and Substance," *Philosophical Perspectives*, Volume 11: *Mind, Causation, and World*, pp. 283–304.

The sense in which Shoemaker's views are non-reductionist is related to the claim in Strawson (1959) (cited above) that the concept of Person is "primitive." On this claim, see the excellent discussion in:

Ishiguro, Hide (1980) "The Primitiveness of the Concept of a Person," in *Philosophical Subjects: Essays Presented to P. F. Strawson*, edited by Z. van Straaten (Oxford: Clarendon Press), pp. 62–75.

One important but understated feature of Shoemaker's view, which has not I think been fully appreciated, is his taking psychological continuity to include "rationalizing" (but not therefore non-causal) relations of the sort defended by Davidson in several essays (most notably "Actions, Reasons, and Causes") reprinted in:

Davidson, Donald (1980) *Essays on Actions and Events* (Oxford: Clarendon Press).

Versions of what I call a "practical not metaphysical view" of personal identity are presented by Olson (cited above) in connection with personal identity in what he calls the "practical" (as opposed to the "numerical") sense, and by:

Korsgaard, Christine (1989) "Personal Identity and the Unity of Agency: A Kantian Response to Parfit," *Philosophy and Public Affairs*, 18, pp. 101–32; reprinted in Korsgaard, *Creating the Kingdom of Ends* (Cambridge: Cambridge University Press, 1996).
Schechtman, Marya (1996) *The Constitution of Selves* (Ithaca, NY: Cornell University Press).
Velleman, David (1996) "Self to Self," *The Philosophical Review*, 105, pp. 39–76.

For and about Hume's view see:

Hume, David (1978) *A Treatise of Human Nature* (with revised texts and notes by P. H. Nidditch) (Oxford: Clarendon Press). Books I and II were originally published in 1739; Hume added Book III and the famous Appendix (which appears to retract his arguments about personal identity) in 1740. The material on personal identity, taken from Section II of Part I, is reprinted in Perry (1975).
Ainslie, Donald (2000) "Hume's Reflections on the Identity and Simplicity of the Mind," *Philosophy and Phenomenological Research*, 62, pp. 557–78.

I discuss the Buddhist view briefly, in a way relevant to the "constitutive move" discussed here, in:

Whiting, Jennifer (1986) "Friends and Future Selves," *The Philosophical Review*, 95, pp. 547–80.

A related discussion appears in:

Johnston, Mark (1989) "Relativism and the Self," in *Relativism: Interpretation and Confrontation*, edited by M. Krausz (South Bend: University of Notre Dame Press), pp. 441–72.

For and about Lewis's view, see:

Lewis, David (1976) "Survival and Identity," in Rorty (1976), pp. 17–40; reprinted with a postscript in Lewis (1983) *Philosophical Papers, Volume I* (Oxford: Oxford University Press).

Parfit, Derek (1976) "Lewis, Perry, and What Matters," in Rorty (1976), pp. 91–107.

On split-brain phenomena, see:

Nagel, Thomas (1971) "Brain Bisection and the Unity of Consciousness," *Synthese*, 20; reprinted in Perry (1975) and in Nagel (1979) *Mortal Questions* (Cambridge: Cambridge University Press).

Marks, Charles (1980) *Commissurotomy, Consciousness, and Unity of Mind* (Montgomery, Vermont: Bradford Books).

For Butler's view, see:

Butler, Joseph (1736) *The Analogy of Religion*, the relevant passages of which are reprinted in Perry (1975).

For Nozick's "closest continuer theory," which involves denying the common view that identity cannot depend on "extrinsic" factors, see chapter 1 of:

Nozick, Robert (1981) *Philosophical Explanations* (Cambridge, MA: Harvard University Press).

For the suggestion that we treat quasi-memory as derivative from ordinary (identity-involving) memory, see:

McDowell, John (1997) "Reductionism and the First Person," in Dancy (1997), pp. 230–50; reprinted in McDowell (1998) *Mind, Value, and Reality* (Cambridge, MA: Harvard University Press).

Please note however that McDowell does not acknowledge the plausibility of this suggestion in the context of a non-reductionist alternative (à la Shoemaker) to Parfit's strong reductionist development of Locke's basic view. Related objections to Parfit's view including the objections to his "impersonal reduction" discussed in Section III – objections to which Shoemaker's non-reductionist view is not *obviously* vulnerable – are presented in:

Cassam, Quassim (1992) "Reductionism and First Person Thinking," in *Reduction, Explanation, and Realism*, edited by D. Charles and K. Lennon (Oxford: Clarendon Press), pp. 362–80.

Campbell, John (1992) "The First Person: The Reductionist View of the Self"; also in Charles and Lennon (1992), pp. 381–419; reprinted as chapter 3 of Campbell (1994), *Past, Space, and Self* (Cambridge, MA: MIT Press).

For related discussion of "quasi-memory" and the functional characterization of Idea-types, see Gareth Evans (1982) *The Varieties of Reference*, edited by John McDowell (Oxford: Clarendon Press).

On "personal" projects see:

Perry, John (1976) "The Importance of Being Identical," in Rorty (1976), pp. 67–90. (Perry's views are discussed in Parfit [1979] and Whiting [1986].)

The normative dimension of psychological continuity is rightly stressed, but (as I argue in a review forthcoming in *The Philosophical Review*) not appropriately related to the causal dimension, by:

Rovane, Carol (1998) *The Bounds of Agency* (Princeton: Princeton University Press).

Other important works relevant to the present discussion include:

Wiggins, David (1979) "The Concern to Survive," *Midwest Studies in Philosophy*, 4.

Johnston, Mark (1989) "Fission and the Facts," *Philosophical Perspectives*, 3, pp. 85–102.

Rovane, Carol (1990) "Branching Self-Consciousness," *The Philosophical Review*, 99, pp. 355–95.

Sosa, Ernest (1990) "Surviving Matters," *Noûs*, 24, pp. 305–30.

Unger, Peter (1990) *Identity, Consciousness and Value* (New York and Oxford: Oxford University Press).

Martin, Raymond (1998) *Self-Concern: An Experiential Approach to What Matters in Survival* (Cambridge: Cambridge University Press). (This contains a useful account of the late seventeenth and early eighteenth century antecedents of the debate about "what matters.")

Chapter 11

Idealism

T. L. S. Sprigge

Definition of Idealism

A possible definition of what it is to be an idealist, in the sense most common now among philosophers, is that it is to be one who believes at least one of the following propositions.

(1) Nothing really exists which is not mental or mind-dependent.
(2) Physical things are really mental.
(3) Physical things are really mind-dependent.
(4) The fact that a physical thing exists is really simply the fact that it would be perceived under certain circumstances.

The following points are to be noted.

(i) To be mental, in the relevant sense, is to be a mind or a component of a mind, while to be mind-dependent is to exist only as an object of some kind of mental awareness.

(ii) Idealism may be monistic or pluralistic. For the monistic idealist there is one cosmic mind, or mind-like reality, which includes all other mental phenomena. For the pluralistic idealist, in contrast, there are many distinct minds or instances of the mental, not belonging together in any overarching mind or mental reality.

(iii) There is a tendency to restrict the term "idealism" to theories which give a more fundamental role to higher forms of mind than lower ones.

(iv) The word "really" indicates that these propositions are metaphysical propositions. As such they purport to tell us something which, while literally true, can be conveniently ignored for many practical purposes. This must be understood in terms of the goal of metaphysics. Metaphysics, at any rate of the type usually referred to as "speculative metaphysics," attempts to make us conscious of the nature of reality, or the nature of things (if a plural is preferred), in a peculiarly literal way which may contrast with our usual cognitive dealings with the world. The linguistic expressions which we affirm in daily life are components in a linguistic mechanism which helps us (whatever WE really are) deal with REALITY (whatever it really is) in a way which is practically useful. Many of our ordinary conceptions are self-contradictory or incoherent, or alternatively simply linguistic devices. At the moment (as it happens) it is rather useful for me to affirm the sentence "it is raining." It functions to make me do what is ordinarily called "putting on a mackintosh," or "uplifting an umbrella" when I "go out of the house" to "catch a bus." The utility of this sentence in guiding my behavior does not depend upon its summoning to my mind (or doing so if required) the real character of the state of affairs which has prompted this utterance. A scientist could give a description of this state of affairs which would bring anyone who understands it to a much deeper grasp of its true nature, but the metaphysician, of an idealist persuasion, may think that even the scientific account is more an instrument for dealing with the world than a prompter to a grasp of its *real* (it's hard to avoid the word) nature.

Main Idealist Thinkers

(a)   Berkeley's theistic idealism

The most famous and influential of historical idealists are George Berkeley (1685–1753) and Immanuel Kant (1724–1804).

Berkeley was the first clear cut idealist in Western thought. His allegiance is to propositions (1) and (3) above, though at times he inclines also to accept (4).

Thus Berkeley claims that the only things which exist are *spirits* and *ideas*. By a spirit he does not mean a ghost, but rather a mind, or, as one might call it, a center of consciousness, while by *ideas*, he means primarily the immediate appearances of physical things to our minds, and images which represent these in thought. Physical things are not an extra to this for they are simply groups of those more vivid ideas which we would usually call their appearances to a mind.

Berkeley argues in a thorough way, to which we cannot do justice here, that the belief that there is something more to a physical thing than the ideas which are its appearances is incoherent and thus false. However, the existence of an idea (and *a fortiori* of a collection of ideas) consists in its being perceived, which implies that physical things can only exist when perceived (and, even then, strictly only their perceived aspects do so).

Berkeley, however, also thinks that it would be foolish to doubt that physical things go on existing when no human or animal perceives them. Since no other *natural* perceivers suggest themselves, there must be something *supernatural* which is perceiving them all the time. Moreover, the orderliness of the world suggests that there is just one supernatural perceiver which keeps things going by perceiving them all the time (rather than, say, a committee of angels, even if such exist, who might disagree as to what to perceive), and that being is what we refer to as "God."

The argument is strengthened by reference to *will*. Some of our ideas occur as a result of our own willing them into existence, and change in virtue of our willing them to change. This is true of those less forceful ideas which arise in me when I am thinking of something rather than perceiving it. For example, I can will an idea of a unicorn into existence, and I can make it prance about simply by willing it to do so. (If this requires some qualification, that will not affect the main line of thought.) But the more forceful ideas which I perceive, and regard as the appearances of physical things, exist and change without being caused to do so by either my willing this or any other natural being doing so. But just as an idea cannot exist without being perceived, so also can its existence and changes only come about through the willing of a mind. For, argues Berkeley, this is the only kind of causation of which sense can be made, since causation must consist in something more than a mere tendency for one thing to follow on another and can only be what we experience directly when we ourselves produce our own ideas. Thus the existence and changes of the physical world must be due to the divine willing of this.

The example of the unicorn may suggest that our will can only affect our private imagery. But this is not so, as Berkeley is well aware. For when I raise my hand, or talk or walk, I am bringing about changes in what is called the public world by willing them. Berkeley is not as clear as one might like here, but basically his view is this. When I wake up I find myself aware of various physical things around me, and of my own body. This is not due to an act of my will. However, I can thereafter bring about changes in my body, in particular by moving my limbs, and use these changes in the world around me to bring about other changes less directly.

The Berkeleyan explanation of this is that the initial ideas which I perceive on waking are determined by God, but that this being so, God will co-operate with me in bringing about movements of my limbs etc. and will *will* the changes to occur which *I* bring about less directly by means of these.

Such is a rough account of one strand in Berkeley's thought. However, he sometimes implies a version of the fourth disjunct (in our opening definition), namely that the existence of physical things, when not perceived by finite minds, consists in the fact that spirits such as ourselves would perceive them if they did certain things (e.g., directly willed movements of their limbs in certain ways). Thus the existence of the wall behind me consists in the fact that I would perceive the ideas which I would count as appearances of it if I effected the change in my idea of my head and shoulders which would be called "turning round to look at it," or "putting out my hand to feel it", etc. The role of God, on this view, is to be ready to evoke the relevant ideas (i.e., perceptual appearances) of a physical thing in someone who takes the steps (gives himself the right ideas of his own movements) required to perceive it. But does not God, on this view also, perceive them all the while, as well as being ready to cause us to do so? The best answer seems to be that God does indeed perceive them all the time and that they are his cues as to what ideas he shall cause finite spirits to have when they will certain ideas of their own bodily movements.

There are, of course, many difficulties in this view. Are God's ideas of things not bound to be pretty different from ours? For God's visual and tactile fields etc., must surely be much less restricted than ours, and that must make them very different. Or does he, like perhaps spiders do, have lots of different sensory fields? Possibly, but it seems odd that he does not synthesize them into one. Moreover, our sensory fields are all in some sense perspectival. But from what point of view are God's perceptual fields presented?

But I do not think this really undermines Berkeley's position. He can allow that the details of God's experience are unknown to us. It is enough that he must be there as the constant perceiver and will-er of ideas which would be recognizably of the same objects as those which we perceive under suitable conditions, and that these ideas of his serve him as cues as to what ideas to evoke in us.

Another question is whether two different spirits can perceive the same thing. Berkeley's answer is that the notion of "the same" is so slippery that it can be true in one sense that they can and in another sense that they cannot and that there is no alarming sense in which my world has to be private. In any case since a physical thing is a collection of ideas, rather than just one idea, ideas perceived by different minds can be related in such a way as to belong to the same collection. Relevant factors here are that they all change together in ways with a certain correspondence, and that there is a strong element of likeness between them.

Berkeley's argument is sometimes condemned as simply assuming, as something established by other philosophers (in particular John Locke, 1632–1704), that all we can perceive are ideas, and that therefore, granted we perceive physical objects, these must consist of ideas. But this does less than justice to Berkeley's arguments, most of which could be stated without speaking of ideas at all. And it is time now to go briefly into what some of his arguments are.

There are certain apparent characteristics or qualities of things which philosophers have found good reason for supposing are mind-dependent, that is, can only exist when perceived by a mind. These are the so-called secondary qualities, such as colors, smells, tastes, sounds, heat, and coldness, as what we really feel (as opposed to what science puts in their place). The reason for regarding these as mind-dependent are several, but turn especially on the extent to which they alter, as objects of our experience, as a result of changes which seem, from an objective point of view, to take place in us rather than in the object perceived. Thus colors radically alter when we look at things through a microscope, sounds get much less loud if we block our ears, smells and tastes when we have a cold, heat changes from being a pleasure to being a pain as our relation to its source changes, and so on.

The many thinkers who have concluded that these secondary qualities are mind-dependent have thought that they cannot belong to the true character of the physical objects which we see, touch or smell or sounds which we hear. What is more, as scientific explanation advances, there seems no need to include them in our account and explanation of what goes on in the physical world. But here they contrast with the primary qualities, such as shape, size, movement, and mass (and number, for whatever apples are, the distinction between one of them and two of them is surely not mind-dependent).

But in rebuttal of this, Berkeley has several arguments; for the reasons which show that the secondary qualities are mind-dependent apply equally to the primary qualities, which vary in several ways according to the state or position of the observer. Thus things double if we press on one of our eyes, size alters (if we are honest about what we see) when our distance from things changes, the shapes of surfaces change according as to how they are placed in relation to us, weight seems to vary with our present strength, and so forth. Moreover, we cannot conceive of something with primary, but not secondary qualities. Therefore these primary qualities are just as mind-dependent as the secondary ones.

Thus an unperceived physical object would be lacking all the qualities which we have in mind when we call it physical. Such an object is an impossibility. It follows that physical objects can only exist when perceived, and the argument for the existence of God follows, as much as if we frankly called them "ideas." Or if they can exist unperceived this can only be as mere possibilities which God is ready to bring into existence when we take the appropriate steps.

The main difficulty of Berkeley's brilliantly argued for position, I believe, is that it is hard to see how there can be causal interaction between me and God if there is no conceivable larger whole of which we are both part. (See below.)

To this we may add the usual difficulties critics find in the existence of God, in particular the problem of evil, which seems to be exacerbated on this form of theism. For if someone is caught in a fire the painful sensations he experiences are at that very moment only occurring because God wills them to. (This seems more cruel than a God who, having set an independent world going, leaves human beings to live in it more or less comfortably as they use or misuse their free will. Moreover, some suggest that if God perceives a fire as it is from inside it, he must experience pain, in which case lighting a fire is a way of hurting God, which seems a little bizarre. Berkeley, however, denies this implication because God's idea of it is more by way of a thought than a perception.) Still, we cannot dismiss an argument as unsound just because the conclusion troubles us. The idea that Berkeley saves his system by a convenient *deus ex machina* fails to recognize that his theism is not a presupposition but something he claims to have proved. The difficulty mentioned in the previous paragraph is, however, more serious and we shall return to it later.

(b) Kant's transcendental idealism

The second historically most important idealist is Immanuel Kant (1724–1804). For Kant the physical world, qua physical, has only a phenomenal reality, that is to say, it is the way some reality, of a totally unknowable character (thinks Kant), presents itself to minds like ours. Kant's arguments for this conclusion are pretty complicated. The general thrust of them all is to show that the physical world has features which are evidently the product of our own manner of perceiving and thinking, and which therefore cannot belong to something which is not the product of these. It can, therefore, only exist as something presenting itself to human beings.

One argument for this concerns the nature of space and time. Kant supposed that we know certain things about objects located in space and changing in time, a priori, that is to say not as generalizations from particular experiences but as somehow presenting themselves as necessary. Kant thought that this was so with the axioms of Euclid. We do not learn of the truth of these by measuring perceived objects but rather recognize that they simply must be true. Kant thought the only possible explanation of this was that these axioms describe characteristics imposed on anything we perceive by our own minds, and thus we can discover them simply by a kind of introspection. Other features, which we recognize that the physical world simply must have, come from our thinking (rather than our perceptual) apparatus. We know, for example, (thinks Kant) that every event in the physical world must have a cause. This is because we cannot think of any physical event without conceiving it as having been caused by another (normally previous) event, most obviously a physical event but in the case of human action perhaps rather a mental event. Therefore any physical event we perceive will somehow be interpreted by our minds as a link in a causal chain.

Kant's particular examples of the way in which the more general characteristics of the physical world are imposed on it by our minds are questionable today. For scientists have come to think that perhaps not every event at a submicroscopic level does have a cause, while they have also concluded that physical space does not, in fact, answer quite to Euclid's axioms. Perhaps it was the character of our minds which once made us think that these things were necessary but further reflection has shown us capable of thinking otherwise.

But, whatever inadequacies there may be in such details, Kant's general view, that how the world appears to us is to some considerable extent determined by the nature of our own minds rather than by the nature of what is appearing, remains a very plausible viewpoint.

According to Kant, then, the physical world is the appearance to us of "things in themselves" of the real character of which we must be complete agnostics. Moreover, although I have spoken of its owing much of its character to the nature of our own minds, in fact what our own minds *really* are is also something of which we are completely ignorant. Thus the world of daily life and scientific investigation is the joint product of two things, an unknowable something which appears to us as our physical environment and an equally unknowable something which appears to us as our own mind.

That we do not know the real character of either of these does not prevent us making certain surmises about them. One such surmise concerns free will. Our actions considered as physical events must be the inevitable results of certain previous causes. This seems to rule out the freedom of the will which we must possess if moral judgment applies to us, for a deterministic machine cannot be praised or blamed for what it does. But if the natural world (the physical world plus our own minds as they appear to us) is only an appearance, then perhaps the freedom required by morality may be a feature of the unknown reality of which it is the appearance. Then again God and immortality, though our way of apprehending, and thereby determining, the character of nature can find no room for them, are perhaps somehow true of things as they are in themselves as opposed to how they appear.

(c)   Hegel and absolute idealism

Many philosophers have been persuaded of the truth of Kant's view that the general character of nature, as it presents itself to us, is the product of our own minds (whatever they may really be). But many of them felt that it was otiose to postulate the things in themselves of which Kant supposed it to be the appearance. Why not just conclude that nature as a whole is the product of our own minds, something which only exists as a presentation which our minds somehow give themselves?

This, however, is a very tough stance to take if the minds in question are simply human minds. Moreover, why is it that each mind creates a world so accordant with that of others? And how is it that I can change what is going on in the world as it is for you by changing the world as it is for me (as must be so if we are to communicate with each other)? One solution would be to suppose that I am the only mind and the world as it appears to me the only world. But this solipsistic position is one which no one, except in the madhouse (as Schopenhauer said), can take seriously.

But there is a solution which has seemed to many people irresistible, and that is that the world and its character is the product or the appearance of one great Cosmic Mind (or mind-like reality) of which our minds are somehow parts or aspects. This view is known as absolute idealism because the Cosmic Mind is often called "the Absolute."

If we call this Cosmic Mind "God" we seem to be back with Berkeley and so up to a point we are. But there is a big difference. For Berkeley there were an indefinite number of finite "spirits" or minds and one great infinite spirit, God. But the finite spirits were not parts or aspects of God, but rather something which

He had created (and with which He was in continual causal relation) without including them as parts of Himself.

The individual usually thought of as the leading figure in absolute idealism was G. W. F. Hegel (1770–1831). (Important too are such other German idealists as Fichte, 1762–1814, Schelling, 1775–1854, and Schopenhauer, 1788–1860.)

The natural world, and human beings in it, are, according to Hegel, the product of a process of self-alienation on the part of what he calls the Absolute Idea. The world stands in the puzzling relation to the Absolute Idea of both *being it* and *not being it*. For it is the Idea in a state of alienation from itself. Gradually, through the minds of human beings, it recognizes itself as being everything, although some of this everything is hidden from itself until this self-recognition via human minds. As the Idea grasps its own nature it realizes too that it is essentially Spirit or Mind (*Geist*).

The Idea tends to be identified with God by Hegel. What is not agreed upon by his readers is whether the Idea has any consciousness apart from that which it lives through in the minds of human beings. Nor is it clear whether the natural world is an illusion which the Idea gives itself, or rather an emanation from it, infused with it, but still with a kind of being in its own right.

However that may be, everything which in any sense there is, issues from the Idea, which conceives itself first as pure being, and then passes through a dialectical sequence of self-conceptions (only chronological towards its end) in which each successive conception resolves contradictions inherent in its predecessors, until it reaches a stage at which, via the consciousness of human beings, it grasps its own nature as spirit.

Great thinker, in his strange way, as Hegel was, the absolute idealists who most impress the present writer are certain philosophers writing in English towards the end of the nineteenth century, who were much influenced by both Kant and Hegel, and indeed also by Berkeley. Chief figures here are the British philosophers T. H. Green (1836–82), Edward Caird (1835–1908), F. H. Bradley (1864–1924), Bernard Bosanquet (1848–1923), the American philosopher Josiah Royce (1855–1916) and, earlier, James Ferrier (1808–64).

The present writer is himself an absolute idealist. This being so, since an examination of each of these philosophers is impractical, he will now present the case for a form of absolute idealism on his own behalf. His outlook is closest to Bradley's, but owes a good deal to Royce too.

Absolute Idealism Vindicated

Absolute idealism of the type we are about to describe is based upon five main claims.

(1)   Every thing stands in real relations to every other thing.

(2)   Every thing which exists is either an experience or a part of an experience.
(3)   Two (or more) things can be *really* related to each other if and only if EITHER there is a whole, which is as genuinely concrete an individual as is each of them, and which they help to constitute as parts thereof, OR alternatively, one of them is similarly a part of the other.
(4)   Each such part of such a whole has a character within its own bounds which it is impossible that anything not just such a part of that whole could possess.
(5)   If it is ever true that an event E occurred then it is thenceforth always true that E occurred.

Note that "thing" here refers to particular things only (not universals).

(1)   *Everything stands in real relations to everything else*

Relations are, *prima facie*, of two distinct types, which may be called "real relations" and "ideal relations" respectively. For simplicity I shall speak mostly only of two-term relations, but the same points apply to relations with three or more terms.

An ideal relation is one which relates terms simply in virtue of, and as a necessary consequence of, the inherent character of each. (An inherent character or property is one which does not consist in the fact that it is related in some specified way to something else.) A real relation is one which is not an ideal relation. The most obvious prima facie examples are spatial and temporal relations and the mental relation of co-presence in a single state of consciousness; also, some would add, the relation between a thought and its object.

If x IS A SQUARE and y IS A TRIANGLE the relation of *having one more side than* holds between them. If one object is *darker in color than* another, that must follow from THE PRECISE COLOR which each has within its own bounds. Since the expressions in capitals refer to inherent characters of the objects in question, it follows that the relations italicized are ideal relations.

In contrast, if two objects are *a mile distant from one another* that seems not to be a consequence of any non-relational properties on the part of the objects. They could remain (or so it seems) just the same in character and the distance between them alter. Thus the italicized expression denotes a real relation between them.

If ideal relations are included it is difficult to reject the idea that everything is in some relation to everything else. For whatever real relations may or may not hold between things there must surely be some truth as to how far their character is similar or dissimilar and in what ways.

But the absolute idealist, as we shall see, requires not merely that every thing be in *some* relation to every other thing but that every thing be in some *real* relation to every other thing.

There are two possible ways in which he might try to establish this.

(1) The first suggestion is that things cannot be in merely ideal relations, – that is, to be in an ideal relationship with something else a thing must also be in a real

relation to it. The main reason for suggesting this is the supposition that there cannot be ideal relations between things which cannot be compared. And this requires the possibility of some kind of transaction between these things and a comparing mind, a transaction which would require that they be in a relation – not merely a matter of a contrast or affinity between the characters of the three things involved, the mind, and the two terms compared.

If so, things cannot be in ideal relations unless they are in real relations. But since it has supposedly been established that everything is at least in some ideal relation to everything else, it follows that everything must be in some real relation to everything else.

But not a few would reject this, claiming rather that things belonging to worlds absolutely cut off from each other, with no spatial, temporal or mental relations between them, must still have ideal relations of contrast or affinity to each other, even though no one could become aware of this. For a surface, qua square, in another world will relate to a surface, qua triangular, in our world, in an ideal way just as it does within our world. (This would be seen as following from what might be called the Platonic relation between the universals which they respectively exemplify – squareness and triangularity.)

It is quite difficult to decide on this matter. Therefore there is something to be said for playing safe by adopting the following strategy.

(2) According to this we should interpret the statement that everything is in some real relation to everything else as concerning only things in *our* world. This may be explained as follows. My world is the totality of things with which I can have anything whatever to do, using "having to do with something" as including the case where I have to do with something else which has something to do with it, and so on recursively. Now you and I and anyone else who has anything to do with either of us belong to the same world because we can and do have something to do with each other however remotely.

We may then say that every thing in *our* world is in real relations to every other thing, and think that it is enough for metaphysics to give an account of our world, without bothering its head with whether there may be other worlds with the contents of which we have, and can have, nothing whatever to do.

This being so we can be confident of the truth of proposition (1) either because it is restricted to things in our world, or because its doing so follows from the truth that everything must have some ideal, and therefore some real, relation to everything else.

(2)   *Everything which exists is either an experience or a part of an experience*

My argument for this has two stages.

(a)   We cannot conceive of anything as unexperienced

Try to imagine something which is unexperienced.[1] Since physical things are the most obvious candidates for things which can exist unexperienced, choose some physical scene which is supposed not to be revealed to any mind. Note that the instruction is not to imagine something without bothering as to whether it is experienced or not, but to imagine something where its being unexperienced is part of what you are imagining.

That one cannot do this is a first phase in the argument of many idealists. But in evaluating this claim one must dissociate it from an entirely bogus reason for making it, namely that what you imagine is experienced by you, and hence not something unexperienced. (This is an argument many think Berkeley used, though I think this rests on a misunderstanding.) This is a bogus reason because, though when you imagine something, it can be said plausibly (though doubtfully) that your imagining it is a way of experiencing it, nonetheless the fact that you are imagining it is not, in relevant cases, part of what you are imagining. If it were, then you could not imagine an experience as that of someone else. But this is definitely false. If you have experienced a particular kind of sensation and you think that someone else is having it now, you can imagine it as being experienced by them, and not by you. (When you see someone else hit very hard you can imagine, up to a point, the pain he is feeling, but you are neither having, nor imagining yourself as having, that pain yourself.)

The question of what the difference is between imagining an experience as your own and as someone else's, requires a more complex answer than can be given here. A brief answer is that in the latter case you imagine it as part of a totality including a perspective on the world from a position in space and time, and perhaps with emotional feelings about things, which could not be yours. The elements of what you imagine, though based on your own experience, make a totality which you can imagine but could not actually live through.

But that bogus reason rejected, what is the correct reason for saying that you cannot imagine a physical thing or scene as unexperienced?

First, a point about the nature of imagination should be noted, namely that what you imagine only includes those characteristics which you use to "describe" what you are imagining. (Imagining something by a fuzzy image is not imagining the thing as fuzzy.) Thus while you can certainly imagine a physical thing without bothering your head as to whether it is experienced or not, you cannot imagine it as positively, so to speak, unexperienced. For you cannot include in the content of what you are imagining anything implying the absence of features the presence of which in anything marks it as an experience or as experienced (as you can imagine a man without hair on his head).

Thus you cannot imagine something as lacking all aesthetic qualities, as perceived from no particular position, and as without a certain organization into *gestalten* which reflect the concerns of an observer. The banks of a river cannot be imagined as lacking colors which are either beautiful, pretty, boring or something of that sort; moreover the image of it, if it is being imagined visually, cannot be deprived of a character which marks it as seen from some particular position, nor can it be imagined as without any organization into a pattern of individuated wholes.

Is it possible to imagine a flower, say, as without color? (Black, white and grey, of course, count as colors in this connection.) Well surely not visually, but perhaps you can do so through imagery pertaining to other senses. Thus purely tactile imagery may allow you to imagine the shapes and texture of its petals, leaves, and stem. Combined with olfactory imagery this may enable you to imagine a flower as it presumably figures in the colorless world of a man born blind. But the imagery is still bound to be replete with qualities that it seems clear could not be found outwith all consciousness, the possession of which prevents its use as a basis for imagining anything as unexperienced. I refer to the roughness and smoothness of surfaces, which varies with how you stroke them, and which will have some specific hedonic character, as more strikingly will all images of smell, – nor will some *gestalt* organization be absent.

But granted, it may be objected, that you cannot imagine a physical thing or scene as lacking features which it could only have within consciousness, does it follow that you cannot conceive of such a thing?

Here I must recall the reader to my claim that the metaphysician wants to have the real character of things made peculiarly perspicuous to him, and that means that something of that character must be at least adumbrated by something which falls within his own consciousness. And this, I believe, must consist in imagining it (or actually experiencing it, of course, but I leave this to be understood).

There is, however, a *via media* between what is imaginable and what is unimaginable. This consists of things which are *indirectly* imaginable. Something is indirectly imaginable if one can specify its character as that which stands in an ideal and imaginable relation to what is imaginable (directly or indirectly). A simple example is this. One can imagine a human being, or something very like one, with four arms, with six arms, and so forth, but one can hardly imagine such a being with a million arms. Yet insofar as *having two more arms than*, is an imaginable ideal relation, one can specify the character of possessing a million arms by steps which, starting from the character of possessing two arms, lead on to that of possessing a million arms. I suggest that a four-dimensional space may be indirectly imaginable in a kindred way, though that does not prove that there actually is, or even could be, such a thing.

But it seems to me impossible that one can specify the quality of being unexperienced as indirectly imaginable in this way. One can imagine a physical reality and remove, in imagination, more and more of the features which mark it as present in or to a mind, or mark them as present in an ever feebler degree. But I do not see that this reduction of marks of mentality can ever lead to something totally lacking in such signs.

Another thing which suggests that a physical thing or scene cannot be imagined as unexperienced is that it seems impossible to imagine a thing external to your body as not figuring as an element in some scene (such as a "view") which has its own vague limits, such as do our perceptual fields. Yet an unexperienced physical world would presumably have no articulation into anything at all like these.

But after all, you may say, conceiving or thinking of something is not the same as imagining it. But here I repeat that the metaphysician, if he is serious, wants to know what reality is truly like in an intimate way, which amounts to imagining it, if not directly, then indirectly. If, for any reason, he decides that there are things which we none of us can imagine, even so far as their general character goes, then he must take refuge in "things in themselves" of whose real character we must remain ignorant. I should add, briefly, that he will regard himself as referring to a particular outside his current experience if and only if he conceives it either as in an imaginable relation to something falling within it or is experiencing what he believes somehow to be its unique "tug" upon him.

The demand for imaginability is not a case of special pleading on the part of one cast of mind, as some philosophers may suggest. For imagining thus answers essentially one of the most traditional ways of explicating what it is to know a thing's character, namely that it is for the feature "formally" existing in the thing to exist "objectively" in the mind (which means existing as an object in the mind, hence rather "subjectively" in the modern sense). What is more it seems to me that many philosophers who have scorned what they have called the imagination have in fact rested their case on what is the same thing under another name. In particular I think that those who have claimed that they could not form a clear and distinct idea of such and such, have meant what I would call being unable to imagine it. Why has the mind/body problem, as it has presented itself since Descartes, been so striking? Surely because we cannot imagine any kind of totality including brain and mind, but can only imagine each separately. That people who use what is essentially the same method come to different results is, I suggest, because they are concentrating on different aspects of the matter in question.

If the metaphysician has to give up on the idea of *unexperienced physical reality*, he will have to find something else if he is to claim that he can conceive of anything at all existing unexperienced. I do not see what this could be.

One solution is certainly to speak of things in themselves à la Kant. But if one can find a positive view of the world which is genuinely explanatory there seems no need to postulate things in themselves. And anyway, further phenomenological experimentation may lead one to think that *being* or at least *existing*, itself can only be imagined as being experienced.

Thus one who agrees with my argument will acknowledge that we cannot conceive of anything as existing unexperienced, in particular that we cannot conceive of physical things as existing unperceived.

(b)   What follows from the inconceivability of unexperienced physical reality?

What follows is this. In attempting to give some general characterization of the nature of reality the metaphysician ought to drop the notion of unexperienced physical reality out of the picture. He must form a view of the world in which there is no such thing. But since our prime example of unexperienced reality is physical nature, it seems that he must really give up the idea of postulating any-thing at all which is unexperienced – his world must be an idealist one in which everything is experienced.

The only two things which may hold him back from complete commitment to this are, first, that he may hold that there are universals (something on the line of Platonic forms) which can exist unexperienced. Secondly, he may be tempted to postulate unknowable things in themselves.

As regards universals, we may remark *en passant* that in an older use of the expression "idealism," it refers precisely to the thesis that forms or universals are in some manner the basic source of reality. However, I think it best to say that universals *are*, that is, possess *being*, but do not exist, and that what exists is the particular things which exemplify them. Then, one can say that universals have *being*, even perhaps that they are fundamental to existence, but still stick to the idealist view that nothing does, or can, *exist* except the experienced. This will amount to saying that universals of their very nature can only be exemplified in experiences. (Whether their *being* depends upon their being experienced or not, we need not say, though, when we come to the Absolute, we can reasonably hold that all are somehow at least the object of thoughts which it contains.)

As regards things in themselves, reminding ourselves firmly that they are not physical things, let us keep them up our sleeve for the moment.

What view of unexperienced physical objects are we now forced to, granted that there can be no such thing? For we are apparently bound to believe in them for practical purposes and the metaphysician must explain how this is so, granted that there is no such thing.

There seem to me to be four possibilities.

(1)   Phenomenalism

This has been described as "Berkeley without God." Its best known proponents are J. S. Mill and the early A. J. Ayer. A phenomenalist like Ayer tends to be denied the label "idealist" because his outlook is too "unspiritual" to be graced with this expression. See (c) above.

For the phenomenalist, when conditions are such that it is appropriate to speak of some physical thing as existing unperceived, the real truth behind this is that the object would be perceived, if we, or someone else, took certain steps. If those steps are taken and the thing really is perceived then the thing (or as much of it as is perceived) really exists, but if not it does not exist, but is only something which certain steps of ours would call into existence.

Some phenomenalists will say that the unperceived object really does exist since the existence of a physical thing is simply the fact that it would be perceived under certain conditions. But surely something whose existence is a matter of what would be the case if something else were the case does not really exist at all in the proper sense; it is not part of the real concrete filling of reality.

It is worth remarking in passing that the phenomenalist must make some distinction between actions which would ordinarily be described as changing something and those which would ordinarily be described as simply taking steps to perceive it. For otherwise he would have to ascribe existence to all things which we might manufacture, inasmuch as they would be perceived if certain steps were taken, such as making the thing and then looking at it.

The main difficulty with phenomenalism is that it holds that innumerable counterfactual conditionals are true, which are not adequately grounded in what is actual. What makes it the case that I would perceive something if I took certain steps? It cannot be the existence of the thing itself, since this only exists in the sense that it would exist if I took those steps.

There seem but two possible answers. The **first** is the more or less Kantian view that there is a system of unknowable things in themselves which grounds the truth of these conditionals. The **second** is that there is a system of experiences which grounds this truth.

The first view may be called agnosticism about the sources of our perceptual experiences. One objection to this is that if we have decided that *to be* (or at least *to exist*) is *to be experienced*, then this agnosticism collapses into the second view. But even if this be denied, agnosticism remains a form of idealism in the sense that it accepts proposition (4) in our opening definition.

Now let us consider the second answer. This amounts to saying that there is a system of experiences which constitutes the thing in itself behind the existence of the physical world conceived as a system of possibilities. However, in giving this limited description of things in themselves it amounts virtually to acceptance of proposition (1) that nothing really exists except experienced reality, since the one plausible example of such a thing, unperceived physical objects, has been discounted.

(2)   The Physical World as Imaginative Construction

Phenomenalism seems wrong as an account of what we ordinarily mean in affirming the existence of unperceived physical things. For surely we think of them as actualities. How is this conception formed, erroneous as it may be? I suggest my answer briefly. Our experience of the physical world is of it as a sensory reality of which our experienced body is in a certain sense the center, felt from within and experienced as acting on what surrounds it to satisfy our felt needs. This sensory reality, which is the physical world as experienced by us at any moment, may be called a somatico-perceptual field (in which the contributions of all the senses, outer and inner, and a sense of their possibilities for action and reaction, are

synthesized). We think of our somatico-perceptual fields as fragments of an in-
definitely much larger reality of essentially the same sort, and we suppose that the
somatico-perceptual fields of others are fragments of the same thing. The physical world is conceived therefore as a totality rather like a somatico-perceptual field
of which all experienced such fields are, as it were, peculiarly illuminated parts.

As an adumbration of our ordinary conception of the physical world as something partly unperceived this seems to me largely right. But it is not a coherent
conception. First, there is some difficulty as to how this totality can be conceived
as other than a kind of divine sensory field, implying a cosmic mind to whose experience it belongs. But secondly it is incoherent because there could not be such
a whole, since each experience supposed to be a fragment of it is ranged round
an active "center" (the "lived body") and there is no way in which your such field
and mine could be parts of a whole at all of the same sort, since being thus ranged
round one body is incompatible with being ranged round another.

All the same our minds are certainly fed with experiences, which constitute such
fields, and there must be some explanation for this. It can hardly just be an ultimate fact. And the possible answers seem again two, either things in themselves
or some system of experiences.

(3)   The Purely Structural View of the Physical World

According to this there is some mystery as to what physical objects inherently are.
What we know about them is the general structure of physical reality and the particular structures within this general structure which pertain to particular physical
things. A structure is something which can be defined in highly abstract terms.
But the structuralist, as we may call such a philosopher, if he is sensible, will grant
that nothing can be merely structure, and that structures if they exist, are actualized in something more concrete. As to what this more concrete something is, the
structuralist may say he simply does not know.

Now the structuralist may be happy with this essentially agnostic position about
the more concrete nature of the physical, but some are not. And some of these
suggest that this concrete nature of the physical world consists in a system of
streams of experience. This is a form of panpsychism, to which I now turn.

(4)   Panpsychism

Each of the three positions, phenomenalism, constructionism, and structuralism
has left us with a choice between agnosticism as to the real source of our somatico-
perceptual experiences (at least in its full concrete reality) and the view that this

reality consists in a system of experiences. Panpsychism faces this choice boldly and opts for the second alternative.

Its case can be made, expressed only a little differently, whichever of the previous three positions is most favored. But essentially it is the view that what appears to us as the physical world, and which possesses the structure spoken of by the structuralist, is really a vast system of interacting centers or streams of experience.

I say centers or streams because there is some awkwardness as to whether to specify the ultimate ingredients of the world in terms of a continuant or an event (and series of events) ontology. To say that a certain thing exists over time can always be translated into a statement of the effect that there is a series of events related in some peculiarly intimate way (depending on the kind of thing in question) each of which counts as a state of that thing and a translation back seems always possible (though the shorter the time for which the thing exists the less helpful this form of speech). Since our physical object language is a continuant one, while (I believe) the most philosophically convenient way of describing experience is an event one, there is a certain awkwardness in stating panpsychism quite satisfactorily. It is perhaps best to push the physical object language towards an event ontology. In that case we can say that the existence of a physical thing over time, in short its history, consists in a series of momentary events, and that what this series really is, is a stream of experience.

Actually panpsychism requires a more complex account. Not every physical thing has a single stream of experiences as the *in itself* of its history. Thus the ultimate physical particles constituting a chair may do so, but it is implausible to suppose that the chair does. The *in itself* of its history must consist, rather, in *a complex of such streams* in intimate interaction with each other. However, it is not only the minutest of physical things whose history consists in an individual stream of experience. For it would seem that when minute physical things are arranged in certain ways they produce something which might be called the psyche of the whole. And this psyche (while it may itself be conceived of physically) will have a single stream of experience as the *in itself* of its history. The consciousness of a human being may be, from a physical point of view, such a psyche, but in itself it is a single stream of experience.

It should be clear at this stage that some form of idealism is compulsory. For we cannot conceive of an existing physical world which is unexperienced, and cannot think of anything else which might so exist, once it is granted that we cannot conceive of anything as unexperienced. We may be agnostic idealists in the style of Kant, or we may be panpsychist idealists, but (if my arguments are right) there is no further alternative. And it seems to me that we should embrace the latter, at least in the sense of attempting to understand the world in terms of it, because otherwise we sit complacently behind a brick wall without even attempting to get over it in the only possible way.

How far panpsychism is a possible way of getting over the wall turns on its more detailed answer to various problems, of which the most significant one is the relation between the mind and the brain. But one may also favor it because one has come to believe that *to exist* and *to be experienced* are the same thing.

> *(3)   Two (or more) things can be really related to each other if and only if EITHER there is a whole, which is as genuinely concrete an individual as is each of them, and which they help to constitute as parts thereof, OR alternatively, one of them is similarly a part of the other*

The next stage in the case for absolute idealism consists in establishing that all real relations are "holistic."

If we attempt to imagine, directly or indirectly, the holding of a real relation between two or more terms, I suggest that we will always find that this consists in thinking of a whole to the overall character of which each contributes its bit, as a part thereof; to forming a whole, moreover, which is at least as much a genuine individual as they are. Think of discovering the spatial relation between the streets of a town. Is not this to grasp how each thus helps to give the townscape the overall pattern which it possesses? And the town is surely at least as much an individual as each street is.

The one exception to this is the part/whole relation itself. To imagine this holding between terms is to imagine the part as making its own particular contribution to the character of the whole.

Such relations may be called holistic relations. (For simplicity I shall drop reference to the part/whole relation itself since the extension of my claims to this should be obvious.)

Well, I certainly cannot imagine two or more terms as relating to each other in a real way (not merely an ideal way) without imagining them as each part of such a whole, nor I suspect can you.

The position which we have reached so far, then, is that the universe consists of innumerable streams of experience, interacting with each other, and such that some of them constitute the mental histories of conscious persons to whom the system as a whole appears as a physical world. But if they are to be in any kind of real relation to each other, I claim that there must be some whole which they constitute together and which is at least as genuinely an individual as they are. What kind of whole could this be?

Ordinary thought sees no great difficulty here. For it thinks of your consciousness as somehow located in your body, and mine in my body, and that the bodies play each its own little part in constituting a spatially extended world. But this will not do once the metaphysical claims which I have been making are granted. For what each of our bodies really is, is a system of lower level streams of consciousness, and the bodies are therefore only related to each other in the way in which streams of consciousness can be, and it is precisely what this is which is our problem. For space, on our account, is either (1) an ultimately illusory construction which each of us makes on the basis of our own somatico-perceptual experience, an unreal whole of which our somatico-perceptual fields are supposed to be fragments or (2) an abstract structure pertaining to our interacting streams of experience.

It may be said that the relation between them is causal and that distinct streams of experience can interact causally. But the causal relation will not do the trick. Not, at least, on the usual view that for an event X to cause an event Y is for there to be a law from which it follows that if an X-type event occurs a Y-type event will occur which is in a certain relation R to it. For clearly this relation R cannot itself be the causal relation without an unsatisfactory regress. Popularly it is usually thought of as the relation of *immediately preceding in the same or adjacent place.* But subtler accounts of R will still leave causation "parasitic" upon another real relation, and cannot therefore act as the "cement of the universe" as it has been said to do.[2]

To me it seems that the only genuine wholes to which experiences can belong are wholes which are themselves experiences. One person's sensations relate to his conscious thought processes in virtue of the fact that they help to constitute together a single experience. And to me it seems inconceivable that there should be any whole within which they belong together, and which is at least as individual as they are, other than a "vaster" experience. This may or may not be a mental whole which includes absolutely every experience which there is. But if it is not, then it must be related to other experiences in, or constituting, the universe, in virtue of the fact that they contribute to the constitution of a still "vaster" experience. In this way there must eventually be reached an experience so "vast" that it includes everything else which there is, that is, includes all the experiences which make up the world, which is to say itself.

There are undoubtedly difficulties in this idea. It amounts to the claim that the universe is what may loosely (rather than mathematically) be called an infinitely comprehensive mental whole, mind or consciousness, which includes all our mental states. Yet we have a sense of being separate beings in a way that such parts of our consciousness as, for example, our individual sensations clearly do not. However, we are not entirely lacking in examples of pieces of our personality held together in one consciousness and yet having their own sense of self. In any case, I do not see any alternative view, and it is not surprising that there are puzzling features to the Absolute as we may now call this infinite mental whole or mind. It has been objected that the infinite mind can hardly include bits of itself which are as ignorant as we are. But they are only ignorant, and only mistaken, insofar as they lack the supplementations which are other parts of that same infinite consciousness.

We thus reach the conclusion that there is one total cosmic consciousness which includes all other experiences, that is, includes everything else or everything whatever if we speak of it as including itself.

(4)   *Each part of such a whole has a character within its own bounds which it is impossible that anything not just such a part of that whole could possess*

This is not a claim essential to absolute idealism, but absolute idealists usually make it. My own experience suggests its truth. For no bit of my experience at any moment has an inherent character which is altogether independent of its position in the whole experience. Or so it seems to me. For example a shape seen at the edge of the visual field is inherently other than it would be at its center, and pain is not quite the same when accompanied by one thought as by another. (This somewhat muddies the contrast between ideal and real relations in ways which we cannot explore.)

(5)   *If it is ever true that an event E occurred then it is thenceforth always true that E occurred*

I have been deliberately vague on the matter of time so far. Does the Absolute change with time? Is it a stream of consciousness which at any moment includes all experiences occurring at that moment, but not experiences which have occurred, except perhaps as some kind of memory, or experiences which will occur except as something anticipated? If the answer were *yes*, then we would have to worry about simultaneity, but since the answer is *no* we can bypass the question.

The view here taken is that it includes all experiences of all times and that time is in a certain sense unreal. A finite stream of experiences, such as yours or mine, consists of a large number of "total" experiences (each constituting one specious present) and each of these (the first and last in a single stretch of experience excluded) has a sense of emerging from another one of these total experiences and of debouching into another. The one it feels itself as emerging from is its immediate past, the one it feels itself as debouching into is its immediate future while its total past and future consists in all such experiences (at any rate roughly) as are related to it by the ancestral of the relation of *being the immediate past or future of.* All such total experiences, however, are just there together in the Absolute. Of course, they are ordered for the Absolute not just as a jumble but as a vast historical process which it tells itself timelessly. As for what a timeless experience is, it is as it were a frozen specious present which has no sense of emerging from or debouching into anything else.

The reason for holding this view is that, quite apart from its idealist elaboration, total reality must eternally include all that we, at any moment, call the past, the present, and the future.

This follows from proposition (5), that if it is ever true that an event E occurred then it is thenceforth always true that E occurred. For this shows that even if all mortal minds forget what happened on a certain day, and if no evidence to establish it is available, it still remains true that it did happen. But it can only be true that an event E happened in the past, if, in the most basic sense of what there is, there is such a thing as the event E. But what can E be? If it is a kind of shadow, or divine recollection, or anything like that of E, then it is not E itself, but E's simulacrum, or something of that sort. However, if E's simulacrum is to be of any use as what makes it true that E occurred, it must be a correct reproduction of E. But this requires that E be part of what there is else there is nothing for it to reproduce correctly. However, it can only be part of what there is if this includes all events, be they past or present, from any particular perspective within reality. And from this it follows that all events which from the point of view of any particular moment are future, are equally part of what there is. And this they can only be if they are eternally present from their own point of view. (Any cosmic memory or other simulacrum would be of no use unless E is part of reality eternally but with its own urgent feel of belonging momentarily to a unique NOW.) Thus my experience as of now is a perfect example of an event which lies in the future of an event which in itself is present and thereby shows us what the future is. (I have presented this argument more fully in other places.)

I have now done what I can within a short compass to make my case for the truth of absolute idealism. Reality is composed of innumerable finite experiences, many or most of them feeling as though they were but stages in a stream of consciousness within which they have taken over, and are about to be taken over, by other experiences. Many of these streams constitute the mental history of conscious individuals capable of quite elaborate processes of thinking. Such streams see themselves as the consciousness of organisms moving about in a space and time, these being their way of representing to themselves (in a manner practically useful for their success in continuing to flow) their position within reality. And all these experiences belong to an eternal cosmic consciousness which we may call "the Absolute." I add that, since the Absolute can, in the nature of the case (having no past or future), not be striving for any change in itself its state must be one of overall satisfaction rather than dissatisfaction, satisfaction perhaps with its own on balance worthwhile necessity despite all the sorrow which it contains. What bearing this view of the world has on ethics and religion cannot be considered here.

Notes

1   To be experienced, as I understand the expression, is either to be an experience or to be a component in an experience. A "total" experience typically divides into a self aspect and a not-self aspect. The former and its components are naturally called "experiences," the latter not so readily. Thus pains and emotions are said to be experiences, but the objects around you *just as they look (or otherwise present themselves) to you* are usually not, but both are experienced. (I am not begging the question in favor of idealism by this usage since it does not verbally exclude the possibility that they also exist outwith

experience.) A "total experience" is a unit like some experienced specious present. "Consciousness" refers to such total units and sequences thereof. Upon the whole, my arguments should carry through on the basis of various slightly different ways of conceptualizing such things and I have sometimes expressed myself in ways intended to conciliate their patrons.

2   The only at all promising alternative to this account of causation is that it is the felt fulfillment of some individual's will in something external to it, but this is impossible unless will and fulfillment flow into one another within a single stream of experience, or more truly within a single specious present. For even though we readily think of a stream of experience as an experienced unity, ultimately this distorts the facts which even here call for the conception of a supra-temporal whole which our experience only adumbrates.

Bibliography

A chronological list of the chief metaphysical works of all the idealist philosophers cited in the chapter. Date after title is that of first edition (in original language) where this differs from the edition listed; some of these works were substantially revised later. Only English translations are listed of the works written in German (often not of the first edition).

George Berkeley (1710). *A Treatise concerning the Principles of Human Knowledge.*
——(1713). *Three Dialogues between Hylas and Philonous.* (Both works are in volume 2 of *The Works of George Berkeley*, ed. A. A. Luce and T. E. Jessop. Thomas Nelson and Sons Ltd, 1949.)
James Ferrier (1854). *Institutes of Metaphysics: the Theory of Knowing and Being.* Edinburgh: W. Blackwood.
Immanuel Kant [1781] (1963). *Critique of Pure Reason*, trans. Norman Kemp Smith. London: Macmillan and Co.
J. G. Fichte [1794] (1982). *The Science of Knowledge*, ed. and trans. Peter Heath and John Lachs. Cambridge University Press.
F. W. J. Schelling [1800] (1981). *System of Transcendental Idealism*, trans. Peter Heath. University Press of Virginia.
G. W. F. Hegel [1807] (1931). *The Phenomenology of Mind*, trans. and ed. J. B. Baillie. London: George Allen and Unwin Ltd.
——[1807] (1977). *The Phenomenology of Spirit*, trans. A. V. Miller with analysis of the text by J. N. Findlay. Oxford University Press. (Of these two translations the first is more readable, the second more accurate.)
——(1988). *Lectures on the Philosophy of Religion* (lectures given in 1827), one volume edition translated by R. F. Brown and others and edited by Peter C. Hodgson. University of California Press.
Arthur Schopenhauer [1818] (1969). *The World as Will and Representation*, trans. E. F. J. Payne, two volumes. Dover Publications.
F. H. Bradley (1930). *Appearance and Reality: A Metaphysical Essay* (first edn. 1893; second edn. 1897). Oxford: Clarendon Press.
Bernard Bosanquet (1912). *The Principle of Individuality and Value.* London: Macmillan.
——(1913). *The Value and Destiny of the Individual.* London: Macmillan.
Edward Caird (1893). *The Evolution of Religion.* Glasgow: J. Maclehose.

Josiah Royce [1899 and 1901, first and second series] (1959). *The World and the Individual*. New York: Dover Publications Inc.

Recent books of an idealist tendency or studies of idealism in order of publication. Most of the authors have written other important and relevant books.

Leslie Armour (1972). *Logic and Reality. An investigation into the Idea of a Dialectical System*. Assen, van Gorcum.

Nicholas Rescher (1973). *Conceptual Idealism*. Oxford: Blackwell.

T. L. Sprigge (1983). *The Vindication of Absolute Idealism*. Edinburgh University Press.

T. L. S. Sprigge (1993). *James and Bradley: American Truth and British Reality*. Chicago: Open Court Press.

Paul Coates and Daniel D. Hutto (eds) (1996). *Current Issues in Idealism*. Bristol: Thoemmes Press.

David Boucher (ed.) (1997). *The British Idealists*. Cambridge University Press.

John Foster (1982). *The Case for Idealism*. London: Routledge and Kegan Paul, 1982.

Vitorrio Hösle (1998). *Objective Idealism, Ethics, and Politics*. University of Notre Dame Press, Notre Dame, Indiana.

Karl Ameriks (ed.) (2000). *The Cambridge Companion to German Idealism*. Cambridge University Press.

John Leslie (forthcoming 2002). *Infinite Minds*. Oxford: Oxford University Press.

Chapter 12

An Idealistic Realism: Presuppositional Realism and Justificatory Idealism

Nicholas Rescher

Aspects of Realism

Preliminaries

Realism is the doctrine that things are generally mind-independent, that what exists generally does so in ways unaffected by what mind-endowed beings think about it. Idealism, by contrast, is the doctrine that the way things are is in general dependent upon what and how minds think about it. These two doctrines are usually viewed as diametrical opposites locked into a position of conflict that extends through virtually the whole of the history of philosophy.

Often, however – and in metaphysics almost always – when discordant doctrines manage to maintain themselves over many generations – it transpires that there is really much to be said on all sides and that the most appropriate and tenable view of the matter is one that somehow manages to combine the best elements of both. Accordingly, the challenge that confronts the metaphysician in such cases is the shaping of a more complex doctrine that manages to effect a higher synthesis among the conflicting contentions by introducing whatever distinctions and sophistications are needed to achieve a reconciliation that accommodates the strong point of each rival position. The present discussion will endeavor to implement such a compromise.

Existence

We humans are amphibians equipped with minds to function in the realm of thought and with bodies to operate in the natural world of space–time and causality. Accordingly, when philosophers talk of existence they generally mean *physical existence* in the natural world. And here the term admits both a narrower and a broader construction. In its narrower construction, to exist physically is to be an object in space and time: to occupy a place here in the manner in which cats and trees and water molecules do. And to exist physically in the broader sense of the term is to play a role in the causal commerce of such things – and thus to represent features or activities of spatiotemporal things so as to exist in the manner in which headaches or human desires do, thereby figuring as part of the world's processual development. On this basis, existence can be specified in an essentially recursive manner as follows:

1 the things we experience with our internal and external senses exist;
2 the things whose existence we need to postulate to realize an adequate causal explanation of the things that exist also exist.

Accordingly, "to exist" (pure and simple) is to feature as a component or aspect of the causal commerce in the real world. And some jargon-expression such as "to subsist" needs to be coined for contextualized existence within a framework of supposition at issue with fictions or hypotheses. Thus merely possible objects – or *possibilia*, for short – are those things that merely "exist" in the sense of subsistence within a hypothetical realm on a fictional make-believe world.

Is man the measure?

Just exactly how is reality, so construed, related to knowledge? Whatever can be *known* by us humans to be real must of course, for that very reason, actually be real. But does the converse hold? Is humanly cognizable reality the only sort of reality there is? Some philosophers certainly say so, maintaining that there actually is a fact of the matter only when "we [humans] could in finite time bring ourselves into a position in which we were justified either in asserting or in denying [it]" (Dummett, 1958–9, p. 160). On such a view all reality is inevitably *our* reality. What we humans are not in a position to domesticate cognitively – what cannot be brought home to us by (finite!) cognitive effort – simply does not exist as a part of reality at all. Where we have no cognitive access, there just is nothing to be accessed. On such a perspective we are led back to the *homo mensura* doctrine of Protagoras: "Man is the measure of all things, of what is, that it is, of what is not, that it is not."

However, in reflecting on the issue in a modest mood, one is tempted to ask: "Just who has appointed us to this exalted role? How is it that *we humans* qualify as the ultimate arbiters of reality as such?"

Regarding this doctrine that what is real must be knowable, traditional realism takes an appropriately modest line. It insists on preserving, insofar as possible, a boundary-line of separation between ontology and epistemology; between fact and knowledge of fact, between truth-status possession and truth-status decidability with respect to propositions, and between entity and observability with respect to individual things. As the realist sees it, reality can safely be presumed to have depths that cognition may well be unable to plumb.

To be sure, it is possible to reduce the gap between fact and cognition by liberalizing the idea of what is at issue with cognizers. Consider the following series of metaphysical theses: *For something to be real in the mode of cognitive accessibility it is necessary for it to be experientiable by,*

- Oneself.
- One's contemporary (human) fellow inquirers.
- Us humans (at large and in the long run).
- Some actual species of intelligent creatures.
- Some physically realizable (though not necessarily actual) type of intelligent being – creatures conceivably endowed with cognitive resources far beyond our feeble human powers.
- An omniscient being (i.e., God).

This ladder of potential knowers is critically important for our present deliberations regarding the idea that to be is to be knowable. For here the question "By whom?" cannot really be evaded.

The idea of an experiential idealism that equates reality with experientiality is one that can accordingly be operated on rather different levels. Specifically, the "i-th level" idealist maintains – and the "i-the level" realist denies – such a thesis at stage number i of the preceding six-entry series. On this approach, the idealist emerges as the exponent of an experientiability theory of reality, equating truth and reality with what is experientially accessible by "us" – with different, and potentially increasingly liberal, constructions of just who is to figure in that "us group" of qualified cognizers. But of course no *sensible* idealist maintains a position as strong as the egocentrism of the first entry on the list. Equally it is presumably the case that no *sensible* realist denies a position as weak as the deocentrism of the last. The salient question is just where to draw the line in determining what is a viable "realistic/idealistic" position.

For present purposes we may leave God aside. He is notoriously a very special case – an exception to all the usual rules. Instead, let us focus for a time upon the third entry of the above listing, the "man is the measure," *homo mensura* doctrine. Now the bone of contention between a "man is the measure" realism and a sensible idealism is the question of a surplus – of whether reality may have parts or aspects that outrun altogether the reach of human cognition. And on this basis the *homo mensura* doctrine is implausible. For in the end, what we humans can know is not and cannot be decisive for what can (unqualifiedly) be known.

Undoubtedly, a mind that evolves in the world via natural selection has a link to reality sufficiently close to enable it to secure *some* knowledge of the real. But the converse is eminently problematic. It is a dubious proposition that the linkage should be so close that *only* what is knowable for some actual being should be real – that reality has no hidden reserves of fact that are not domesticable within the cognitive resources of existing creatures (let alone one particular species thereof!).

Accordingly, it seems sensible to adopt the "idealistic" line only at the penultimate level of the above listing and to be a realist short of that. Essentially this is the position of the causal commerce realism espoused at the outset of the present discussion. As such a position sees it, the most plausible form of idealism is geared to that next-to-last position which takes the line that "to be real is to be causally active – to be a part of the world's causal commerce." And since one can always hypothesize a creature that detects a given sort of causal process, we need not hesitate to equate reality with experientiability in principle. We thus arrive at an idealism which achieves its viability and plausibility through its comparative weakness in operating at the next-to-last level, while at all of the earlier, more substantive levels our position is effectively realistic. The result is a halfway-house compromise position that combines an idealism of sorts with a realism of sorts.

A conservative idealism of this description holds that what is so as a "matter of fact" is not necessarily cognizable by "us" no matter how far – short of God! – we extend the boundaries of that "us-community" of inquiring intelligences. On the other hand, one cannot make plausible sense of "such-and-such a feature of nature is real but no possible sort of intelligent being could possibly discern it." To be real is to be in a position to make an impact somewhere on something of such a sort that a suitably equipped mind-endowed intelligent creature could detect it. What is real in the world must make some difference to it that is *in principle* detectable. Existence-in-this-world is coordinated with perceivability-in-principle. And so, at this point, there is a concession to idealism – albeit one that is relatively weak.

But in any case, traditional *homo mensura* realism is untenable. There is no good reason to resort to a hubris that sees our human reality as definitive on grounds of being the only one there is. Neither astronomically nor otherwise are we the center around which all things revolve. After all, humans have the capacity not only for knowledge but also for imagination. And it is simply too easy for us to imagine a realm of things and states of things of which we can obtain no knowledge because "we have no way to get there from here," lacking the essential means for securing information in such as case.

Nevertheless an important point remains to be made in the light of the aforementioned hierarchy of potential knowers. Since to be physically real is to be part of the world's causal commerce, it is always in principle possible for an intelligent sentient being of a suitable sort to enter into this causal situation so as to be able to monitor what is going on. Accordingly *being* and *being knowable-in-principle* can plausibly be identified. The crucial contrast thus is not that between existence and knowability but rather between what is knowable by us and what is knowable in principle, all parochialism aside. Ironically, however, this relationship between knowledge and existence also has a reverse side.

Realism and incapacity

What is perhaps the most effective impetus to realism lies in the limitations of man's intellect, pivoting on the circumstances that the features of real things inevitably outrun our cognitive reach. In placing some crucial aspects of the real together outside the effective range of mind, it speaks for a position that sees mind-independence as a salient feature of the real. The very fact of fallibilism and limitedness – of our absolute confidence that our putative knowledge does *not* do full justice to the real truth of what reality is actually like – is surely one of the best arguments for a realism that turns on the basic idea that there is more to reality than we humans do or can know. Traditional scientific realists see the basis for realism in the substantive knowledge of the sciences; the present metaphysical realism, by contrast, sees its basis in our realization of the inevitable *shortcomings* of our knowledge – scientific knowledge included.

This epistemic approach accordingly preempts the preceding sort of objection. If we are mistaken about the reach of our cognitive powers – if they do not adequately grasp "the way things really are" – then this very circumstance clearly *bolsters* the case for the sort of realism now at issue. The cognitive intractability of things is something about which, in principle, we cannot delude ourselves altogether, since such delusion would illustrate rather than abrogate the fact of a reality independent of ourselves. The very inadequacy of our knowledge is one of the most salient tokens there is of a reality out there that lies beyond the inadequate gropings of mind. It is the very limitation of our knowledge of things – our recognition that reality extends beyond the horizons of what we can possibly know or even conjecture about it – that betokens the mind-independence of the real.

A meaningful realism can only exist in a state of tension. For the only reality worth having is one that is in some degree knowable. And so it is the very limitation of our knowledge – our recognition that there is more to reality than what we do and can know or ever conjecture about it – that speaks for the mind-independence of the real. It is important to stress against the sceptic that the human mind is sufficiently well attuned to reality that *some* knowledge of it is possible. But it is no less important to join with realists in stressing the independent character of reality, acknowledging that reality has a depth and complexity of make-up that outruns the reach of mind.

On the complexity of reals

As we standardly think about particulars within the conceptual framework of our factual deliberation and discourse, *any* real concrete particular has more features and facets than it will ever actually manifest in experience. For every objective property of a real thing has consequences of a dispositional character and these are never surveyable *in toto* because the dispositions which particular concrete things inevitably have endow them with an infinitistic aspect that cannot be comprehended within experience.[1] This desk, for example, has a limitless manifold of phenomenal features of the type: "having a certain appearance from a particular point of view." It is perfectly clear that most of these will never be actualized in experience. Moreover, a thing *is* what it *does*: entity and lawfulness are coordinated correlates – a good Kantian point. And this consideration that real things must exhibit lawful comportment means that the finitude of experience precludes any prospect of the *exhaustive* manifestation of the descriptive facets of any actual existents.[2]

Moreover, concrete things not only have more properties than they ever *will* overtly manifest, but they have more properties than they ever *can* possibly actually manifest. The existence of this latent (hidden, occult) sector is a crucial feature of our conception of a real thing. Neither in fact nor in thought can we ever simply put it away. To say of this apple that its only features are those it actually manifests is to run afoul of our conception of an apple. To deny – or even merely to refuse to be committed to the claim – that it *would* manifest particular features *if* certain conditions came about (for example, that it would have such-and-such a taste if eaten) is to be driven to withdrawing the claim that it is an apple. The latent, implicit ramifications of our objective factual claims about something real are potentially endless. The totality of facts about a thing – about any real thing whatever – is in principle inexhaustible and the complexity of real things is in consequence descriptively unfathomable. Endlessly many true descriptive remarks can be made about any particular actual concrete object. For example, take a stone. Consider its physical features: its shape, its surface texture, its chemistry, etc. And then consider its causal background: its subsequent genesis and history. Then consider its multitude of functional aspects as relevant to its uses by the stonemason, or the architect, or the landscape decorator, etc. There is, after all, no end to the perspectives of consideration that we can bring to bear on things. The botanist, herbiculturist, landscape gardener, farmer, painter, and real estate appraiser will operate from different cognitive "points of view" in describing one selfsame vegetable garden. And there is in principle no theoretical limit to the lines of consideration available to provide descriptive perspective upon a thing.

The properties of any real thing are literally open-ended: we can always discover more of them. Even if we were (surely mistakenly) to view the world as inherently finitistic – espousing a Keynesian principle of "limited variety" to the effect that nature can be portrayed descriptively with the materials of a finite taxonomic scheme – there will still be no a priori guarantee that the progress of science will not lead *ad infinitum* to changes of mind regarding this finite register of descriptive materials. And this conforms exactly to our expectation in these matters. For where the real things of the world are concerned, we not only expect to learn more about them in the course of scientific inquiry, *we expect to have to change our minds about their nature and modes of comportment*. Be the items at issue elm trees, or volcanoes, or quarks, we have every expectation that in the course of future scientific progress people will come to think about their origin and their properties differently from the way we do at this juncture.

Our characterization of real things can accordingly become more *extensive* without thereby becoming more *complete*. New descriptive features ongoingly come into view with the progress of knowledge. (Caesar not only did not, but in the existing state of knowledge could not have known that his sword contained tungsten.) Real things are – and by their very nature must be – such that their actual nature outruns any particular description of it that we might venture.

It follows from these considerations that we can never justifiably claim to be in a position to articulate "the whole truth" about a real thing. The domain of thing-characterizing fact inevitably transcends the limits of our capacity to *express* it, and *a fortiori* those of our capacity to canvas completely. In the description of concrete particulars we are caught up in an inexhaustible detail: There are always bound to be more descriptive facts about things than we are able to capture with our linguistic machinery: the real encompasses more than we can mange to say about it – now or ever.

The progressive nature of knowledge

The existence of this latent (hidden, occult) sector is a crucial element of our conception of a real thing. In this regard, however, real things differ in an interesting and important way from fictive ones. To make this difference plain, it is useful to distinguish between two types of information about a thing, namely that which is *generic* and that which is not. Generic information tells about those features of a thing which it has in common with everything else of its natural kind or type. For example, a particular snowflake will share with all others certain facts about its structure, its hexagonal form, its chemical composition, its melting point, etc. On the other hand, it will also have various properties which it does not share with other members of its own "lowest species" in the classificatory order – its particular shape, for example, or the angular momentum of its descent. These are its non-generic features.

Now a key fact about *fictional* particulars is that they are of finite cognitive depth. In discoursing about them we shall ultimately run out of steam as regards their non-generic features. A point will always be reached when one cannot say anything further that is characteristically new about them – presenting non-generic information that is not inferentially implicit in what has already been said. New *generic* information can, of course, always be forthcoming through the progress of science. When we learn more about coal-in-general then we know more about the coals in Sherlock Holmes' grate. But the finiteness of their cognitive depth means that the presentation of ampliatively novel *non-generic* information must by the very nature of the case come to a stop when fictional things are at issue.

With *real* things, on the other hand, there is no reason of principle why the provision of non-generically idiosyncratic information need ever be terminated.

On the contrary, we have every reason to presume these things to be cognitively inexhaustible. The prospect of discovery is open-ended here. A precommitment to description-transcending features – no matter how far description is pushed – is essential to our conception of a real thing. Something whose character was exhaustible by linguistic characterization would thereby be marked as fictional rather than real.[3]

This cognitive opacity of real things means that we are not – and will never be – in a position to evade or abolish the contrast between "things as we think them to be" and "things as they actually and truly are." Its susceptibility to further elaborate detail – and to changes of mind regarding this further detail – is built into our very conception of a "real thing." To be a real thing is to be something regarding which we can always, in principle, acquire further new information – information that may not only supplement but even correct that which has previously been acquired. Further inquiry can always, in theory, lead us to recognize the error of our earlier ways of thinking about things – even when thoroughly familiar things are at issue. It is, after all, a fact of life that scientific progress generally entails fundamental changes of mind about how things work in the world. And of course what is true of us will be true of all other finite knowers as well.

Hidden depths: realism and objectivity

The fact that we do and should always think of real things as having hidden depths inaccessible to us finite knowers – that they are always cognitively opaque to us to some extent – has important ramifications that reach to the very heart of the theory of communication.

Any particular thing – the moon, for example – is such that two related but critically different versions can be contemplated:

(1)   the moon, the actual moon as it "really" is

and

(2)   the moon as somebody (you or I or the Babylonians) conceives of it.

The crucial fact to note in this connection is that it is virtually always the former item – the thing itself – that we *intend* to communicate or think (= self-communicate) about, the thing *as it is*, and not the thing *as somebody conceives of it*. Yet we cannot but recognize the justice of Kant's teaching that the "I think" (I maintain, assert, etc.) is an ever-present implicit accompaniment of every claim or contention that we make. This factor of attributability dogs our every assertion and opens up the unavoidable prospect of "getting it wrong."

Communication requires not only common *concepts* but common *topics* – shared items of discussion. However, this fundamental objectivity-intent – the determination to discuss "the moon itself" (the real moon) regardless of how untenable one's own *ideas* about it may eventually prove to be – is a basic precondition of the very possibility of communication. It is crucial to the communicative enterprise to take the egocentrism-avoiding stance of an epistemological Copernicanism that rejects all claims to a privileged status for *our own* conception of things. Such a conviction roots in the fact that we are prepared to "discount any misconceptions" (our own included) about things over a very wide range indeed – that we are committed to the stance that factual disagreements as to the character of things are communicatively irrelevant within enormously broad limits.

We are able to say something about the (real) Sphinx thanks to our subscription to a fundamental communicative convention or "social contract": to the effect that we *intend* ("mean") to talk about it – the very thing itself as it "really" is – our own private conception of it notwithstanding. When I speak about the Sphinx – even though I do so on the basis of my own conception of what is involved here – I will nevertheless be taken to be discussing "the *real* Sphinx" in virtue of the basic conventionalized intention at issue with regard to the operation of referring terms.

Any pretentions to the predominance, let alone the correctness of our own potentially idiosyncratic conceptions about things must be put aside in the context of communication. The fundamental intention to deal with the objective order of this "real world" is crucial. If our assertoric commitments did not transcend the information we ourselves have on hand, we would never be able to "get in touch" with others about a shared objective world. No claim is made for the *primacy* of our conceptions, or for the *correctness* of our conceptions, or even for the mere *agreement* of our conceptions with those of others. The fundamental intention to discuss "the thing itself" predominates and overrides any mere dealing with the thing as we ourselves conceive of it.

The information that we may have about a thing – be it real or presumptive information – is always just that, viz. information that WE lay claim to. We cannot but recognize that it is person-relative and in general person-differentiated. Our attempts at communication and inquiry are thus undergirded by an information-transcending stance – the stance that we communally inhabit a shared world of objectively existing things – a world of "real things" amongst which we live and into which we inquire but about which we do and must presume ourselves to have only imperfect information at any and every particular stage of the cognitive venture. This is not something we learn. The "facts of experience" can never reveal it to us. It is something we postulate or presuppose to be able to put experience to cognitive use. Its epistemic status is not that of an empirical discovery, but that of a presupposition that is a product of a transcendental argument for the very possibility of communication or inquiry as we standardly conceive of them.

What is at issue here is not a matter of *discovery*, but one of *imputation*. The element of community, of identity of focus is not a matter of *ex post facto* learning from experience, but of an a priori predetermination inherent in our approach to language-use. We do not *infer* things as being real and objective from our phenomenal data, but establish our perception as authentic perception OF genuine objects through the fact that these objects are given – or rather, *taken* – as real and objectively existing things from the first.[4] Objectivity is not deduced but imputed. We do, no doubt, *purport* our conceptions to be objectively correct, but whether this is indeed so is something we cannot tell with assurance until "all the returns are in" – that is, never. This fact renders it critically important *that* (and understandable *why*) conceptions are communicatively irrelevant. Our discourse *reflects* our conceptions and perhaps *conveys* them, but it is not in general substantively *about* them but rather about the things on which they actually or supposedly bear.

We thus reach an important conjuncture of ideas. The ontological independence of things – their objectivity and autonomy of the machinations of mind – is a crucial aspect of realism. And the fact that it lies at the very core of our conception of a real thing that such items project beyond the cognitive reach of mind betokens a conceptual scheme fundamentally committed to objectivity. The only plausible sort of ontology is one that contemplates a realm of reality that outruns the range of knowledge (and indeed even of language), adopting the stance that character goes beyond the limits of characterization. It is a salient aspect of the mind-independent status of the objectively real that the features of something real always transcend what we know about it. Indeed, yet further or different facts concerning a real thing can always come to light, and all that we *do* say about it does not exhaust all that *can and should* be said about it. Objectivity and its concomitant commitment to a reality beyond our subjective knowledge of it is thus a fundamental feature of our view of our own position in the world's scheme of things.

The Idealistic Dimension

The rationale of realism

So much for the case for realism. Let us now take a fork in the road and turn towards idealism.

What is it – brute necessity aside – that validates those communicative presuppositions and postulations of ours? The prime factor at work here is simply our commitment to utility. Given that the existence of an objective domain of impersonally real existence is not a *product* of but a *precondition* for empirical inquiry, its acceptance has to be validated in the manner appropriate for postulates and prejudgments of any sort – namely in terms of its ultimate utility. Bearing this pragmatic perspective in mind, let us take a closer look at this issue of utility and ask: What can this postulation of a mind-independent reality actually do for us?

The answer is that we need that postulate of an objective order of mind-independent reality for at least six important reasons.

(1)   To preserve the distinction between true and false with respect to factual matters and to operate the idea of truth as agreement with reality.
(2)   To preserve the distinction between appearance and reality, between our *picture* of reality and reality itself.
(3)   To serve as a basis for inter-subjective communication.
(4)   To furnish the basis for a shared project of communal inquiry.
(5)   To provide for the fallibilistic view of human knowledge.
(6)   To sustain the causal mode of learning and inquiry and to serve as a basis for the objectivity of experience.

The long and short of it is that the assumption of a mind-independent reality is essential to the whole of our standard conceptual scheme relating to inquiry and communications. Without it, both the actual conduct and the rational legitimation of our communicative and investigative (evidential) practice would be destroyed. Nothing that we do in this cognitive domain would make sense if we did not subscribe to the conception of a mind-independent reality.

To begin with, we indispensably require the notion of reality to operate the classical concept of truth as "agreement with reality" (*adaequatio ad rem*). Once we abandon the concept of reality, the idea that in accepting a factual claim as true we become committed to how matters actually stand – "how it really is" – would also go by the board. The very semantics of our discourse constrain its commitment to realism; we have no alternative but to regard as real those states of affairs claimed by the contentions we are prepared to accept. Once we put a contention forward by way of serious assertion, we must view as real the states of affairs it purports, and must see its claims as facts. We need the notion of reality to operate the conception of truth. A factual statement on the order of "There are pi mesons" is true if and only if the world is such that pi mesons exist within it. By virtue of their very nature as truths, true statements must state facts: they state what really is so, which is exactly what it is to "characterize reality." The conception of *truth* and of *reality* come together in the notion of *adaequatio ad rem* – the venerable principle that to speak truly is to say how matters stand in reality, in that things actually are as we have said them to be.

In the second place, the nihilistic denial that there is such a thing as reality would destroy once and for all the crucial Parmenidean divide between appearance and reality. And this would exact a fearful price from us: we would be reduced to talking only of what we (I, you, many of us) *think* to be so. The crucial contrast notion of the *real* truth would no longer be available: we would only be able to contrast our *putative* truths with those of others, but could no longer operate the classical distinction between the putative and the actual, between what people merely *think* to be so and what actually *is* so. We would not take the stance that, as the Aristotelian commentator Themistius put it, "that which exists does not conform to various opinions, but rather the correct opinions conform to that which exists" (Maimonides, *The Guide for the Perplexed*, I, 71, 96a).

The third point is the issue of cognitive coordination. Communication and inquiry, as we actually carry them on, are predicated on the fundamental idea of a real world of objective things, existing and functioning "in themselves," without specific dependence on us and so equally accessible to others. Inter-subjectively valid communication can only be based on common access to an objective order of things. The whole communicative project is predicated on a commitment to the idea that there is a realm of shared objects about which we as a community share questions and beliefs, and about which we ourselves as individuals presumably have only imperfect information that can be criticized and augmented by the efforts of others.

This points to a fourth important consideration. Only through reference to the real world as a *common object* and shared focus of our diverse and imperfect epistemic strivings are we able to effect communicative contact with one another. Inquiry and communication alike are geared to the conception of an objective world: a communally shared realm of things that exist strictly "on their own" comprising an enduring and independent realm within which and, more importantly, with reference to which inquiry proceeds. We could not proceed on the basis of the notion that inquiry estimates the character of the real if we were not prepared to presume or postulate a reality for these estimates to be estimates of. It would clearly be pointless to devise our characterizations of reality if we did not stand committed to the proposition that there is a reality to be characterized.

The fifth item is a recourse to mind-independent reality which makes possible a "realistic" view of our knowledge as potentially flawed. A rejection of this commitment to reality *an sich* (or to the actual truth about it) exacts an unacceptable price. For in abandoning this commitment we also lose those regulative contrasts that canalize and condition our view of the nature of inquiry (and indeed shape our conception of this process as it stands within the framework of our conceptual scheme). We could no longer assert: "What we have there is good enough as far as it goes, but it is presumably not 'the whole real truth' of the matter." The very conception of inquiry as we conceive it would have to be abandoned if the contract conceptions of "actual reality" and "the real truth" were no longer available. Without the conception of reality we could not think of our knowledge in the fallibilistic mode we actually use – as having provisional, tentative, improvable features that constitute a crucial part of the conceptual scheme within whose orbit we operate our concept of inquiry.

Reality (on the traditional metaphysicians' construction of the concept) is the condition of things answering to "the real truth"; it is the realm of what really is as it really is. The pivotal contrast is between "mere appearance" and "reality as such," between "our picture of reality" and "reality itself," between what actually is and what we merely think (believe, suppose, etc.) to be. And our allegiance to the conception of reality, and to this contrast that pivots upon it, roots in the fallibilistic recognition that at the level of the detailed specifics of scientific theory, anything we presently hold to be the case may well turn out otherwise – indeed, certainly will do so if past experience gives any auguries for the future.

Our commitment to the mind-independent reality of "the real world" stands together with our acknowledgment that, in principle, any or all of our *present* scientific ideas as to how things work in the world, at *any* present, may well prove to be untenable. Our conviction in a reality that lies beyond our imperfect understanding of it (in all the various senses of "lying beyond") roots in our sense of the imperfections of our scientific world-picture – its tentativity and potential fallibility. In abandoning our commitment to a mind-independent reality, we would lose the impetus of inquiry.

Sixthly and finally, we need the conception of reality in order to operate the causal model of inquiry about the real world. Our standard picture of man's place in the scheme of things is predicated on the fundamental idea that there is a real world (however imperfectly our inquiry may characterize it) whose causal operations produce *inter alia* causal impacts upon us, providing the basis of our world-picture. Reality is viewed as the causal source and basis of appearances, the originator and determiner of the phenomena of our cognitively relevant experience. "The real world" is seen as causally operative both in serving as the external moulder of thought and as constituting the ultimate arbiter of the adequacy of our theorizing.

The conception of a mind-independent reality accordingly plays a central and indispensable role in our thinking about communication and cognition. In both areas alike we seek to offer answers to our questions about how matters stand in this "objective realm" and the contrast between "the real" and its "merely phenomenal" appearances is crucial here. Moreover, this is also seen as the target and *telos* of the truth-estimation process at issue in inquiry, providing for a common focus in communication and communal inquiry. The "real world" thus constitutes the "object" of our cognitive endeavors in both senses of this term – the *objective* at which they are directed and the *purpose* for which they are exerted. And reality is seen as pivotal here, affording the existential matrix in which we move and have our being, and whose impact upon us is the prime mover for our cognitive efforts. All of these facets of the concept of reality are integrated and unified in the classical doctrine of truth as it corresponds to fact (*adaequatio ad rem*), a doctrine that only makes sense in the setting of a commitment to mind-independent reality.

Accordingly, the justification for this fundamental presupposition of objectivity is not *evidential* at all; postulates are not based on evidence. Rather, it is *functional*. We need this postulate to operate our conceptual scheme. The justification of this postulate accordingly lies in its utility. We could not form our existing conceptions of truth, fact, inquiry, and communication without presupposing the independent reality of an external world. We simply could not think of experience and inquiry as we do. (What we have here is a "transcendental argument" of sorts from the character of our conceptual scheme to the acceptability of its inherent presuppositions.) The primary validation of that crucial objectivity postulate lies in its basic functional utility in relation to our cognitive aims.

What we have here is a "trans-continental deduction" of the following generic structure: If you want to achieve certain communicative ends then you must function as the basis of certain substantive commitments of a realistic and objectivistic sort. The fact of it is that our concept of a *real thing* is such that it provides a fixed point, a stable center around which communication revolves, an invariant focus of potentially diverse conceptions. What is to be determinative, decisive, definitive, etc., of the things at issue in my discourse is not my conception, or yours, or indeed anyone's conception at all. The conventionalized intention to a discursive coordination of *reference* means that a coordination of *conceptions* is not decisive for the possibility of communication. Your statements about a thing will and should convey something to me even if my conception of it is altogether different from yours. To communicate we need not take ourselves to share views of the world, but only take the stance that we share the world being discussed. This commitment to an objective reality that underlies the data at hand is indispensably demanded by any step into the domain of the publicly accessible objects essential to communal inquiry and interpersonal communication about a shared world. We could not establish communicative contact about a common objective item of discussion if our discourse were geared to the substance of our own idiosyncratic ideas and conceptions.

The ontological thesis that there is a mind-independent physical reality to which our inquiries address themselves more or less adequately – and always imperfectly – is the key contention of realism. But on the telling of the presenting analysis, this basic thesis has the epistemic status of a presuppositional postulate that is initially validated by its pragmatic utility and ultimately retrovalidated by the satisfactory results of its implementation (in both practical and theoretical respects). Our commitment to realism is, on this account, initially not a product of our *inquiries* about the world, but rather reflects a facet of how we *conceive* the world. The sort of realism contemplated here is accordingly one that pivots on the fact that we *think* of reals in a certain sort of way, and that in fact the very conception of the real is something we employ because doing so merits our ends and purposes. The rationale of a commitment to ontological objectivity is in the final analysis functionally or pragmatically driven. Without a presuppositional commitment to objectivity with its acceptance of a real world independent of ourselves that we share in common, interpersonal communication would become impracticable. Realism, then, is a position to which we are constrained not by the push of evidence but by the pull of purpose. Initially, at any rate, a commitment to realism is an *input* into our investigation of nature rather than an *output* thereof. At bottom, it does not represent a discovered fact, but a methodological presupposition of our praxis of inquiry; its status is not constitutive (fact-descriptive) but regulative (praxis-facilitating). Realism is not a factual discovery, but a practical postulate justified by its utility or serviceability in the context of our aims and purposes, seeing that if we did not *take* our experience to serve as an indication of facts about an objective order we would not be able to validate any objective claims whatsoever. (To be sure, what we can – and do – ultimately discover is that by taking this realistic stance we are able to develop a praxis of inquiry and communication that proves effective in the conduct of our affairs.)

Now insofar as realism ultimately rests on such a pragmatic basis, it is not based on considerations of independent substantiating evidence about how things actually stand in the world, but rather on considering, as a matter of practical reasoning, how we do (and must) think about the world within the context of the projects to which we stand committed. In this way, the commitment to a mind-independent reality plays an essentially utilitarian role as providing a functional requisite for our intellectual resources (specifically for our conceptual scheme in relation to communication and inquiry). Realism thus harks back to the salient contention of classical idealism that values and purposes play a pivotal role in our understanding of the nature of things. And we return also to the characteristic theme of idealism – the active role of the knower not only in the constituting but also in the constitution of what is known.

To be sure, this sort of idealism is not substantive but justifactory. It is not a rejection of real objects that exist independently of mind and as such are causally responsible for our objective experience; quite the reverse, it is designed to facilitate their acceptance. But it insists that the justificatory *rationale* for this acceptance lies in a framework of mind-supplied purpose. For our commitment to a mind-independent reality is seen to arise not *from* experience but *for* it – for the sake of putting us into a position to exploit our experience as a basis for validating inquiry and communication with respect to the objectively real.

A position of this sort is in business as a realism, all right. But seeing that it pivots on the character of our concepts and their *modus operandi*, it transpires that the business premises it occupies are actually mortgaged to idealism. The fact that objectivity is the fruit of communicative purpose allows idealism to infiltrate into the realist's domain.

And the idealism at issue cuts deeper yet. No doubt, we are firmly and irrevocably committed to the idea there is a physical realm out there which all scientific inquirers inhabit and examine alike. We hold to a single, uniform physical reality, insisting that all investigations exist within and investigate IT: this one single shared realism, this one single manifold of physical objects and laws. But this very idea of a single, uniform, domain of physical objects and laws represents just exactly that – *an idea of ours*. And the idea is itself a matter of how we find it convenient and efficient to think about things: it is no more – though also no less – than the projection of a theory devised to sort the needs and conveniences of our intellectual situation.

This approach endorses an object-level realism that rests on a presuppositional idealism at the justificatory infralevel. We arrive, paradoxical as it may seem, at a realism that is founded, initially at least, on a fundamentally idealistic basis – a realism whose ultimate *justificatory basis* is ideal.

Conceptual Idealism

The pivotal thesis of conceptual idealism is that real things *as we conceive of them* are infused with mind-supplied aspects. Of course there is nothing mental about a clue once the object at issue is characterized as such. But its being so characterizable in the first place is something that requires the interventions of mind.

The line of thought at issue can be set out as follows:

1 Any real object, anything that actually exists is in principle cognizable. For the item at issue, whatever it is, could not be all it is if it were not identifiable as such.

2 Something is cognizable (and identifiable) only under a description. To be real is to be a certain sort of thing – its identity can only be established under a certain sortal characterization.

3 Sortalization (characterization, description) and with it identification is a mind-involving operation. It can only be accomplished by mind-endowed beings.

The argument is thus straightforward: The fact that real things must be identifiable means that reality is a matter of existence-as; to exist at all is to exist as a certain sortal type of thing. And sortalization depends on mental operations (as William James rightly maintained, our interests determine our descriptive and classificatory schemata). And on this basis a realism of identifiable individuals is operatable only on the basis of an idealism of mental capacities in identification, description, and sortalization.

The very idea of an individual thing is thus mind-infected. For to identify something is to characterize it descriptively or to indicate it ostensively or somehow else distinguish if from other things. Identification is thus a process in which one person so acts as to indicate something to a comprehending interlocutor; all acts of identification have the common feature that *the attention of a mind is so directed as to be brought to focus upon something*. Accordingly, it should be an unproblematic and indeed even a superficial point that all modes of identification are mind-involving interactions. A basically interpersonal *transaction* is at issue here, namely – describing, discriminating, pointing out, distinguishing, and so forth, all of which invariable have a person as indirect object: they are transactions involving what one, some agent, does for another (or for himself – in the special case).[5] Identification is, by its very nature, a mentalistic act: "to identify" is an intellectual process and "to be identified" is accordingly a mind-involving condition. The very concept of identification involves an intrinsic reference to the directable attention of a comprehending intelligence.

Thought or discourse cannot coherently deal with a particular as "a thing as it is in itself" but must consider things under such-and-such a description. Objects must be *thought of* – exactly as they must be *seen* – from a perspective or "point of view." (Of course, with thought, unlike seeing, it is an *intellectual* perspective and not an optical one that is at issue: the perspective of a certain family of concepts.) But even as it is a virtually trite point that the *description* of any real thing or state of affairs is conceptually perspectival, so it is not hard to see that this must also hold for *identification*. Just as physical objects cannot be seen free from the limitations of a *physical* point of view, so things cannot be considered or discussed free from the limitations of a conceptual point of view. Just as things must always be seen from a spatial perspective, so they must be conceived or considered from a conceptual perspective "under a certain description," as current jargon has it. One can separate the particular itself from any one particular single description or mode of reference to it, but if this thing is going to be considered or discussed at all, this must, of course, be done from *some* conceptual perspective or other. And so, to return to the pivotal point, it is clear that particularity, which depends on identificatory individuation, is thereby something mind-involving.

It is sometimes said that idealism is predicated on a confusion of objects with our knowledge of them and conflates the real with our thought about it. But this charge misses the point. Conceptual idealism's thesis is not the trivial one that mind makes the *idea* of nature, it is not open to Santayana's complaint against Schopenhauer that "he proclaimed that the world was his idea, but meant only (what is undeniable) that his *idea* of the world was his idea." Rather, what is at issue is that mind-patterned conceptions are built into our idea of nature: that the way we standardly conceive of real things is in some crucial respects patterned on our self-conceptions as mind-endowed agents.

Conceptual idealism is predicated upon the important distinction between conceptual mind-involvingness and explicit mind-invokingness, illustrated in the contrast between a *book* and a *dream*. To characterize an object of consideration as a *dream* or a *worry* is explicitly mind-invoking. For dreams and worries exist only where there is dreaming and worrying, which, by their very nature, typify the sorts of things at issue in the thought-processes of mind-endowed creatures: where there are dreams or worries, there must be mind-equipped beings to do the dreaming and worrying. A book, by contrast, seems at first sight entirely non-mental: books, after all, unlike dreams or worries, are physical objects. If mind-endowed beings were to vanish from the world, dreams and worries would vanish with them – but not books! Even if there were no mind-endowed beings, there could certainly be naturally evolved book-like objects, objects *physically indistinguishable from books as we know them*. Nevertheless there could not be *books* in a world where minds had never been in existence. For a book is, by definition, an artifact of a certain purposive (i.e., communicative) sort equipped with pages on which "reading material" is printed. Such purposive artifacts all invoke goal directed processes of a type that can exist only where there are minds. To be a book it must have *writing* in it, and not just *marks*. And writing is inherently the sort of thing produced and employed by mind-endowed beings. In sum, to explain adequately what a *book* is we must thus make reference to writing and thereby in turn, ultimately to minds. The point is not that the book is mentalesque as a physical object, but rather that to explicate what is involved in characterizing that object as "a book" we must eventually refer to minds and their capabilities, seeing that a book is by its very nature something for people to read. A world in which there neither are nor ever have been minds can contain objects physically indistinguishable from our books and nails, but books and nails they could not be, since only artifacts created for a certain sort of intelligence-invoking purpose can correctly be so characterized. And so, while books – unlike dreams – are not mental items, their conceptual-ization/characterization must nevertheless in the final analysis be cast in mind-involving terms of reference.

And this sort of thing is true of real things in general, since to be real is to be knowable in principle by intelligent, mind-endowed beings. Accordingly, *concep-tual* idealism sees mind not as *causal source* of the materials of nature, but as indis-pensably furnishing some of the *interpretative mechanisms* such as individuality and agency in whose terms we standardly conceive of them.

A commitment to the existence of a realm of mind-independent reality is unquestionably part and parcel of our standard conceptual scheme for thinking about the world. Nevertheless, it is clear that to be a particular is to be identifi-able as an individual item with a nature and identity of its own: to be distin-guishable as one discrete item in contra-distraction to others. But even as what makes something a book is that it is readable, so what makes something an object in the real world is that it is experientiable. In its very nature, particularity con-sists in identifiability, distinguishability, discriminability. The prospect of identi-fication is crucial for objectivity: to be an object – even merely an object of consideration – it is requisite to have an identity, to be individualizable. But all of these processes (identifying, distinguishing, discriminating) are fundamentally mind-involving; each involves attention-directing and is accordingly the sort of thing that mind-endowed beings – and only mind-endowed beings – can do.

The impact of this argument that identification is mind-involving may be tempered by the following line of objection:

> Let it be granted (says the objector) that your argument has shown that to say 'X is *identified*' is to make a mind-referential claim. But this does not mean that 'X is *identifiable*' is mind-involving. Your approach slurs the cru-cial distinction between actuality and possibility. For consider the pairs: described/describable, mentioned/mentionable, indicated/indicatable, and identified/identifiable. If one grants that the first member of such a pair is mind-involving, one does not thereby concede that the second member is. Thus, saying that a certain particular is *identified* may well carry a covert reference to a mind, but this does not show that its *identifiability* is mind-dependent. Consequently, since generic particularity demands only identifi-ability, and not actual identification, your argument that actual identification is mind-involving does not show that *identifiability* is, and so does not suffice to establish the conclusion that particularity is.

This objection is to some extent well taken and specifically so insofar as its aim is to make the point – surely correct – that *actual* identification is not a necessary requirement for being a particular, since there is no contradiction in saying that there are particulars which are not identified (though obviously one cannot give an example of one). But the impetus of the objection can be deflected by recognizing the fundamental difference between identification on the one hand,

and description, indication, and the rest, on the other. For identification is, in the present context, entirely unique and *sui generis* in a way that impedes straight-forward application of the analogy of the actual and the potential on which the objection rests.

It makes perfectly good sense to say of something that it is describable but not described or indicatable but not indicated. The actual/potential distinction is indeed operative in these cases. *But this is not so with identification*: We cannot in principle meaningfully say *of something that IT* is identifiable but not identified, because to say this is to commit a literal nonsense. One would be saying expli-citly that one doesn't know what one is speaking of; where the item at issue is not identified there is nothing that we can say about it in specific terms. Until it has been identified (however imperfectly) we simply are not dealing with a particular individual thing: we cannot appropriately be held to say anything about "it" – not even that it is identifiable. To say this is not, of course, to deny that we can speak of otherwise unspecified particulars, as in a statement like "One of the trees in this forest has treasure buried beneath it." But cases of this sort pose no difficulty for our position. For if indeed there is treasure buried under just one tree, then we have, in effect, succeeded in making an identifying reference to it (as "the tree that has treasure beneath it"); but if there are several trees above the treasure (or none at all), then there just is no "it" about which we can be said to be speaking: our purportedly identifying reference fails to refer, so that our statement becomes – under these circumstances – semantically untenable.

To summarize: only two conceptual routes lead into the realm of the particu-lar, that of actual identification and that of potential identifiability. The former – identification – is conceptually mind-invoking because identification is an attention-directing, and thus an overtly mental process. The latter – identifiability – is implicitly mind-involving because of the mentalesque nature of *identification* itself.

It is useful in this connection to reemphasize once more the important dis-tinction between the *ontological* mind-dependency of mind invokingness and the *conceptual* mind-dependency of mind involvingness. Granted, only identification is mind-dependent in the strong sense of mind involvingness, and not identifia-bility. But that of course does not prevent identifiability from being *conceptually* mind involving – as it indeed is, seeing that the issue pivots on the focusing of attention. To say of something that it is related to minds in a certain way (specif-ically in the way of admitting being identified by them) is obviously to character-ize it in conceptually mind-referring terms (even as describing it as *visible* would be to characterize it in conceptually sight-referring terms of reference).

Acknowledgment

I am grateful to Richard Gale for constructive criticism.

Notes

1   To be sure, various *abstract* things, such as colors or numbers, will not have dispositional properties. For being divisible by four is not a *disposition* of sixteen. Plato got the matter right in Book VII of the *Republic*: in the realm of mathematical abstracta there are not genuine *processes* – and process is a requisite of dispositions. Of course, there may be dispositional truths in which numbers (or colors, etc.) figure that do not issue in any dispositional properties of these numbers (or colors, etc.) themselves – a truth, for example, such as my predilection for odd numbers. But if a truth (or supposed truth) does no more than to convey how someone *thinks* about a thing, then it does not indicate any property of the thing itself. (Fictional things, however, *can* have suppositional dispositions: Sherlock Holmes was addicted to cocaine, for example.)

2   This aspect of objectivity was justly stressed in the "Second Analogy" of Kant's *Critique of Pure Reason*, although his discussion rests on ideas already contemplated by Leibniz. See G. W. Leibniz, *Philosophische Schriften*, edited by C. I. Gerhardt, Vol. VII, pp. 319ff.

3   This also explains why the dispute over mathematical realism (Platonism) has little bearing on the issue of physical realism. Mathematical entities are akin to ficitonal entities in this – that we can only say about them what we can extract by deductive means from what we have explicitly put into their defining characterization. These abstract entities do not have non-generic properties since each is a "lowest species" unto itself.

4   The point is Kantian in its orientation. Kant holds that we cannot experientially learn through our perceptions about the objectivity of outer things, because we can only recognize our perceptions as perceptions (i.e., representations of outer things) if these outer things are given as such from the first (rather than being learned or inferred). As Kant summarizes his "Refutation of Idealism": "Idealism assumed that the only immediate experience is inner experience, and that from it we can only *infer* outer things – and this, moreover, only in an untrustworthy manner. . . . But on the above proof it has been shown that outer experience is really immediate. . . ." (*Critique of Pure Reason*, B276).

5   Thus spots in the visual field, identifiable to no one save the subject himself, qualify as identifiable items. The identificatory transaction is multi-personal in the *standard* cases, but not always; paradigmatically and generally, but not inevitably.

Bibliography

Brandom, Robert (1994). *Making it Explicit*. Cambridge, MA: Harvard University Press.

Causey, R. L. (1977). *Unity of Science*. Dordrecht: Reidel.

Davidson, Donald (1980). *Essays on Actions and Events*. New York: Oxford University Press.

Dummett, Michael (1958–9). "Truth," *Proceedings of the Aristotelian Society*, vol. 59, p. 160.

Eddington, Arthur S. (1929). *The Nature of the Physical World*. New York: The Macmillan Company, and Cambridge: Cambridge University Press.

Ewing, A. C. (1934). *Idealism: A Critical Survey*. London: Methuen.

Kant, Immanuel, *Critique of Pure Reason*.

McDowell, John (1994). *Mind and World*. Cambridge, MA: Harvard University Press, second edn. 1996.

Peirce, Charles S. (1931–58). Charles Hartshorne et al. (eds.), *Collected Papers of Charles S. Peirce*. Cambridge, MA: Harvard University Press, 8 vols.

Putnam, Hilary (1988). *Representation and Reality*. Cambridge, MA: Harvard University Press.

——(1990). *Realism with a Human Face*. Cambridge, MA: Harvard University Press.

Rescher, Nicholas (1978). *Scientific Progress*. Oxford: Basil Blackwell.

——(1982). *Empirical Inquiry*. Totowa, NJ: Rowman & Littlefield.

——(1984). *The Limits of Science*. Berkeley and Los Angeles: University of California Press.

——(1985). *The Strife of Systems*. Pittsburgh: University of Pittsburgh Press.

——(1987). *Scientific Realism*. Dordrecht: D. Reidel.

——(1988). *Rationality*. Oxford: Oxford University Press.

——(1989). *Cognitive Economy*. Pittsburgh: University of Pittsburgh Press.

——(1990). *A Useful Inheritance*. Savage, MD: Rowman & Littlefield.

——(1994). *Philosophical Standardism*. Pittsburgh: University of Pittsburgh Press.

——(1995). *Satisfying Reason*. Dordrecht: Kluwer.

——(1996). *Priceless Knowledge?* Lanham, MD: University Press of America.

——(1997). *Predicting the Future*. Albany: State University of New York Press.

Rorty, Richard (1982). *Consequences of Pragmatism*. Minneapolis: University of Minnesota Press.

Russell, Bertrand (1948). *Human Knowledge: Its Scope and Limits*. Simon & Schuster.

Salmon, Wesley C. (1989). *Four Decades of Scientific Explanation*. Minneapolis: University of Minnesota Press.

Simon, Herbert A. (1969). *The Sciences of the Artificial*. Cambridge, MA: MIT Press, 2nd edn. 1981.

Wigner, E. P. (1949). "The Limits of Science," *Proceedings of the American Philosophical Society*, vol. 93, pp. 521–6.

——(1960). "The Unreasonable Effectiveness of Mathematics in the Natural Sciences," *Communications on Pure and Applied Mathematics*, 13, pp. 1–14.

Chapter 13

Overcoming a Dualism of Concepts and Causes: The Basic Argument of "Empiricism and the Philosophy of Mind"

Robert Brandom

Some of the most interesting and important metaphysics of the last 400 years addresses the nature of intentionality: our capacity to direct our activity by our beliefs about the things around us. Intentionality – the aboutness or representational character of thought – is the most fundamental feature of our mindedness. The metaphysics of intentionality during the early modern period has been structured by an overarching distinction that shows up in many more specific forms: body vs. mind, order of things vs. order of ideas, representings and representeds, causal vs. conceptual. A distinction qualifies as a dualism when it is drawn in a way that makes unintelligible the relations between what is distinguished, and this fundamental distinction in the metaphysics of intentionality has often threatened to become a dualism.[1] The Cartesian variety had special features that seemed to be important for the difficulties faced by the whole picture. It understood the subjective in terms of the theoretical transparency, incorrigibility, or certainty of the mental, and its practical indefeasibility, dominion, or local omnipotence. (Descartes was impressed by the fact that one can be wrong about how things *are*, but not about how they *seem*, and that while it may not be in one's power to *do* something, it is always in one's power to *try* to do something.) This understanding of the subjective is one of the reasons that without what can seem as a metaphysical detour through God, Descartes cannot explain how the physical world can affect our thought through perception, or how thought can affect the physical world through action. Important as his more particular ideas about subjectivity were, rejecting these features of Descartes' view turned out to be far from sufficient to avoid the danger of commitment to various other forms of what is broadly the same sort of dualism, however. Even philosophical approaches that have rejected much of the specifically Cartesian metaphysics of the subject can have trouble with their accounts of the interactions between the causal order and the conceptual order. And this ought not to surprise us. After all, it didn't turn out to help very much with this problem to give up the specifically Cartesian metaphysics of the physical in terms of pure extension.

The rise of modern philosophy is coeval with the rise of modern science. Descartes, of course, was a major player in both fields. He crystalized the problem that was to engage philosophers down to our own day: how to understand the place of *minds* in the physical world revealed to us by the new science. That was a *causal* world: a world, in the familiar slogan, of atoms in the void. A new kind of mathematized theoretical understanding was revealing that world to us as never before. But it was by no means clear that there was room in that emerging picture for the theorists themselves. How could *understanding* or *thinking* something be understood to fit into this picture? The activity of classifying something under the concepts of physics – as extended, with a certain size, shape, position, and motion – did not itself seem obviously to be itself intelligible in terms of the sorts of physical properties science was discovering. Intentionality is our capacity to represent things, to understand them, to think *about* them (including the ability to think about things that are distant in space or time, or even nonexistent). The best Descartes himself could do was to postulate the existence of a special kind of stuff, mindstuff, which was understood as essentially representative in nature – by contrast to physical stuff, which by nature could only be represented. But he was wholly unable to say how the two sorts of stuff interacted, and so unable to say anything helpful about what it is for a thought or concept to be about something in the causal order, where laws of nature hold sway. This response has been almost universally found to be unsatisfactory.

One of the most distinctive attempts to offer a new diagnosis of and therapy for the ills of broadly Cartesian dualisms of the causal and the conceptual is to be found in the work of one of the great systematic metaphysicians of the midtwentieth century: Wilfrid Sellars. Like Descartes (and Plato), his metaphysics grows out of his epistemology. The connection between the two subjects is different for him, because he does *not* (as Descartes does) subscribe to the Platonic principle that fundamental differences in kinds of being can be read off of structural differences in the ways we know them. (For instance, for reasons discussed below, Sellars opposes the instrumentalist thought that purely theoretical objects, which are known only inferentially, are ontologically – rather than methodologically – of a different kind from observable objects, which are known perceptually.) The epistemological diagnosis that funds Sellars' metaphysical reconciliation of the causal and the conceptual is set out in his master-work: *Empiricism and the Philosophy of Mind* (Sellars, 1956; hereafter *EPM*).

That essay is one of the great works of twentieth-century philosophy. It is rich, deep, and revolutionary in its consequences. It cannot, however, be ranked among the most *perspicuous* of philosophical writings. Although it is fairly easy to discern its general tenor and tendency, the convoluted and digressive order of exposition pursued in the essay has obscured for many readers the exact outlines of such a fundamental concept as *givenness* – with the result that few could at the end of their reading accurately trace its boundaries and say what all its species have in common, being obliged instead to content themselves with being able to recognize some of its exemplary instances. Again, I think that partly for this reason, readers of *EPM* seldom realize just how radical is its critique of empiricism – just how much of traditional empiricist ways of thinking must be rejected if Sellars' arguments are accepted. And if the full extent of the work's conclusions is hard to appreciate, all the more difficult is it to follow its argumentative path through all its turnings. In what follows my aim is to lay out one basic idea of Sellars', which I see as underlying three of the most important arguments he deploys along the way to his conclusions. My concern here will not be in how those arguments contribute to his overall enterprise, but rather in how they are rooted in a common thought. Sellars does not make this basic idea as explicit as one would like, and does not stop along the way to observe how each of the three individual arguments depends on it. But if I am right, we will understand the essay better by being able to identify and individuate this thread in the tapestry.

The master idea I want to start with is Sellars' understanding of observational capacities: the ability to make noninferential reports of, or to form perceptual judgments concerning, perceptible facts. My claim is that he treats them as the product of two distinguishable sorts of abilities: the capacity reliably to discriminate behaviorally between different sorts of stimuli, and the capacity to take up a position in the game of giving and asking for reasons. The three central strategic moves in the essay I will seek to understand in terms of that two-factor approach to observation are: first, the way he dissolves a particular Cartesian temptation by offering a novel account of the expressive function of "looks" talk; second, his rationalist account of the acquisition of empirical concepts; and third, his account of how theoretical concepts can come to have observational uses.

Sellars' Two-Ply Account of Observation

If we strip empiricism down to its core, we might identify it with the insight that knowledge of the empirical world depends essentially on the capacity of knowing organisms to respond differentially to distinct environing stimuli. I'll call this claim "*basic*," or "stripped down" empiricism; it could equally well be called the *trivial* thesis of empiricism.[2] Surely no rationalist or idealist has ever denied *this* claim. While differential responsiveness is obviously a necessary condition for empirical knowledge, it is clearly nothing like a sufficient condition. A chunk of iron responds differentially to stimuli, for instance by rusting in some environments, and not in others. To that extent, it can be construed as *classifying* its environments, taking or treating them as being of one of two kinds. In the same way, as Hegel says, an animal takes something as food by "falling to without further ado and eating it up."[3] But this sort of classificatory taking something *as* something should not yet be classed as a *cognitive* matter, on pain of losing sight of the fundamental ways in which genuine observationally acquired knowledge differs from what is exhibited by merely irritable devices such as thermostats and land mines.

A parrot could be trained to respond to the visible presence of red things by uttering the noise "That's red." We might suppose that it is disposed to produce this performance under just the same circumstances in which a genuine observer and reporter of red things is disposed to produce a physically similar performance. There is an important respect in which the parrot and the observer are alike. We could call what they share a *reliable differential responsive disposition* (which I'll sometimes shorten to "RDRD"). RDRDs are the first element in Sellars' two-ply account of observational knowledge. At least in the basic case, they are characterizable in a naturalistic, physicalistic vocabulary.[4] The concept of an RDRD is meant to capture the capacity we genuine knowers share with artifacts and merely sentient creatures such as parrots, that the basic thesis of empiricism insists is a necessary condition of empirical knowledge.

The second element of Sellars' two-ply account of observational knowledge is meant to distinguish possessors of genuine observational belief and knowledge from merely reliable differential responders. What is the crucial difference between the red-discriminating parrot and the genuine observer of red things? It is the difference between *sentience* and *sapience*. For Sellars' purposes in *EPM*, the difference between merely differentially responding artifacts and genuinely sentient organisms does not make an essential cognitive or epistemological difference. *All* we need pay attention to in them is their exercising of reliable differential responsive dispositions. But he is very concerned with what distinguishes both of these sorts of things from genuine observers. His thought is that the difference that makes a difference is that candidates for observational knowledge don't just have reliable dispositions to respond differentially to stimuli by *making noises*, but have reliable dispositions to respond differentially to those stimuli by *applying concepts*. The genuine observer responds to visible red things by coming to believe, claiming, or reporting *that* there is something red. Sapient awareness differs from awareness in the sense of mere differential responsiveness (the sort exhibited by any organism or device that can for instance be said in the full sense to be capable of avoiding obstacles) in that the sapient being responsively classifies the stimuli as falling under concepts, as being of some conceptually articulated kind.

It is obvious that everything turns on how one goes on to understand concept application or the conceptual articulation of responses. For Sellars, it is a linguistic affair: grasping a concept is mastering the use of a word. Then we must ask what makes something a use of a word, in the sense relevant to the application of concepts. Sellars' answer is that for the response reliably differentially elicited by the visible presence of a perceptible state of affairs to count as the application of a concept, for it to be properly characterized as a reporting or coming to believe *that* such-and-such is the case, is for it to be the making of a certain kind of move or the taking up of a certain kind of position in a game of giving and asking for reasons. It must be committing oneself to a content that can both serve as and stand in need of *reasons*, that is, that can play the role both of premise and of conclusion in *inferences*. The observer's response is conceptually contentful just insofar as it occupies a node in a web of inferential relations.

What the parrot lacks is a *conceptual understanding* of its response. That is why it is just making noise. Its response means nothing to the parrot – though it may mean something to us, who *can* make inferences from it, in the way we do from changes in the states of measuring instruments. The parrot does not treat *red* as entailing *colored*, as entailed by *scarlet*, as incompatible with *green*, and so on. And because it does not, uttering the noise "red" is not, for the parrot, the adopting of a stance that can serve as a reason committing or entitling it to adopt other stances, and potentially in need of reasons that might be supplied by still further such stances. By contrast, the observer's utterance of "That's red," is making a move, adopting a position, in a game of giving and asking for reasons. And the observer's grasp of the conceptual content expressed by her utterance consists in her practical mastery of its significance in that game: her knowing (in the sense of being able practically to discriminate, a kind of knowing *how*) what follows from her claim and what it follows from, what would be evidence for it and what is incompatible with it.

Although Sellars does not carefully distinguish them, two different strands can be discerned within this second element of his account. First is the idea that for performances (whether noninferentially elicited responses or not) to count as *claims*, and so, as expressions of *beliefs* or *judgments*, as candidates for *knowledge*, they must be in what he calls "the dimension of endorsement."[5] This is to say that they must have a certain sort of pragmatic significance or force: they must express the endorsement of some content by the candidate knower. They must be the adoption of a certain kind of normative stance: the undertaking of a *commitment*. Second, that the commitment is a *cognitive* commitment, the endorsement of a *conceptual content*, is to be understood in terms of its *inferential* articulation, its place in the "space of reasons," its being a move in the "game of giving and asking for reasons."[6] This is to say at least that in making a claim, one commits oneself to its suitability as a premise from which conclusions can be drawn, a commitment whose entitlement is always at least potentially liable to demands for vindication by the exhibition of other claims that can serve as reasons for it.

This two-factor account of perceptual judgments (claims to observational knowledge) is a version of a broadly Kantian strategy: insisting on the collaboration of capacities characterizable in terms of receptivity and spontaneity. It is a pragmatic version, since it is couched in terms of know-*how*: practical abilities to respond differentially to nonlinguistic stimuli, and to distinguish in practice what inferentially follows from or serves as a reason for what. The residual empiricism of the approach consists in its insistence on the need for the exercise of some of our conceptual capacities to be the exercise of RDRDs. Its residual rationalism consists in its insistence that the responses in question have cognitive significance, count as applications of concepts, only in virtue of their role in reasoning. What otherwise would appear as language-entry moves, without language-language moves, are blind. What otherwise would appear as language-language moves without language-entry moves, are empty. (I say "what otherwise would appear" as moves because such blind or empty moves do not for Sellars qualify as moves in a *language* game at all.)[7]

It follows from this two-pronged approach that we must be careful in characterizing perceptual judgments or reports of observations as "noninferential." They are noninferential in the sense that the particular acts or tokenings are noninferentially *elicited*. They are not the products of a process of inference, arising rather by the exercise of reliable capacities to noninferentially respond differentially to various sorts of perceptible states of affairs by applying concepts. But *no* beliefs, judgments, reports, or claims – in general, no applications of concepts – are noninferential in the sense that their content can be understood apart from their role in reasoning as potential premises and conclusions of inferences. Any response that does not at least potentially have an inferential significance – which cannot, for instance, serve as a premise in reasoning to further conclusions – is cognitively idle: a wheel on which nothing else turns.

This rationalist claim has radical consequences. It means that there can be no language consisting only of noninferential reports, no system of concepts whose *only* use is in making perceptual judgments. Noninferential reports do not form an autonomous stratum of language: a game one could play though one played no other. For that they are *reports* or *claims*, expressions of *beliefs* or *judgments*, that they are applications of *concepts* at all, consists in their availability to serve as premises and conclusions of inferences. And this is so no matter what the subject matter of the reports might be – even if what is reported, that of which one is noninferentially aware, is one's own current mental states. Awareness that reaches beyond mere differential responsiveness – that is, awareness in the sense that bears on *cognition* – is an essentially inferentially articulated affair.

So observational concepts, ones that have (at least some) noninferential circumstances of appropriate application, can be thought of as *inference laden*. It does not follow, by the way, that they are for Sellars for that reason also *theory laden*. For, as will appear below, Sellars understands theoretical concepts as those that have only inferential circumstances of appropriate application – so that noncompound claims in which they occur essentially are ones that one can only become entitled to as the result of an inference. His rationalist rendering of the notion of conceptual contentfulness in terms of role in reasoning only commits Sellars to the claim that for any concept to have noninferential uses, it must have inferential ones as well. He is prepared to countenance the possibility of an autonomous language game in which every concept has noninferential, as well as inferential uses. Such a language game would be devoid of theoretical terms.

"Looks" Talk and Sellars' Diagnosis of the Cartesian Hypostatization of Appearances

One of the central arguments of *EPM* applies this two-legged understanding of the use of observational concepts to the traditional understanding of claims about how things *look* as reports of *appearances*. The question he addresses can be variously put. In one form it is the question of whether *looks-red* come before *is-red* conceptually (and so in the order of explanation). Put in a form more congenial and comprehensible to a pragmatist – that is, in a form that concerns our abilities to *do* something – this becomes the question of whether the latter can be defined in terms of the former in such a way that one could learn how to use the defining concept (*looking-φ*) first, and only afterwards, by means of the definition, learn how to use the defined concept (*is-φ*). Since Sellars understands grasp of a concept in terms of mastery of the use of a word, this then becomes a question about the relation between practices of using "look-φ" talk and the practices of using "is-φ" talk. This is a relatively clear way of asking about an issue that goes to the heart of the Cartesian project of defining the ontological realm of the mental in terms of epistemic privileged access in the sense of incorrigibility of mental occurrences.

Descartes was struck by the fact that the appearance/reality distinction seems not to apply to appearances. While I may be mistaken about whether something *is* red (or whether the tower, in the distance, *is* square), I cannot in the same way be mistaken about whether it *looks* red to me now.[8] While I may legitimately be challenged by a doubter: "Perhaps the item is not *really* red; perhaps it only *seems* red," there is no room for the further doubt, "Perhaps the item does not even *seem* red; perhaps it only *seems* to seem red." If it seems to seem red, then it really does seem red. The *looks, seems,* or *appears* operators collapse if we try to iterate them. A contrast between appearance and reality is marked by the distinction between *looks-φ* and *φ* for ordinary (reality-indicating) predicates "φ". But no corresponding contrast is marked by the distinction between *looks-to-look-φ* and *looks-φ*. Appearances are reified by Descartes as things that really are just however they appear. He inferred that we do not know them mediately, by means of representings that introduce the possibility of *mis*-representing (a distinction between how they really are and how they merely appear, i.e., are represented as being). Rather, we know them *immediately* – simply by having them. Thus appearings – thought of as a realm of entities *reported* on by noninferentially elicited claims about how things *look* (for the visual case), or more generally *seem*, or *appear* – show up as having the ideal qualifications for epistemologically secure foundations of knowledge: we cannot make mistakes about them. Just *having* an appearance ("being appeared-to φ-ly," in one of the variations Sellars discusses) counts as *knowing* something: not that something is φ, to be sure, but at least that something *looks-, seems-,* or *appears-φ*. The possibility accordingly arises of reconstructing our knowledge by starting out only with knowledge of this sort – knowledge of how things look, seem, or appear – and building up in some way to our knowledge (if any) of how things really are (outside the realm of appearance).

This project requires that concepts of the form *looks-φ* be intelligible in principle in advance of grasping the corresponding concepts *φ* (or *is-φ*). Sellars argues that Descartes got things backwards. "Looks" talk does not form an autonomous stratum of the language – it is not a language-game one could play though one played no other. One must already be able to use "is-φ" talk in order to master "looks-φ" talk, which turns out to be parasitic on it. In this precise practical sense, *is-φ* is *conceptually* (Sellars often says "logically") *prior* to *looks-φ*.

His argument takes the form of an account of how "looks" talk can arise piggy-backed on "is" talk. In *EPM* Sellars does not try to support the strong modal claim that the various practices *must* be related in this way. He thinks that his alternative account of the relation between these idioms is so persuasive that we will no longer be tempted by the Cartesian picture. It is an interesting question, which I will not pursue here, whether his story can be turned into a more compelling argument for the stronger claim he wants to make. What he offers us is the parable of John in the tie shop.

At the first stage, John has mastered the noninferential use of terms such as "green" and "blue." So he can, typically, reliably respond to green things by applying the concept *green*, to blue things by applying the concept *blue*, and so on. To say that his responsive dispositions are reliable is to say that he usually turns out to be right – so the inference from his being disposed to call something "green" or "blue" to its being green or blue is a generally good (though not infallible) one.

At the next stage, electric lights are installed in the shop, and John discovers that they make him prey to certain sorts of systematic errors. Often, when under the electric lights inside his shop he observes something to be green, it turns out in fact – when he and others examine it outside in daylight – to be blue. Here it is obviously important that John have access to some ways of entitling himself to the claim that something is blue, besides the term he is initially disposed to apply to it. This can include his dispositions to respond to it outside the shop, together with his beliefs about the circumstances in which ties do and do not change color, the assessments of others, and the fact that the proper use of color terms was originally keyed to daylight assessments. At this point, John becomes cautious. When viewing under the nonstandard conditions of electric lighting, he does not indulge his otherwise reliable disposition to respond to some visible ties by calling them green. Instead he says something like: "I'm disposed to call this green, and if I didn't know that under these circumstances I'm not a reliable discriminator of green things, I would give in to that temptation and call it green."

At the final stage, John learns under these circumstances to substitute the expression "It *looks* green," for this long expression of temptation withstood. Using the expression "looks-φ" is doing two things: first, it is evincing the same usually reliable differential responsive disposition that in other circumstances

results in the claim that something *is*. But second, it is *withholding* the endorsement of the claim that something is green. In other words, it is doing something
that agrees with an ordinary noninferential report of green things on the first component of Sellars' two-ply account of observation reports – sharing an RDRD –
but disagrees with it on the second component, withholding endorsement instead
of undertaking the commitment.

The idea is that where collateral beliefs indicate that systematic error is likely,
the subject learns not to make the report "*x* is φ," to which his previously incul-
cated responsive dispositions incline him, but to make a new kind of claim: "*x*
looks (or seems) φ." The Cartesian temptation is to take this as a new kind of
report. This report then is naturally thought of as reporting a minimal, noninferentially ascertainable, foundationally basic item, an appearing, about which each
subject is incorrigible. Sellars' claim is that it is a mistake to treat these as reports
at all – since they *evince* a disposition to call something φ, but do not do so. They
do not even *report* the presence of the disposition – that is, they are not ways of
saying that one has that disposition.

This analysis of what one is doing in using "looks" explains the incorrigibility
of "looks" talk. One can be wrong about whether something *is* green because the
claim one endorses, the commitment one undertakes, may turn out to be incor-
rect. For instance, its inferential consequences may be incompatible with other
facts one is or comes to be in a position to know independently. But in saying that
something *looks* green, one is not endorsing a claim, but *withholding* endorsement
from one. Such a reporter is merely evincing a disposition to do something that
for other reasons (e.g., suspicion that the circumstances of observation lead to
systematic error) he is unwilling to do – namely, endorse a claim. Such a reporter
cannot be wrong, because he has held back from making a commitment. This is
why the *looks, seems,* and *appears* operators do not iterate. Their function is to
express the withholding of endorsement from the sentence that appears within the
scope of the operator. There is no sensible contrast between "looks-to-look φ"
and "looks-φ," of the sort there is between "looks-φ" and "is-φ" because the first
"looks" has already withheld endorsement from the only content in the vicinity
to which one might be committed (to something's being φ). There is no further
withholding work for the second "looks" to do. There is nothing left to take back.
Since asserting "X looks φ" is not undertaking a propositionally contentful commitment – but only expressing an overrideable disposition to do so – there is no
issue as to whether or not that commitment (which one?) is correct.

Sellars accordingly explains the incorrigibility of appearance-claims, which had
so impressed Descartes. He does so in terms of the practices of using words, which
are what grasp of the relevant appearance concepts must amount to, according to
his methodological linguistic pragmatism. But once we have seen the source and
nature of this incorrigibility – in down-to-earth, practical, resolutely nonmeta-
physical terms – we see also why it is precisely unsuited to use as an epistemological foundation for the rest of our (risky, corrigible) empirical knowledge. For, first,
the incorrigibility of claims about how things merely *look* simply reflects their

emptiness: the fact that they are not really claims at all. And second, the same story shows us that "looks" talk is not an autonomous language game – one that could be played though one played no other. It is entirely parasitic on the practice of making risky empirical reports of how things actually are. Thus Descartes seized on a genuine phenomenon – the incorrigibility of claims about appearances, reflecting the non-iterability of operators like *looks, seems,* and *appears* – but misunderstood its nature, and so mistakenly thought it available to play an epistemologically foundational role for which it is in no way suited.

Two Confirmations of the Analysis of "Looks" Talk in Terms of the Two-Ply Account of Observation

Sellars finds that the analysis of "looks" talk in terms of the two-pronged account of perceptual judgments is confirmed by its capacity to explain features of appearance-talk that are mysterious on the contrasting Cartesian approach.

  (i)   The apple over there is red.
 (ii)   The apple over there looks red.
(iii)   It looks as though there were a red apple over there.

Utterances of these sentences can express the same responsive disposition to report the presence of a red apple, but they endorse (take responsibility for the inferential consequences of) different parts of that claim. (i) endorses both the existence of the apple, and its quality of redness. (ii) endorses only the existence of the apple. The "looks" locution explicitly cancels the qualitative commitment or endorsement. (iii) explicitly cancels both the existential and the qualitative endorsements. Thus, if someone claims that there is in fact no apple over there, he is asserting something incompatible with (i) and (ii), but not with (iii). If he denies that there is anything red over there, he asserts something incompatible with (i), but not with (ii) or (iii). Sellars' account of the practice of using "looks," in terms of the withholding of endorsement when one suspects systematic error in one's responsive dispositions, can account for the difference in scope of endorsement that (i)–(iii) exhibit. But how could that difference be accounted for by an approach that understands "looks" talk as reporting a distinctive kind of particular, about which we are incorrigible?

    Sellars finds a further confirmation of his account of "looks" talk – and so of the two-factor account of observational capacities that animates it – in its capacity to explain the possibility of reporting a merely *generic* (more accurately, merely determinable) look. Thus it is possible for an apple to look merely red, without its looking any specific shade of red (crimson, scarlet, etc.). It is possible for a plane figure to look many-sided without there being some particular number of sides (say 119) which it looks to have. But if "looks" statements are to be understood as reports of the presence before the eye of the mind of a particular which *is*, how can this possibility be understood? Particulars are completely determinate. A horse has a particular number of hairs, though as Sellars points out, it can *look* to have merely "a lot" of them. It is a particular shade of brown (or several shades), even though it may look only darkly colored. So how are such generic, merely determinable, looks possible? Sellars' account is in terms of scope of endorsement. One says that the plane figure looks "merely many-sided" instead of "119-sided" just in case one is willing only to endorse (be held responsible for justifying) the more general claim. This is a matter of how far one is willing to trust one's responsive dispositions, a matter of the epistemic credence one feels they deserve or are able to sustain. Particulars, even if they are sense contents, cannot be colored without being some determinate color and shade. How then can the sense datum theorist – who wants to say that when something *looks* φ to S, something in S *is* φ – account for the fact that something can look colored without looking to be any particular color, or look red without looking to be any particular shade of red? So Sellars' account of "looks" talk in terms of endorsement can account for two aspects of that kind of discourse that no theory that invokes a given can explain: the scope distinctions between qualitative and existential lookings, and the possibility of merely generic or determinable lookings.

A Rationalist Account of the Acquisition of Empirical Concepts

It is characteristic of empiricism as Sellars understands (and rejects) it, that it countenances a notion of awareness or experience meeting two conditions. First, it goes beyond mere differential responsiveness in having some sort of cognitive *content* – that is, content of the sort that under favorable circumstances amounts to knowledge. This is the idea of a notion of awareness or experience *of* a red triangle in one's visual field that can at the same time be (or be one's evidence for) knowledge *that* there is a red triangle in one's visual field. Second, this sort of awareness is *preconceptual*: the capacity to be aware in this sense or have experiences of this sort is prior to and independent of the possession of or capacity to apply concepts. The idea of a kind of awareness with these two features is what Sellars calls the "Myth of the Given."

Whatever difficulties there may be with such a conception – most notably the incoherences Sellars rehearses in the opening sections of *EPM* – it does provide the basis for a story about concept acquisition. Concepts are understood as acquired by a process of *abstraction*, whose raw materials are provided by exercises of the primitive capacity for immediate, preconceptual awareness.[9] One may – and Sellars does – raise questions about whether it is possible to elaborate this story in a coherent fashion. But one ought also to ask the corresponding question to the empricists' rationalist opponents. Rationalists like Sellars claim that *all* awareness is a conceptual affair. Being aware of something, in any sense that goes beyond mere responsiveness in its potential cognitive significance – paradigmatically in its capacity to serve as *evidence* – is bringing it under a concept. Sense experience cannot be the basis for the acquisition of concepts, since it presupposes the capacity to apply concepts. So how *do* knowers acquire concepts? At this point in the dialectic, classical rationalists such as Leibniz threw up their hands and invoked innate ideas – denying that at least the most basic and general concepts *were* acquired at all. Sellars owes either a defense of innatism, or an alternative account of concept acquisition.

Sellars rejects innatism. Grasp of a concept is mastery of the use of a word, so concepts are acquired in the process of learning a language. But if we don't acquire the concept *green* by noticing green things, since we must already have the concept in order to notice green things as such (by applying the concept to them), how is it possible for us to learn the use of the word "green," and hence acquire the concept? We each start by learning the corresponding RDRDs: being trained to respond to visibly green things by uttering what is still for the novice just the *noise* "green." This much, the parrot can share. Besides these language-entry moves, the language learner must also master the inferential moves in the vicinity of "green": that the move to "colored" is OK, and the move to "red" is not, and so on. Training in these basic language-language moves consists in acquiring more RDRDs, only now the stimuli, as well as the responses, are utterances.

If a two-year old wobbles into the living room and utters the sentence "The house is on fire," we will not generally take him to have claimed or expressed the belief that the house is on fire. He does not know what he is saying – in the sense that he does not yet know what he would be committing herself to by that claim, or what would be evidence for it or against it. If a five-year-old child utters the same sentence, though, we may well take the utterance to have the significance of a claim, the expression of a belief. We take it to be the adoption of a stance in the dimension of endorsement, to be the undertaking of a commitment, by *holding* the child responsible for her claim: asking for her evidence, asking her what she thinks we should to about it, and so on. For it is now presumed that she can tell what she is committing herself to, and what would entitle her to that commitment, and so knows what she is saying, what claim she is endorsing, what belief she is expressing. When the child masters enough of the inferential moves in the vicinity of a responsively elicited utterance of "That is red," she is taken to have endorsed a claim, and so to have applied a concept.

On the inferential account of distinctively conceptual articulation, grasping a concept requires mastering the inferential connections between the appropriate use of some words and the appropriate use of others. So on this account there is no such thing as grasping just one concept: grasping *any* concept requires grasping *many* concepts. Light dawns slowly over the whole.

How good must one be at discriminating the appropriate antecedents and consequents of using a word in order to count as grasping the concept it expresses? Sellars does not explicitly address this question in *EPM*, but I think his view is that whether or not one's utterance has the significance of endorsing a claim, and so of applying a concept, is a question of how it is treated by the other members of the linguistic community. The normative status of committing oneself – taking up a position in the dimension of endorsement – is a social status. One must be good enough at anticipating and fulfilling one's responsibilities in order to be *held* responsible, and so for one's remarks to be accorded authority, in the sense of being treated as providing suitable premises for inferences by others. How much is enough is not a metaphysical matter of recognizing the crossing of some antecedently specifiable boundary, but a social matter of deciding when to recognize a performance as authoritative and hold the performer responsible. It is a question that belongs in a box with: When does writing one's name at the bottom of a piece of paper count as committing oneself to pay the bank a certain sum of money every month for thirty years? Some seventeen-year olds may actually understand what they would be committing themselves to better than some twenty-two-year olds. But the community is not therefore making a metaphysical mistake in treating the latter but not the former as able genuinely to commit themselves.

Sellars' account of concept acquisition starts with reliable differential responsive dispositions to respond to environing stimuli by uttering sentences. What is then required is that one's utterance come to have the significance of making a move in the game of giving and asking for reasons. That requires two elements: the practical inferential know-how required to find one's way about in the inferential network connecting different sentences, and the social acknowledgment of that know-how as sufficient for one's performances to have the significance in the linguistic community of commitments to or endorsements of the inferentially articulated claims expressed by those sentences. This story is structured and motivated by Sellars' two-pronged account of observation reports, as noninferentially elicited endorsements of inferentially articulated claims.

Giving Theoretical Concepts an Observational Use

As a final example of the work Sellars calls on his two-pronged analysis of observational capacities to do in *Empiricism and the Philosophy of Mind*, we might consider his account of how theoretical concepts can acquire an observational use. His reason for addressing the issue is that he wants to make intelligible the idea that some sorts of paradigmatic mental occurrences – thoughts and sense impressions – might first become available to us purely theoretically, and only later come to be observable by us. For showing that such a development in our capacities *is* intelligible provides a means of confounding the Cartesian idea of immediate (that is, noninferential) observability as *essential* to the very idea of mental occurrences. But my concern here is with the general point, rather than this particular application of it.

The first point to realize is that, as I mentioned above, according to Sellars' view, the distinction between theoretical objects and observable objects is *methodological*, rather than *ontological*. That is, theoretical and observable objects are not different kinds of thing. They differ only in how we come to know about them. Theoretical objects are ones of which we can only have *inferential* knowledge, while observable objects can also be known noninferentially. Theoretical concepts are ones we can only be entitled to apply as the conclusions of inferences, while concepts of observables also have noninferential uses. But the line between things to which we have only inferential cognitive access and things to which we also have noninferential cognitive access can shift with time, for instance as new instruments are developed. Thus when first postulated to explain perturbations in the orbit of Neptune, Pluto was a purely theoretical object; the only claims we could make about it were the conclusions of inferences. But the development of more powerful telescopes eventually made it accessible to observation, and so a subject of noninferential reports. Pluto did not then undergo an ontological change. All that changed was its relation to us.[10]

It might be objected to this view that when the issue of the ontological status of theoretical entities is raised, they are not considered merely as objects in principle like any others save that they happen at the moment to be beyond our powers of observation. They are thought of as *unobservable* in a much stronger sense: permanently and in principle inaccessible to observation. But Sellars denies that anything is unobservable in this sense. To be observable is just to be noninferentially reportable. Noninferential reportability requires only that there are circumstances in which reporters can apply the concepts in question (the dimension of inferentially articulated endorsement) by exercising reliable differential dispositions to respond to the objects in question (the causal dimension), and know that they are doing so. In this sense, physicists with the right training can *noninferentially* report the presence of mu mesons in cloud chambers. In this sense of "observation," nothing real is in principle beyond the reach of observation. (Indeed, in Sellars' sense, one who mastered reliable differential responsive dispositions noninferentially to apply *normative* vocabulary would be directly observing normative facts. It is in this sense that we might be said to be able to *hear*, not just the noises someone else makes, but their *words*, and indeed, *what they are saying* – their *meanings*.) It is an empirical question what circumstances we can come reliably to respond to differentially. The development of each new sort of measuring instrument potentially expands the realm of the here-and-now observable.

Once one sees that observation is not based on some primitive sort of preconceptual awareness, the fact that some observation reports are riskier than others and that when challenged we sometimes retreat to safer ones from which the originals can be inferred will not tempt one to think that the original reports were in fact the products of inference from those basic or minimal observations. The physicist, if challenged to back up his report of a mu meson, may indeed justify his claim by citing the distinctively hooked vapor trail in the cloud chamber. This is something else observable, from which the presence of the mu meson can, in the right circumstances, be inferred. But to say that is not to say that the original report was the product of an inference after all. It was the exercise of a reliable differential responsive disposition keyed to a whole chain of reliably covarying events, which includes mu mesons, hooked vapor trails, and retinal images. What makes it a report of mu mesons, and not of hooked vapor trails or retinal images, is the inferential role of the concept the physicist noninferentially applies. (It is a consequence of something's being a mu meson, for instance, that it is *much* smaller than a finger, which does *not* follow from something's being a hooked vapor trail.) If *mu meson* is the concept the physicist applies noninferentially, then if he is sufficiently reliable, when correct, that is what he *sees*. His retreat, when a question is raised, to a report of a hooked vapor trail, whose presence provides good inferential reason for the original, noninferentially elicited claim, is a retreat to a report that is safer in the sense that he is a *more* reliable reporter of hooked vapor trails than of mu mesons, and that it takes less training to be able reliably to report vapor trails of a certain shape, so that is a skill shared more widely. But the fact that an inferential justification can be offered, and that the demand for one may be in order, no more undermines the status of the original report as noninferentially elicited (as genuinely an observation) than does the corresponding fact that I may under various circumstances be obliged to back up my report of something as red by invoking my reliability as a reporter of red things in these circumstances – from which, together with my disposition to call it red, the claim originally endorsed noninferentially may be inferred. Thus one can start with grasp of a concept that consists entirely in mastery of its use as a premise and conclusion in inferences – that is, as a purely theoretical concept – and by the addition of suitable RDRDs come to be able to use them observationally, perhaps in observations whose standard conditions include not only such items as good light (as in the tie shop case) but also the presence of various sorts of instruments. This argument once again appeals to and depends upon Sellars' understanding of observational capacities as the product of reliable noninferential responsive dispositions and mastery of inferential norms.

Conclusion: On the Relation Between the Two Components

Sellars' primary explanatory target in *Empiricism and the Philosophy of Mind* is our knowledge of the current contents of our own minds. He wants to rethink our understanding of the way in which we experience or are aware of what we are thinking and how things perceptually seem to us. The point I have been trying to make in this essay is that the master idea that guides his argument is a particular way of thinking, not about our knowledge of the contents of our own minds, but about our observational knowledge of ordinary empirical states of affairs. It is because he understands perceptual awareness of a red apple in front of one as he does that Sellars rejects a host of traditional ways of thinking about awareness of having a sense impression of a red apple or the thought that there is a red apple in front of one.

I have claimed Sellars understands the sort of perceptual awareness of external objects that is expressed in observation reports as the product of exercising two different sorts of capacities: the capacity reliably to respond differentially to stimuli (which we share both with merely sentient creatures such as parrots and with merely irritable devices such as thermostats and landmines) and the capacity to take up positions and make moves in a game of giving and asking for reasons. I have rehearsed the way I see some of the major arguments and conceptual moves in the essay as rooted in this two-ply conception: the account of the use of "looks" talk that underlies the incorrigibility of sincere contemporaneous first-person reports of how things perceptually seem to one, including the treatment of scoped and generic "looks" claims, Sellars' approach to the issue of concept acquisition, which caused so much trouble for traditional rationalists, and his rendering of the distinction between theoretical and observational concepts.

I would like to close with some observations and questions about the relations between the two kinds of ability whose cooperation Sellars sees as required for observation. The two sorts of capacities define dimensions of perceptual aware-ness that are in a certain sense orthogonal. We saw in the discussion of concept acquisition the broad outlines of a story about how one might move from pos-session of mere RDRDs to the capacity to apply observational concepts. And we saw in the discussion of theoretical and observational concepts how one might move from the purely inferential capacity to apply a concept, by the addition of suitable RDRDs, to mastery of a fully observational concept. That is, we saw in the case of particular observational concepts how one could have either of the two components without the other, and then move to having both.

But this shows only *local* independence of the two components: that one can have the RDRD of an observational concept without having the concept, and one can have a concept without having the RDRD needed to be able to apply it obser-vationally. The corresponding global independence claim is not true. Purely theor-etical concepts do not form an *autonomous* language game, a game one could play though one played no other. For one must be able to respond conceptually to the utterances of others in order to be talking at all. So one could not play the game of giving and asking for reasons at all unless one could apply at least *some* con-cepts noninferentially, in the making of observation reports. But this does not mean that there could not be an *insulated* region of purely theoretical concepts, say those of pure mathematics – "insulated" in the sense that they had no infer-ential connection to anything inferentially connected to a concept that had an observational use. I don't say that any actual mathematics is like this, though it may be. Pure mathematics, I think, is in principle *applicable* to ordinary empirical objects, both those accessible through observation and those (now) accessible only inferentially. Applying an abstract mathematical structure to concrete objects is using the former to guide our inferences concerning the latter. But this relation ought not to be assimilated to that between theoretical objects and observable objects. It is not clearly incompatible with a kind of inferential insulation of the game of giving and asking for reasons concerning the mathematical structures. I think there are many interesting issues in the vicinity that are as yet not fully explored.[11]

It might seem that there could be no interesting question concerning the potential independence of RDRDs, corresponding to this question about the potential independence of the game of giving and asking for reasons. For it seems obvious that there can be reliable differential responsive dispositions without conceptual capacities. That is what mere sentients and artifacts have. But I think in fact there is a subtle question here, and I want to end by posing it. To begin with, what is obvious is at most that the RDRD's corresponding to *some* observational concepts can be exhibited by creatures who lack the corresponding concepts. And we might doubt even this. The story of John in the tie shop reminds us that our dispositions actually to call things *red* can be quite complex, and interact with our background beliefs – for instance about what are standard conditions for observing red things, and what conditions we are in – in complex ways. Though this claim goes beyond what Sellars' says, I think that learning about systematic sources of error can lead us to alter not just how we express our dispositions (substituting "looks φ" for "is φ"), but eventually even those dispositions themselves. I think, though I cannot say that I am sure (a condition that itself ought to give some sorts of Cartesians pause), that familiarity with the Müller–Lyer illusion has brought me to a state in which one of the lines no longer even *looks* to me to be longer than the other. The more theoretically laden our concept of standard conditions for some sort of observation are (think of the mu-meson case, where those conditions involve the presence of a cloud chamber), the less likely it is that a creature who could deploy no concepts whatsoever could master the RDRDs of a sophisticated observer.

Besides creatures who lack concepts entirely (because they are not players in any game of giving and asking for reasons), we could ask about which RDRDs are in principle masterable by concept users who for some reason lack the specific concepts that for the genuine observer are keyed to the RDRDs in question. It might be, for all I know, that by suitable reinforcement I could be trained to sort potsherds into two piles, which I label with the nonsense terms "ping" and "pong," in such a way that I always and only put Toltec potsherds in the "ping" pile, and Aztec ones in the "pong" pile. What would make my noises *nonsense* is that they do not engage inferentially with my use of any other expressions. And we might suppose that I do not have the concepts *Toltec* and *Aztec*. If told to substitute the labels "Toltec" and "Aztec" for "ping" and "pong," I would then be a kind of idiot savant with respect to the noninferential applicability of those concepts (which I would still not grasp). Perhaps there are no conceptual limits to such idiot savantry. But I find it hard to conceive of cases in which someone who lacks all the relevant concepts nonetheless can acquire the RDRDs necessary to serve as a measuring device (not, by hypothesis, a genuine reporter) of observable instances of the applicability of thick moral concepts such as *courage, sensitivity, cruelty, justice,* and so on. Of course, unless one endorses something like Sellars' account of what is required for something to be observable, it will seem that such properties are not suitable candidates for being observable by *anybody*, never mind by idiot savants. But for those of us who do accept his approach, this sort of question is one that must, I think, be taken seriously. That is the thought I want to leave you with.

Reference

Wilfrid Sellars, 1956, *Empiricism and the Philosophy of Mind*, with an Introduction by Richard Rorty and a Study Guide by Robert Brandom (Harvard University Press, 1997). Original publication in *Minnesota Studies in the Philosophy of Science*, vol. 1, ed. Herbert Feigl and Michael Scriven (University of Minnesota Press, 1956).

Notes

1   I tell this story in a great deal more detail in *Tales of the Mighty Dead*, forthcoming from Harvard University Press, in which a version of this essay also appears.

2   I would call it "minimal empiricism," except that John McDowell (in the Introduction to the paperback edition of *Mind and World* [Harvard University Press, 1996]) has adopted that term for a *much* more committal thesis.

3   *Phenomenology*, paragraph 109 (in numeration of A. V. Miller's translation [Oxford University Press, 1979]).

4   They would not be so characterizable in cases where the response is specified in, say, normative or semantic vocabulary – for instance, as *correctly* using the word "red," or as applying the *concept red*.

5   Sellars' discussion begins at *EPM*16. All references are to section numbers of Sellars' *Empiricism and the Philosophy of Mind*, reprinted with an Introduction by Richard Rorty and a Study Guide by Robert Brandom (Harvard University Press, 1997).

6   See for instance *EPM*36.

7   The idiom of "language-language" moves and "language-entry" moves is drawn from Sellars' "Some Reflections on Language Games" (in *Science, Perception, and Reality* [London: Routledge, Kegan Paul, 1963]).

8   I might be mistaken about whether *red* is what it looks, that is, whether the property expressed by the word "red" is the one it looks to have. But that, the thought goes, is another matter. I cannot be mistaken that it looks that way, like *that*, where this latter phrase is understood as having a noncomparative use. It *looks-red*, a distinctive phenomenal property, which we may inconveniently only happen to be able to pick out by its association with a word for a real-world property.

9   It is tempting to think that on this line concepts are related to the contents of pre-conceptual experiences as universals to particulars. But as Sellars points out, the empiricists in fact took as primitive the capacity to be aware already of *repeatables*, such as redness and squareness. This might suggest that the relation is better understood as one of genus to species. But *scarlet* is not strictly a *species* of the genus *red*, since there need be no way to specify the relevant differentiae without mentioning the species. (Compare the relation between the phenomenal property of redness and that of being

colored.) So the relation between immediately experienceable contents and the concepts under which they are classified is better understood as that of *determinate* repeatable to *determinables* under which it falls.

10 Notice that this realism about theoretical entities does not entail scientific realism in the sense that privileges science over other sorts of cognitive activity, although Sellars usually discusses the two sorts of claims together.

11 See for instance McDonnell's discussion in "Brandom on Inference and Representation," *Philosophy and Phenomenological Research*, 57(1), March 1997, pp. 157ff, and my reply at pp. 189ff, and a paper by John MacFarlane entitled "McDowell's Kantianism" forthcoming in a volume devoted to McDowell's work.

Chapter 14

Metaphysical Realism and Logical Nonrealism

Panayot Butchvarov

According to metaphysical realism, the existence or at least the nature of things, "reality," is independent of our cognition of them, whether in perception, conception, or description. Metaphysical nonrealism denies this. It comes in many varieties, as different as Berkeley's subjective idealism and Kant's transcendental idealism in the eighteenth century, Hegel's objective idealism in the nineteenth century, and in contemporary philosophy what Michael Dummett and Hilary Putnam call antirealism and Nelson Goodman calls irrealism. Berkeley held that the existence of the things we perceive is dependent on our perception of them, Kant that their nature is dependent on our understanding, on our concepts, and Wittgenstein and Heidegger that it is dependent on our language. Metaphysical realism is the bedrock of everyday and scientific thinking, but nonrealism has dominated modern philosophy, in one form or another, at least since Berkeley and Kant. The reasons for accepting it, however, have seldom been stated in detail and usually have consisted in rhetorical generalities such as "Nothing can be conceived that cannot be perceived" or "Thought without language is impossible," which are not plausible. But a specific and not implausible reason is provided by *logical* nonrealism.

The logical nonrealist denies that there are objects ("logical objects") corresponding to the expressions distinctive of logic but also essential to any developed language, the so-called logical expressions ("constants"). Standard examples are the sentential operators: "not" ("~"), "and" ("•"), "or" ("v"), "if . . . then . . ." ("⊃"); the quantifiers: "all" ("∀"), "some" ("∃"); the verb "to be" in its senses of predication ("Socrates is human"), identity ("Socrates is Plato's teacher"), and existence ("God is"). The logical realist, on the other hand, holds that at least some of the logical expressions do correspond to objects in reality, that there are logical objects. Gottlob Frege and Bertrand Russell (at one central stage of his philosophy) were logical realists. A noteworthy logical nonrealist was Ludwig Wittgenstein, in *Tractatus Logico-Philosophicus*.

Both metaphysical realism and logical nonrealism have been considered obviously true, and few have felt their inconsistency. Few have seen that if logical nonrealism is true, then metaphysical realism is largely false. In this essay I argue that this indeed is so. Section I develops the essentially negative thesis of logical nonrealism. Section II offers a positive account of how, even though logical nonrealism is true, the logical expressions and thus logic itself do relate to the world.

I

Contemporary metaphysical realism and nonrealism are best understood by recalling Kant's transcendental idealism. Kant argued that although there is reality as it is in itself ("things-in-themselves"), we can know it only as it is for us ("things-for-us"). Indeed, not only our knowledge but all judgments, whether true or false, are shaped by our cognitive faculties, by our senses and our concepts. We can no more get at what reality is in itself, independently of us, than we can get outside our skins. In Putnam's words, if not sense, the proposition that nothing unconceptualized can enter in epistemic relations with judgments and thus lead to knowledge is a "virtual tautology" (Putnam, 1994, p. 513). But to state it as an explicit tautology would require extensive accounts of the notions it involves, which would rely on similar and no less controversial other propositions. (This is a familiar predicament in philosophy.) The proposition should not be confused with the thesis of ordinary idealism. Kant did not hold, as Berkeley did, that everything is mental. Nor should it be confused with the general thesis of nonrealism – that reality is dependent for its existence or nature on us – which is hardly a tautology. Nonrealism does not follow from our inability to "get at what reality is in itself"; at most, skepticism follows. This is why Kant described his view as only a *transcendental* idealism. Contemporary nonrealists are seldom sensitive to the distinction. Nevertheless, demonstrative proof of nonrealism should not be expected, just as usually it should not be expected elsewhere in philosophy. Good reasons must suffice. And what I called a virtual tautology is a very good reason for nonrealism, even though nonrealism itself is not a tautology at all.

My central concern, however, will not be the general and rather amorphous dispute between realism and nonrealism. It will be the specific and well-defined version of metaphysical nonrealism I called logical nonrealism. It resembles Kant's view but places the dependence of reality-as-it-is-for-us on our language rather than on our mental faculties, and even then only with respect to the logical expressions in language. I shall begin by explaining how and why logical nonrealism is a version of metaphysical nonrealism.

The subject matter of metaphysics is said to be reality, being, what there is, or in the mundane terminology of contemporary philosophy, "the world." Various answers have been given to the question of what is real or exists: e.g., that only material entities exist (Hobbes), or that only mental entities exist (Berkeley), or that also abstract entities exist (Plato), or that also God exists (Aquinas). But however we answer the question, reality or at least the world has a structure, it is not a mere collection or assemblage of isolated items.

What kind of structure of the world is fundamental, absolutely necessary, one that is acknowledged by everyone? Not a causal structure: Hume rejected causal connections, except in the bland sense of spatiotemporal correlation. Nor a spatial structure: the dualist holds that in addition to material entities there are mental entities, such as thoughts and feelings, and the idealist even holds that everything is mental; but (irreducibly) mental entities are not in space (do not enter in relations such as two-miles-from). Nor a temporal structure: the Platonist holds that there are abstract entities, e.g., universals and numbers, which are not in time (do not enter in relations such as two-years-earlier-than), and the theist holds that there is a nontemporal but concrete entity that created the spatiotemporal world and time itself. The fundamental structure of the world, denied by no one though seldom mentioned, is logical. If the first question of metaphysics is what kind of structure the world *must* have, then the first proposition of metaphysics is that it must have a logical structure. Indeed, according to Aristotle, the "science of being qua being," i.e., metaphysics, begins with the study of the principles of the "syllogism," i.e., logic (Aristotle, 1993, 1005b 7–35).

But what is meant by "logical structure"? The answer lies in what is meant by "logic," and the best guide to that are the classics of modern logical theory: Frege, Russell, and Wittgenstein. Logic is concerned with the relations between propositions (sentences, statements, judgments) that hold in virtue of their "logical form." According to Russell's canonical account, propositions are either atomic (e.g., "Socrates *is* human"), or molecular (e.g., "Socrates is human *and* Plato is human"), or general (e.g., "*All* humans are mortal") in respect to logical form (Whitehead and Russell, 1962, Introduction). And the key to discerning their logical form is the presence of certain words, the so-called logical expressions mentioned earlier and exemplified by the words I have italicized. To say that the world has a logical structure is to say that any description of it employs such expressions. But we have no conception of a world that is even in principle not describable. Therefore, we have a good reason for holding that the world must have a logical structure and must be describable with sentences employing logical expressions.

Now the question immediately arises whether the world has a logical structure independently of language. The logical nonrealist holds that it does not. Logical nonrealism can thus be seen as a restrained version of contemporary metaphysical nonrealism and an heir of Kant's transcendental idealism.

Kant focused on the spatial, temporal, and causal structure of the world, not on its logical structure, and on its dependence not on language but on our mental faculties, what he called "sensibility," i.e., sense perception and introspection, and "understanding," i.e., concepts and judgments. Contemporary nonrealism insists chiefly on its dependence on the understanding, on that in virtue of which the world may be conceptualized rather than just felt. So it may be described as *con-*

ceptual nonrealism. But it focuses on language rather than on (irreducibly) mental items, such as Kantian concepts, and so it may be described also as *linguistic* nonrealism. For it finds appeals to mental items questionable or at least unhelpful. As David Armstrong has remarked, "Concepts [so understood] are a more mysterious sort of entity than linguistic expressions" (Armstrong, 1978, p. 25). Indeed, reasons for skepticism about the existence of any "inhabitants of consciousness" have been offered both in continental philosophy (e.g., by Sartre, 1956, 1957) and in the English-speaking world (e.g., by Wittgenstein, 1953, 1958). Such skepticism may be motivated, as in Armstrong's case, by fondness for materialism, or, as in the case of Sartre and Wittgenstein, by aversion to the seventeenth-century view of the mind as a "place" where various items are "stored."

In *Tractatus Logico-Philosophicus* Wittgenstein declared: "*The limits of my language mean the limits of my world*" (Wittgenstein, 1922, 5.6, italics in original). This seems to imply the general thesis of linguistic nonrealism. What might have been Wittgenstein's reason? The second sentence of the work reads: "The world is the totality of facts, not of things." Indeed, two worlds may contain the same things, have the same "inventory," but differ in how these things "hang together." For example, both may contain Jill and Jane, as well as the relation of admiring, but differ because in one Jill admires Jane and Jane does not admire Jill, while in the other Jane admires Jill and Jill does not admire Jane. The worlds contain at least two different "facts," though the same "things."

As this example suggests, a "fact" seems to be something propositional, linguistic, in the sense that, even though not a part of language, it is distinguishable from a "thing" only if thought of as the correlate in the world of a sentence. A fact is a complex entity that has a structure or form that resembles the structure or form of a sentence. For example, Russell's requirement that an atomic fact "contain" particulars and properties or relations seems to be an image of the grammatical requirement that a simple sentence contain a subject and a predicate, and his distinction between atomic and molecular facts seems to be an image of the grammatical distinction between simple and compound sentences (Russell, "The Philosophy of Logical Atomism," in Marsh, 1956). This correspondence of images was codified by Wittgenstein in the Tractarian doctrine that sentences are logical pictures of facts. It is fairly clear that when describing the obscure ontological characteristics of facts Russell and Wittgenstein relied on the familiar grammatical characteristics of sentences. Of course, they were concerned not with the "surface" grammatical form of a sentence but with what they called its logical form. But they arrived at the latter only as a transformation of the former. Logic does not include ordinary grammar, but it has been described as including logical grammar. And we have little if any conception of logical grammar apart from our conception of ordinary grammar.

This reliance on sentences, on language, is explicit in Frege's technical notion of a thought. (Russell's and Wittgenstein's heavy indebtedness to Frege in logical theory was freely acknowledged by both.) Fregean thoughts belong neither in the physical nor in the mental world, but "in a third realm," he says (Beaney, 1997, p. 337). Like Russell's and Wittgenstein's "facts," they are understood through analogy with sentences: "The world of thoughts has a model in the world of sentences, expressions, words, signs. To the structure of the thought there corresponds the compounding of words into a sentence" ("Negation," in Beaney, 1997, p. 351). And: "[T]he structure of the sentence serves as an image of the structure of the thought" ("Compound Thoughts," in Klemke, 1968, p. 537). Although in German Frege's term *Gedanke* is a synonym of "thought," as used by him it has no obvious English translation, "proposition" perhaps being least misleading as long as we think of a proposition as an objective item distinct from both the sentences in the various languages that express it and our ideas and judgments about it. If so, there is no clear difference between a true Fregean thought and a fact: "What is a fact? A fact is a thought that is true" ("Thought," in Beaney, 1997, p. 342). Frege's view that thoughts are neither mental nor physical may seem mysterious, but this is true also of Russell's and Wittgenstein's facts, which are not "things" and therefore do not enter in physical, spatial relations, nor are they mental images or judgments. The fact that this computer is two feet from me is not itself two feet or any other distance from me, and is no more mental than the computer.

Indeed, in logic we often do speak of propositions, rather than of sentences or of facts. This may be a symptom of our ambiguous conception of the subject matter of logic, of our uneasy attempt to straddle across the apparent chasm between the logic of sentences and the logic of facts. The thesis of logical non-realism is that the chasm is only apparent, that the logic of the world is not distinguishable from the logic of words, that Wittgensteinean and Russellian facts, as well as Fregean thoughts, are merely hypostatized sentences, shadows that sentences cast upon things. P. F. Strawson wrote: "Of course, statements and facts fit. They were made for each other. If you prise the statements off the world you prise the facts off it too; but the world would be none the poorer" (Strawson, 1950, p. 137).

The general thesis of metaphysical nonrealism now receives clear and compelling support. What makes a world a *world*, rather than a mere assemblage of items, is what requires sentences, rather than mere lists of names, for our description of it, namely, a logical structure, a structure that any world must have. This is a requirement even more basic than that a world must be "logically possible," meaning by this that it must not involve a contradiction, for even a contradiction has logical structure: that of "p and *not-p*." But the only conception we have of logical structure is that of the logical structure of sentences. This is why in speaking of a world we must appeal to the category of facts or of Fregean thoughts. Sentences, of course, are parts of language, and their logical structure is a feature of language, of something that is human, "ours." We have no genuine conception of a language that is both nonhuman and in principle untranslatable into a human language. As Quine says, "illogical cultures are indistinguishable from ill-translated ones" (Quine, 1966, p. 105). Therefore, insofar as we can conceive of the structure of the world and thus of the world itself *as a world*, they are "ours," "human," they "depend" on us. Of course, that the only conception of logical structure we have is that of sentences, of language, does not entail that the world does not have that or some other kind of structure independently of language. But it is a very good reason for reaching such a conclusion. For it does entail that our *cognition* of the world, insofar as it involves logical concepts, depends on language, and that so does *the world insofar as it is cognized by us.*

I have used the word "cognition" because here it is preferable to the more common word "knowledge." In conformity with the nonrealist's intent as well as current usage in the cognitive sciences, cognition need not be knowledge or even veridical. We may think of cognition as the employment of our capacities for knowledge, identified by means of examples – perception, introspection, intellectual intuition, induction, deduction, abduction – and of knowledge as our success in their employment. In his project to uncover the necessary conditions of knowledge Kant did not beg the question against the Humean skeptic, as many suppose, because he was concerned chiefly with the necessary conditions of cognition, of understanding, judgment, whether true or false, and with knowledge only by implication. We may engage in cognition even if never achieving knowledge. Therefore, a dependence of cognition on language is much more radical than a dependence of knowledge on language. And the traditional skeptical challenge concerns knowledge, not cognition. The skeptic does not question the possibility of false judgments.

Many twentieth-century philosophers, on both sides of the Atlantic, seem to have held that *all* cognition, not just that involving logical concepts, is dependent on language. For example, Heidegger wrote that "Language is the house of being" ("Letter on Humanism," in Krell, 1977, p. 193), and that "language is the happening in which for man beings first disclose themselves to him each time as beings . . ." (*Poetry, Language, Thought*, 1971, p. 74). I have already cited Wittgenstein's assertion "*The limits of my language* mean the limits of my world." And, as recently as 1995, Quine writes: "thought, as John B. Watson claimed, is primarily incipient speech" (Quine, 1995, pp. 88–9). Such opinions exemplify an extreme form of what has been called the linguistic turn in twentieth-century philosophy. It is more fundamental than earlier metaphysical "turns," such as the Platonic turn in antiquity, the theological turn in the Middle Ages, and the idealist turn in the eighteenth and the nineteenth century. For it applies to everything we think is real, including abstract entities, God and angels, and minds and ideas. It is a turn at least to the view that all cognition is dependent on language, and in its extreme form to what I have called linguistic nonrealism.

If we hold that reality as it is cognized (as it is "for us") is dependent on our language insofar as our cognition of it involves logical expressions, then we subscribe to a limited though in its implications far-reaching version of linguistic nonrealism and thus we take the linguistic turn ourselves. But we should not agree that *all* cognition is dependent on language. We must avoid the highhandedness often characteristic of philosophers. We must not suppose that we can give a general and a priori answer, whether affirmative or negative, to the question whether all cognition depends on language. To a large extent this is an empirical question, one for scientists – neurologists, psychologists, linguists – to investigate. And the proper answer may well vary from one kind of putative *objects* of cognition to another. Rocks are very different from headaches, both are different from electrons, and all three are very different from numbers. It would be rash to suppose that what is true of our cognition of some is true of our cognition of all. Also there are many, very different *kinds* of cognition. Some may depend on language while others do not. Surely, there is cognition in the form of sense perception, enjoyed by infants and nonhuman animals, which does not involve language. Recognition is a fundamental form of cognition, and surely it occurs in children before they learn to speak. Driving a car and professional boxing involve specialized cognition that only superficially finds expression in language. Creative work in music or painting only minimally involves talking. Worldly people, especially in the law, politics, and diplomacy, rely heavily on "reading" facial expressions. But language notoriously fails us when we try to describe facial expressions.

Our topic, however, is not this general and ill-defined question of the dependence on language of cognition. It is the specific and focused question of the dependence on language of cognition that requires for its expression sentences containing logical expressions. For lack of a better term, let us call such cognition, as well as the words and the sentences or propositions expressing it, logical, thus not limiting the word to the branch of philosophy called logic. All propositions of logic are logical propositions, but not all logical propositions are propositions of logic.

We achieve even greater specificity and focus when we ask, Does logical cognition have a *distinctive* subject matter, is it, at least in part, about anything distinctively logical? If not, then *to that extent* it would appear to be nothing but (use of) language, since it would lack the nonlinguistic feature essential to other kinds of cognition: a subject matter, things they are about, which make them, at least in part, the cognitions they are. Seeing a cat differs from seeing a dog partly because cats differ from dogs. And hearing a cat or a dog differs from seeing it partly because sounds differ from colors and shapes. Of course, we do not want to say that *all* there is to logical cognition is language. I said "distinctive subject matter" precisely because outside logic sentences containing logical expressions do have a subject matter, namely, whatever is denoted by the nonlogical expressions (the so-called "descriptive words") they also contain. But our question is whether they have a subject matter insofar as they are logical, i.e., a distinctive subject matter. The world may have a logical structure that is supplied by language, but it does not have *only* a logical structure: it also contains the entities that are structured. The tendency to forget this may explain why philosophers have paid little attention to the nonrealist implications of logical nonrealism. They say, for example: "Of course 'All humans are mortal' is about the world – it is about humans and the property of being mortal. They overlook the fact that while what the sentence says does depend on more than the presence in it of the logical expressions "all" and "are," it does depend on them nonetheless. Its truth-value depends on *both* the nonlogical and the logical expressions in it.

The propositions belonging in logic employ only logical expressions. If logical expressions stand for nothing, then these propositions have no extralinguistic significance – a consequence commonly even if rashly accepted. But, beyond that of babes, all human cognition, not just that expressible in statements made by logicians, must be expressible with statements that (in English) employ the verb "to be" at least in its sense of predication, sentential operators, or quantifiers, even if, unlike those of logic, they also employ nonlogical, descriptive, expressions. All developed human cognition is logical, in this broad sense. A language that lacked them would be either primitive or untranslatable. And if logical cognition *insofar as it is logical* can be nothing but (use of) language, then no developed human cognition is possible without language. This would be a good reason for holding that the world, insofar as it is the object of such developed cognition, cannot have a character fundamentally other than what we humans take it to have.

What I mean by developed cognition would include that expressed by "All the sheep in the field are black" – it does not require higher education. If we could not say that all the sheep in the field are black, then there would be precious little we could say. But while the words "sheep," "field," and "black" stand for things in the world, "all" does not. (And, so, neither does the sentence "All the sheep in the field are white" stand for anything distinctive in the world, a "fact.") The *all* is not among the "things themselves." It is not an individual thing, or a property or relation of an individual thing. This is why the phrase I have just used, "the all," is a grammatical monstrosity that only a philosopher would concoct. If we take advantage of the familiarity of Kant's sense of the word "transcendental," we may say that logical concepts and the expressions for them, such as "all," are transcendental. They are essential to our developed cognition and our description of the world, but stand for nothing in the world. This is another way of stating the thesis of logical nonrealism.

Logical nonrealism is hardly news. Philosophers and grammarians used to call the logical expressions syncategorematic, and in the *Tractatus* Wittgenstein declared: "My fundamental thought is that the 'logical constants' do not represent" (Wittgenstein, 1922, 4.0312). But little argument was offered, and the general nonrealist implications were seldom seen. Perhaps the closest to an argument was Wittgenstein's distinction between "saying" and "showing," which initially seems mysterious, but an application of it is familiar even to beginning students of logic. That a proposition is logically true, i.e., such that its negation is a contradiction, "shows" itself, it can be "seen" in its logical form, without reference to what it is about. That it is true in any other way, however, does not show itself, cannot be seen just in its form. We must also know what it is about, what it "says," by attending to the descriptive expressions it contains and what they stand for. This familiar distinction suggests that the logical form itself is not about anything, that it stands for nothing.

To make the thesis of logical nonrealism focused, let us take the words "all" and "not" as our paradigms of a logical expression. They are fundamental not only to logic but to all developed cognition. They express, respectively, the logical concepts of generality and negation. It would suffice for the thesis of logical nonrealism that it should be accepted for them. And as our realist foil, let us take Frege's and Russell's classic discussions of these concepts. It is to these discussions that Wittgenstein's "fundamental thought" was opposed.

Frege wrote: "It is surely clear that when anyone uses the sentence 'all men are mortal' he does not want to assert something about some Chief Akpanya, of whom perhaps he has never heard" (Geach and Black, 1970, p. 83). Frege classified what is expressed by "all" as a *second-level function*, which is "saturated" by *first-level functions*, which themselves are saturated by individual objects ("Function and Object" and "Concept and Object", both in Beaney, 1997). A function is logically unsaturated, or incomplete, dependent, in that it requires "attachment" to something else, somewhat as the grammatically incomplete expression "is human" requires attachment to a grammatically complete expression such as "Socrates," an analogy to which Frege often appealed. A predicate, e.g., "is human," stands according to Frege for a first-level function, what we call a property. Frege called it a concept (*Begriff*), but in common with other philosophers of the time, including G. E. Moore in Britain, he did not mean by "concept" something mental. In the thesis of materialism, "$(\forall x)(x$ is material)," i.e., "Everything is material," the quantifier "$\forall x$" represents a second-level function, and what follows it, "x is material," represents a first-level function that completes it. The latter is also incomplete, but what completes it is an individual thing, e.g., a rock, which is logically complete. Frege's terminology is awkward, but what matters for our purposes is his explicit acknowledgment of something corresponding to the word "all." To be sure, it is something "incomplete," but so is a property such as being human.

In a similar vein, Russell wrote: "When you have taken all the particular men that there are, and found each one of them severally to be mortal, it is definitely a new fact that all men are mortal" ("The Philosophy of Logical Atomism," in Marsh, 1956, p. 236). For "In order to arrive [by 'complete induction'] at the general proposition 'All men are mortal', you must already have the general proposition 'All men are among those I have enumerated'" (p. 235). General propositions, such as "All men are mortal" and "Some men are mortal," stand (if true) for "general facts." So, "there are general facts" (p. 236). Moreover, because "You cannot ever arrive at a general fact by inference from particular facts, however numerous," "there must be *primitive* knowledge" of some general facts (p. 235). There is "the necessity of admitting general facts, i.e., facts about all or some of a collection" (p. 289).

Frege held that there are negative thoughts, in his technical sense of "thought," since "for every thought there is a contradictory thought," which "appears as made up of that thought and negation," though not as "mutually independent" parts. For, "The thought does not, by its make-up, stand in any need of completion; it is self-sufficient. Negation on the other hand needs to be completed by a thought. The two components are . . . quite different in kind. . . . One completes, the other is completed. And it is by this completion that the whole is kept together" ("Negation," in Beaney, 1997, p. 358). Negation is incomplete just as the second-level functions expressed by the quantifiers are incomplete. The difference is that negation is completed by a complete entity, a thought, while a second-level function is completed by an incomplete entity, a first-level function. But negation is not anything mental or subjective. It is not "the act of denial" (ibid., p. 358). It is not a kind of judging: "Negation does not belong to the act of judging, but is a constituent of a thought" (ibid., p. 363). It is an objective part of a no less objective entity that Frege calls a thought. The sentence "It is not the case that Socrates is feline" consists of two parts: "it is not the case that" and "Socrates is feline." The latter could stand by itself, the former could not. And what the whole sentence says is no more psychological or subjective than what "Socrates is feline" says.

Russell argued at considerable length that "there are negative facts" (Marsh, 1956, p. 215) and that "negativeness is an ultimate" (p. 216). He wrote: "There is implanted in the human breast an almost unquenchable desire to find some way of avoiding the admission that negative facts are as ultimate as those that are positive . . . Usually it is said that, when we deny something, we are really asserting something else which is incompatible with what we deny. If we say 'roses are not blue', we mean 'roses are white or red or yellow'. But such a view will not bear a moment's scrutiny. . . . The only reason we can deny 'the table is square' by 'the table is round' is that what is round is *not* square. And this has to be a *fact*, though just as negative as the fact that this table is not square" ("On Propositions: what they are and what they mean," in Marsh, 1956, p. 288; italics in original).

In a discussion of our topic, one faces three options: logical realism, logical reductionism, and logical nonrealism. For example, in the case of universal statements, the realist would hold that the word "all," the universal quantifier, stands for a real entity, whether a Russellian "logical object" or Fregean "second-level function." The reductionist, finding the reality of such an entity implausible (as Wittgenstein did, almost immediately upon meeting Russell in 1911), would translate universal statements as conjunctions of the singular statements that instantiate them. And the nonrealist, finding the reality of an entity represented by the conjunction sign just as implausible, would deny that there are logical entities of any sort. Sometimes the would-be reductionist avoids appealing to other logical concepts, and thus is no longer properly called "reductionist," by implicitly appealing to the very same concepts as those to be explained. An example is the claim that the propositional operators are "defined" by the corresponding truth-tables and that this is "all there is to them," that, for example, *not-p* is "merely a truth function" of p because *not-p* is true if and only if p is false. But we have no grasp of falsity except as the negation of truth, regardless of what theory of truth we hold. As Russell remarked, it is "extremely difficult to say what exactly happens when you make a positive assertion that is false, unless you are going to admit negative facts" (Marsh, 1956, p. 214). Another example is the following: "$\forall x\Phi(x)$ asserts the property of universality of the property Φ, and $\exists x\Phi(x)$ asserts the property of nonemptiness to it" (Carnap, 1958, p. 107). But these "properties' are just what the quantifiers "$\forall x$" and "$\exists x$" express.

Now Frege's and Russell's views are explicit espousals of both logical non-reductionism and straightforward logical realism. Not only are Russell's general and negative facts not reducible to any other logical facts, they are objective constituents of the world. Therefore, what makes them general or negative must also be in the world, though Russell was perhaps unclear about this. But Frege was quite clear: negative thoughts must have negation as one of their two components. Surely, this is so also in the case of Russell's negative facts. How do they differ from the corresponding positive facts? If there is an item in the world represented by "not-p," as Russell held, as well as an item represented by "p," how do these two items differ if not in virtue of "something" in one of them that is not in the other, presumably something that "not" represents? For the difference is in the facts, in the world, not in our language or minds, according to Russell. According to Frege, the presence of negation in negative thoughts is essential to the truth-values of negative sentences, just as the presence in general thoughts of the second-level functions expressed by the quantifiers is essential to the truth-values of general sentences. Surely, the presence of negation in Russell's negative facts is essential to the truth-values of negative sentences, and the presence of what is irreducibly expressed by the quantifiers, let us call it generality, is essential to the truth-values of general sentences. If, as Russell held, truth depends on what is in the world, then what is essential to truth must also be in the world.

The logical nonrealist thus faces two tasks. The first, perhaps accomplished by Frege and Russell, is to combat logical reductionism, the view that "upon analysis" the question of the reality of logical objects does not even arise because the logical constants that appear to represent them have been "analyzed away." The value of logical nonreductionism is to show that this is not so, to force us to abandon comforting slogans such as "General statements are just conjunctions or disjunctions of singular statements" and "Molecular statements are just truth-functions of their components." But the second task the logical nonrealist faces is to insist that, even though logical reductionism is false, the logical constants still fail to represent. The plausibility of Frege's and Russell's views attaches to their nonreductionism, not to their realism. In fact, the latter is quite implausible.

For example, nonrealism about negation seems inescapable. (But see Peterson, 1986 and 1989). That *negation* corresponds to *nothing* in the world seems almost a tautology. Sartre claimed that consciousness "introduces" negation into the world precisely because it is not "already" there (Sartre, 1956, pp. 21–45). "No" and "not" are learned early in childhood, to signal the absence or nonexistence of a thing, to reject an object or a suggestion offered by someone, to deny the truth of what has been said. But they are neither names of any entity such as absence or nonexistence, nor names of such signaling, rejecting, or denying.

The idea that the words "all" and "some" correspond to entities also has seldom been entertained. Indeed, Gustav Bergmann, one of the few philosophers who thought deeply about our topic, did write: "Each quantifier represents something which is sometimes presented. Had it never been presented, we would not know what the quantifier meant" (Bergmann, 1964, p. 70). To respond to Bergmann's argument by saying that he relies on a naive conception of meaning would itself be naive. Nevertheless, it is an (abductive) *argument* for a statement of phenomenological observation, a statement about what is "presented," not a *report* of phenomenological observation, which it should have been, had it been true. But at least Bergmann was aware of what is necessary if logical realism is to be defended. Perhaps Frege and Russell were not.

In denying that logical expressions stand for entities, the logical nonrealist is not just denying the simplistic "Fido"–Fido principle, according to which every word is a name. What is denied is the natural, not at all simplistic though ultimately also mistaken, assumption that if a word serves a cognitive role then it relates to *something*, in a distinct, comprehensible way, even if it does not name it, that there must be something in what is cognized that grounds that role even if it is not named by the word, and that this "something" is accessible to us, if not directly in perception as colors and books perhaps are, then indirectly in sophisticated thought as quarks, relations, and God perhaps are. The logical nonrealist holds that none of this is true in the case of the logical expressions.

The nonrealist's claim should not be confused with the much weaker claim that language is *causally* necessary for logical cognition. Presumably, a human being who lacks a language cannot have detailed knowledge of astronomy or of the history of Spain. But surely God can, and for all we know so can intelligent beings in outer space. We may not understand what such knowledge would be like, but neither can we visualize a non-Euclidean space or have auditory images of the high-frequency sounds that dogs but not humans can hear. The same may be said about humdrum cognitions like that expressed in an inventory by location of the chairs in a large university. We cannot think, without writing, of everything such a sentence is about, i.e., chair1, chair2, chair3, chair4. . . . This is the point of making an inventory. But, surely, God can.

Could not the thought expressed in a universal statement such as "All my toys are upstairs" be entertained by a child before learning the word "all"? Perhaps it could, if it were just a collection of several singular thoughts – e.g., that the doll is upstairs, that the ball is upstairs, and that the whistle is upstairs – if the child is somewhat destitute. But a collection of thoughts is not what a conjunctive statement, a statement requiring the operator "and," expresses. And even if it were, it would not be what a universal statement, a statement requiring the quantifier "all," expresses. A universal statement is not equivalent to the conjunction of the singular statements that are its instantiations, it is not "made true" only by them. As Russell would have pointed out, the conjunctive statement would also have to include as an additional conjunct the *universal* statement "These are all the toys I have," if it is to be true (Marsh, 1956, p. 235). A universal statement is "made true" not just by the "atomic facts" corresponding to its singular instantiations, but also by "the further fact about the world that those are all the [relevant] atomic facts . . . [which] is just as much an objective fact about the world as any of them are" (Marsh, 1956, p. 236).

Would God be capable of cognition of such an objective fact without using a language? He would know all the individual things there are, perhaps an infinity of them, without employing a language, but what would it be for him to know that these are all the individual things there are? God's "vision" of all of them would not be enough. The thought that they are *all*, that none has been omitted, would also be needed. In our case, it seems, that thought could only be linguistic. In God's case, to literally attribute to him use of language would be blasphemy, but an analogical attribution might be theologically defensible.

II

So far what I have said about logical cognition has been negative. Can anything positive be said? Perhaps logical cognition corresponds to nothing distinctive in the world. But, surely, there is a connection between it and the world. After all, we employ logical expressions in most, if not all, statements we make, in everyday life as well as in science, not just in logic where lack of such a connection has seemed acceptable. And surely those statements are true because the world is as they say it is, or false because the world is not as they say it is. To acknowledge this need not be to accept a theory of truth as correspondence to "facts." It is just to acknowledge what is obvious.

We face here a predicament analogous to the one Wittgenstein faced when he denied that the use of words for sensations depends on anything they refer to. They refer neither to anything "outer" such as behavior, nor – this is the point of his private-language argument – to anything "inner" (Wittgenstein, 1953, § 243–72). But this tells us what their use does *not* depend on. What *does* it depend on? To just say that it depends on nothing is deeply unsatisfactory, even if true, as most readers of Wittgenstein would testify. Wittgenstein offered an answer by introducing his notion of a "defining criterion" (as contrasted with a mere "symptom"), which in the case of such words replaced the notion of reference yet stood for a connection between their use and the world. Holding one's cheek in a certain distinctive way may be a criterion for saying that the person has a toothache (Wittgenstein, 1958, pp. 24–5), in the sense of grounding the learning and then governing the use of the expression. On the other hand, the person's facial expression may be merely a symptom. Of course, holding one's cheek and having a toothache are not the same. Nor do we infer inductively from our own case that they are connected; this would not be a serious induction, since it is necessarily based on only one case (p. 24). Perhaps holding one's cheek is not a criterion for the use of "toothache" (Wittgenstein mentioned it only as a possible example), but surely some patterns of behavior, however complex, are such criteria, in the sense that, though logically neither sufficient nor necessary for its correctness, if they are not at least occasionally satisfied the use of "toothache" would be bewildering and presumably never mastered. One can have a toothache without holding one's cheek or doing anything else expressive of a toothache, and one can smile, sing, and dance despite an aching tooth, but if this were usually or even often the case we would have doubts not only about the truth of the assertion that one has a toothache but about its being a proper use of the word.

Our predicament is even closer to one Kant faced: There seems to be no connection between what he called the pure concepts of the understanding (e.g., the concept of causation), which according to him are necessary for cognition of the world of experience but stand for nothing in experience, and the world of experience to which nevertheless they apply. To deal with this problem, Kant proposed his doctrine of the schematism of the pure understanding. He wrote: "[P]ure concepts of the understanding being quite heterogeneous from empirical intuitions, and indeed from all sensible intuitions, can never be met with in any intuition. For no one will say that a category, such as that of causality, can be intuited through sense and is itself contained in appearance. How, then, is the *subsumption* of intuitions under pure concepts, the *application* of a category to appearances, possible? . . . We must be able to show how pure concepts can be applicable to appearances . . . Obviously there must be some third thing . . ." (Kant, 1950, A137/B176 – A138/B177). What is this "third thing"? A few pages later Kant says, "The schema of cause, and of the causality of a thing in general, is the real upon which, whenever posited, something else always follows" (A144/B183). This seems to be what Hume had called constant conjunction. If so, then Kant agreed that it is what we must depend on in applying the concept of causality, what mediates its application, but of course he sharply denied that causality is the same as constant conjunction.

These were Wittgenstein's and Kant's ways of dealing with difficulties they faced. The analogous difficulty the logical nonrealist faces is that there seems to be no connection between the use of logical expressions and the world. We cannot deal with it by just copying Kant's way or Wittgenstein's way, for these were concerned with very different topics and depended on specific psychological and linguistic assumptions that we cannot make. Instead, I shall appeal to certain distinctive *experiences* as a "third thing" that seems to mediate between the use of logical expressions and the world. We may call them logical experiences. They are *associated* with the expressions and *govern* their use, consciously or unconsciously. They *anchor* them. They are not experiences *of* logical objects, or of any other objects. They are experiences in the ordinary, natural, and innocuous, not the philosopher's or the introspective psychologist's technical and suspect sense of "experience." In that ordinary sense the paradigms of experience are pains and pleasures, itches and shivers, joy and misery, not anything supposedly present, for example, in all visual perception. Of course, they need not occur whenever the expressions are used, just as one need not be holding one's cheek whenever one has a toothache. Language is much too subtle to conform to such rigid requirements.

What are these logical experiences? We should not assume that there must be a different one for every logical expression. We do not have to be logical reductionists in order to allow that some logical expressions are genuinely reducible to others. Nevertheless, several logical experiences are familiar and arguably also central because they are associated with central logical concepts.

Consider the concept of identity, that expressed by the verb "to be" in one of its senses, e.g., in "This is the dog I saw yesterday." It is essential to our cognition of the world but stands for nothing in the world. If identity were something in the world, presumably it would be a relation, but, as Hume, Hegel, Wittgenstein, and others have pointed out, no such relation is observable or indeed imaginable, even when supposed to hold between observable or imaginable things (cf. Wittgenstein, 1953, § 215). And application of the concept seldom if ever requires determination of "indiscernibility." You saw a dog yesterday, you see a dog now, and you correctly judge that they are identical, that they are one and the same dog, but you don't see or remember a relation of identity between "them," nor do you establish that *every* property the one has the other also has. Nevertheless, to say that there are only the linguistic expressions for identity (from the plain "same" and "is," to the fancy "identical" and "=") would be misleading because *identification* in the form of recognition occurs in humans before the acquisition of language, indeed in animals incapable of language. But even if we suppose that in preverbal or nonverbal recognition we apply a concept, e.g., the concept of dog, to the object recognized, this does not mean that we also apply the concept of identity. Even if a prelinguistic child applies the concept of dog to what the child sees, surely it does not apply the concept of identity to what it sees now and what it saw earlier. Such a child can hardly be credited with possession of the concept of identity; perhaps many adults, already in possession of language, cannot.

However, though standing for nothing, the concept of identity is associated with an experience, namely, the experience of familiarity. It is not a coincidence that this is also the experience essential to recognition. It is the bridge between cognition as mere cognition and cognition as verbal description. It serves as a steadying anchor for our use of identity expressions ("same," "identical," "="), and perhaps without it they could not have been learned. (Even if logical concepts are "innate," the actual expressions for them in the various languages are not.) The experience of familiarity is not itself identity, it is not what the expressions for identity would denote if they did denote. Nor is it consciousness of identity, since there is nothing to be conscious of. And it is not the application of a concept or the utterance of an expression even when it accompanies them – it is an *experience*, something one feels, not something one does.

Indeed, because of its role in recognition the experience of familiarity enjoys special dignity. It is involved in the acquisition and application of all concepts, not just that of identity. To acquire and then apply the concept of dog we must be able to find certain objects familiar, whether dogs or pictures of dogs. To learn and then use the word "dog" we must find certain phonemes familiar, we must recognize them (Price, 1953, p. 38). So there is every reason to believe that the experience occurs before conceptual cognition and the acquisition of language, even though it bears intellectual fruit only when concepts are acquired and expressed in language. But any sophisticated command of a language would require more than recognizing and learning words – it would require also being able to make identity judgments about them, most obviously when the word is pronounced or inscribed in different ways. The word "dog" is the *same* word as "DOG," even though at least two of the letters look very different. The level of sophistication that knowledge of such matters involves is not lofty. It is plain literacy.

Unfamiliarity, strangeness, is also a distinctive and familiar experience. It is associated with the use of identity expressions in negative statements. It is not just the nonoccurrence of familiarity, but a genuine (and sometimes disconcerting) experience in its own right. Its importance ought to be evident but is often overlooked. Nothing would be a world in which nothing is familiar, as Plato pointed out in the *Theaetetus* when arguing against Protagorean skepticism. But also nothing would be a world in which nothing is unfamiliar, strange. A world is something we explore, and strangeness both prompts the exploration and often faces us in its results. In general, we must allow that logical experiences have opposites, contraries, which too are logical experiences and may be no less important.

There seem to be experiences associated also with at least some of the other logical expressions. They too serve as steadying anchors. There seems to be such an experience associated with implication ("if . . . then . . ." "⊃"). In his noteworthy discussion of what he calls the logic of sign-cognition, Price speaks of "a feeling of *if*" and suggests that it "arises through the experience of questioning or doubting" (Price, 1953, p. 134). And Sartre held that questioning is what "introduces nothingness in the world" (Sartre, 1956, pp. 21–45). There is important insight in both views, which complement each other, and I shall return to them in connection with negation. But the notion of questioning is too intellectual for our purposes, though it was not intended by Price or Sartre to be intellectual at all. I suggest, instead, that implication is associated, though indirectly, with the experience of expectation, of which also cats and rats are capable. Expectation is not just predicting or imagining a future event – it indeed is better described as the *feeling* of expectation. And surely it occurs in infants as well as nonhuman animals. Whether disappointed or fulfilled, expectation includes consciousness (perception, thought, imagination) of what is expected, and often also of its ground or basis. Expectation of rain includes thinking of rain, and may also include seeing dark clouds. But the *feeling* of expectation is distinct from both. They may occur without any feeling, without genuine experience. This becomes clearer when we distinguish (1) pure expectation, which does not even appear to have a ground ("I just know it will rain tonight"), (2) inferential expectation ("it's cloudy, so it will rain"), in which a ground is explicit, and (3) conditional expectation ("if it's cloudy, it will rain"). The experience, feeling, of expectation is palpable in (1), but not in (2) or (3). Yet (1) is probably a vestige and usually a guise of (2), which seems to be the original phenomenon of expectation. Indeed, it is (3) that explicitly involves the logical concept of implication, and often if not always is purely intellectual in character, "empty of feeling." But (3) is implicit in (2): corresponding to every inference, there is a conditional proposition the antecedent of which is the premise(s) and the consequent the conclusion of the inference.

Negation seems associated with an experience of a striking and much discussed character, vividly described by Sartre. Looking in a café for someone you eagerly expect but fail to find involves, often, a distinctive and much too familiar experience (Sartre, 1956, pp. 9–11). It is not the intellectual performance of making the negative judgment that the person is not there, which one could do even if not expecting the person. It is an experience, a feeling – usually the feeling of *disappointment,* in one of its many degrees and forms. Indeed, on the other side of the English Channel, H. H. Price wrote: "Disappointed expectation is what brings NOT into our lives" (Price, 1953, p. 124, upper case in original). Disappointment, as the experience associated with negation, is not the same as feeling of expectation, the experience associated with implication. Nevertheless, they are obviously and intimately related. This suggests that together they constitute the experiential core of propositional logic. It also suggests that implication and negation are the natural (not necessarily the formal) primitive propositional operators. And like familiarity and strangeness, expectation and disappointment too seem essential to any life deserving to be called cognitive. So is surprise, which presumably is the opposite of expectation. If the world is the world we live in (which other world might it be?), then we may say that all of these experiences are essential also to the world. But though we may say this, it is not entailed by what precedes it. At most, we have before us an extension of the essentially Kantian thesis that the distinction between the world as it is in itself and the world as it is for us is empty. But this is not a tautology. Those who disagree with Kant do not contradict themselves.

Are there distinctive experiences associated with generality and thus constituting the experiential core of quantified logic? In the case of the particular ("existential") quantifier ("some," "there is," "∃") we may be tempted to say that it is the experience of existence. But even if there were such an experience, this would be a misunderstanding, despite what conventional philosophy tells us. To say that there are many things Jack fears is not to imply that they exist, that they are real. Just the opposite might be the point of saying it. Some of the things we fear are real but fortunately many are not, though unfortunately we fear them nonetheless. But whether or not we follow convention and restrict quantification to existent objects ("beings," "entities"), there seems to be a characteristic experience associated with the particular quantifier. It is the experience of being-there, of standing up or out, of *presence,* whether real or imaginary. An example might be the experience of the presence of the *Times* on the rack when I eagerly look for it and do find it. It should not be confused with my seeing the newspaper or even seeing *that* it is there. I see many newspapers on the rack and, if it matters to me, also see that they are there, but usually experience nothing. Another example might be the stubborn presence before Jack's "mind" of what he fears most, imaginary though it is – e.g., a fatal accident involving his daughter.

In the case of the universal quantifier, the associated experience seems to be the experience of *absence*, for example the absence of the *Times* from the rack when I eagerly look for it but fail to find it. It should not be confused with seeing the newspapers that are there, or with the judgment that the *Times* is not among them, an intellectual performance I can engage in with respect to many newspapers I never look for. The experience need not be that of disappointed expectation (perhaps I hoped but did not expect to find it), which is associated with negation, but surely the two are closely related. This may be why we find plausible the interdefinability of the universal quantifier and the particular quantifier by way of *negation*, the equivalence of "$(\forall x)\ \Phi x$" and "$\sim(\exists x)\sim\Phi x$." (If everything is material then it is not the case that something is not material, and if it is not the case that something is not material then everything is material.)

I have used the words "presence," "absence," and "being-there" in their ordinary senses. For example, "presence" is not confined to the present. A person could be said to have been present at a meeting last week and to be expected to be present also next week. My intention has not been to allude to the important use of these words by philosophers such as Heidegger and Sartre. Nevertheless, it is to such philosophers that we should go for detailed phenomenological accounts, even when they differ from what I have said. And we should also go to trail-blazing philosopher/psychologists such as William James, who preceded continental phenomenology. James dwelt in detail on the richness of what he called "the stream of thought," the place of language in it, the role of "relations" and not just of "substantives," the inadequacy of both "sensationalism" and "intellectualism." He acknowledged the occurrence of "a feeling of *and*, a feeling of *if*, a feeling of *but*, and a feeling of *by*," and pointed out the dependence of the thought of something as "existent *extra mentem*" on "repeated experiences of the *same*." (See James, 1983, especially ch. IX.) In general, much more needs to be said about what I have called logical experiences. I have not even attempted an exhaustive taxonomy of them. I have only scratched the surface.

The brute fact of the experiences associated with logical expressions is a further limitation on the role of language in cognition. Indeed, those expressions correspond to no objects. But it is not true that all there is to logical cognition is language. There are also the associated experiences. This may be why it strikes us as incredible that such cognition should be "nothing but language." There is more to logical cognition than language, there are also certain distinctive experiences. The occurrence of these experiences, which is hardly accidental, shows that the linguistic turn in philosophy ought to be even more confined than I urged earlier. It ought not to be purely linguistic even where it is most plausible – in logic.

Logical experiences are essential not only to the uses of logical expressions, they are essential to our world, the world in which we live. Our world is a world of action. It is not like a planet viewed from orbit. We are immersed in it. And it is essentially a world of familiarity and strangeness, expectations and disappointments, presences and absences. It is to this world that the logical experiences are essential. Is this not enough to explain why they serve to anchor in the world the logic of our cognition of the world, to keep logic in touch with earth?

We thus arrive at a sensible, moderate metaphysical nonrealism, which unlike Kant's is linguistic and unlike current versions is limited to the logical structure of the world. Nevertheless, it is a nonrealism with very much the bite that any other properly motivated nonrealism, such as Kant's, might have. Logical structure, though not the substance, is hardly an accident of the world. (The things structured, the "objects," are the substance, Wittgenstein held in the *Tractatus*.) This is why Aristotle charged the science of being qua being with the study first of "the most certain principles of all things," the principles of the syllogism. What is true of logic directly affects what is true of being, or, in a mundane terminology, of the world.

Our nonrealism acknowledges the virtual tautology that nothing unconceptualized can be the content of judgments or statements and thus serve as evidence or enter in other epistemic relations. But, unlike most current versions of nonrealism, it does not deny the need for something like Kant's distinction between things-in-themselves and things-for-us. It avoids what might be called conceptual or linguistic creationism, the heady view that there is nothing we have not conceptualized or verbalized. Nor does it deny, on the side of things-for-us, the difference between what Kant called sensibility and understanding. That there is such a difference is evident, however difficult it may be to state it. We might say that understanding is up to us, while sensibility is not, but this, though in the right direction, would be misleading or at least vague. It would be better to say that we have some idea of how we may choose to conceptualize differently the things we find, but not of how we may choose to find different things. "The only objective criterion of reality is coerciveness, in the long run, over thought," William James wrote (1983, p. 21). The logical experiences of unfamiliarity, disappointed expectation, and absence make this coerciveness especially vivid. They occur in the coercive context of "things as we find them," not of "things as we make them."

Bibliography

References

Aristotle (1993). *Metaphysics*. New York: Oxford University Press.

Armstrong, D. M. (1978). *Nominalism and Realism: Universals and Scientific Realism*, Vol. 1. Cambridge: Cambridge University Press.

Beaney, M. (1997). *The Frege Reader*. Oxford: Blackwell.

Bergmann, G. (1964). *Logic and Reality*. Harper & Row.

Berkeley, G. (1999). *A Treatise Concerning the Principles of Human Knowledge*. New York: Oxford University Press.

Carnap, R. (1958). *Introduction to Symbolic Logic and its Applications*. New York: Dover.

Dummett, M. (1976). *The Logical Basis of Metaphysics.* Cambridge: Harvard University Press.

Geach, P. and Black, M. (eds.) (1970). *Translations from the Philosophical Writings of Gottlob Frege.* Oxford: Blackwell.

Goodman, N. (1978). *The Ways of WorldMaking.* Indianapolis: Hackett.

Heidegger, M. (1971). *Poetry, Language, Thought* (A. Hofstadter, trans.). New York: Harper & Row.

——(1977). "Letter on Humanism," in Krell.

——(1996). *Being and Time* (Joan Shambaugh, trans.) Albany: State University of New York Press.

James, W. (1978). *Essays in Philosophy.* Cambridge, MA: Harvard University Press.

——(1983). *The Principles of Psychology.* Cambridge: MA: Harvard University Press, 1983.

Kant, I. (1950). *Critique of Pure Reason* (N. K. Smith, trans.). London: Macmillan.

Klemke, E. D. (ed.) (1968). *Essays on Frege.* Urbana: University of Illinois Press.

Krell, D. F. (ed.) (1977). *Martin Heidegger: Basic Writings.* New York: Harper & Row.

Marsh, R. C., (ed.) (1956). *Logic and Knowledge.* London: Allen & Unwin.

Peterson, P. E. (1986). "Real logic in philosophy." *The Monist,* 60 (2).

——(1989). "Logic knowledge." *The Monist,* 72 (1).

Price, H. H. (1953). *Thinking and Experience.* London: Hutchinson's University Library.

Putnam, H. (1994). "The Dewey Lectures 1994," *Journal of Philosophy,* 61.

Quine, W. V. (1951). *Mathematical Logic.* Cambridge, MA: Harvard University Press.

——(1966). *The Ways of Paradox.* New York: Random House.

——(1995). *From Stimulus to Science.* Cambridge, MA: Harvard University Press.

Sartre, J.-P. (1956). *Being and Nothingness* (Hazel Barnes, trans.). New York: Philosophical Library.

——(1957). *The Transcendence of the Ego* (Forrest Williams and Robert Kirkpatrick, trans.) New York: Noonday.

Strawson, P. F. (1950). "Truth." *Aristotelian Society, Supplementary Volume 24.*

Whitehead, A. N. and Russell, B. (1962). *Principia Mathematica.* Cambridge: Cambridge University Press.

Wittgenstein, L. (1922). *Tractatus Logico-Philosophicus.* London: Routledge & Kegan Paul.

——(1953). *Philosophical Investigations.* London: Macmillan.

——(1958). *The Blue and the Brown Books.* Oxford: Oxford University Press.

Suggested Further Reading

Alston, W. B. (1997). *The Realist Conception of Truth.* Ithaca: Cornell University Press.

Bergmann, G. (1994). *New Foundations of Ontology* (William S. Heald, ed.). Madison: University of Wisconsin Press.

Blackburn, S. (1990). *Spreading the Word.* New York: Oxford University Press.

Bradley, F. H. (1897). *Appearance and Reality.* Oxford: Clarendon Press.

Butchvarov, P. (1979). *Being Qua Being: A Theory of Existence, Identity, and Predication.* Bloomington: Indiana University Press.

——(1998). *Skepticism About the External World.* New York: Oxford University Press.

Dejnozka, J. (1996). *The Ontology of Analytic Philosophy and its Origins.* Lanham: Rowman & Littlefield.

Devitt, M. (1997). *Realism and Truth*. Princeton: Princeton University Press.

Diamond, C. (1995). *The Realistic Spirit*. Boston: MIT Press.

Fodor, J. A. (1975). *The Language of Thought*. Cambridge: Harvard University Press.

Kant, I. (1950). *Prolegomena to Any Future Metaphysics*. New York: Prentice-Hall.

Katz, J. J. (1997). *Realistic Rationalism*. Boston: MIT Press.

Landini, G. (1998). *Russell's Hidden Substitutional Theory*. New York: Oxford University Press.

Maddy, P. (1992). *Realism in Mathematics*. New York: Oxford University Press.

McDowell, J. (1996). *Mind and World*. Cambridge: Harvard University Press.

Putnam, H. (1990). *The Many Faces of Realism*. LaSalle: Open Court.

Quine, W. V. (1988). *Word and Object*. Boston: MIT Press.

——(1988). *From a Logical Point of View*. Cambridge: Harvard University Press.

——(1989). *Methods of Logic*. Cambridge: Harvard University Press.

Stern, D. (1994). *Wittgenstein on Mind and Language*. New York: Oxford University Press.

Wright, C. (1987). *Realism, Meaning, and Truth*. London: Blackwell.

Chapter 15

The Metaphysics of Possibilia

William G. Lycan

Everyone knows there are things that aren't real, that don't exist: poltergeists, the Easter Bunny, Lady Macbeth, the free lunch. That fact was especially emphasized by Alexius Meinong (1904/1960), who took it to be entirely obvious that there are nonexistent possibles (and even nonexistent impossibles, such as the round square). But in that simple assertion lies a puzzle, which W. V. Quine (1948/1963) once called "*Plato's beard*": How can there be a thing that isn't? If we can think about a nonexistent individual, and even say truly of it that it does not exist, must the thing not, in some sense, be? We refer to such things by means of names and descriptions; and they are often objects of our thought.

1 *The uses of nonexistence and nonexistents.* It is not only middle-sized individual things that sometimes aren't real. There are complex situations or states of affairs that are unreal, such as Napoleon's having won at Waterloo or my being President of the United States. Indeed there are whole nonexistent universes – imaginary alternatives to the actual world we inhabit. Such universes are called "possible worlds." (Of course our own world, the real one, is a possible world too, but it is no *merely* possible world, because it is actual.)

Philosophers speak seriously of "other" possible worlds for any number of reasons: By positing nonactual worlds, we may give illuminating semantics for modal logics, identifying *possibility* with truth at some possible world and *necessity* with truth at every world. Contemporary logical theory has already furnished us with an elegant formal account of words like "some" and "every"; the standard predicate calculus represents such words as *quantifiers*, and exhibits their complex inferential properties. Once necessity and possibility are understood respectively in terms of "some" and "every" (as applied to worlds), their own logical features fall neatly out of quantifier logic. For example, take the trifling logical facts that what is necessarily true is actually true, and what is actually true is possibly true. Those two facts obtain, respectively, because what is true in every world is true in this the actual world, and what is true in this world is true in some world.

Besides the fully general modalities, necessity and possibility, philosophers like to talk of more specialized versions as well: natural-scientific or nomic necessity, epistemic or legal possibility. Possible-worlds semantics explicates such notions by introducing an *accessibility relation* defined on worlds. Thus, for it to be nomically necessary that P is, for P to be true in every world nomically accessible from ours (intuitively, in every world that shares our world's natural laws); for it to be legally possible that P is, for P to be true in at least one world that is legally accessible from ours, i.e., that shares the civil and criminal codes of the relevant actual polity. (The accessibility relation is also technically important to modal logicians because the formal features ascribed to it by a particular semantic interpretation explain the truth of the characteristic axioms of the formal system being interpreted.)

Ordinary people mobilize more specialized and idiosyncratic modalities, usually corresponding to modal auxiliary verbs or to suffixes such as "-able." In fact, virtually every homely modality is restricted, and relative to contextually determined sets of background assumptions. Interestingly, very few of those street-level restricted modalities correspond to recognizable philosophical categories. (Even the concept of nomic necessity is hardly better known to everyday English than are the fully general alethic modalities.) Consider "I have to, but I can't"; "May I have some?"; "as soon as possible"; "I need help"; "an unspeakable act"; "inedible food"; "chewable aspirin." It would take considerable work to describe the exact accessibility relation underlying any of those comparatively local modalities.

By positing possible worlds, as the preceding examples suggest, we can also make progress in the semantics of natural languages, appealing to worlds in explaining the behavior of, e.g., conditional sentences or propositional-attitude constructions, or, at another level of theory, fictional discourse. In metaphysics, worlds are used to model abstract entities such as propositions and Fregean senses, and to explain the relations between such things as laws of nature, counterfactual truths, and universals. Probability theory and decision theory are usefully interpreted in terms of worlds.

Thus, mere possibilia and nonactual possible worlds, or effective proxies for them, now seem indispensable in philosophy and in linguistics. That is not to say that the nonactual worlds must exist in any ontologically ultimate sense, for they might be façons de parler or otherwise fictive. But I believe most philosophers would agree that some respectful account must be given of apparent references to them.

2   *Trouble*. And yet most philosophers are at the same time uneasy about mere possibilia. For as Russell and Quine have emphasized, the idea of a *thing that does not exist* or of a *nonactual world* also seems paradoxical. Meinong's thesis raises any number of problems. For example: (a) Russell (1905) asked whether *the existent round square* exists. (b) Quine (1948/1963) has demanded identity and individuation-conditions for mere possibilia; when have we one possible elephant and when have we two, or nineteen, or four million, three thousand and ninety-two? (c) If Sherlock Holmes lived in Baker Street, is it true of (the real) Baker Street that it had Holmes as a resident? And (d) though Holmes had hair, there

is no specific number of hairs that he had; how can there be, or even "be," a person who has hair but who has no particular number of hairs?

A friend of possibilia can answer such questions by grouping possible people etc. into whole possible worlds and by making various choices – some motivated, some legitimately stipulative – resulting in an elegant theoretical apparatus. (See Castañeda (1974, 1989); Parsons (1980); Rescher (1975); Rapaport (1978); Routley (1980); Zalta (1983, 1988)). And it has been vigorously argued that the theory has great, even indispensable explanatory power (Montague (1974), Cresswell (1972, 1973, 1985), Stalnaker (1976), Lewis (1973, 1986).

But there is a further worry, about parsimony. Most philosophers subscribe to some version of Occam's Razor; at least, few philosophers posit entities that they admit to be totally gratuitous for purposes of philosophical explanation. Quine accused Meinong of bloating ontology, by believing not only in all the things there could possibly be, but also in all the things there could not be. The problem is not just that Meinong has overposited; it is that since he has already posited every-thing that could (or even could not) be, how can he explain or even allow con-tinuing appeals to parsimony in philosophy and in science?

Meinong has an obvious rejoinder: that Occam's Razor applies only to exis-tents. No one endorses the positing of entities *as existing* if those entities are not needed for purposes of explanation; but mere possibilia are nonexistents, and so are unthreatened by Occam's Razor.

Yet the suggestion that we should posit possibilia, but not posit them "as exist-ing," leads directly to the crucial and worst difficulty.

3   *Bigger trouble.* Sometimes when philosophers posit entities of a given type – say propositions, negative facts, Cartesian egos, or even sets – other philosophers have complained that those entities were queer and obscure, and/or that they did no valuable explanatory work. But in each case it was the entities themselves that were disputed; we understood the *positing* part of positing those entities, even if we mistrusted the nature or the role of the entities themselves. And this is what distinguishes nonexistent possibles from posits of all the other kinds. Meinong saw the puzzle himself: "Those who like paradoxical modes of expression could very well say, 'There are objects of which it is true that there are no such objects'" (1904/1960, p. 83). Humdrum as our casual references to nonexistents are, Meinong's explicitly formulated view sounds self-contradictory.

We can sharpen the quandary by turning to the standard predicate calculus. In that system of logic, the expression "There are" is normally represented as an *exis-tential quantifier*, because it is normally used to assert the existence of things of a given kind. Meinong asks us in effect to "quantify over" nonexistent items. When we translate Meinong's "paradoxical" formulation fully, we get

$$(M) (\exists x) \sim (\exists y)(y = x)$$

And this formula *provably is* a contradiction. The positing of a "nonexistent" thing or world, unlike that of a proposition or a Cartesian ego, courts overt self-inconsistency. The most urgent task for a friend of possibilia, then, is to resolve the prima facie contradictoriness of Meinong's formulation. Let's call that the "Contradiction Problem."

4   *Approaches.* Recent modal metaphysics has come up with surprisingly many palliative strategies in response to the Contradiction Problem. And the various contemporary metaphysical theories of possibility are usefully seen as competing ways of resolving the contradiction.

Clearly, the friend of possibilia must disambiguate the English phrase "There are," and replace (M) with a quantificational formula that is no contradiction. Thus s/he must distinguish two different operators, one continuing to indicate actual existence and the other, Meinongian quantifier expressing some other notion yet to be explained.

To date there are six basic approaches. (They are not mutually exclusive; some current views fall into more than one of the six categories.)

(i) The *Paraphrastic* approach. Some philosophers have suggested informally that apparent reference to and quantification over nonexistent possibles could be eliminated by paraphrase, that is, that such references could be paraphrased away from the sentences in which they occur. Possible individuals and possible worlds would then be treated as façons de parler.

(ii) The *Quantifier-Reinterpreting* approach. Marcus (1975–6) has attempted to solve the Contradiction Problem by providing a nonstandard semantic interpretation for the Meinongian quantifier which preserves its familiar inferential properties but requires no nonactual entities. She advocates the "substitution" interpretation originally due (I believe) to Lesniewski, which would make reference only to the actual linguistic expressions purporting to designate mere possibilia, rather than the possibilia themselves.

(iii) The *Fictionalist* approach. Armstrong (1989) has proposed to treat mere possibilia as fictions, on the model of ideal entities in science such as perfect vacuums and frictionless planes. There are truths, even existentially quantified truths, about nonexistents just as there are truths about such ideal items. Rosen (1990) offers a slightly different fictionalism.

(iv) The *Ersatz* approach, as it is called by David Lewis (1973, 1986). An Ersatzer leaves both quantifiers standardly interpreted, but construes "possibilia" as being actual objects of some suitable kind. The Ersatzer tries to find some actual entities that are collectively analogous or isomorphic to an adequate system of possible objects and worlds, and which therefore can serve as or *do duty for* possibilia; s/he may then let the apparently Meinongian quantifiers range over these objects. Proposed ersatz worlds or world-surrogates include: sets of sentences or propositions, massive recombinations of the basic elements of our own world, types of mental act, and what Stalnaker (1976) calls "ways things might have been."

(v) The *Relentlessly Meinongian* approach. This is simply to embrace Meinong's two distinct quantifiers and refuse to explicate either in terms of the other. The Relentless Meinongian contends in particular that since ordinary people understand Meinong's distinctive "There are" perfectly well without special training, there is no philosophical need to analyze it in other, somehow more acceptable terms.

(vi) David Lewis's (1986) view, which can be called *Hyper-Realism*. Like the Relentless Meinongian, Lewis countenances nonactual entities, and like the Ersatzer he explicates one of the quantifiers; but he explicates, not the Meinongian quantifier, but the narrower quantifier expressing actuality or real existence. For him, imaginary things and other worlds *exist* just as you and I do, though we parochially call ourselves and our worldmates "actual." For a thing to be actual, if the word is in our mouths, is just for the thing to inhabit the same world we do.

5   *Actualism and Concretism.* I shall use the term "Actualism" to cover approaches (i)–(iv) and any other position that deflates or apologizes for Meinongian quantification and refuses to countenance nonactual entities. I shall call (v) and (vi) "Concretist." The "Actualist"/"Concretist" division has become tolerably clear within modal metaphysics, especially as applied to worlds in particular.

Actualists hold that there is only one *world*, the actual, blooming, buzzing physical world of earth and fire and iron and concrete and flesh and blood, and there is only the actual class of existent things; the "other, nonactual possible worlds" invoked by the friend of possibilia are only other ways the world might have been, which "ways" can be represented by perhaps flimsy abstracta, either abstract entities or idealizations or mental constructs of some sort.

Concretism is the thesis that all the worlds are *worlds*, not just world-simulacra such as sets of sentences or whatever (and possible human beings are human beings, not mental entities or the like). Alongside our concrete world, there are other equally concrete worlds, whose "nonactuality" is less obviously a matter of ontological kind; every world, in addition to our preferred "real" one, is physical, made of ingredients as physical as earth or iron. The Concretist denies that our own world is distinguished from the others in any ontological way. Lewis adds the further claim that words like "actual" are locative indexical terms, on the model of "here" or "in this county" or "on this planet": What we call the "real" or "actual" world is *this* world, the one we live in; but inhabitants of other worlds are equally correct in using the same words "real" and "actual" to refer to those worlds of their own.

Lewis (1973) did not distinguish as in Lewis (1986) between Relentless Meinongianism and Lewis's mature Hyper-Realism, but it was forthrightly Concretist even then. Ersatzers have included Cresswell (1972), Plantinga (1974), Stalnaker (1976), Lycan (1994). (Plantinga and Lycan appeal to sets of propositions. Cresswell uses combinatorial rearrangements of the actual world's basic constituents. Stalnaker's proposed world-surrogates are "ways things might have been," *sui generis* abstract entities; Forrest offers "world-natures," which are very complex (usually) unexemplified properties.) In what remains of this chapter I shall concentrate on those dominant approaches, and then turn briefly to Fictionalism, neglecting (i)–(ii) above. (I have discussed each of (i) and (ii) at length in Lycan, 1994.)

6   *Concretists* vs. *Ersatzers.* I begin by noting several generic differences between Concretist and Ersatz theories.

(1) The two views treat the notion of *truth* differently: They agree that since worlds differ in their constituent facts, a given sentence or proposition is true "at" some worlds but false at others. But Concretists generally see "true" itself as defined in terms of the "truth-at" relation: A sentence or proposition is "true" when it is true-at the *actual* world (@, as it is called following a tradition inaugurated by Lewis). This means that, for Lewis, truth is entirely world-relative, since actuality itself is world-relative. By contrast, Ersatzers think of plain old truth as primary, and not as world-relative: Truth is correspondence to the (one) *world*, while "truth-at" is some constructed, parasitic relation of correspondence between the given sentence or proposition and another abstract or ideal or mental object that only represents a concrete world (for example, if the "world" just is a set of sentences, the given sentence *is a member of* that set).

(2) What separates one world from another? (In virtue of what, are you and I worldmates, as Lewis puts it, but the Wife of Bath inhabits and invigorates a different world from ours?) The Ersatzer may take the distinctness of "worlds" for granted, since s/he has essentially constructed the nonactual ones, stipulating what goes on "in" each. But the Concretist must give some account of distinctness, for s/he takes worlds to pre-date the discussion and in no way to be under our stipulative control. (Lewis (1986) offers a spatiotemporal criterion: X and Y are worldmates just in case they are related spatiotemporally, as you and I are but you and the Wife of Bath are not.)

(3) In some sense, particular individuals must persist from world to world. Since I might have become a chemist rather than a philosopher, there is some world at which I am a chemist, and so in some sense I must exist at that world as well as in ours. On the Ersatzer's picture, there is no special problem about this identity across world boundaries. If, for example, "other worlds" are big sets of some sort, actual individuals such as you or I can be members of those sets. But on the Concretist view, one finds it hard to imagine one and the same physical individual's persisting across the boundaries that separate one concrete physical world from another. According to Lewis, that idea is as loony as if someone were to suggest that I am *strictly identical with* a rather similar but contemporaneously existing denizen of a planet in another solar system. According to Lewis, *I* do not inhabit any world but @; it is only a "counterpart" of mine who pursues chemistry at another world. Taking this position obligates Lewis to provide an account of the putative "counterpart" relation, which he has attempted (1983, 1986). (He must suppose that there is some particular fact about my various individuals in virtue of which they do bear that curiously intimate relation to me.)

(4) A closely related point: Tony Blair might have been an Austrian Olympic swimmer. And he might also have been the fourth Austrian swimmer in a seated row of identical sextuplets. Indeed, it seems he might instead have been the second swimmer in the same row in a qualitatively identical entire world. Now, the Ersatzer is free to take Kripke's (1972/1980) stipulative view of transworld identity: *On my*

say so, the fourth swimmer in the row in world w_1 is Blair, because world w_1 is my imaginative creation and I have stipulated that we are talking about Blair's having been a swimmer instead of a British politician; I am equally free to stipulate a world w_2 in which Blair is the second swimmer in the row, without there being any special qualitative difference between the w_1 and w_2 swimmers that would make one Blair's counterpart at w_1 but the other Blair's counterpart at w_2. But the Concretist cannot take the stipulative position, for her/his other worlds physically exist, and their occupants do what they do independently of what we do or say here at @. Thus the Concretist must look at other worlds as through a telescope (Kripke's simile) and must *make a substantive case for* identifying a particular other-worldly swimmer – the fourth or the second – as a counterpart of Blair's.

(5) Formally, "worlds" are analogous to *times*, in being parameters of truth; just as a tensed sentence such as "George is at the racetrack" can be true at one time but not at another, so the sentence can be true at one world but not at another. On the Ersatzist picture, this is entirely natural, since it explicates "truth-at" as set membership or something like it; different "worlds" obviously have different sentences or propositions as members. But because of (3), no Concretist who accepts persistence of particular individuals from one time to another can accept the world/time analogy.

(6) As we saw in section 1, possible-worlds semantics brilliantly translates assertions of possibility and necessity into quantificational terms: "It is possible that P" is rendered as "*There is* at least one world at which P is true," and "Necessarily, P" as "P is true at *every* world." For that reason, we may hope for a philosophical reduction of the metaphysically troublesome modal notions of possibility and necessity to an entirely nonmodal mode of discourse. But Lewis (1986) argues that every Ersatzer forfeits that hope, for in constructing Ersatz worlds, s/he must appeal to some modal notion in guaranteeing that they correspond to possibilities. For example, if worlds are sets of propositions, they must be *consistent* sets of propositions, i.e., sets of mutually *compatible* propositions, i.e., sets whose members *could* simultaneously all be true. By contrast, the Concretist explicates modality just in terms of individual physical things, worlds, which are just collections of smaller physical objects; Lewis claims not to presuppose any primitive notion of possibility or necessity in describing his apparatus, though that claim remains controversial.

(7) As Meinong realized and emphasized, it seems there are *impossible* things, such as squaring the circle, as well as possible nonexistents. And it seems there are impossible worlds, say, a world corresponding to a particular human subject's inconsistent belief system. An Ersatzer has no problem with impossible worlds. Like a possible world, an impossible world is just (e.g.) a set of propositions – one which happens to be inconsistent. But a Concretist has a hard time saying how a physical, flesh-and-blood world could have logically incompatible constituents. Lewis himself (1986) refuses to countenance impossible worlds.

7   *Lewis's Concretism.* Stalnaker (1976) distinguishes four component theses of Lewis's (1973). I quote and interpolate:

(1) *Possible worlds* [and smaller possibles] *exist*. Other possible worlds are just as real as the actual world [@]. They may not *actually* exist, since to actually exist is to exist in the actual world, but they do, nevertheless, exist.

(And quantifiers range over not all the actual individuals that there are but all the nonactual ones that there are as well, unless their ranges are explicitly or tacitly restricted in context.)

(2) *Other possible worlds are things of the same sort as the actual world* . . .

(And smaller nonactual objects are things of the same sort as their actual counterparts; nonactual dinner plates are physical objects with physical uses; nonactual human beings are made of flesh and blood. This is a strong version of Concretism, stronger than Meinong's own, since Meinong did not require nonactual individuals to have complete sets of properties.)

(3) *The indexical analysis of the adjective 'actual' is the correct analysis.* 'The inhabitants of other worlds may truly call their own worlds actual . . .'.

(And when we, in this (our) world @, call some object "actual," that term abbreviates the indexical expression "worldmate of *ours*"; every possible individual is actual "at" the world it inhabits.)

(4) *Possible worlds cannot be reduced to something more basic*. . . . It would be a mistake to identify them with some allegedly more respectable entity. . . .

To which we may add, as we saw: (5) Every individual, actual or merely possible, is world-bound; there is no genuine identity of individuals across worlds. You and I merely have counterparts in other worlds who resemble us for certain purposes but are distinct individuals in their own right. And (6) there are no impossible worlds or things; everything is possible.

It is important to see that several of the foregoing claims are independent of one another and that one may well accept some of them but disagree with Lewis over others. Stalnaker argues in particular that although (1) and (3) are fairly commonsensical, (3) does not entail (2), and (4) is a highly contentious addition. (Stalnaker accepts Lewis's indexical analysis of "actual," but regards it as metaphysically uninteresting, since there is only one *world* for entities to be actual "at.") (5) is certainly reasonable given (2), but (6) is disputed even by Lewis's fellow Concretist Meinong.

Lewis (1986) adds the crucial claim that distinguishes him from the Relentless Meinongian and makes him what I called a Hyper-Realist. Until that point he had not addressed the Contradiction Problem as such, much less tried to explicate the broad Meinongian quantifier. But then he did so: (7) We should explicate, not the inclusive quantifier, but *the narrow Actualist quantifier*. On Lewis's mature view, the more inclusive "Meinongian" quantifier is not Meinongian at all, but just the ordinary quantifier, and has its everyday, (usually) physical meaning; it needs no explication or interpretation whatever. Instead, Lewis defines the narrow quantifier. It is of course understood as the inclusive quantifier restricted to the actual, but now Lewis introduces the novelty mentioned above: He explicates "actual" in terms of the concept of a worldmate, and he offers his independent account of worldmateship in turn, as spatiotemporal relatedness. (The latter account is independently motivated, for as we saw, the Concretist has the problem of distinguishing one world from another.)

8 *Lewis against the Ersatzers.* Lewis defends his Concretism in part by attacking the alternatives, principally Ersatzism. (His eventual criticisms of Relentless Meinongianism are given in Lewis (1990).) His main objection to Ersatzing was mentioned in section 6 above: that every Ersatzer of his acquaintance takes some modal notion as primitive, and if one leaves even one modal concept unexplicated, one is left without a theory of modality itself, and has explained the modal only in terms of the modal. (However, Forrest (1998) maintains that his "world-nature" theory avoids this liability.)

There is a further objection to the set-of-propositions account in particular, that reveals another serious failing: The account sacrifices the elegant practice of explicating propositions themselves in terms of worlds. If we reduce "worlds" to sets of propositions, we cannot then reduce propositions to sets of worlds or to functions from worlds to truth values. The same goes for other familiar abstract entities appealed to by Ersatzers, such as the properties and relations of which Forrest (1998) constructs his world-natures. This is a nasty price to pay, and Concretism has the advantage here.

Lewis has further sorts of objections to more detailed Ersatzist programs. Against specifically linguistic Ersatzism, which construes "worlds" as sets of sentences, he complains that there are not enough actual sentences available to distinguish all the genuine possibilities that there are, for those possibilities are mathematically more numerous than any earthly system of representation could in principle capture. In particular, he adds (1986), there might have been alien "natural properties," properties which do not actually exist but do inhabit worlds having (e.g.) an alien physics. Since those properties do not exist here, we have no way to name them, and so we cannot describe worlds in which they do exist, worlds in which they are switched around, and the like.

Against Quine's (1969) suggestion (implemented by Cresswell (1972)) that "worlds" can be represented by recombinations of the basic matter-elements that occupy the real world's space–time points, Lewis objects in effect that certain choices of the elements, the actual things we are to count as being the fundamental building blocks of the universe, will commit the theorist to strong modal theses which would better be left as open questions. For example, it presumably is possible that the world should have contained either more or less fundamental stuff. How might Quine/Cresswell construct an arrangement corresponding to an increase in the amount of fundamental matter? It further seems that there could have been irreducibly mental or spiritual entities, and that the world might have operated according to an entirely different physics and even according to a radically different geometry, but neither of those possibilities can easily be represented as or by a recombination of the matter that makes up @.

Chapter 3 of Lewis (1986) explores further versions of Ersatzism and wages criticism in more depth.

Finally, one might add that even if one throws together a system of actual objects that *ape* the group of "nonactual" things or worlds we need, in the sense of being structurally isomorphic to that group of things, why should we suppose that real *possibility* and other modalities in this world have anything to do with specially configured sets of items, whether sentences or propositions or matter-elements? It seems unlikely that what fundamentally makes it true that there could have been talking donkeys is that there exists a fabulously complex set of some sort. In this regard, Stalnaker (1976) does well to leave his "ways things might have been" unarticulated.

9   Vs. *Lewis*. I shall summarize some objections in turn to Lewis's Concretism. The first three we have already seen in section 6 above: that the Concretist is saddled with the problem of providing a credible criterion for separateness of worlds, that s/he must also come up with an effective analysis of the "counterpart" relation that serves as Lewis's surrogate for transworld identity, and that s/he forfeits the otherwise useful formal analogy between worlds and times.

A fourth objection is based on the also noted fact that Lewis rules out impossible worlds. This, I believe, is a serious liability. For linguistic semantics needs impossible worlds. Conditional sentences can have impossible antecedents, as in "If there were round squares, . . . ," and people can often be described as having contradictory beliefs. (Moreover, I can think of no direct argument for "nonexistents" that does not support impossibilia by parity of reasoning; I would not expect anyone to find a reason, independent of Concretism, for countenancing nonactual possible worlds but refusing to acknowledge impossible ones.)

The fifth objection: Given that other worlds are all "out there" in logical space independently of our mental activity and that they are causally and spatiotemporally inaccessible to us, how is it possible for us to know anything about them, or that they exist at all? (Richards (1975), Rescher (1975) and Skyrms (1976) have pressed this point.) If it be replied that just the same nasty epistemological question arises for numbers and other indispensable abstracta, remember that, for the Concretist, worlds are collections of *physical* objects. The point is well put by Skyrms: "*If* possible worlds . . . are supposed to exist in as concrete and robust a sense as our own . . . , then they require the same sort of evidence for their existence as [do] other constituents of physical reality" (p. 326). But there is not the slightest physical evidence for the existence anywhere of, e.g., donkeys that talk. (Lewis, 1986, attempts a reply to Skyrms.)

The sixth objection: As I have noted, Lewis addresses the Contradiction Problem by insisting that "actual" entities constitute only a tiny subclass of all the entities that exist, understanding "actual" as meaning roughly "worldmate of mine," and then (1986) explicating the crucial worldmateship relation by proposing his spatiotemporal criterion. But the last of those moves incurs two new objections. The first is that Lewis's theory now gets the truth-conditions of modal sentences grotesquely wrong. Consider Lewis's example of talking donkeys. Lewis claims that the possibility of talking donkeys obtains in virtue of there *existing*, in the everyday physical sense of "exist," at least one donkey that has the two extraordinary physical properties of talking and of being spatiotemporally disjoint from us. What reason could we have for believing the latter statement? And even if it is true, is *that* what constitutes the fact that there could have been talking donkeys?

The second new objection is due to Plantinga (1987): Suppose we were somehow to find out that there do exist scads and scads of other physical worlds, all spatiotemporally disconnected from us and from each other. (God, or quantum physicists, might reveal this.) But then surely we would have discovered something about reality, that there *actually* exist other physical space–times merely dislocated from ours. The space–times would be actual regions of reality, rather than merely possible "worlds." Further, Plantinga argues, no one would think the discovery had anything to do with *modality* in particular, at all; it would not be taken as vindicating any thesis about possibility.

10   *Fictionalism*. Fictionalists eschew the Actualist–Concretist debate by refusing to admit that apparent quantification over mere possibilia carries genuine existential commitment (even to abstract or mental Ersatzes); they hold that apparent reference to nonactual entities and worlds is only a kind of fiction or pretense. As Rosen (1990) says, it is a deflationist view: "You can legitimately say in one breath . . . 'there is a world where blue swans exist' and in the next breath[,] . . . 'but really, I don't believe in possible worlds'" (p. 330).

Armstrong (1989) compares possible worlds to ideal entities in science such as perfect vacuums, ideal gases and "economic men." He insists that there are scientific truths about such unreal entities even though those items are known not to exist.

But how are such scientific truths to be understood? Armstrong gives us little guidance as to that. One obvious suggestion would be to read them counterfactually or hypothetically: "If there were a perfect vacuum, then light would travel through it in such-and-such a way." But it is a little hard to extrapolate that practice to possible worlds. "If there were a pluriverse of unfathomably many nonactual possible worlds, then there would be a world that contained blue swans" is hard to process, and I think its antecedent is genuinely hard to interpret, especially when one adds as Armstrong would, "which there is not in any sense at all." A worse difficulty for the counterfactual strategy is that counterfactuals themselves are, as a class, badly in need of semantic interpretation, and by far the most compelling extant semantics for counterfactuals is a possible-worlds semantics (e.g., Lewis, 1973). On pain of circularity, one cannot both give a counterfactual explication of possible-worlds talk and maintain a possible-worlds semantics for counterfactuals.

Perhaps Armstrong would do better to join Rosen in mobilizing an "In fiction F" operator or as Rosen calls it (p. 331), a "story prefix," as in "According to Conan Doyle's Sherlock Holmes stories, a famous detective lived in Baker Street and solved many mysteries." On this approach, a fictional truth such as "Holmes captured Sebastian Moran" is taken as elliptical for the corresponding story-prefixed statement: "According to the Sherlock Holmes stories, Holmes captured Sebastian Moran," which is literally true and which of course makes no commitment to the existence of Holmes or Moran.

So instead of Conan Doyle's oeuvre, let there be a big Lewisian story about a panoply of alternate possible worlds; Rosen calls the story "PW." (PW actually needs to be somewhat complex, in order to be sure that the fictional worlds contain enough denizens to ensure that all the right modal statements will come out true on the resulting semantics.) Then a modal statement such as "There might have been blue swans" and its possible-worlds explication "There is a world in which there are blue swans" will both be translated as, "According to PW, there is a world in which there are blue swans." This clearly avoids the existential commitment to nonactual worlds and to blue though nonactual swans.

It is perhaps no worse than odd to think that our ordinary modal statements are true in virtue of the literal existence of a specific theory invented by philosophers. But Rosen's proposal shares two of the liabilities incurred by previous views. First, as he grants (p. 344), he has not eliminated modality (any more than has the Ersatzer), for his story prefix is itself a modal operator and he takes it as primitive. Second, we badly need a semantics for the story prefix itself, and as in the case of counterfactuals, the best going semantics for modal operators is a possible-worlds semantics; hence Rosen faces a threat of circularity just as does the counterfactual move I offered to Armstrong.

Rosen himself raises an interesting further objection to his own theory. (A similar point has been urged against Lewis, but not as effectively.) Some modal facts rightly elicit emotional responses. For example, we regret what might have been but was not, and we are frightened and chastened by what might easily have happened to us. But if modal facts are at bottom only facts about PW, such emotions are inappropriate. PW is only a philosophical story. It might frighten and chasten me that my Lewisian counterpart in a very nearby concrete world is killed as a result of taking a foolish risk, but it should not frighten or chasten me that *according to a story* (PW) told by David Lewis, I have a counterpart who is killed. For on Rosen's view the killing did not happen to anyone, not even to a non-actual person.

Rosen replies only briefly. He suggests that PW is not an ordinary story, but has a "special authority" that warrants emotional responses. The authority derives "from being an explicit formulation of our imaginative habits" (p. 353).

Further criticisms of Rosen's proposal are made by Brock (1993), Vision (1993), and Divers (1995).

11   *Prospects.* It will not be easy to resolve the issues between Actualists and Concretists, nor to refute or establish Fictionalism. Replies have already been made to the various objections I have catalogued, and there will be further objections, countercharges and rejoinders to be made in connection with any theory currently

in the field. Unfortunately, no extant theory is at all satisfactory, nor are we likely to see a new and plausible metaphysic of modality anytime soon.

References

Armstrong, D. M. (1989). *A Combinatorial Theory of Possibility*. Cambridge: Cambridge University Press.

Brock, S. (1993). "Modal Fictionalism: a response to Rosen," *Mind*, 102, pp. 147–50.

Castañeda, H.-N. (1974). "Thinking and the Structure of the World," *Philosophia*, 4, pp. 3–40; reprinted in Castañeda (1989).

——(1989). *Thinking, Language, and Experience*. Minneapolis: University of Minnesota Press.

Cresswell, M. J. (1972). "The World Is Everything That Is the Case," *Australasian Journal of Philosophy*, 50, pp. 1–13; reprinted in Loux (1979).

——(1973). *Logics and Languages*. London: Methuen.

——(1985). *Structured Meanings*. Cambridge, MA: Bradford Books/MIT Press.

Divers, J. (1995). "Modal Fictionalism Cannot Deliver Possible Worlds Semantics," *Analysis*, 55, 81–8.

Forrest, P. (1998). "Ways Worlds Could Be," in S. Laurence and C. MacDonald (eds.), *Contemporary Readings in the Foundations of Metaphysics*. Oxford: Blackwell.

Kripke, S. (1972/1980). "Naming and Necessity," in Davidson and Harman (1972), pp. 253–355; republished (1980) as *Naming and Necessity*. Cambridge, MA: Harvard University Press. Page references are to the latter.

Lewis, D. (1973). *Counterfactuals*. Cambridge, MA: Harvard University Press.

——(1983). "Individuation by Acquaintance and by Stipulation," *Philosophical Review*, 92, pp. 3–32.

——(1986). *On the Plurality of Worlds*. Oxford: Basil Blackwell.

——(1990). "Noneism or Allism?" *Mind*, 99, pp. 23–31.

Loux, M. (1979) (ed.). *The Possible and the Actual*. Ithaca, NY: Cornell University Press.

Lycan, W. G. (1994). *Modality and Meaning*. Dordrecht and Boston: Kluwer Academic Publishers.

Marcus, R. B. (1975–6). "Dispensing with Possibilia," *Proceedings and Addresses of the American Philosophical Association*, 44, pp. 39–51.

Meinong, A. (1904/1960). "The Theory of Objects," in *Realism and the Background of Phenomenology* (ed. R. M. Chisholm). Glencoe, IL: Free Press, pp. 76–117.

Montague, R. (1974). *Formal Philosophy*. New Haven: Yale University Press.

Parsons, T. (1980). *Nonexistent Objects*. New Haven: Yale University Press.

Plantinga, A. (1974). *The Nature of Necessity*. Oxford: Clarendon Press.

——(1987). "Two Concepts of Modality: Modal Realism and Modal Reductionism," in J. E. Tomberlin (ed.), *Philosophical Perspectives, 1: Metaphysics, 1987*. Atascadero: Ridgeview Publishing.

Quine, W. V. O. (1948/1963). "On What There Is," *Review of Metaphysics*, 2, pp. 21–38. Reprinted in *From a Logical Point of View*, second edition. New York: Harper Torchbooks.

——(1969). "Propositional Objects," in *Ontological Relativity and Other Essays*. New York: Columbia University Press.

Rapaport, W. J. (1978). "Meinongian Theories and a Russellian Paradox," *Noûs*, 12, pp. 153–80.

Rescher, N. (1975). *A Theory of Possibility*. Pittsburgh: University of Pittsburgh Press.

Richards, T. (1975). "The Worlds of David Lewis," *Australasian Journal of Philosophy*, 53, pp. 105–18.

Rosen, G. (1990). "Modal Fictionalism," *Mind*, 99, pp. 327–54.

Routley, R. (1980). *Exploring Meinong's Jungle and Beyond*. Canberra: Departmental Monograph #3, Philosophy Department, Research School of Social Sciences, Australian National University.

Russell, B. (1905). Critical Notice of Meinong (ed.), *Untersuchungen zur Gegenstandstheorie und Psychologie, Mind*, 14, pp. 530–8.

Skyrms, B. (1976). "Possible Worlds, Physics and Metaphysics," *Philosophical Studies*, 30, pp. 323–32.

Stalnaker, R. (1976). "Possible Worlds," *Noûs*, 10, pp. 65–75; reprinted in Loux (1979).

Vision, G. (1993). "Fiction and Fictionalist Reductions," *Pacific Philosophical Quarterly*, 74, 150–74.

Zalta, E. (1983). *Abstract Objects: An Introduction to Axiomatic Metaphysics*. Dordrecht, D. Reidel.

——(1988). *Intensional Logic and the Metaphysics of Intentionality*. Cambridge, MA: Bradford Books/MIT Press.

Chapter 16

The Actual and the Possible

Alexander R. Pruss

Introduction

We use alethic modal language all the time. For instance, we say that someone did not do something she could have done, or that the existence of unicorns is possible, or that $2 + 2 = 4$ could not have failed to be true. We make counterfactual assertions such as "Were I to drop this glass, which in fact I do not, it would fall." We think it might have been the case that Hitler had never existed. In these locutions we are speaking about situations and things that are not actual, of ways the universe might have been but was not.

Moreover, alethic modal language could not play the kind of role it has in our lives if we did not take a realist stance towards it. For instance, to decide rationally between alternatives, we often need to consider what consequences would result from each alternative. To decide questions of moral responsibility we often need to decide what else could have been done. The laws of nature by which we navigate the world have counterfactual force. If we did not take our alethic modal claims to express objective truths, modal language could not play the role it does in these cases.

A useful way of clarifying modal discourse is to introduce the notion of a *possible world*, or *world* for short, which is a complete way that a universe might have been. The term "possible" refers here not to physical possibility, but to a broad notion of logical or metaphysical possibility, which lets one ask questions such as whether it would be metaphysically possible for a horse to beget an owl. Once possible worlds are introduced, one can say a proposition is possible if it is true at some world, necessary if true at all worlds, and contingent if true at some but not all, so that modal operators can be replaced by quantifiers. It is possible that there is a unicorn if and only if there is a possible world at which there are unicorns.

Many ordinary language modal claims seem local. "It might have been that Hitler had never been born" sounds like it is a claim merely about the circumstances around Hitler's birth. However, in fact, it is a global claim. We do not simply mean that a world in which Hitler is not born is logically possible. What we mean is that there is a world like ours in relevant respects, for instance sharing the same laws of nature and initial conditions, or maybe even the same historical conditions up to the late nineteenth century, but in which Hitler is not born. Specifying what these relevant respects are may well be a global task, especially if laws of nature are global. So we need possible worlds for clarification and disambiguation.

Moreover, possible worlds can be used to clarify modal claims that one could not easily explicate in other ways. For instance, a claim that people's having virtue or vice supervenes on natural facts is a claim that there are no possible worlds which share the same natural facts but which differ in respect of someone's virtue or vice. Likewise, David Lewis has shown us how to explain counterfactuals in terms of possible worlds. Assuming I do not drop the glass, it is true that *were I to drop the glass, it would fall* provided that some world in which I drop the glass and it falls is more similar to our world in relevant ways, especially in nomic structure, than any world in which I drop the glass but it does not fall.

Two Interrelated Problems

If we are to be realists about alethic modal truths, then the natural question is: What makes modal propositions *true*? What are they true *of*? In general, an objectively true proposition must be true *of* some aspect of reality. One way of spelling out this intuition is to say that in order for a proposition to be true, it must have a *truthmaker*, something in virtue of which it is true. The truthmaker is something worldly, and for propositions about concreta, it is something concrete. Thus, the truthmaker of the proposition that Smith is bald is the concrete baldness of Smith, or else Smith's being bald.

Truthmaker-based arguments have been common in philosophy, starting with Parmenides who argued that there are no true propositions about the future on the presentist premise that future worldly states do not exist and hence the truthmakers for propositions about the future do not exist. Alternately, one could use *modus tollens* and argue that since it is true that tomorrow the sun will rise, some future worldly states *do* exist and make true propositions about the future true. Similarly, many have argued that there are no ethical truths, because the truthmakers of ethical propositions would allegedly have to be queer non-physical entities.

The claim that true propositions require truthmakers has been challenged. For instance, one might worry what existent reality can make a negative claim such as that there are no seven-legged dogs true. One could posit a negative state of affairs, such as *there not being any seven-legged dogs*, but that would trivialize the truthmaker theory. Alternately, one could say that what makes it true that there are no seven-legged dogs would be everything's being either A_1, or A_2, ... or A_n and A_1's having some positive property incompatible with being a seven-legged dog, A_2's having some positive property incompatible with being a seven-legged dog, ... and A_n's having some positive property incompatible with being a seven-legged dog.

What, then, are the truthmakers of alethic modal claims? This question is deeply puzzling, since many alethic modal claims *prima facie* concern non-existent things such as unicorns. One proposed answer is that the truthmakers of alethic modal claims are possible worlds, and we have already seen that we have good reason to believe in possible worlds even apart from this. So this brings us to the second question: What *are* possible worlds?

In his essay in this volume, William G. Lycan discusses six approaches to the problem of how to make sense of talk of non-existent possibilia, grouped into two wide groups. The *actualist* accounts reject any non-actual entities, any entities not found in the actual world, and thus must provide an account of the truth of modal claims in terms of this-worldly actual entities. The *concretist* accounts, on the other hand, say that there are concrete non-actual entities, such as unicorns existing concretely in concrete physical worlds different from ours, which serve as the truth-makers of modal propositions.

I will critically evaluate the most prominent contemporary concretist account, that of David Lewis, according to which possible worlds are just concrete physical universes on a par with ours, and the most promising contemporary actualist account, that of Robert M. Adams (1974) and Alvin Plantinga (1974), which claims that possible worlds are Platonic entities constructed from abstracta such as propositions or properties. I will argue that both of these kinds of accounts fail to provide an adequate theory of the truthmakers of alethic modal propositions, and sketch an alternate actualist account based on ideas of Aristotle and Leibniz. Interestingly, the actualist account I will sketch will make the truthmakers be *concrete* entities.

Lewis's Solution

David Lewis has an elegant and thoroughly worked out concretist answer to both the problem of truthmakers of modal claims and the problem of what possible worlds are. A Lewisian world is, by definition, a maximal physical spatiotemporally connected aggregate. Every way that a world could have been is a way that some existing, physical world really is. This I call "Extreme Modal Realism." According to the Extreme Modal Realist, there are infinitely many existing island universes, and unicorns and witches do exist, but not in our world. What makes it true to say that something could happen is just that it does happen in one of these island universes.

Lewis has a two-fold argument for positing the infinitude of physical universes that he needs. The first is a cost–benefit theoretic-utility argument. Supposing there are such universes solves the problem of what makes true modal statements true, and Lewis thinks it useful for many other philosophical purposes, such as for saying that a proposition is nothing but the set of worlds at which it is true. Given the usefulness of the theory, Lewis concludes that it is probably true.

The second argument for the theory is to argue that like indexical terms such as "I," "here," and "now," the word "actual" and its cognates depend for their reference on the context in which they are tokened. If someone says "There actually exist horses," according to Lewis she is saying that there exist horses in the universe in which she is speaking. This makes the word "actual" and its cognates into indexical terms. But all the referents of indexical terms are ontologically on par. All referents of "I" are ontologically on par with me: there is no absolute property of I-ness that accrues to me and me alone. (This is not so obvious in the case of "now," though it will be true even there on Lewis's way of looking at time.) By analogy, all the referents of "actual" are also ontologically on par. Thus, the universe which is actual is not ontologically special. It must be ontologically on par with all the other non-actual universes, and hence all possible non-actual universes must exist, Lewis concludes, and must be ontologically on par.

Note, then, that considering "actual" to be an indexical gives one a good argument for believing in Extreme Modal Realism. Conversely, if one accepts Extreme Modal Realism, there is good reason to consider "actual" to be an indexical term, or at least a term that is relevantly similar to an indexical term. To see this, Lewis argues as follows. According to Extreme Modal Realism, every way that a world could have been is a way some concretely existing world is. Now, if actuality were an absolute property of a world, then there would be exactly one world which had that property. But "[s]urely it is a contingent matter which world is actual. A contingent matter is one that varies from world to world. At one world, the contingent matter goes one way; at another, another. So at one world, one world is actual; and at another, another. How can this be *absolute* actuality? – The relativity is manifest!" (Lewis, 1986, p. 94). Next, however, one can argue that our best account of something's actuality being relative in this way is to suppose that actuality is indexical, or at least relevantly similar to indexical claims.

All this means that Extreme Modal Realism goes hand-in-hand with a relative, indexical theory of actuality. But is "actual" an indexical? Richard Gale (1991, ch. 5) has noted that the indexical account of actuality fails to give correct truth values for various sentences. For example, the sentence "I might not have been I" is false, because an indexical like "I" is a *rigid designator*, that is a term which has the same referent in counterfactual as in non-counterfactual contexts. On the other hand, Gale has argued that "the actual world" is a definite description just like "the tallest person in the world." Just as the tallest person in the world might not have been the tallest person in the world, likewise it is true to assert: "The actual world might not have been the actual world," which is disanalogous to the indexical case and shows that "the actual world" is non-indexical. In the latter sentence, "the actual world" is used non-rigidly: its second occurrence refers to the world that would be actual in the counterfactual case.

A defender of Lewis might say that the above is a non-central use of "the actual world" and point to the central use as occurring in sentences like: "It could have been the case that Smith was taller than she is *in the actual world*." In this sentence, "the actual world" is indeed used rigidly the way an indexical is, since it refers not to the counterfactual world where Smith is taller, but to the world in which the sentence is tokened.[1] However, first of all, the very existence of a non-rigid use, even if non-central, already shows a crucial disanalogy between indexicals and "actual." Secondly, ordinary definite descriptions also have an analogous rigidified use. For instance, one can say, with only a little awkwardness: "It could have been the case that John was faster than *the fastest person alive*." Here, "the fastest person alive" acts as rigid designator: in the counterfactual context it refers to the same person who in our world is the fastest person alive, though this person is obviously not the fastest person alive in the counterfactual world.

Thus the presence of both a non-rigid and a rigid use make "the actual world" much more closely analogous to definite descriptions. This and other logico-linguistic disanalogies between "the actual world" and paradigmatic indexical terms undercut the argument for Extreme Modal Realism from the supposed indexicality of actuality. However, if one accepts Extreme Modal Realism for other reasons, such as theoretic utility, one *will* see a crucial analogy between actuality and indexical terms, namely the systematic shift in reference between different contexts of use: what "the actual world" refers to when used by a speaker in one world is not what it refers to when used by a speaker in another. The Lewisian will then say that "the actual world" is an indexical term, albeit one that is sometimes linguistically treated differently from paradigmatic ones. What will be decisive as an argument against this claim will be that in addition to the linguistic disanalogies, we will see that there is a crucial analogy in the way we treat actuality and ordinary indexicals in our inductive reasoning.

Now, if we do accept the plausibility of Lewis's account of actuality, the Extreme Modal Realism account attractively answers the two basic questions of the nature of possible worlds and modality. Possible worlds are not queer ghostly might-have-beens but are full-blooded physical beings, universes like ours. And we have an apparently reductive physicalist account of possibility: A proposition is possible if and only if there is a maximal spatiotemporally connected aggregate of which it is true.

When we say that unicorns can exist, there is no semantic problem of explaining what we are doing when talking of unicorns given there are no unicorns. We are simply saying that somewhere in the totality of all physical universes there are unicorns. But of course the unicorns are not actual; they are not a part of the aggregate of all physical objects spatiotemporally related to my present tokening of this sentence.

Inductive Paradox

Lewis's theory radically revises our notions of the range of things that exist to include the things that we thought to be merely possible. Not surprisingly, this creates a number of unacceptable paradoxes.

The first of these shows that if Lewis's theory of actuality is right, then we are never justified in making any inductive inferences about the future. But certainly we are justified in inferring on the basis of past data that, e.g., something approximately like the universal law of gravitation will continue to hold tomorrow. If tomorrow I drop a glass, it will fall – and Lewis will surely not want to deny I have reason to believe this. However, I will show that if Lewis is right that actuality is indexical, then this is an unjustified inference. Since the inference that gravity will hold tomorrow *is* a justified one, *pace* the skeptics, by *modus tollens* it follows that actuality is not indexical, and so this argument is a *reductio* of Lewis's claims about the indexicality of actuality.

To see this, suppose for a *reductio* that actuality is indexical. Let D be a complete description of the actual world up to the present, that is t_0, in non-future-involving terms. Intuitively, a non-truth-functionally complex sentence about a time t is "non-future-involving" provided it does not entail the existence of any instants of time after t and is compatible with the truth of an arbitrary number of tokenings of that sentence after t. Now, there are at least as many possible worlds satisfying D but at which the law of gravitation fails a day after t_0 as there are worlds satisfying D but at which gravity continues to work a day after t_0. This is just a statement about logical space, one that David Lewis certainly accepts, and one that both sides in the Humean debate on induction can accept.

Suppose then I have a possible world w about which the only thing I know is that it satisfies D. I am not justified in inferring just from *this* information that gravity will work a day after t_0 in w. Since I am only talking about possible worlds at this point, this is merely a statement about logical space, and my claim follows from the fact that there are at least as many worlds satisfying D at which gravity will fail a day after t_0 as there are ones at which it will continue to hold. This, too, is a statement that people on both sides of the Humean debate can accept, and should not be controversial. The mere facts that w is possible and w satisfies D do not give one reason to think gravity will continue to hold in w.

Before continuing, we need to observe one crucial fact about theoretical reason, and specifically about inductive reason. Theoretical reason is impartial with regard to merely indexical facts. If some set of non-indexical facts did not justify an inference to some further non-indexical proposition, then adding a purely indexical claim to the evidence, such as "The time described is *now*" or "This took place *here*," cannot by *itself* give justification for inferring the non-indexical proposition we could not infer before. Purely indexical data is irrelevant for objective reason. If, for instance, I cannot infer from some non-indexical inductive data about people that Alexander Pruss will do the right thing under some circumstances, then neither can I infer it when I add the additional premise that *I* am Alexander Pruss – to do so would be to commit a fallacy of partiality.

Now suppose I find out one more piece of information about w in addition to knowing that it satisfies D: I find out that w is actual. If I take the claim that actuality is indexical seriously, then just as merely learning that t_0 is now does not give me any information relevant for inferring that gravity will continue to function a day after t_0, analogously, learning that w is actual will not give me any information relevant for inferring that the law of gravitation will be true in w a day after t_0. Therefore, if actuality is indexical, I cannot infer from the fact that w satisfies D and w is actual that gravity will hold a day after t_0. Since in fact we do not have any further relevant information about our world beyond D and the fact that this world is actual, neither can *we* infer that gravity will function tomorrow, assuming that actuality is indexical. But this conclusion is absurd: we certainly are justified in inferring that if we drop something tomorrow, it will fall. By *modus tollens*, it follows that actuality is not indexical.

More formally, the *reductio* is as follows:

(1)   Let D be a complete non-indexical description of the actual world up to the present (t_0) in non-future-involving terms. (Definition.)

(2) D contains the claim that gravity has always held prior to t_0. (Premise.)

(3)   Conclusions about the actual world reached by reasoning in accordance with the canons of inductive reasoning are justified, and in particular knowing that gravity has always actually held prior to t_0 justifies one in believing it will continue to hold after t_0. (Premise.)

(4)   There are at least as many worlds satisfying D in which the law of gravitation fails after t_0 as there are worlds in which it continues to hold. (Premise.)

(5)   *Therefore, knowing that an entity w is a world satisfying D does not by itself epistemically justify inferring that w is a world at which gravity holds after t_0. (Premise, justified intuitively by appeal to (4).)

(6)   *Theoretical reason is impartial with respect to merely indexical facts: If knowing that x is F (where F is purely non-indexical and x is a definite description or proper name) does not epistemically justify inferring that x is G (where G is purely non-indexical), then neither does knowing x is F and that x is I (now, here, etc.: any pure indexical will do) justify inferring that x is G. (Premise.)

(7)   *Actuality is indexical. (Premise.)

(8)   Therefore, knowing that an entity w is a world satisfying D and that w is actual does not epistemically justify inferring that w is a world at which gravity holds after t_0. (By (5)–(7).)

(9)   *But knowing that the actual world satisfies D and that w is actual epistemically justifies inferring that gravity holds in w after t_0. (By (2) and (3).)

(10)   Therefore, knowing that the actual world satisfies D and that w is actual both does and does not epistemically justify inferring that gravity holds in w after t_0, which is absurd. (By (8) and (9).)

The premises marked with an asterisk form an inconsistent quadruple. All of them, except (7), are highly plausible, and hence we need to reject the premise (7) that actuality is indexical. Another way to look at this argument is to see it as showing that if actuality is indexical, then inductive reasoning violates (6) and hence is guilty of the fallacy of partiality. But in fact we take inductive scientific reasoning to be a paradigm of impartial reason, and hence actuality is not indexical.

Note that a pragmatic will-to-believe argument for accepting inductive consequences such as that gravity will continue to function cannot help Lewis. Will-to-believe arguments presuppose that we have reason to think that one belief *will* be more beneficial than another, and if inductive reasoning about gravity is undercut as above, likewise we do not have any information either way as to which beliefs are more likely to be beneficial.

Identity versus Counterpart Theory

A proposition is possible if and only if it is true at some world. Taking this at face value, it is possible that I be a biologist if and only if there is some world at which I am a biologist. Since I was never a biologist in the actual world, the true claim that it was possible for me to have been a biologist seemingly implies that at some non-actual world I am a biologist, which in turn implies that I exist not only at the actual world but at at least one non-actual world as well. Moreover, *prima facie*, for grounding the truth of the claim that it is possible that I be a biologist it is irrelevant whether *other* people at this or other worlds are biologists or not.

There are now two different kinds of possible world theories. An identity theorist like Saul Kripke insists on taking these intuitions at face value. Thus, I myself, exist at a number of possible worlds, at one of which I am a biologist. David Lewis, on the other hand, is a counterpart theorist and holds that each concrete entity exists in only one world. What makes it true, however, to say that I could have been a biologist is that there is a possible world at which my *counterpart* is a biologist, where my counterpart in a given world is (roughly) that person there, if he exists, who resembles me most in the relevant respects and whose resemblance to me is sufficiently close. The identity theorist will, of course, insist that what people very similar to me do in other worlds does not *make* it true that I could do those things. Although their doings would be *evidence* for my being able to do it, these doings would not be a *truthmaker* for the proposition that I can do it.

Lewis's Extreme Modal Realism now faces a dilemma. Either counterpart theory, as Lewis himself thinks, is right, or identity theory is right. Each horn of the dilemma leads to two problems: one ethical and one metaphysical.

Suppose both identity theory and Extreme Modal Realism are true. Then the following paradox results. Whatever I choose to do, in the sum total of reality, I perform all the choices that it is logically possible for me to perform. I claim that this means that what I do overall does not matter and ethics breaks down.

First of all, as has often been noted, on Lewisian grounds what I choose does not matter for the totality of reality at large, since according to Extreme Modal Realism the totality of all real worlds is fixed, as this totality corresponds to the logical space of all possibilities. However, this is not itself enough to generate the breakdown of ethics, as Lewis has argued. According to a non-consequentialist like Lewis, what matters is not that the sum total of all reality should be positively affected by one's actions, but that one's own actions be the right ones, that one be oneself virtuous, even if there are infinitely many vicious people who undo the good effects of one's actions.

However, if one adds identity theory to Extreme Modal Realism, then the ethical paradox becomes much more formidable. For then my actions do not even affect overall what kind of a person *I* am, because I really exist in infinitely many worlds, and I cannot change which ones I exist in. In some worlds I am a mass murderer, in others I am a great philanthropist, and in yet others I am a venal liar. Whatever I do, facts like this will not change. I know that if I choose between a virtuous and a vicious action in favor of a virtuous action, I will do the vicious one anyway, in worlds equally real as ours and in a way that is as real as the one in which I do the virtuous action. Hence, moral choice does not have significance for building one's moral character, since one's overall character as a person is fixed. This is paradoxical, and hence we cannot have both identity theory and Extreme Modal Realism.

Note that this argument does not apply under counterpart theory. It is true that if I act virtuously, then infinitely many counterparts of mine will act viciously. But they are not literally *I*, and hence a non-consequentialist can still insist that I should do my duty, not minding them, for what they do is not my business. On the identity theory, however, what they do is literally my business, since they are I.

Besides paradox, there is a serious metaphysical difficulty for Extreme Modal Realism if identity theory is adopted. We have seen that Extreme Modal Realism cannot tolerate an absolute theory of actuality. Lewis's indexical alternative, however, fails given the identity theory. Recall that on the indexical account of actuality, a given instance of a tokening of "the actual world," at least in central cases, refers to that world in which it was tokened.

However, according to the identity theory, that very tokening occurs in more than one world. For suppose I token the sentence: "In the actual world, a cure for cancer is found in the year 2020," and suppose that the sentence is in fact false. Nonetheless, it is logically possible that I make *this* very tokening in a world in which it expresses a true proposition. After all, according to the identity theorist, there will be a world in which this sentence-type expresses a true proposition, and in which I token the sentence at numerically the same place and time as I do, having the same history, and I perform the tokening in the same way. It is highly plausible to suppose that under these circumstances it follows that in that world I make numerically the same tokening.

But if the very same tokening of a sentence containing the phrase "the actual world" occurs in more than one world, then one cannot define the extension of the phrase "the actual world" as being *the* world in which it occurs. Nor can one allow the phrase to refer to more than one world, for then it would be the case that both a world where a cure for cancer is found in 2020 is actual and a world where such a cure is not found is actual, and this entails the self-contradictory statement that actually the cure for cancer is both found and not found in 2020. Therefore the indexical theory of actuality is not available on the identity variant of Extreme Modal Realism, and it is difficult to see what could replace it, given the unavailability for a Lewisian of an absolutist theory of actuality.

However, the counterpart horn of the dilemma is no more congenial. First of all, we have to contend with the strong Kripkean metaphysical intuitions that what my counterparts might do in other worlds cannot be what makes it true that *I* could have been a biologist. Facts about people other than I are irrelevant interlopers with respect to questions about *my* capabilities.

Secondly, a variant ethical paradox can also be given, albeit one which for technical reasons has to be run in a counterfactual world and which needs the plausible technical assumption that there are no indiscernible worlds, a question Lewis himself remains agnostic about. It is indeed plausible that there are no indiscernible possible worlds. First of all, the usual tool for individuating indiscernible objects is by their spatiotemporal relations. But possible worlds do not stand in spatiotemporal relations to one another. Moreover, if there were indiscernible possible worlds, one could ask the question: How many indiscernible copies of a given possible world are there? Whatever answer one gave would seem arbitrary: even if the number were infinite, it would seem arbitrary that it has the precise cardinality it does.

Imagine then that I am in a possible world containing a number of persons, but only one of the persons ever makes a free choice, and suppose this choice is nondeterministic and is the only nondeterministic event physically possible in that world. The choice in question is whether I should stick my wet thumb in a light socket. Suppose I know this would not kill me and would have no ethically significant consequences for anybody in that world other than that it would cause severe pain for a while to me. It would clearly be irrational, indeed crazy, of me to perform that action.

However, if a counterpart version of Extreme Modal Realism is true, then this would not only not be crazy, but it would be heroic. For supposing that the world described above is actual, there is a non-actual world which shares the same initial conditions and laws of nature, but in which my counterpart makes the choice opposite to mine. If I stick my thumb in the light socket, my counterpart does not. If I do not stick my thumb in the light socket, my counterpart does. Therefore, there is a real sense in which by sticking *my* thumb in the light socket, I save someone else from horrible pain. This then is a heroic act of supererogation rather than a crazy act. Therefore, the counterpart version of Extreme Modal Realism is absurd.

Thus, Lewis's Extreme Modal Realism leads to ethical paradoxes, albeit different ones, whether one adopts identity theory or counterpart theory. Both horns of the identity-*vs.*-counterpart theory dilemma involve other difficulties for Lewis's Extreme Modal Realism. Moreover, the argument from inductive reasoning applies on either horn of the dilemma. Therefore, we have a strong cumulative case against Extreme Modal Realism on the basis of paradoxical conclusions. One paradox does not completely destroy a theory, but a large number of serious ones puts it in grave doubt.

Platonism: The Main Realist Alternative to Lewis

The most promising contemporary realist alternatives to Lewis's account of possible worlds are the abstract worlds accounts promoted by Robert M. Adams and Alvin Plantinga. On their accounts, worlds turn out to be abstract Platonic entities, exactly one of which is instantiated by the universe, where "the universe" is defined to be the aggregate of all existing or occurring concrete entities, and this is the world that is absolutely actual. I will focus primarily on the Adams permutation of this account.

We thus start off by introducing *propositions* as theoretical abstract entities that are the bearers of truth-values and are needed to explain what it is that sentences express, what the objects of beliefs and propositional attitudes are and what paraphrases preserve, somewhat as electrons are needed to explain various physical phenomena. Some propositions, namely the true ones, are related to things and events in the universe, with the relation being one of the propositions *being made true by* or *representing* these things and events in the universe. If things in the universe were otherwise than they are, then different propositions would stand in these relations to things in the universe – if there were unicorns, then the proposition that there are unicorns would stand in the relation of *being made true by* to some things, namely the unicorns in the universe.

Note that the theoretical reason for believing in these Platonic propositions is largely independent of issues of modality. Adams then constructs a possible world as a maximal consistent collection of propositions. (An argument is needed that such collections exist, but as a matter of fact an argument can be supplied.) Exactly one world is then absolutely actual: it is the one all of whose propositions are true. A proposition can be said to be true *at* a world providing it is one of the propositions that are a member of the collection of propositions that the world is identical with. Note that because the worlds are Platonic entities, I had to distinguish between the concrete *universe*, which we physically inhabit, and the actual *world* which is the collection of all true propositions.

One might object to the Platonic approaches on the grounds that they all involve queer entities. Not only are we required to believe in Platonic beings, but, as Lewis notes, we are to believe that there is a magical relation of representation holding between Platonic beings such as propositions and the concrete entities that make them true, with it being contingent which propositions enter into those relations since it is contingent which propositions are true. What is it, then, that picks out one relation in the Platonic heaven rather than another as *the* relation of representation?

The proponent of these Platonic worlds can argue, however, that she has no need to answer this question. The relation of representation is one of the primitive terms in her theory, and it is not even a primitive chosen *ad hoc* to explain possible worlds, but a primitive needed for other explanatory purposes, such as of making sense of our practices of claiming, believing and paraphrasing. Nonetheless, if we had some way of pointing out this relation within the Platonic universe of all relations, then we would be happier as theorists.

Secondly, the Platonic theories are expressly non-reductive as accounts of possibility, unlike Lewis's theory. For Adams, a possible world is a maximal consistent collection of propositions, which is just the same as saying it is a maximal *compossible* collection of propositions. On this theory, there is a primitive abstract property of possibility or consistency that applies to individual propositions and to collections of them. One could also take necessity to be the primitive concept, but this would not change anything substantially.

That the Platonic accounts are non-reductive is only a problem if a reductive account of possibility is available. However, the most plausible account claiming to be reductive is Lewis's, which is too paradoxical to accept. But while a complete reduction is probably impossible, it would be desirable to give at least a partial reduction, on which the whole realm of alethic possibility would be seen to have its root in some more comprehensible subclass. The Platonic accounts do not succeed in performing this more limited reduction either.

Adams' theory is an *actualist* one. His possible worlds are built up out of things that are actual. These abstracta actually exist – indeed, necessarily so – and an actualist theory is one that grounds possibility in actually existent realities. On the other hand, Lewis's other worlds are not actual entities by Lewis's indexical criterion, as they are not the world in which my tokening of the word "actual" in this sentence occurred. If we think of possible worlds as possibilities for our universe, then there is a sense in which Adams and Plantinga have grounded possibilities in actuality, thereby answering to the Aristotelian maxim that actuality is prior to possibility.

However, in a deeper way, the Platonic approach is not faithful to what the Aristotelian maxim affirms. When an Aristotelian says a possibility is grounded in an actuality, she means that the actuality has some powers, capacities or dispositions capable of producing that possibility, which of course once produced would no longer be a mere possibility. This is clearest in the paradigm case where the actuality is temporally prior to the possibility. Aristotle's favorite illustration is how the actuality of one man makes possible the existence of a future man through the first man's capability for begetting a descendant. If we find attractive the idea that possibilities should be grounded in actuality in the stronger Aristotelian sense, then the Platonic approach will be unsatisfactory, because Platonic entities, in virtue of their abstractness, are categorially barred from entering into causal relations, and hence cannot make possibilities possible by being capable of producing them.

Moreover, the Aristotelian can argue that in fact there *are* capabilities and dispositions sufficient to ground the truth of at least *some* possibility claims. That I could have been a biologist is very plausibly made true by my capacities and dispositions and those of various persons and things in my environment. These capacities and dispositions are concrete real-worldly things, albeit ones having modal force. Hence, in fact, we do not need a Platonic realm to make at least some possibility claims true. Indeed, the facts about the Platonic realm – about propositions having or not having some primitive property – are interlopers here. Just as the statement that I could have been a biologist was not made true by what my Lewisian counterparts in other worlds do, so too it is not made true by abstract properties of Platonic abstracta. The common intuition behind both cases is that it is something in me and my concrete environment that makes the statement true.

This, however, creates a major problem for the Platonic approach. On the Platonic approach, what makes it possible that I was a biologist is that the abstract proposition – which is an entity in the Platonic heaven – that I was a biologist has the abstract property of possibility. But we have just seen that there are concrete capacities and dispositions in the universe that are by themselves sufficient to make it possible that I was a biologist. We thus have two different ways of characterizing possibility: one is via concrete this-worldly Aristotelian properties of concreta which really do exist – the Platonist should not deny this – and the other is via some abstract Platonic primitive properties of abstracta. Moreover, anything that is possible on the Aristotelian grounds will be physically possible, and hence also logically possible, and hence possible on Platonist grounds (though *prima facie* perhaps not conversely). But now we can ask: Why is this so? Why is there this apparent coincidence that anything made possible by this-worldly powers and capacities and dispositions happens to correspond to a proposition in the Platonic realm that has a certain abstract property? The Platonist is unable to explain this coincidence between powers in our universe and abstract facts about the Platonic realm, given the lack of causal interaction between the two realms.

An Aristotelian Alternative

If one shares the Aristotelian intuition that this-worldly capacities, powers and dispositions can make modal statements true, one might opt for a fully Aristotelian definition of mere possibility: A non-actual state of affairs is possible if there actually was a substance capable of initiating a causal chain, perhaps non-deterministic, that could lead to the state of affairs that we claim is possible. We can then say that something is possible if it is either actual or merely possible.

An approach like this has a number of benefits. Capacities, powers, and dispositions are probably the concepts closest to ordinary language notions of possibility. They are things we arguably have direct experiential knowledge of, *pace* Hume, by ourselves being capable of producing effects, and we can at least point out by ostension what, say, a capacity is. Moreover, though, while having modal force, they are concrete. Reducing all possibility to this subclass of modal notions would thus increase the comprehensibility of what we mean in saying something is possible – at least if one finds Aristotelian intuitions appealing. The account is not a full reduction, since powers and capacities are modal notions, but it does reduce all of modality to a more basic subclass.

There are, however, two closely related difficulties facing any such approach. The fist is that while this works fine for *local* possibilities, such as of my having been a biologist, it is difficult to see how one could get possible *worlds* out of it.

The second problem is the following argument. Consider the set of all contingent beings in the universe, namely beings that could have failed to exist. It is highly plausible that if we have a set of beings, every member of which is contingent, then it is a contingent fact that *any* of the beings in the set exist. But if this is right, the Aristotelian has a problem. For the possibility that *none* of those contingent beings that exist in the universe had existed cannot be grounded in the causal powers of any actual contingent being. Note that we are talking here not about the controversial possibility that there should exist no contingent beings, but about the much less controversial one that *those* contingent beings that exist might not exist, though perhaps other ones might then exist in their stead.

Neither is it clear how the Aristotelian could account for the possibility of the laws of nature having been different. Again, we see that the Aristotelian account has trouble with global possibilities.

Leibniz's Account

Consider now a somewhat different answer to the question of what possible worlds are. Leibniz, who started the whole debate about possible worlds, argued that necessary truths, including modal truths such as that unicorns are possible, must exist *somewhere*. Finding Platonic entities too queer, he wanted to locate these truths as acts of thought or ideas in the mind of an omniscient, necessarily existent God who contemplates them. He then gave an account of possible worlds that matched this. A Leibnizian possible world is a maximally specific consistent thought in the mind of God of a way for the world to be.

These acts of thought are actual entities, then, and so Leibniz has an answer as to what possible worlds are. Moreover, one might argue that Leibniz's account makes some progress with respect to the question of how it is that the entities which are possible worlds represent concrete things. Recall that one difficulty with the Platonic approach was that of picking out *which* relation between concrete

things and propositions was to count as *the* relation of representation. If one takes
the controversial view that our thoughts are innately representative, the Leibnizian account may get around this problem by saying that the relation between divine
thoughts and concrete things counts as the relation of representation which is the
relation produced by that faculty in God's mind which is analogous to the faculty
of intentionality in us, and we can perhaps point out which of our faculties is the
faculty of intentionality by ostension. There are many difficulties here, including
first of all the Leibnizian's very controversial commitment to thoughts being
innately representative or to a faculty of intentionality. But if we find appealing
the intuition that we can have a better grasp of what thoughts are, even divine
thoughts, than we can of Platonic entities, because thoughts are something that
we after all have direct experiential knowledge of, then we might prefer the
Leibnizian account.

However, this does not solve the main problem with the Platonic approach,
which was its failure to give an adequate account of what makes possibilities possible. The Leibnizian account does not help there at all, since those divine ideas
that are singled out for being dubbed "worlds" are singled out in virtue of being
consistent – that is, possible. Their possibility is prior in the order of explanation
to their being known by God to be possible (cf. Adams, 1994, p. 191). And so
this approach is not relevantly different from singling out some collections of
propositions for being dubbed "worlds" on the grounds of their being consistent.
Positing a God who contemplates possible worlds as described above does not in
any way help with Aristotelian intuitions about possibility being grounded in actuality, since, as far as the account goes, the thoughts could be just as causally inert
as Platonic abstracta.

A Combined Account

But now go back to one of the arguments against the Aristotelian view. The argument was that the Aristotelian cannot posit a contingent substance that would
ground the possibility of our whole past history having been different. But if the
Aristotelian is brave enough, she can say that what this shows is that if the Aristotelian notion of possibility is correct, and if we accept the intuition that none of
those contingent beings that exist might have existed, then we are committed to
the claim that there is a non-contingent being which grounds the possibility of
none of the contingent beings having existed. In fact, with a little work, this argument can be extended to show that the Aristotelian notion of possibility commits
one to the existence of a necessary first cause (perhaps a non-unitary cause which
is an aggregate of causes) that non-deterministically produces the historical universe and grounds the possibility of other histories, and indeed of there being
other laws of nature.

A sketch of the argument is as follows. Let S be the set of all actually existing contingent beings, and let w_0 be the actual world. Then, let w_1 be a possible world in which no member of S exists. It is then true at w_1 (technically, by the axiom S5 of modal logic) that it might have been that w_0 was actual. Then, by the Aristotelian account, there is a substance x in w_0 which could have initiated a causal chain that could lead to w_0 being actual. But x cannot start any chain of causes that can lead to actuality's not including x. Therefore, x must also exist in w_0. Thus, x exists in both w_0 and w_1. Since no member of S exists in w_1 while x exists in w_0, it follows that it is true at w_0 that x is not a member of S and hence is a necessary being. A further argument along similar lines can be used to show that in fact x must be the first cause of all contingent beings in w_0.

To some, of course, this will count as a *reductio ad absurdum* of the Aristotelian approach. However, if we do not count it as such, there is a natural way to combine this account with Leibniz's, by identifying the Aristotelian first cause with Leibniz's necessarily existent God. Then, one could have *both* possible worlds, namely certain thoughts in the mind of God, *and* an answer to the problem of what makes these worlds possible, namely God's power for initiating a causal chain capable of leading to their existence. The God of this theory would be not only omniscient but also omnipotent, then. Of course how attractive one will find this account will depend on one's assessment of *other* evidence for and against the existence of such a God.

If one decides not to take this theistic route, one might well have to go with a Platonic account of what possible worlds are, at the cost of having possibility be a primitive property of abstracta and of not being able to do justice to the Aristotelian intuition that actuality is prior to possibility; or else with an Aristotelian account of possibility, at the cost of not having possible worlds or global possibilities. Alternately, as far as a theory of possibility goes, one might give up on possible worlds, but allow for global possibilities such as of the laws of nature being different or of none of the actual contingent beings existing, by invoking a *non-theistic* first cause for history, such as some event prior to the Big Bang in some superuniverse.

There is hope, however, that the theistic account, once elaborated sufficiently, would end up combining the strengths of the Platonic, Aristotelian and Leibnizian accounts while avoiding most of their weaknesses. Of course this requires that there be an essentially omniscient and omnipotent necessary being, but just as Lewis thinks that the theoretical usefulness of his Extreme Modal Realism is an argument for the existence of his concrete physical worlds, so too one can argue that the theoretical usefulness of a theistic account like this provides some grounds for thinking it is true, and in particular that there is a God.

Acknowledgment

I am grateful to Robert Brandom, Wayne Davis, James Dreier, Richard Gale, Jeremy Heis, David Manley, Thane Naberhaus, Alvin Plantinga, Nicholas Rescher,

Ernest Sosa and Peter van Inwagen for encouragement, discussions, comments and/or suggestions.

Note

1   *Technical note:* It might be argued that in fact even in this example "the actual world" is not used rigidly but simply has wide scope within the sentence it is tokened in. To see this, consider the following dialogue (with a slight change of example). A: "It could have been the case that Smith was less intelligent than she is *in the actual world.*" B: "This is true, but it might not have been true." In this dialogue, B makes the arguably true claim that it might have been the case that Smith had such a level of intelligence that she could not have had a lower (this would be true if it was possible for Smith to have had *no* intelligence at all). However, if "in the actual world" were a rigid designator, and the actual world were w_0, then B would be making the claim that although it could have been the case that Smith was less intelligent than she is in w_0, it could have been the case that it could not have been the case that Smith was less intelligent than she is in w_0, a claim that is evidently false if S5 is true (i.e., if the possibly possible is necessarily possible). If we take it that B's claim is not evidently false, then we have to grant that although "in the actual world" has wide scope relative to the rest of A's assertion, it is not rigid.

Bibliography

Adams, Robert M. (1974). "Theories of Actuality," *Noûs*, 8, pp. 211–31.
——(1994). *Leibniz: Determinist, Theist, Idealist.* Oxford University Press.
Gale, Richard M. (1991). *On the Nature and Existence of God.* Cambridge University Press.
Lewis, David (1986). *On the Plurality of Worlds.* Basil Blackwell.
Plantinga, Alvin (1974). *The Nature of Necessity.* Oxford University Press.

Index

A-series, time, 68–9
A-theories, 131–5, 136–7, 141
absence, 299
absolute idealism, 66, 187n, 225–39
  causation, 237, 240n
  consciousness, 236–7, 239
  events, 238–9
  experience, 228–32, 236–9, 239–40n
  God, 225–6
  mind, 226
  parts, 236–8
  space, 236–7
  time, 238–9
  wholes, 236–8
abstract particulars, 45, 113, 125
abstract thought, 105–6
abstract universals, 45, 120
abstraction, 103–4
acceleration, 6, 7–8
accessibility relation, 304
accident, 90–4, 96–7, 98, 99–100, 102,
  112
action, 46, 60–1, 91
activity, 100, 101
actualism, 307, 319, 327–32
actuality
  indexical account of, 307, 320–4,
    325–6, 328
  thomist metaphysics, 107
Adams, Robert M., 319, 327, 328, 331
adverbs, 62–3
Aeterni Patris, 88
agency, 101
agency-based disanalogies, 70–8, 84
  definition of agent, 70–1

agreement, method of, 23–4
Albert the Great, 90
Ambrose, St., 92
analogy, 102–3
analytical thomism, 88
Anaxagoras, 165–6
angels, 98
animals, 192
Anscombe, G. E. M., 60, 62, 100, 139,
  176
Anselm, Saint, 107
anticipation, 68, 202
antirealism, 282
antiscientism, 161
antiskeptical epistemology, 156
appearance, and reality, 252, 269–73
Aquinas, Thomas, 87–90
  activity, 101
  anti-Cartesianism, 105
  causation, 101, 102
  Commentary, 103
  Commentary on the Sentences, 106–7
  doctrine of analogy, 102
  essence, 102
  "five ways," 106
  God, 106–7, 284
  individuation, 98
  induction, 103, 104
  kinds of predication, 91
  knowledge, 102, 104
  matter, 95, 96
  nominal and real definitions, 101
  On Being and Essence, 88
  On the Principles of Nature, 88
  soul, 104

space, 98
substance and accident, 92–3, 94, 97,
   102
Summa Theologiae, 92, 107
transubstantiation, 92–3
Aristotelians
   and Aquinas, 88–90
   dense time, 67
   possible worlds, 328–9
   scientific explanation, 8–9, 12–13
Aristotle, 88, 90, 319
   A-theories, 131
   animal capacities, 192, 208
   anti-Cartesianism, 105
   being, 300
   capacities of souls, 192
   causation, 101
   concept of category, 91, 110
   controlled equivocation, 102
   essence, 66
   kinds of predication, 91
   law of noncontradiction, 69
   logic, 284
   matter, 95
   nominal and real definitions, 101
   personal identity, 194, 208
   possible worlds, 328–30, 331–2
   Posterior Analytics, 103
   potentiality, 146
   properties, 69
   relationism, 1
   space, 1
   subject, 138
   substance, 69, 91, 97, 110
   time, 1, 66
Armstrong, D. M.
   A-theory of universals, 131, 132, 133,
      134–6, 137
   concepts, 285
   possible worlds, 306, 313, 314
   predicate nominalism, 148*n*
   type-token distinction, 143
arrow paradox, 33–5
art restoration, 95
artefacts, 95
astrophysics, 160–1
"at–at" theory, 34–5
atom, 125, 126
atomist metaphysics, 100
atomistic adequacy, 170
atomistic equivalence, 170
attractions, Newton, 14–15

attributes *see* properties
Augustine, Saint, 68
Augustineanism, 89
autonomous self-perpetuators, 181
awareness, 273–5, 277–8
Ayer, A. J., 232

B-series, time, 68, 69, 70
Bacon, J., 125, 129
Baier, Annette, 75
Baldwin, Th., 122
bare particulars, 111, 133, 134, 136
Barrow, Isaac, 4
Beaney, M., 286, 290, 291
being, 66, 67, 87
   Aristotle, 300
   universals, 232
Belloc, Hilaire, 143
Bennett, Jonathan, 47, 54, 55, 60, 63,
      188*n*
Bergmann, Gustav, 293
Bergson, Henri, 67
Berkeley, George, 90, 229
   causation, 221
   God, 221–2, 223, 225–6
   mind, 45, 220–3, 225–6, 283, 284
   perception, 45, 220–3, 282
   spirits, 220–3, 225–6
   theistic idealism, 220–3, 282
   things, 220–3
   will, 221–2
Bernstein, Richard, 78
big bang theory, 161–2
Black, M., 290
bodily resurrection, 104–5, 194
bodily transfer, 179–87, 191
Bosanquet, Bernard, 226
Bouilleau, 13
Bradley, F. H., 226
brain, 180
brain transplant, 179, 191, 195
Brand, Myles, 57
Brandom, R. B., 122
Brock, S., 314
Bruno, Giordano, 2
bundle theories, 113, 124–8
Butler, Joseph, 196
"by"-locution, 60–2

Caird, Edward, 226
calculus, 33–4
Campbell, John, 209–10

Campbell, K., 113, 122, 129, 131, 132
Carnap, R., 292
Cartesians
    matter, 9, 96
    scientific explanation, 8–10, 12–13
    subjectivity, 263–4
Castañeda, H.-N., 305
categories, 91, 110–30
causal explanation, 38–9
causal influence, 29, 31, 35
causal interactions, 31–3, 35–6, 37
causal judgments, 37
causal line, 29
causal order, 264
causal preemption, 27
causal processes, 28–31, 33, 35–6, 37
causal structures, 35–6
causal transmission, 33–5, 36, 37
causation, 19–42
    absolute idealism, 237, 240n
    agency-based disanalogies, 70–2
    Aquinas, 101, 102
    Aristotelians, 9, 12–13
    Aristotle, 101
    Berkeley, 221
    Cartesians, 9, 12–13
    constant conjunction, 21, 25, 100, 295
    and effects, 37–8
    Hume, 19–22, 24, 25, 26, 27, 28, 33,
        37, 100, 101, 284
    Kant, 22–3, 224, 225, 295
    Mackie, 24–8, 37
    Mill, 23–4, 26, 28, 39
    in the objects, 26, 28–36
    property-instances, 45
    spatiotemporal contiguity, 21, 25, 100
    temporal priority, 21, 25, 100
    thomist metaphysics, 99–103
The Cement of the Universe (Mackie), 24
central nervous system, 180
cerebral cortex, 180
cerebrum transplant, 179, 191, 195
change, 67
    Aristotelians, 9
    Cartesians, 9
    thomist metaphysics, 90, 95, 96–7
Cherfas, Jeremy, 149n
Chesterton, G. K., 87, 90
Chisholm, R. M., 133–4, 136, 180
choice, 71
Christian metaphysics, 127
Christian mysticism, 89

Christian theology, 88–9
Clarke, Samuel, 2, 6
classes, 138–9
Cleland, Carol, 54
cluster, 113
cognition
    language, 287–90, 293, 299
    nonrealism, 287–94
    reality, 243–6, 254
cognitive content, 273
cognitive coordination, 253
coincidences, 21
collection, 113
collisions
    Hume, 20–1, 33, 37
    Newton, 14–15
color-resemblance, 137
Commentary (Aquinas), 103
Commentary on the Sentences (Aquinas),
        106–7
common sense
    composition, 152, 154, 155–8
    compositional nihilism, 157–8
    unrestricted composition, 155–7
communication, 249–50, 252, 253, 254–5
complex pristate, 121
composition
    appeal to science, 160–6
    common sense, 152, 154, 155–8
    as a fiction, 151–74
    reflexivity, 153
    thomist metaphysics, 90
    transitivity, 153
    uniqueness of, 153, 154
    unrestricted, 153, 154, 155–7, 166–8
compositional nihilism, 152, 154, 155,
        162
    common sense, 157–8
    and the self, 159–60
    universalism, 166–8
Compositionality Principle (PSCP), 111,
        115–16, 119, 128
compound entity, 125
compresence, 114
concept acquisition, 273–5, 278
concepts, 139–40, 141–4, 145–7
conceptual idealism, 256–60
conceptual nonrealism, 284–5
conceptual order, 264
conceptual understanding, 267
concomitant variation, method of, 24, 39
concrete particulars, 45, 111–12, 113, 114

concretism, 307–11, 312–13, 319–27
conditional statements, 25–7, 100
conditioned response, 21
configuration, 113, 124–8
conjunctive statements, 293
conscious intentions, 22
consciousness
    absolute idealism, 236–7, 239
    continuity of, 191, 193, 207
conserved quantities, 32–3, 36
constant conjunction, 21, 25, 100, 295
constructionism, 233–4
Context Principle, 111, 119–28
contextual constancy, 80
contingency, 91, 101
continuity, 90
continuum, 162
Contradiction Problem, 306–7, 310–11,
    312–13
controlled equivocation, 102
Copernicus, Nicolaus, 2
cosmic forces, 16
Cosmic Mind, 225
cosmos, 2
counterfactual conditionals, 27–8, 233
counterfactuals, possible worlds, 313, 318
counterpart theory, 308, 324–7
Cover, J. A., 114
creation, 154
Cresswell, M. J., 305, 307, 311
criterion, 94, 294–5

Daly, Ch., 113
Darwin, Charles, 1
Davidson, Donald, 53–4, 57, 58, 60, 62–3
death, 125
decision theory, 304
deductive reasoning, 15, 103
deep structure level analyses, 124
defining criterion, 94, 294–5
deliberation, 71
demonology, 157
Denkel, A., 111
Descartes, René, 14, 15, 88, 180, 191
    appearances, 269, 270, 271, 272
    causation, 40n
    cosmic motions, 11
    independence of substance, 112
    inertia law, 13
    matter, 96, 108n
    mind and soul, 175
    mindstuff, 264

motion, 2, 5, 13
relationism, 1, 2, 6, 10
scientific explanation, 8
self and the world, 175
space, 4
subjectivity, 263
"this I," 175
description, 257–60
descriptive metaphysics, 90, 118
developed cognition, 289–90
difference, 90, 98
difference, method of, 23–4
differential calculus, 33–4
differential responsiveness, 265–6, 274,
    276–7, 278
disanalogies
    agency-based, 70–8, 84
    objectivity-based, 78–84
disappointment, 298, 299
diseases, 38
dispositional properties, 246–7, 261n
dispositions, 102, 147
    see also reliable differential responsive
        dispositions (RDRDs)
distinctness, 90–1
distributive singular terms (DSTs), 143,
    144–5, 146
Divers, J., 314
Dowe, Phil, 36, 41n
DSTs, 143, 144–5, 146
dualism, 263, 284
    identity theory, 177–9, 191–2
    thomist metaphysics, 105
Dummett, Michael, 139, 243, 282
dummy predicates, 142

earth, motion of, 6
Edwards, Jonathan, 177
effects, 37–8
efficient causation, 101
ego, 175
egocentrism, 201–3
Einstein, Albert, 1, 30
embodiment, 104–5
emergence, 108n
empiricism, 99, 265–6, 273–5
endorsement
    dimension of, 267, 274–5
    scope of, 273
    withholding of, 271, 272
enduring/temporally extended, reference
        to "I," 177, 178, 186, 187, 188n

ersatz worlds, 306, 307, 308–9, 311–12
essence
   Aristotle, 66
   thomist metaphysics, 101, 102–3, 106–7
eternity, 66
ethers, 11
ethical truths, 318
eucharistic transubstantiation, 92–3
Euclid, 224
Euclidean geometry, 22, 40–1n
Euler, Leonhard, 13
event names, 47
event-identity
   non-duplication principles, 57–8
   parts and wholes, 58–60
events, 43–65
   absolute idealism, 238–9
   adverbs, 62–3
   Aristotelians, 12–13
   "by"-locution, 60–2
   facts, 44, 46, 49, 50–2
   Kant, 224, 225
   ontological category, 123, 125
   panpsychism, 235
   as property-exemplifications, 46–7,
      48–50
   as property-instances, 45–7
   temporal relations, 3, 66, 68–9
   tropes, 47, 49–50, 55–6, 57, 58
   zonal fusion of, 56–7
   see also causation
evil, 223
evolution, 125
exemplification, 123
existence, 106–7, 159–60, 242–3, 282,
   298–9
existential quantifier, 305
expectation, 297–8, 299
experience, 156
   absolute idealism, 228–32, 236–9,
      239–40n
   constructionism, 233–4
   empiricism, 99, 273–5
   Kant, 22, 295
   panpsychism, 234–6
   personal identity, 190, 196–7, 203–7,
      210, 212
   phenomenalism, 232–3
   thomist metaphysics, 90, 98, 99, 100,
      106
extension, Cartesians, 9
extensionality, 154

Extreme Modal Realism, 319–21, 324–7,
   332

facial expressions, 288
factor, 122
facts
   events, 44, 46, 49, 50–2
   nonrealism, 285–6
   Russell, 285, 286, 290, 291, 292
   Wittgenstein, 285, 286
   see also prifacts
fallibilism, 246, 253–4
familiarity, 296–7
feature-placing sentences, 118
Fermat, Pierre de, 13
Ferrier, James, 226
Fichte, J. G., 226
fictional particulars, 248
fictionalism, 169–71, 306, 313–14
final causation, 101
fission, 190, 194, 195–9, 202, 210–12
flux, 90, 98
forces, Newton, 7, 10, 12
formal causation, 101
forms, 91, 94–7, 98, 99, 101, 103, 104
Forrest, P., 307, 311
four-dimensional, identity theory, 177,
   186, 188n
Francken, Patrick, 61
free will, 225
Frege, G., 138, 150n, 282, 284
   Context Principle, 119
   facts, 122
   generality, 290, 292
   negation, 290–1, 292
   thought, 285–6, 290–1
future, 68–9
   agency-based disanalogies, 71–8, 84
   objectivity-based disanalogies, 78–84
fuzzy classes, 140–1

Gale, Richard, 320
Galileo, 2, 10, 13, 14
Gallagher, Sean, 85n
Geach, P., 290
general relativity (GR), 161
generality, 290, 292, 298–9
generalizations, 25
generic individuation, 98
genetic relationships, 201
geometry, 22–3, 40–1n
gerundial nominals, 51–4, 60–1

God, 66, 73
    absolute idealism, 225–6
    Aquinas, 106–7, 284
    Berkeley, 221–2, 223, 225–6
    idealistic realism, 244
    Leibnizian possible world, 330–1, 332
    thomist metaphysics, 89, 99, 106–7
Goodman, Nelson, 15, 144–5, 153, 154,
    282
De Gravitatione (Newton), 5
gravity, 8, 10, 11, 14, 15–17, 161
Green, T. H., 226
Gribben, John, 149*n*
gunk, 164–5

Haldane, J., 88, 104, 107
Halley, Edmund, 14
hardness, Newton, 10, 16
heavenly motions, 15–17
Hegel, G. W. F., 90, 226, 266, 282, 296
Heidegger, Martin, 282, 287, 299
Helm, Paul, 188*n*
Hero of Alexandria, 13
Hobbes, Thomas, 284
Hoffman, J., 112
Holistic Contextuality Principle (PHCT),
    128
holistic relations, 236–7
homo mensura doctrine, 243–5
Hooke, Robert, 13–14
Hubble expansion, 161–2
Hume, David, 15
    causation, 19–22, 24, 25, 26, 27, 28,
        33, 37, 100, 101, 284
    collisions, 20–1, 33, 37
    "I," 176, 187*n*
    constant conjunction, 21, 25, 100, 295
    identity, 296
    inductive skepticism, 103
Huyghens, Christiaan, 1, 7, 13, 14
hyper-realism, 307, 310
hypothetico-deductive reasoning, 15

"I," 175–89
    bodily transfer, 179–87
    enduring/temporally extended, 177,
        178, 186, 187, 188*n*
    material/immaterial, 177, 179–87
    and self, 175–6
    transitory/lasting, 177
ideal relations, 227–8
idealism, 2, 219–41, 242, 251–6

conceptual idealism, 256–60
    definition, 219–20
    identity theory, 177–8
    mental, 219, 284
    mind-dependence, 219, 222–3, 256–60
    reality, 219–20, 229–32, 244–5, 256
    theistic idealism, 220–3, 282
    transcendental idealism, 224–5, 282,
        283, 284
    see also absolute idealism
ideas, 176
    Berkeley, 220–3
identification, 257–60
identity
    as logical experience, 296–7
    thomist metaphysics, 90, 94–7, 98
    see also "I"; personal identity
identity crises, 199
identity theory, 124, 324–7
Identity Theory of Truth, 122
illusions, 212
imagination, 229–31, 245
immanent causation, 181
immortality, 225
impenetrability, Newton, 10, 16
imperfect gerundial nominals, 51–4, 61
implication, 297–8
impossible worlds, 309, 312
impressions, 176
independence, 112
indeterminate causation, 39
individuals, 103–4
*Individuals: an essay in descriptive
    metaphysics* (Strawson), 90
individuation, 98–9, 123
inductive reasoning, 15, 103, 104, 322–4
inferences, 267–8, 276–7, 278–9, 322–3
informational content, 120
innatism, 274
inquiry, 252, 253, 254–5
inscriptions, 144–5, 147
instantaneous velocity, 34
instantiation, 112, 113, 123
intellect, 104, 246
intellection, 99, 104
intellectual mysticism, 67
intelligence, 127
intention-connectedness, 196, 197
intentionality, 263–4
    Leibnizian possible worlds, 331
intentions, 22, 71, 75
inter-subjective communication, 253

introspection, 176
intuitions
    events, 47–8, 56
    Kant, 295
    trope theory, 113–14
INUS condition, 26, 27, 37
irrealism, 282

James, William, 67, 77, 257, 299, 300
Jesus Christ, 104
Jupiter, 16, 24

Kant, Immanuel, 88, 90, 226, 235, 249,
        289, 298
    causation, 22–3, 224, 225, 295
    events, 224, 225
    experience, 22, 295
    geometry, 22–3, 40–1n
    intuitions, 295
    knowledge, 287
    mind, 224–5
    natural world, 224–5
    nonrealism, 300
    objectivity of outer things, 261n
    perception, 224, 284
    a priori categories, 110
    sensibility, 284, 300
    "things in themselves," 224–5, 231,
        233, 283
    transcendental idealism, 224–5, 282,
        283, 284
    understanding, 284, 295, 300
Kepler, Johannes, 16
Kilwardby, Archbishop of Canterbury,
        89
Kim, Jaegwon, 43, 44, 46–51, 53–4, 59
kind, concept of, 111–12
Klemke, E. D., 286
Kline, George, 73
knowledge
    Aquinas, 102, 104
    empiricism, 265–6, 273
    Kant, 287
    nonrealism, 287
    progressive nature of, 248–9
    reality, 243–6, 248–9, 253–4
    thomist metaphysics, 102–3, 104
    see also observational knowledge
Krell, D. F., 287
Kripke, S., 101, 308–9, 324

lambda type intersections, 32–3
language
    cognition, 287–90, 293, 299

nonrealism, 284–8
legal possibility, 304
legal responsibility, 38–9
Leibniz, Gottfried Wilhelm, 5, 90, 319
    events, 43, 46
    innatism, 274
    motion, 6–7
    possible worlds, 330–1, 332
    relationism, 1, 2–4
Leo XIII, Pope, 88, 89
Lesniewski, Stanislaw, 152, 306
Lewis, David, 102, 305
    concretism, 307, 308, 309–11, 312–13,
        319–27
    Contradiction Problem, 310–11, 312–
        13
    counterfactuals, 313, 318
    counterpart relation, 308, 324
    ersatz worlds, 306, 308, 309, 311–
        12
    Extreme Modal Realism, 319–21, 324–
        7, 332
    hyper-realism, 307, 310
    impossible worlds, 309, 312
    indexical account of actuality, 307, 320–
        4, 325–6, 328
    mereology, 153, 154, 186–7
    personal identity, 186–7, 194
    predication, 135–6
    properties, 139
    truth, 308
    universals, 135–6
    worldmates, 308, 311, 312–13
Liddell, Henry George, 140
light, Newton, 11, 12, 14
likeness, 57
limitedness, 246
linear momentum, 32–3
linguistic ersatzism, 311
linguistic nonrealism, 285, 287
linguistic turn, 287
Locke, John, 147, 222
    causation, 22
    events, 43, 45–6
    nominal and real definitions, 101
    particulars, 133
    personal identity, 178–9, 182, 187,
        188n, 191, 196, 199, 205–8
    psychological continuity, 191, 196
    substance, 99, 102
Lockean dualism, 191–2
locomotion, 81–2
logic, 284, 286

logical atomism, 126
logical cognition, 288–94, 299
logical constructs, 182
logical experiences, 295–300
logical expressions, 282, 284, 287,
    288–90, 293, 294
    and logical experiences, 295–300
logical form, 284, 285, 289
logical grammar, 285
logical nonrealism, 282–300
    cognition, 287–94
    facts, 285–6
    knowledge, 287
    language, 284–8
    objects, 282
    personal identity, 282
    predications, 282, 289
    sentences, 285–7
    things, 285
logical nonreductionism, 292
logical propositions, 288–9
logical reductionism, 291, 292
logical structure, 284, 286–7, 288, 300
logico-semantic devices, 116–18
Lombard, Lawrence Brian, 55, 61
"looks" talk, 269–73, 278
Loux, M., 111–12
Lowe, E. J., 112
Lycan, W. G., 307, 319

McCool, G., 88
McDowell, John, 208
McFall, Lynne, 72
Mach, Ernst, 6, 12
McInerny, R., 103
Mackie, J. L., 24–8, 37
McTaggart, J. M. E., 68, 69
Maddy, Penelope, 162
Maimonides, M., 252
Marcus, R. B., 306
Marsh, R. C., 285, 290, 291, 292, 293,
    294
Martin, C. B., 102
mass
    causal interactions, 33
    causal transmission, 35
    Newton, 10, 16, 17
Material Beings (van Inwagen), 152
material causation, 101
materialism, 90, 290
    identity theory, 177, 179–87, 192
mathematical realism, 261n
mathematical topology, 125

matter
    Cartesians, 9, 96
    Descartes, 96, 108n
    Newton, 10, 11, 12, 16–17
    thomist metaphysics, 94–7, 98, 101
Maupertuis, Pierre Louis Moreau de,
    13
Meinong, Alexius, 303, 304, 305–6, 309,
    310
memory
    Augustine, 68
    personal identity, 178–9, 188n, 190,
        196–7, 202, 207, 209, 212–13
mental, idealism, 219, 284
mental pristates, 124
mental states, 199–200
mereological closure, 170
mereological summation, 182–7
mereology, 125, 152–7, 162–6
metaphors, 140
Mill, John Stuart, 23–4, 26, 28, 39, 232
mind, 175
    absolute idealism, 226
    Berkeley, 45, 220–3, 225–6, 283, 284
    Cartesians, 9
    Christian metaphysics, 127
    Kant, 224–5
    thomist metaphysics, 104–6
mind-dependence
    idealism, 219, 222–3, 256–60
    qualities of things, 222–3
mindstuff, 264
modal disanalogies
    agency-based, 70–8, 84
    objectivity-based, 78–84
momentum, 32–3
monads, 2–3
monistic idealism, 219
Montague, R., 305
moon, 16–17
Moore, G. E., 290
moral responsibility, 38–9
More, Henry, 4
Mormann, Th., 125, 129
motion
    as an illusion, 33
    Aristotelians, 8–9
    arrow paradox, 33–5
    "at–at" theory of, 34–5
    Cartesians, 8–10
    circular, 7
    Descartes, 2, 5, 13
    forced, 8–9

motion *cont.*
　heavens, 15–17
　inertial, 9
　Leibniz, 6–7
　natural, 8–10
　Newton's dynamics, 1–2, 5–6, 7–8,
　　9–11
　relationism, 1–4, 6–7
　straight-line, 5–6, 7
multiple personality, 200–1

natural language, 114, 116
natural world
　Hegel, 226
　Kant, 224–5
　thomist metaphysics, 99
natures
　A-theories, 131, 133
　thomist metaphysics, 94, 101, 103–4
necessary conditions, 25–6, 100
necessary connection, 21, 25, 100
necessary truths, 73, 74, 75, 77, 81, 83,
　330
necessity, 303–4, 309
negation, 290–2, 298, 299
neo-Platonism, 89
Neptune, 24
Newton, Isaac
　attractions, 14–15
　collisions, 14–15
　forces, 7, 10, 12
　De Gravitatione, 5
　gravity, 8, 10, 11, 14, 15–17
　hardness, 10, 16
　impenetrability, 10, 16
　light, 11, 12, 14
　mass, 10, 16, 17
　matter, 10, 11, 12, 16–17
　motion, 1–2, 5–6, 7–8, 9–11
　Opticks, 11, 12
　physical objects, 55
　Principia, 1, 7–8, 11, 12, 13, 14, 15
　rules of reasoning, 13–17
　scientific explanation, 8, 9–12
　space, 1–2, 5, 10
　time, 1–2, 5, 10
nihilism *see* compositional nihilism
nomic necessity, 304
nominal definitions, 101–2
nonbeing, 67
nonexistence, 303–5
noninferential reports, 267–8, 276–7

nonrealism *see* conceptual nonrealism;
　linguistic nonrealism; logical
　nonrealism
norms, 147
nuclear theory, 114
numerical individuation, 98

object-stages, 44
objectivity, realism, 249–51
objectivity-based disanalogies, 78–84
　non-selective, 79–82
　shared-perspectives, 83–4
objects
　as aggregates of spatiotemporal zones,
　　55
　causation in, 26, 28–36
　inherent characters, 227
　Kant, 224
　logical nonrealism, 282
　phenomenalism, 232–3
　real relations, 227–8
　spatial relations, 3
　temporal/spatial parts, 81–2
　see also motion
observation sentences, 117
observational knowledge, 265–8, 272–3,
　275–7, 278
Occam's Razor, 305
O'Leary-Hawthorne, J., 114
Olson, Eric, 199
On Being and Essence (Aquinas), 88
On the Plurality of Worlds (Lewis), 139
On the Principles of Nature (Aquinas), 88
ontological atomism, 126
ontological category, 110–30
Opticks (Newton), 11, 12
organicism, 152
organization, 90, 94
ourselves, 176

P-theories, 131, 132, 138–42, 146–7,
　150*n*
pain, 76–7, 85*n*, 207
panpsychism, 234–6
paraphrase, 306
Parfit, Derek
　personal identity, 192, 193, 195–6, 197,
　　198–9, 203–6, 208, 209
　timeless, 75–6
Parmenides, 67, 187*n*, 318
parsimony, 305
Parsons, Terence, 63, 305

particularized properties, 113
particulars
  A-theories, 131, 132–5, 137
  conceptual idealism, 256–60
  fictional, 248
  ontological theories, 113, 118–19
  P-theories, 132
  Plato, 143
  prime, 123
  thomist metaphysics, 103, 104
  trope theories, 132, 135, 137
  see also abstract particulars; bare
    particulars; concrete particulars
parts
  absolute idealism, 236–8
  see also composition
passion, 91
past, 68–9
  agency-based disanalogies, 71–8, 84
  objectivity-based disanalogies, 78–84
Paul, St., 104
Pavlov, Ivan Petrovich, 21
perception
  Augustine, 68
  Berkeley, 45, 220–3, 282
  cognition, 288
  Kant, 224, 284
  Leibniz, 2
  as non-selectivity disanalogy, 79–80
  phenomenalism, 232–3
  thomist metaphysics, 99
perfect gerundial nominals, 52–4
person, 175
personal identity, 190–218
  Aristotle, 194, 208
  experience, 190, 196–7, 203–7, 210,
    212
  fission, 190, 194, 195–9, 202, 210–12
  Lewis, 186–7, 194
  Locke, 178–9, 182, 187, 188*n*, 191,
    196, 199, 205–8
  logical nonrealism, 282
  materialism, 177, 179–87, 192
  memory, 178–9, 188*n*, 190, 196–7,
    202, 207, 209, 212–13
  Parfit, 192, 193, 195–6, 197, 198–9,
    203–6, 208, 209
  psychological-continuity theory of,
    177–8, 185, 191–4, 195–8, 209–10
  soul, 178–9, 182, 191, 192
  strict numerical sense, 194–5, 198–9,
    201, 202–3, 209

subject, 203–7
thought, 203–6
see also "I"
Peter of Ireland, 90
Peterson, P. E., 292
phenomenalism, 2, 232–3
physical world
  constructionism, 233–4
  Kant, 224–5
  panpsychism, 234–5
  structuralism, 234
  see also objects; reality; things
pineal gland, 180
place, 91, 98
Plantinga, Alvin, 307, 313, 319, 327, 328
Plato, 84, 89, 102, 264
  abstract entities, 284
  dialectics, 78
  familiarity, 297
  forms, 66, 140
  particulars, 143
  Republic, 131
  Theaetetus, 297
Platonism, 89–90, 261*n*, 284, 327–9, 332
pleasure, 76–7, 207
Plotinus, 66
pluplural quantifiers, 172–3*n*
plural quantifiers, 162–3, 172–3*n*
pluralistic idealism, 219
plurality, 90, 98
point-sized entities, 165
positivism, 12
possibilia, 139, 303–16, 317–33
  actualism, 307, 319, 327–32
  Aristotle, 328–30, 331–2
  Armstrong, 306, 313, 314
  concretism, 307–11, 312–13, 319–27
  Contradiction Problem, 306–7, 310–11,
    312–13
  counterfactuals, 313, 318
  ersatz worlds, 306, 307, 308–9, 311–12
  fictionalism, 306, 313–14
  Leibniz, 330–1, 332
  nonexistence and nonexistents, 303–5
  Platonism, 327–9, 332
  Quine, 303, 304, 305, 311
  theistic account, 331–2
  trouble, 304–6
Posterior Analytics (Aristotle), 103
posture, 91
potential infinity, 67
potentiality, 96, 107, 146

preconceptual awareness, 273
predications, 115–17, 118, 120–1, 163
  A-theories, 131–2, 135, 136–7
  Aquinas, 91
  Aristotle, 91
  logical nonrealism, 282, 289
  P-theories, 138, 139, 140–1, 142, 147
  thomist metaphysics, 91
  trope theories, 136, 137
  universals, 131–2, 135–8, 139, 140–1,
    142, 145, 146, 147
presence, 298–9
present, 68–9
  agency-based disanalogies, 71–8, 84
  objectivity-based disanalogies, 78–84
Price, H. H., 296, 297, 298
prifacts, 121, 122, 127, 128
prime particulars, 123
prime sentences, 119–22, 126–7
Principia (Newton), 1, 7–8, 11, 12, 13,
  14, 15
pristates, 120–8
probabilistic causation, 39
probability theory, 304
process, ontological category, 123, 125
process philosophy, 67
processes, 28–31, 33, 35–6, 37
properties
  A-theories, 133–4
  Aristotelians, 9
  Aristotle, 69
  Cartesians, 9
  distinctions within, 91
  events, 44–5, 46
  Lewis, 139
  ontological category, 110, 111–12, 115,
    123
  P-theories, 150n
property-exemplifications, 46–7, 48–50
property-instances, 45–7
propositions, 44, 284, 286, 288–9, 327–8
propria, 91
Protagoras, 243
PSCP *see* Compositionality Principle
  (PSCP)
pseudo-processes, 29–31
psychological continuity, 177–8, 185,
  191–4, 195–8, 209–10
Puccetti, Roland, 180
Puntel, L. B., 122
purpose, 101
Putnam, H., 101, 167–8, 282, 283

qualities, 91, 114, 125, 176, 222–3
Quantifier-Reinterpreting approach,
  306
quantifiers, 282, 289, 293, 303, 305–7,
  310–11
  see also plural quantifiers
quantity, 91
quantum field theory, 161
quantum mechanics, 39–40
quasi-memories, 197, 202, 209, 212
questioning, 297
Quine, W. V.
  dummy predicates, 142
  events, 57–8
  illogical cultures, 286
  mereology, 153, 154
  ontological category, 116–18, 119, 121,
    129n
  possible worlds, 303, 304, 305, 311
  thought, 287
Quinn, Phil, 73–4

Rapaport, W. J., 305
rationalism, conceptual acquisition, 273–
  5
rationality, 70, 71
RDRDs (reliable differential responsive
  dispositions), 266, 274, 276–7, 278,
  279
reactivity, 100
Reagan, Ronald, 81
real definitions, 101–2
real relations, 227–8, 236–7
realism, 242–62
  aspects of, 242–51
  complexity of real things, 246–8
  conceptual idealism, 256–60
  and incapacity, 246
  logical nonrealism, 282–94
  man is the measure doctrine, 243–5
  mind-independence, 246, 251–6
  objectivity, 249–51
  rationale of, 251–6
reality, 66, 67, 87
  and appearance, 252, 269–73
  cognition, 243–6, 254
  communication, 249–50, 252, 253,
    254–5
  and concept of truth, 252, 254
  idealism, 219–20, 229–32, 244–5, 256
  inquiry, 252, 253, 254–5
  Kant, 224

knowledge, 243–6, 248–9, 253–4
logical structure of, 284, 286–7, 288, 300
as subject matter of metaphysics, 283–4
reason, 89
recognition, 288, 296–7
reductionism question, 124
reductive physicalism, 124
reference relation, 121–2
reflection, 13, 90, 98
reflexivity, 153
refraction, 13
regularity theories, 25–8
Reid, 156, 188*n*
relational property, 61
relational tropes, 55, 57
relationism, 1–4, 6–7
relations, 91, 227–8, 236–7
relativity, 8, 30
Relentless Meinongian, 306–7
reliable differential responsive dispositions (RDRDs), 266, 274, 276–7, 278, 279
representation, relation of, 327–8, 331
repression, 200
reptiles, 149*n*
Republic (Plato), 131
Rescher, N., 305, 312
residual substance, 105
residues, method of, 24
rest, 2, 67–8
resurrection, 104–5, 194
revisionary metaphysics, 90
Richards, T., 312
RNA world hypothesis, 161
Rosen, G., 306, 313–14
Rosenkrantz, G. S., 112
Ross, J., 103
Routley, R., 305
Royce, Josiah, 226
Russell, Bertrand, 116, 187*n*, 282, 284
  "at–at" theory of motion, 34–5, 41*n*
  causal line, 29
  facts, 285, 286, 290, 291, 292
  generality, 290, 292
  negation, 291–2
  possibilia, 304
  universal statements, 293–4

sameness, 90
Santayana, George, 258
sapience, 266

sarcasm, 140
Sartre, Jean-Paul, 285, 292, 297, 298, 299
Saturn, 16, 24
Schechtman, Marya, 199
Schelling, F. W. J., 226
scholastics, 102
Schopenhauer, Arthur, 225, 226, 258
science
  composition, 160–6
  rise of, 264
  thomist metaphysics, 99–103
scientific explanation, 8–13
scientific realism, 246
scientism, 90
Scott, Robert, 140
secondary qualities, 222–3
self
  and "I," 175–6
  compositional nihilism, 159–60
  Locke, 206
self-alienation, 226
self-consciousness, 70, 71
self-deception, 200
self-realization, 70, 71, 73–5, 77
Sellars, Wilfrid, 143, 144, 145, 264–5, 277–80
  concept acquisition, 273–5, 278
  core person, 180
  "looks" talk, 269–73, 278
  observational knowledge, 265–8, 272–3, 275–7, 278
  theoretical concepts, 275–7, 278
semantico-ontological framework, 114–15
semantics
  Context Principle, 111, 119–28
  substance ontologies, 111–16
  trope theory, 113–14
sense experience, 22, 156
sensibility, 284, 300
sensible species, 45
sentence-tokens, 143, 144–5, 172*n*
sentence-types, 143, 144–5, 172*n*
sentences
  feature-placing, 118
  nonrealism, 285–7
  observational, 117
  see also prime sentences
Sentential Compositionality Principle (PSCT), 111, 119–28
sentential connectives, 27–8
sentential operators, 282, 289

sentience, 266
set theory, 125
Shaffer, Jonathan, 148*n*
shape-resemblance, 137
shared-perspective disanalogies, 83–4
Shoemaker, Sydney, 179–81, 185, 192, 195, 196–7, 199–200
Siger of Brabant, 89
sign-cognition, 297
Simons, P., 113, 114, 125
skepticism, 103, 104, 156
Skyrms, B., 312
Smart, J. J. C., 107
social causation, 39
social entities, 182
social practices, 194
Socrates, 57
somatico-perceptual fields, 233–4
sortalization, 257
sortals, 58, 81–2
soul, 175
    Christian metaphysics, 127
    personal identity, 178–9, 182, 191, 192
    thomist metaphysics, 104–6
space
    absolute idealism, 236–7
    agency-based disanalogies, 71–6, 84
    Aquinas, 98
    Aristotle, 1
    Barrow on, 4–5
    continuity of, 162
    Descartes, 4
    event-identity, 58–9
    Kant, 224
    More on, 4
    Newton's dynamics, 1–2, 5, 10
    objectivity-based disanalogies, 78–84
    as order of possibility, 4
    relationism, 1–4, 6
    substantival position, 3–6
    thomist metaphysics, 98
spatiotemporal contiguity, 21, 25, 100
specific individuation, 98
specious present, 85*n*
Spinoza, Baruch, 55, 112, 187*n*
spirits, Berkeley, 220–3, 225–6
Stalnaker, R., 305, 306, 307, 309–10, 312
"states of affairs," 115
steady state theory, 162
strangeness, 297
Strawson, Peter, 90, 98, 118, 119, 286
stroke-victims, 195

structuralism, 234
subject
    Aristotle, 138
    classification of, 138
    ontological categories, 111–12, 113, 115–16, 118–19, 126
    personal identity, 203–7
subject-attributes, 115
subject-universals, 115
subjection-in-general, 118
subjectivity, 263–4
substance
    Aquinas, 92–3, 94, 97, 102
    Aristotelians, 9
    Aristotle, 69, 91, 97, 110
    Cartesians, 9
    category of, 91, 110
    change of, 95, 96
    different senses of, 111–12
    Locke, 99, 102
    persons as, 191–2
    thomist metaphysics, 90–4, 95, 96–7, 99–103, 105
substance ontology, 111–16, 128
    Sentential Compositionality Principle (PSCT), 120
    trope theory, 113–14
substantial form, 94, 98, 99, 101, 103, 104
substantiation, 118
substitutional quantification, 142, 149*n*
substraction, 120
substratum, 111, 112, 113, 114
sufficient conditions, 25–7, 100
Summa Theologiae (Aquinas), 92, 107
supernatural, 221
supervenience, 108*n*
surface level analyses, 124
surprise, 298
Swinburne, Richard, 188*n*, 198
A System of Logic (Mill), 24

Taylor, Richard, 81
Tempier, Bishop of Paris, 89
temporal becoming, 68, 69–70, 78
temporal priority, 21, 25, 100
temporality, 66
temporally extension, reference to "I," 177, 178, 186, 187, 188*n*
Theaetetus (Plato), 297
theistic idealism, 220–3, 282
Themistius, 252

theodicy, 73
things
  accidents, 94
  Aristotelians, 9
  Berkeley, 220–3
  complexity of, 246–8
  concept of, 45
  conceptual idealism, 256–60
  description, 257–60
  dispositional properties, 246–7, 261n
  distinct from properties, 91
  events, 44, 46
  identification, 257–60
  knowledge of, 243–6, 248–9
  nonrealism, 285
  objectivity, 249–51
  panpsychism, 235
  phenomenalism, 232–3
  primary qualities, 223
  as property-instances, 45
  secondary qualities, 222–3
  temporal part of, 44, 46
  types of information about, 248–9
  as universals, 45
  see also composition; properties
"things in themselves," 224–5, 231, 232,
    233, 283
Thomas, St., 175
thomist metaphysics, 87–109
  abstraction, 103–4
  accident, 90–4, 96–7, 98, 99–100, 102
  causation, 99–103
  change, 90, 95, 96–7
  essence, 101, 102–3, 106–7
  existence, 106–7
  experience, 90, 98, 99, 100, 106
  forms, 91, 94–7, 98, 99, 101, 103, 104
  God, 89, 99, 106–7
  identity, 90, 94–7, 98
  individuals, 103–4
  individuation, 98–9
  knowledge, 102–3, 104
  matter, 94–7, 98, 101
  mind, 104–6
  natures, 94, 101, 103–4
  science, 99–103
  soul, 104–6
  substance, 90–4, 95, 96–7, 99–103,
    105
  thought, 105–6
  universals, 103–4
Thomson, Judith Jarvis, 56, 57, 61

thought
  Cartesians, 9
  first person I-thoughts, 203–6
  Frege, 285–6, 290–1
  Kant, 224
  Leibnizian possible worlds, 331
  personal identity, 203–6
  Quine, 287
  thomist metaphysics, 105–6
three-dimensional, identity theory, 177,
    188n
time, 66–86
  A-series, 68–9
  absolute idealism, 238–9
  agency-based disanalogies, 71–7, 84
  Aristotle, 1, 66
  B-series, 68, 69, 70
  Barrow on, 4–5
  as category, 91
  coercive power of, 78
  continuity of, 162
  definition, 66
  dense time, 67
  discrete time, 67–8
  event-identity, 58–9
  Kant, 224
  Newton's dynamics, 1–2, 5, 10
  objectivity-based disanalogies, 78–84
  as order of possibility, 4
  paradoxes of, 67–70
  relationism, 1–4, 6
  unreality of, 66, 68–9
time-slices, 177, 188n
timelessness, 66
tokens, 143, 144–6, 172n
Tomberlin, James, 149n
Tractatus Logico-Philosophicus
    (Wittgenstein), 282, 285, 289, 300
transcendental idealism, 224–5, 282, 283,
    284
transcendental thomism, 88
transitivity, 153
transitory/lasting, reference to "I," 177
transubstantiation, 92–3
Trent, Council of, 92
trope theories, 113–14, 131, 132, 135,
    136, 137
tropes, 47, 49–50, 55–6, 57, 58, 125, 148n
trouble, 304–6
truth, 121, 122, 252, 254, 308, 317, 318
truthmaker-based arguments, 318–19, 324
types, 143, 144–5, 172n

understanding
   Kant, 284, 295, 300
   thomist metaphysics, 99
unfamiliarity, 297
Unger, Peter, 187*n*
uniqueness of composition, 153, 154
universal properties, 45
universal statements, 291, 293–4
universals, 131–50
   A-theories, 131–7, 141
   nihilism, 166–8
   ontological theories, 113, 114, 125
   P-theories, 131, 132, 138–42
   predications, 131–2, 135–8, 139,
      140–1, 142, 145, 146, 147
   thomist metaphysics, 103–4
   trope theories, 131, 132
   unexperienced, 232
   see also abstract universals
unrestricted composition, 153, 154,
   155–7, 166–8
Uranus, 24
utility, 251, 254
utterances, 147

vague words, 140–2
value, causal theory of, 70–1
van Inwagen, Peter, 149*n*, 152, 307
Vendler, Zeno, 51–2, 53, 54
vesture, 91
Vision, G., 314
visual perception, 79–80

Wallis, John, 13, 14
Watson, John B., 287
weight, Newton, 17
Wetzel, Linda, 144

Whitehead, A. N., 67, 165, 284
Whiting, Jennifer, 206
wholes
   absolute idealism, 236–8
   see also composition
will
   Berkeley, 221–2
   Christian metaphysics, 127
will-to-believe arguments, 324
Williams, Bernard, 196
Williams, D. C., 47, 113, 131
Wittgenstein, Ludwig, 284, 291
   defining criterion, 94, 294
   facts, 285, 286
   fundamental thought, 290
   identity, 296
   limits of language, 282, 285, 287
   logical constants, 289
   Tractatus Logico-Philosophicus, 282, 285,
      289, 300
   words for sensations, 294
Wittgensteinians, 176, 187*n*
word-tokens, 143, 144–5, 172*n*
word-types, 143, 144–5, 172*n*
world-natures, 307, 311
world-surrogates, 306, 307
Wren, Christopher, 13, 14
Wright, Steven, 78

X-type intersections, 32–3
Xantippe, 55, 57

Y-type intersections, 32–3

Zalta, E., 305
Zeno of Elea, 33–4, 67
Zucchi, Alessandro, 53